THEODORE ROOSEVELT

THEODORE ROOSEVELT

Preacher of Righteousness

Joshua David Hawley

Foreword by David M. Kennedy

Yale University Press
New Haven & London

Published with assistance from the Mary Cady Tew Memorial Fund.

Set in Postscript Electra by The Composing Room of Michigan, Inc.
Printed in the United States of America.

Library of Congress Cataloging-in-Publication Data
Hawley, Joshua David.
Theodore Roosevelt : preacher of righteousness / Joshua David Hawley.
p. cm.
Includes bibiographical references and index.
ISBN 978-0-300-12010-3 (hardcover : alk. paper)
1. Roosevelt, Theodore, 1858–1919 — Political and social views.   2. Roosevelt, Theodore,
1858–1919 — Knowledge and learning.   3. Presidents — United States — Intellectual life —
Case studies.   4. United States — Politics and government — 1901–1909.   5. United
States — Foreign relations — 1901–1909.   I. Title.
E757.H37   2008
973.91′1092 — dc22
2007039384

A catalogue record for this book is available from the British Library.

The paper in this book meets the guidelines for permanence and durability
of the Committee on Production Guidelines for Book Longevity
of the Council on Library Resources.

10 9 8 7 6 5 4 3 2 1

To my parents and to Lesley

Roosevelt was the greatest preacher of righteousness in modern times . . . he made right living seem the natural thing, and no man was beyond the reach of his preaching and example.

—*Gifford Pinchot, 1919*

God did not spare angels when they sinned, but cast them into hell and committed them to pits of darkness, reserved for judgment; and did not spare the ancient world, but preserved Noah, a preacher of righteousness.

—*II Peter 2:4–5*

neau. All this Hawley explains with exemplary lucidity, in supple and sinuous prose that Roosevelt himself would surely have admired.

Hawley is especially astute when he takes up the long-vexed question of Roosevelt's precise ideological identity—a question bound up with still unresolved debates about the character of progressivism, the early twentieth century reform movement with which TR is customarily identified. Was he a conservative disguised in reformer's clothing, a cunning trimmer who blunted the movement for transformative change, or an authentic progressive who genuinely sought to use the power of government to temper the wind to the shorn lamb and give the American people a true "Square Deal"? How did his own egregious individualism square with his unapologetically statist nationalism? How did he reconcile his support for immigrants, and his belief in their assimilability, with his often raw racialism? Was he a calculating advocate for America's national interests, or an interventionist busybody with no coherent strategic agenda? In the eternal efforts to balance liberty with equality, individual rights with the claims of the community, what were his dominant values? Did he believe, like Aristotle, that man was destined for society, or, like Benito Mussolini, that the individual must subordinate himself to the state? Was his incessant call for righteousness a heartfelt summons to civic virtue or merely sanctimonious posturing?

Like his subject, Joshua Hawley brings some formidable assets to bear in grappling with those questions—including an unusually questing intelligence, a breadth and depth of learning well beyond his years, and an intolerance for conventional thinking. Trained in both history and the law, Hawley has a historian's sense of context and proportion, and a lawyer's capacity for making fine distinctions. And like Roosevelt, too, Hawley has a rare gift for breathing life into ideas, for braiding a deep understanding of the role of formal thought into his account of the seething, teeming world we inhabit. He turns in his concluding pages to a trenchant examination of the relevance of TR's ideas for our own time, when, as in the progressive era, political identities are again confused and contentious, and when we once more yearn, like William Allen White, for righteousness in our private and public spheres alike, even while we remain, like Mark Hanna, reflexively skeptical of all who preach it.

PREFACE

It is a hard business, finding one's place in the world. But sooner or later every person comes to it. For most, this is the task of a year or a season. For Theodore Roosevelt, it was the work of a lifetime.

Roosevelt was a man always on the make. As numerous contemporaries noted, he seemed congenitally unable to sit still. Always writing, talking, adventuring, improving—Henry Adams called him "pure act." His kinetic activity is legend and has made him a beloved figure in American lore. But what has proved less obvious to observers, in his lifetime and in ours, is the degree to which Roosevelt's strenuousity stemmed from the life of his mind. Roosevelt never came to rest in life because he never fully reconciled himself to the world as he found it or as he found himself within it. He was forever trying to understand better and experience more, to improve himself and his circumstances. Roosevelt was always reforming. In time, he would try to reform himself and his nation with his politics.

Theodore Roosevelt came of age and then to office in a country convulsed by historic change. Factories and railroads and coal mines and telegraphs transformed the American economy. The era of the small, independent producer, long an American ideal, succumbed in the fierce battle of prices and production to larger business conglomerations the press called "trusts." The age of combination was at hand.

American society changed, too. Immigrants streamed to the country's shores in unprecedented volume, straining cities' social infrastructures and upending urban politics. Workers moved from the farm to the city, and everywhere Americans found new trades, enjoyed new domestic comforts, faced new economic perils, and felt connected—even crowded—like never before. As the century wore on, the old urban social elite found themselves increasingly overshadowed and politically marginalized by the industrial *riche* and an upstart, professional middle class. The social strata of the nineteenth century crumbled away.

Social mores and the intellectual edifices that supported them felt the strain as well. New biological discoveries and finds in paleontology produced new scientific theories to explain them, first and foremost the theory of evolution. German higher criticism meanwhile suggested the Bible was itself just a product of evolution, a human work, filled with gaps and oversights and plain old-fashioned mistakes. Beneath the weight of these twin pressures and the industrial juggernaut, the mainstays of American Christianity began to give way. Its power to act as an integrating moral source, providing the framework for science, philosophy, politics, and the arts, would not last out the century.

Americans of all types and regions responded to this upheaval and its severe dislocations with a passion for reform. They called themselves by many names, including Grangers, Mugwumps, and Populists. Others were known less formally, as settlement house workers or good government reformers, as temperance advocates or believers in a social gospel. From wherever they hailed and whatever their cause célèbre, the reformers shared a common concern; their agendas were driven by a common fixation. They were, all of them, unshakably focused on the preservation of American self-government. The challenges of the era led them to take up again the fundamental problems of republican democracy. The health of the republic and the fate of democratic freedom constituted their grand refrain.

Foremost among them stood Theodore Roosevelt. More than any other figure of the era, he embodied the reformist aspirations of the American people. Roosevelt too followed the path of the industrial age to the enduring questions of free government. He too understood the meaning of liberty and the requirements of citizenship to be the central problems of his generation. He addressed these problems, and his age, with his politics.

Today Roosevelt's politics are claimed by all manner of controversialists from across the political spectrum. He is hailed by some as the patron of the modern welfare state, the first great twentieth century champion of social justice through government action. Others claim him as the original neo-conservative, pointing to his hawkish foreign policy and aggressive defense of American interests. There are elements of truth in both these characterizations, and in many of the other images of Roosevelt current in contemporary America. For all his popularity, however, for all the volumes penned about his life and essays appropriating his legacy, surprisingly few historians have paused to consider Roosevelt's political thought as a whole, to mine its origins or trace its effect on his era. Since the Second World War, in fact, most historians have regarded Roosevelt as merely another pragmatic politician and his political ideas as a largely incoherent assortment of various nostrums, plucked up as the need arose and just as easily discarded. This view is mistaken. It is time that Roosevelt the thinker received his due.

Roosevelt's ideas certainly did reflect the major intellectual currents of the day—from the racialism and fascination with science to the abiding faith in human progress. They reflected his personal circumstances and his political needs. But Roosevelt was no crass intellectual opportunist. His political thought was a complex theme that unfolded over multiple movements, taking on subtlety and nuance, gathering depth and resonance, as it progressed. The dominant motif emerged relatively early and waxed grander as he went. In a word, that theme was righteousness. Roosevelt called the nation to live better. He insisted that neither economic systems nor class struggles set the course of history. Individual character did. He preached social reform through personal transformation. This was the gospel of an earlier age set to a new key, with influences buried deep in America's past.

Roosevelt's ideas were consequential. His preaching galvanized a national moment of reform that altered the trajectory of American politics and shaped the American character. In the preceding decades discrete smatterings of reform advocates had pressed for government intervention to meet the challenges of the industrial age. Their agitation was typically confined to the state and city levels. Roosevelt's presidency inaugurated a twenty-year period of reform politics on the national stage, a period that came to be known as the progressive era. In those years Americans acquired a larger, stronger, more activist national state. They acquired a more powerful presidency, a new national regulatory apparatus, a new administrative bureaucracy, and a new role in the world. From the debates of that period came the grammar of our contemporary politics, and from its battles our reigning public philosophy.

Roosevelt made the progressive era possible. His spirit became its ethos. His politics of virtue, his warrior republicanism, was a gauntlet thrown down to an entire country and to himself, a challenge to be better, to be more, to be righteous. It was a challenge that defined his life and his time.

Americans in the early twenty-first century again find themselves beset by bewildering social, economic, and technological change; embroiled in foreign wars; and wondering what it is government should do. We have come to a time, in short, when the purposes of our political life are again in question. All things considered, it is an auspicious moment to examine the ideas of a man who lived in an uncertain milieu much like our own, and whose answers to his era helped make the modern age what it is.

It should go without saying that Theodore Roosevelt's mind was too capacious to be exposited in one modest volume. No historian could hope to capture the teeming variety of his ideas in a few hundred pages, and I do not intend to try. What follows is not a biography of Roosevelt, of which many outstanding instances already exist, or a comprehensive study of his intellect. Instead, these pages are meant as an extended essay about one man's intellectual and even spiritual journey and the politics that journey produced.

Because Roosevelt's political ideas developed in a particular historical context, this story is also necessarily about his time, his teachers, and his intellectual forebears, including those he knew and those he did not. Following Roosevelt on his way we meet many of the grand ideas and figures of turn-of-the-century America. In many cases, we must understand them in order to understand him. To that end, I have attempted to place Roosevelt in conversation with the historical characters whose ideas he drew on and revised. And I have attempted to relate his thought to that of other important thinkers in the Western political tradition that was his own.

To trace the development of Roosevelt's political ideas is to find the story of his character and the character of his time. With any luck, the effort may help us understand the character of our own.

IN THE FATHER'S HOUSE

Toward morning the north wind slackened, and the dawn came milder than those before. Passengers on the ferry to Staten Island were relieved to find the bay relatively calm and the deck free of ice, though elsewhere the gale's handiwork lingered: tides in the East River, swelled to record levels by the October wind, remained high. Still, the morning of the twenty-seventh arrived as a reprieve, a temperate pause before the onset of a bitter season. The year was 1858. In a stately brownstone on East Twentieth Street, a young woman heavy with child set aside her breakfast and ordered a coach. Encouraged by the break in the weather, she would spend the day about town, while she still could.

New York was not a quiet city, not in cold weather or hot or at any time of the day. Over eight hundred thousand souls jostled and traded within its boundaries. Crowded factories clattered with activity hour by hour, slowing only when the workers stumbled home late to their tenements, those twenty-five-by-seventy-foot housing blocks on the city's lower east side that a working family might share with twenty-four others. The dockyards teemed with scores of newcomers fresh from Ireland, Scandinavia, central Europe, and other far regions of the globe, while vendors, panhandlers, and pickpockets roamed the streets between City Hall Park and lower Broadway. Merchants kept their offices farther downtown, and they could sometimes be seen in favorable weather walking about Battery Park with their wives between twelve and two in the afternoon.[1]

Once near the heart of the thirteen states, New York sat now on the country's eastern periphery, its days as the nation's capital long past. It was a world unto itself, this city, profoundly different from any other place in America. Yet for all its difference—for the soot and smog of the wage-paying industries, for the working poor jammed together in makeshift housing, for the stunning ethnic diversity—the fate of New York remained inextricably bound with that of the nation beyond its cobblestone streets. And in 1858, the future of that nation seemed uncertain indeed.

A vast frontier beckoned America in the West, but its promise deepened, rather than relieved, the country's crisis of identity. Would chattel slavery be permitted to spread into the Western territories? With that question's answer rode the fate of the Union. Two days earlier, on the evening of October 25, William H. Seward of the fledgling Republican Party warned a mass audience in Rochester that America harbored competing political systems, one based on slave labor, the other on free, and they could not survive together. Either the sugar plantations of Louisiana would be tilled by free men, Seward predicted, or the wheat fields of the North would be worked by slaves.[2]

He was not alone in his forecast. Northern preachers, abolitionists, free labor advocates, and unionists increasingly believed slavery to be incompatible with free government and healthy capitalism, while Southern slave owners and cultural apologists cast themselves as the defenders of order, aristocracy, and other social mores that made republican government possible. The independent gentleman essential in republican theory would disappear if Northern imperialism succeeded, charged John C. Calhoun and his intellectual apostles. Worse, every city would look like New York, crawling with foreigners and wage workers and municipal corruption. Chattel slavery was a bulwark against a future of deadening, soulless industrialism. It was a shield of the South's proud past, of its schools and churches and social structure. It was a defense of republican government against mass democracy.[3]

Though they were not yet ready to label their Northern brethren as traitors to the Constitution sunk in "erroneous religious belief," those charges leveled by the South Carolina Convention in 1860 were not far off. For their part, many Northerners—many New Yorkers—could not yet imagine a war between the states. That there would be a fight for America's future of some sort was clear to most, however, and while newsboys shouted the headlines and New Yorkers went about their daily tasks, the city, like the country, waited this day in autumn, suspended between past and future at the turn of history.[4]

In the early afternoon Martha Bulloch Roosevelt of East Twentieth Street cut short her shopping and returned to Number 28, suddenly tired. She took a light lunch of bread and butter with ginger preserves and climbed the stairs, heavily, to her bed. An hour later she was in the throes of childbirth. With some effort servants managed eventually to locate a neighborhood physician. He came to her bedside as darkness fell, in time to deliver a son—her first. The time was 7:45 in the evening, October 27, 1858. His name would be Theodore.[5]

If Theodore Roosevelt was, as he would later insist, a "straight New Yorker" by birth, he was first the child of another world: the house of Roosevelt. A member of the eighth generation of his family born in the United States, "Teedie" was named for his father, Theodore Roosevelt, Senior. As the choice suggested, the boy was expected from the beginning to follow his namesake in the Roosevelt world. This was a place of aristocratic leisure and high-minded charity, of uptown homes and European holidays, and of fervent, practiced religious devotion. Amid this world Teedie learned to walk and speak and read; he gained his first lessons in life and acquired the intellectual trappings that defined his later education and public career. "Most American boys of my age," Roosevelt said in retrospect, "were taught both by their surroundings and by their studies." This was especially true for him.[6]

By early twenty-first century standards, his education was unconventional, and even in his day, even among his class, somewhat unusual. Before the age of thirteen, Teedie received no formal education. He never attended primary or secondary school. Instead, his instructors were his parents, his books, his travels and cultural milieu, and, after his thirteenth birthday, a series of private tutors handpicked by his father. With them he studied English, French, German, Latin, and some Greek. He read a bit of European history and mathematics, and enough science to whet a lifelong appetite. But his more important intellectual acquisitions were the core life convictions that he would use to arrange all his other knowledge. In this sense, his early lessons on manhood and God, science, race, and history were among his most significant. Roosevelt's instruction in these subjects in the years preceding his undergraduate career was neither discrete nor chronological. The areas of study overlapped and influenced one another; the lessons were given in various ways by multiple sources over Roosevelt's childhood and youth. But he learned these lessons well. Their echo could be heard years later in the railroad rate debate of 1905 and the Bull Moose crusade of 1912, in his public sermons and his private letters.

His upbringing made virility and faith, science and race, Roosevelt's enduring preoccupations, as they were his family's and his father's. The elder Theodore embraced a fervent Christianity of uncompromising piety and righteous works but worried that his children would be too weak to follow his way. As Teedie grew, the country's cultural consensus was fraying, at least among the Northeastern elite. Torn by religious heterodoxy, by growing popular materialism and the utilitarian philosophical systems that justified it, by ethnic diversity and the revolution in the biological sciences, the amalgam of Protestant Christianity, late Enlightenment rationalism, and republican political theory that served as America's public philosophy was coming apart. Philosophers, politicians, and scientists alike searched for replacements of one sort or another. They struggled to reconcile an older American concern with civic virtue, individualism, and self-government with a new pluralistic, scientific, industrialized America. They sought to preserve biblical mores without biblical religion. Roosevelt lived amid this great cultural conversation. He imbibed its terms and learned its cadences. Like those ideas he found and embraced in youth, as a man he too would straddle old and new. He would speak of faith, but he believed in a salvation found only on earth. He would employ the words of republican liberalism, but in the phrasing of a racialist. He talked as a conservative, but harbored the political ambitions of a radical. This assortment of paradoxes and projects Roosevelt shared with a number of other Americans from backgrounds similar to his, and he would lead them, these progressives, for a time. Their ideas — his ideas — would help make modern America and set the trajectory of twentieth century American politics, if perhaps in ways he did not quite expect. All of these consequences were products in one way or another of Roosevelt's education. It may have been unconventional, but it made the deepest of marks.

When he was small, still in dresses and his blond hair in bangs, Teedie learned to carry his father's Scriptures to him, in the evening, grasping the volume with his small hands. Theodore and his eldest son shared this ritual, and these moments, alone — Martha Roosevelt would not learn of this routine until war had taken her husband from the house and Teedie told the story, longing to see him. Twenty-seven years old when his first boy was born, the elder Theodore ever afterward strode across the landscape of his son's memory in the vigor of his early manhood, before the onset of the cancer that struck him down in middle age. He was a tall, broad-shouldered man, handsome and gregarious, with a special gift for inspiring deep personal admiration, even awe. "My father," Roosevelt later attested, "was the best man I ever knew." He was also the man Teedie wanted most to please. "I am sure there is no one," he wrote his namesake from Harvard, "who has a Father who is also his best and most intimate friend. . . . I shall do my best to deserve your trust."[7]

Teedie had picked a daunting idol to emulate. His father was the fifth son of Cornelius Van Schaack Roosevelt, the latest in a long line of determined, resourceful, prosperous Roosevelt men. The family had come to Manhattan when it was still called New Amsterdam, and though they infrequently ventured beyond its bounds, they made quite a name for themselves there. The Roosevelts had been bank presidents, engineers, state senators. Cornelius's brother James had served in the United States Congress and had been a member of the New York Board of Aldermen, a leader of the New York City faction in the state legis-

lature, a Justice of the State Supreme Court, an ex-officio Judge of the State
Court of Appeals, and a United States district attorney for the Southern District
of New York. Yet even in the company of such distinguished forebears, Theodore
Roosevelt, Senior, was a class to himself.[8]

To his radiant, forceful personality Theodore added physical vigor and a natural athleticism: he was given to long horse rides in Central Park and to driving
his four-in-hand trap at an adventurous pace through the streets of New York. His
physical stamina was legendary. His older daughter remembered outings with
her father so exhausting she would have cried had she not been loath to disap-
point him. Then there was the way he bore the Roosevelt legacy, wielding it with
such élan. The house on East Twentieth Street where Teedie entered the world
had been a gift to Theodore from his father. In a display of generous largesse,
C.V.S. Roosevelt had given Theodore's brother, Robert, the house next door.
The front was brownstone rather than red brick, in keeping with the upper crust
vogue of the 1850s. And while the living space was relatively modest, the extensive library, black haircloth upholstery, French Empire furniture, and coterie of
servants betrayed Theodore's social standing: Cornelius Van Schaack Roosevelt
was an exceptionally wealthy man, the Roosevelt family a multigeneration New
York fixture, and Theodore himself a veritable prince of Manhattan.[9]

He nominally found employment with his older brother James—there were
five brothers in all—at the family's hardware business turned importing firm,
Roosevelt & Son. But Theodore's most time-consuming activity was his philan-
thropy. The New York Newsboys' Lodging House, Miss Sattery's Night School
for Little Italians, the Children's Aid Society, the New York Orthopedic Hospital, the Museum of Natural History, and the Sunday school program at the
Madison Square Presbyterian Church all benefited from the copious attention,
personal and financial, of Theodore Roosevelt. He had a particular way with
children. The urchin, orphan newsboys, who could not have been more different from the heir to the Roosevelt fortune, thrilled to see him and could listen to
his stories for hours. He helped find homes—and a new life—for many of them
in the American West. He cut a striking figure, this great, bearded lion of a man,
galloping through Central Park or dancing with his daughter in tailored evening
attire at the Cotillion Club. He was perhaps the proudest—certainly the most inspiring—son of a storied family.[10]

Theodore was not one to dispirit his own family with constant demands or unrealistic expectations. Nevertheless, the standard set by his example was high,
and he made few if any efforts to ease the pressure. If being a Roosevelt came naturally to him, it was not, for all that, such an easy thing to be. For Teedie, the famous stamina that undergirded all his father's activities and enabled his remark-

able works was particularly intimidating. The younger Roosevelt was a notoriously sickly child, plagued by asthma, poor eyesight, recurring headaches, diarrhea, fevers, and bad dreams, among other things. The man on horseback who carried all the city on his shoulders was a man Teedie could hardly hope to become. Yearn as he might to please his father and join him in his world, the path to Roosevelt manhood was closed to Teedie so long as physical fitness was the entrance fee.

The asthma was the worst of it. Teedie suffered his first attack in June of 1862 at three years old, while his father was away. He would battle the affliction the rest of his life. Once, while vacationing in Europe with his parents and siblings, his breathing became so labored nurses rubbed his chest until he coughed blood. Somewhat less severe but no less dismaying asthmatic fits regularly occasioned hurried trips out of the city and to the New York countryside or, better still, to the sea. The affliction disrupted family travel, ruined holidays, and largely prevented Teedie from attending school. Theodore thought perhaps a total change of climate would help his son and, partly for this reason, packed the family off to Europe for an extended vacation in 1869, six months after Teedie's eleventh birthday. Experience quickly exploded his theory. "On Saturday was exactly the fortnight since we reached Venice. *These entire two weeks* he has had nothing but diarrhea and threats of asthma," Martha Roosevelt wrote a friend from Italy. "[W]hat it is that keeps up the attacks is a mystery." Then, too, from the time he could toddle, Roosevelt had been thin and small for his age. While little brother Elliott grew tall and muscular, Teedie was still losing fistfights to younger boys at age fourteen.[11]

Not surprisingly, Teedie evinced an early and lasting preoccupation with physical strength and prowess, apparent even before his adolescence. The journal the junior Roosevelt kept on his yearlong tour of the European continent from 1869 to 1870, among his earliest literary productions, makes vivid and repeated references to his conquests in war games and other physical contests. His playmates would be "forced to receive me as an honored soldier," after his victory in a romp of military make-believe, Teedie insisted to his diary while in Rome in January of 1870. February found Teedie reading a history of the Greek empire and directing imaginary imperial conquests in the parks of the Italian capital. The family left Rome in March, but Teedie's fascination with soldiers and conquest, military campaigns and other daring exploits involving physical strength, remained as intense as it had been throughout the trip.[12]

This fascination is understandable given his most esteemed role model. While Teedie was reading Greek history and reenacting military campaigns, his father marched the family across Europe, planning exhausting visits to museums, palaces, and gardens, punctuated by rigorous hiking excursions and long country walks. Nor was Theodore's kinetic vacationing philosophy confined to his 1870 European holiday. His family took regular trips to the New York countryside, spending weeks there swimming, walking, and horseback riding in the summer months. A year after their return from the Continent, Teedie wrote that he, his father, siblings, and a handful of other extended family members were in the Adirondack Mountains on another hiking adventure. As if to consecrate the event, Theodore closed each evening in those mountains with the words of one of that era's foremost enthusiasts of battle and victory, James Fenimore Cooper. As the sun set, young Roosevelt told his journal, "Father read aloud to us from the last of the Mohicans [sic]."[13]

Teedie came to understand the importance of bodily strength from other sources as well. The younger Roosevelt may have been physically small and sickly, but he was intellectually robust. By his tenth birthday, Teedie's literary consumption was impressive, though confined to two main staples: natural history books and adventure stories, often some combination thereof. Mayne Reid, J. G. Wood, R. M. Ballantyne, and James Fenimore Cooper were Roosevelt's early and constant literary companions, and they reinforced what his father exemplified: physical strength was the sine qua non of manliness.[14]

But it was Teedie's favorite magazine that put the lesson most bluntly. Well into his fifty-sixth year, with a copy on his shelves of every issue of *Our Young Folks*, Roosevelt insisted that the periodical was "the very best magazine in the world." He doubted "if any magazine for old or young has ever surpassed it." Begun in the waning days of the War between the States, *Our Young Folks* contained tips on farming, appropriate dress, and, most importantly for Teedie Roosevelt, long, detailed, and even occasionally subtle adventure stories involving children. The settings ranged from the Revolutionary War to the Wild West, but always the moral was the same: the children who showed honesty and integrity, the boys who behaved bravely, won the day.[15]

While most of the magazine's story lines were essentially similar to those of Roosevelt's other reading, *Our Young Folks* did something that Reid and Ballantyne and Cooper did not do. It made the quasi-republican premises behind its moral narratives explicit. "A great and good nation is made up of great and good men and women," an article in the January 1865 issue admonished. "A strong building cannot be composed of weak timber." In case the child missed the point, "a complete man," the article went on, "is composed of a healthy body, a cultured brain, and a true heart. Wanting either [sic] he fails." Here was Theodore's life example summarized in the clearest terms. Intellectual knowledge and moral purpose depended on a healthy body to be made useful or, as the junior Roosevelt would put it later, "efficient." And on personal character all depended. So thoroughly did Roosevelt imbibe this logic that he would rehearse it regularly throughout his public life with almost precisely the same words used by *Our Young Folks* in the 1860s.[16]

This teaching shared striking similarities with republican political theory, a body of thought handed down to early Americans by their English forebears that emphasized the relationship between sound personal character and political freedom. The writers at *Our Young Folks*, however, gave the traditional republican reasoning a unique, mid-nineteenth century turn. They insisted that one needed to be physically fit in order to lead an active, involved life beneficial to others. More than that, the magazine directly suggested that physical vigor was a reflection of one's character and moral worth. The child had a moral responsibility to cultivate his or her body. Accordingly, small homilies offered as articles instructed readers on the posture and sleeping habits necessary to develop sound, healthy physiques. Personal happiness and usefulness to society were implicated in the way their bodies developed, children were told. Indeed, the fate of the nation was implicated, and the reader's responsibility to himself and his body was also a responsibility to the nation at large. "What magnificent expansion" awaited the country, one article exulted in 1865. "But what immense responsibilities! Soon they must rest upon you, — your manhood and womanhood. God and the nations will watch you."[17]

This was a weighty burden. And if Teedie found such expectations difficult to shoulder, there is evidence other members of his family did as well. Martha Bulloch Roosevelt, born in 1835, married in 1853, was a daughter of the South. She had been a high-spirited, if somewhat indulged, young lady when Theodore met her on her family's Georgia plantation—Bulloch Hall—in 1850. She was only fifteen. Their courtship, carried on almost entirely by correspondence, sparkled with the playful, coquettish enthusiasm of the woman all the Bullochs called "Mittie." "My dear Thee," she wrote her Northern fiancé in 1853, in a typical flash of debutante flair, "I kiss a great many different people and always expect to, I cannot allow you monopoly there, why, just think," she went on, fairly taunting, "what the world would be without my kisses, I could not think of depriving my friends of that pleasure."[18]

Yet once removed to the North, to New York City, the fiery young Mittie, who had unilaterally chosen her husband's groomsmen, who fed his romantic insecurities, and who dictated his schedule down to the day of their wedding, somehow faded. While Theodore grew increasingly confident, lively, and magnanimous, never again to reveal in correspondence the emotional vulnerability captured in his early letters to the belle of Roswell, Georgia, Mittie seemed to retreat into wistfulness and expensive indulgence. Her daughter Corinne told of hours spent before the vanity mirror, applying makeup, nurturing her glossy, ebony black hair; of repeated baths and pink satin and French hairdressers and a horrible, fastidious hatred of dirt. Daniel, the Roosevelt coachman, was ordered to prepare the coach every weekday at three; many an afternoon, after hours of pacing, he was simply sent away—Mittie could not complete her beautifying routine.[19]

Her financial extravagance grew so extreme that Theodore insisted their eldest child, Anna, take over day-to-day management of the household, though the girl was just fourteen. His wife had become rather a mystery to him, and occasionally a trial, though by all accounts Theodore was a patient man. He seems not to have considered the possibility that his life and his family's expectations might have had something to do with Mittie's transformation. "Goodbye, dearest Thee," she wrote to her husband, almost forlornly, from Paris in 1873. "Don't forget mittie, who loves you very, *very* dearly and devotedly, tho she sometimes troubles you and suffers remorse for afterwards." She signed the note, "One of your babies." Indeed she was.[20]

If she had once captivated Bulloch Hall with her laughter, her witticisms, and her vivacity, now she held her husband's attention with her many needs and delicate health. A tendency toward physical frailty apparent from her early teen years became a pronounced disposition in New York. "Mittie is not well," her mother wrote from East Twentieth Street in 1863, a sentence that would have been true any number of days during the year. "She does not have much palpitation but at times has much pain about the region of the heart. The Dr. thinks it neuralgia."[21]

Neuralgia—clinical nervousness—the bane of the urban upper class, afflicted Theodore's wife with apparently escalating severity. His family was not alone in the suffering. In the years immediately following the outbreak of civil war, concern about physical vitality and mental wellness became so pervasive among segments of the Northeastern elite that it spawned a new field of medical research. Neurologist George M. Beard, an acquaintance of the Roosevelts, and likeminded researchers feared the urban industrial boom was shifting the country's demographic patterns and cultural habits in ways detrimental to physical strength and moral well-being. Beard diagnosed the country's cultural dissensus as a medical condition and prescribed a medical cure to achieve moral renewal.

Theodore had good cause to follow the research and study its recommendations. His wife suffered. More alarmingly, his elder son and heir did too.

Medical professionals eventually settled on "neurasthenia" as the catch-all term to describe the slew of symptoms they believed America's new industrial age was prompting, at least among certain portions of the population. Migraine headaches, insomnia, dyspepsia, depression, alcoholism, hysteria, and asthma were a few of the disorders that field-leader Beard saw as part of the "neurasthenic" condition. Idiosyncratic in the late 1860s and early '70s, Beard's theory of neurasthenia had become widely accepted and its terminology ubiquitous by the time Teedie left home for Harvard in 1876. Part of the theory's attraction was its ability to explain medically—and therefore, with an air of objectivity—the somewhat strange and seemingly recent physical and mental phenomena besetting the upper classes. Neurasthenic studies responded to Americans' concerns about the effects of the urban industrial world on health and character by offering a broader, scientific narrative about the development of American civilization.[22]

"American nervousness is the product of American civilization," Beard wrote in his magnum opus, *American Nervousness*, published in 1881. This neurasthenia was the direct result of modernity. Defined as a progressive disease of the nerves, Beard postulated that neurasthenia began with general nervous excitement which, if unchecked, could end in exhaustion, "brain-collapse," insanity, or even death. The basic contentions sounded plausible enough: every person had a "nerve force" balance, the account of energy one needed to work, think, and conduct common, everyday tasks. If that balance was overtaxed or not properly "reinvested" and thereby resupplied, a nerve force deficit might result, leading to neurasthenia. Larger deficits produced severer neurasthenic symptoms, and the lower the nerve force account balance fell, the harder it was to resupply.[23]

The theory got interesting when Beard specified who was at highest risk, and why. The neurologist-cum-moralist held that the disease attacked only those with the most refined sensibilities: the well-educated and well-read, business owners, salaried workers, artists, and those who did not work for a living at all. In other words, though Beard characterized the affliction as widespread, and though it had, by the late nineteenth century, inspired a whole literature of medical articles, newspaper reports, fiction, and poetry, neurasthenia was confined almost exclusively to members of the upper classes living and working in America's industrial centers, principally Boston and New York. This class of Americans, the Roosevelt class, was most susceptible to neurasthenia, the theory went, because of their work and lifestyles. "Brain workers"—and apparently one could not work with both brain and hands—required more nerve force for their toils than did manual laborers, skilled or unskilled. This was because brain work, according to Beard, or what Americans now might call "white collar" or "desk work," was more intellectually tasking than the most strenuous physical exertion. Factory workers and farmhands might collapse in exhaustion at the end of a day's labor, but their nerve force supply was relatively unaffected.[24]

Tellingly, workers could deplete their nerve force in ways other than mental exertion. Moral vices were the primary examples of this sort of energy-wasting activity. Illicit sex, drinking, gambling, card-playing, and, in the case of adolescent boys especially, masturbation, consumed nerve force to no benefit, short- or long-term. The socioeconomic elite were again more likely to fall prey to these vices because of their greater leisure time as well as the unique social and mental pressures they suffered.[25]

In the peculiar susceptibility of wealthy, white, established urban families to neurasthenia, both Beard and the writers at *Our Young Folks* detected a grave threat to American civilization. According to their view, Northeastern, upper-class families like the Roosevelts who had lived in the United States for a century or more were the caretakers of American culture. As wave after wave of immigration broke over American society, the "native born" elite became increasingly important bridges between the America of the past and that of the future. Should they as a class become enfeebled, the treasures of the country's culture might be submerged and the ship of state robbed of necessary ballast.[26]

On the whole, neurasthenic doctrine was less a medical theory than a moral one, a late nineteenth century iteration of Protestant biblical morality removed from its source and plated with the language of scientific empiricism. As such, it reflected a sharp concern for the decline of social mores coupled with a reluctance to try to rejuvenate those norms through religious commitment. Earlier generations of Americans sought to reform social behavior by proselytizing society's members, by converting them to the straight and narrow way. The loss of the culturally distinct, visible community of Puritan elect in the mid-1700s helped spur the Great Awakening. Concern for the viciousness of life on the frontier—for the drinking and whoring and wanton violence—birthed a generation of circuit riders in the 1820s and '30s and stirred one of the largest, culturewide religious revivals in history.[27]

But the medical moralists of Teedie's boyhood did not preach repentance, at least not biblical repentance in the sense of a return to God in Christ. Beard and his apostles preached a piety of good behavior, clean living, and social altruism. Intriguingly, they felt compelled to endorse evangelical mores only by grounding them in the apparently neutral material of scientific fact. In this light, Beard's theories were one attempt to answer to the loss of a shared public philosophy by recasting one of its central pillars, biblical morality, in a more defensible, scientific form. Neurasthenia was also a cultural theory, as most moral theories eventually are. Neurasthenic doctrine subtly deprecated manual labor, slandered immigration and immigrants, and anointed as worthy the urban elite. Its prescriptions aimed to renew that class, the Northeastern professional and leisured class, reaffirming their cultural authority even as proponents criticized many class members' behavior.[28]

The solution to the gathering crisis menacing America's cultural protectors, and thus America, was also the solution to Teedie Roosevelt's crisis of manhood. The answer to both was to build moral fiber by building physical strength. Exercise and physical fitness helped ward off the debilitating effects of neurasthenia. Moreover, if unhealthy bodies often betrayed unhealthy moral behavior, the converse seemed true: sound bodies reflected sound morals, because morality was good for you, literally. The elder Theodore Roosevelt knew of George Beard, and sometime after 1868, probably following the family's first trip to Europe, took Teedie to his clinic. Beard's colleague Alphonso D. Rockwell diagnosed the boy as suffering from the "handicap of riches." He found the boy effeminate. Teedie had been too weak to attend school with his brother and too weak for sustained physical exertion, and the asthma attacks were unrelenting.[29]

Theodore was determined that Teedie not suffer like his wife—or flounder like her. Apparently the junior Roosevelt came to the same conclusion. He gladly inherited his mother's rapier wit and gift for storytelling. Certainly he always spoke of his mother and her family with warm affection. He deeply admired the courage of his Bulloch uncles who fought in the Civil War. Yet from the time he was ten he habitually and dismissively referred to her as "darling little motherling," a habit he may have taken from his father. She was small, delicate, easily exhausted, and ineffective—everything his father was not, and everything he did not want to be. If his father's example was hard, Teedie would struggle rather than retreat. He would win his father's approval, and win his manhood in the process. "Theodore," the elder Roosevelt addressed his son in the fall of 1870, just shy of the boy's twelfth birthday, "you have the mind but you have not the body, and without the help of the body the mind cannot go as far as it should. You must make your body. It is hard drudgery to make one's body, but I know you will do it."[30]

Theodore Roosevelt, Junior, nodded at his father and through clenched teeth replied, "I'll make my body."[31]

Physical virility was the doorway to manhood and also, Teedie learned, the path to salvation. The purpose of a man's life was not, after all, to gratify his own desires or to bask in luxury. The purpose was to do God's work on earth. Proponents of neurasthenic theory may have been reluctant to seek moral renewal in religious fervor, but the senior Theodore Roosevelt felt no such qualms. "Dearest One," he wrote to Mittie one Sunday afternoon after their marriage, "I have just returned from hearing Dr. Dewitt preach one of his beautiful sermons. . . . His subject was the ascension of Christ and he persuaded us to turn our thoughts above, where he now is." Theodore's thoughts seemed permanently fixed there. He prized the Scripture and apparently spent a portion of each day in prayer and Bible reading. Indeed, he was frustrated when he could not. "I forgot to bring my Bible," he lamented to his wife while traveling on business, "and delayed buying one, hoping that Dodge would get the room next to me and I could use his."[32]

He encouraged intimates to follow his example and make time for prayerful devotion, beginning with his wife. Even before their marriage, Theodore showed a tender concern for her spiritual wellness. He took great delight in sending his fiancée a prayer book to help her in her daily devotions. "Dan has got the prayer book in his trunk," he told her in a letter from New York. "It is a present that gives me great pleasure to give you, always remembering your promise never to think of it as compared with the bible." In the same letter in which he praised the Reverend Dr. Dewitt, he urged his new wife to consider carefully where she would most like to attend services. "Think over it Darling One. [W]e both of us want a settled place of worship. . . . [W]e will talk it over when we meet."[33]

Mirroring his own devotional life, Theodore propounded spiritual exercises for his children. Every morning of the week began with family prayers, which he led. He taught them to memorize Bible verses and frequently offered brief homilies on their meaning. Corinne Roosevelt's daughter would later remember that her mother spoke of Jeremiah's lamentations, King David, the tombs of the Judges, and all manner of events connected with the life of Christ in the most intimate way, "as if they were friends." Young Teedie encountered his first descriptions of war and battle in the Old Testament, and could soon offer detailed analyses of their action. There were prayers before bed, too, led this time by Martha Roosevelt. On Sundays, Theodore took the family en masse to church, and all four children were expected to spend the hours thereafter in quiet reflection and then to recount the sermon that evening to their father's satisfaction. In time, Theodore gave each child his or her own Bible from which to read.[34]

Theodore's faith did not manifest merely in personal piety, however. He turned his famous physical vigor to righteous works. His considerable philanthropic activity flowed directly from his commitment to living God's goodness, and even in addition to his numerous, regular charitable obligations—from the Newsboys' home to the Orthopedic Hospital—he found time to do more. After teaching Sunday school one winter morning in 1860, he told his wife he found one of the boys from another class who had been dismissed for bad behavior. "I gave him a tract on condition that he would go home and read it, which I found an hour or two afterwards he had done by dropping in and examining him on the contents." Not content with this burst of missionary activity, "I laid myself out to see how many I could persuade to meet me at the Mission Church in the evening who would not have come otherwise. About ten came which I thought a pretty good afternoon's work." Still, the elder Theodore often felt he was not doing enough. After hearing a sermon on Luke 12:47–48 — "[E]veryone to whom much was given, of him much will be required" — Theodore wrote that he might devote "all the time and much more than I was now doing to God's service and I would still fall far short of any hope of salvation except through His divine mercy."[35]

Teedie observed his father's strenuous righteousness and accepted wholeheartedly his stern moral code. But there is reason to suspect he may not have understood the elder Theodore's perspective. To be sure, Teedie followed his father's example strictly — even severely. He rejected playmates who failed his moral standards: "Did you hear Percy Cushion was a failure? He swore like a trooper and used disreputable language." Teedie cast him out of the children's circle. Later, he refused to smoke at Harvard, drink to excess, or engage prostitutes. He would teach Sunday school for much of his life and regularly read the Bible. But Teedie did not apparently grasp in his boyhood or later understand the personal devotion to a personal savior from which his father's actions sprang. To him, the senior Theodore's religion, with all its activity, its demanding routine, its emphasis on service, may well have appeared as a piece with his commitment to masculine virility — both were about action, about redemption through doing, righteousness by works. "To love justice, to be merciful. . . . That is my religion, my faith," the younger Roosevelt said once grown. "To me it sums up all religion, it is all the creed I need." Faith, on his interpretation, became a high call to right living, and thus like his father's example of manliness — or perhaps synonymous with it — a high standard to be met.[36]

Mittie Roosevelt might well have encouraged this view of religion, if somewhat inadvertently. Although a lifelong Presbyterian, she did not share her husband's evangelical fervor. Her letters contain virtually no references to private devotion beyond that prescribed by her husband. And though she participated in the familial exercises, and said prayers with the children and by herself each night before bed, a white sheet spread beneath her knees to guard her from any dirt, the children make no reference to regular religious instruction from their mother. Theodore had worried about Mittie's spiritual health before their marriage, and, tellingly, Mittie's mother worried too. Martha Stewart Bulloch lived in the Roosevelt brownstone almost continuously from Teedie's birth until her death in 1864 and was a devoted Christian. She frequently attended midweek prayer meetings in the city and recommended religious tracts to friends; she thanked God in her prayers for revivals in Ireland and longed for one at home. Though an unrepentant Southerner who loathed Abraham Lincoln and all he stood for, she possessed religious sensibilities that had more in common with her Northern son-in-law than with her daughter. She fretted over Mittie. "If she was only a christian, I think I could feel more satisfied," she told a family friend. "Susy dearest," she added in a perhaps oblique comment on Mittie's love of luxury, "this world is a great enemy to grace."[37]

"Grace" was not a word Teedie heard much from his mother or, though Theodore meditated on God's mercy in his personal writings, apparently from his father, either. But then, "grace" was not a concept in great favor in the religious conversation of the day. It had come to seem superfluous—or worse, ominous, a faint suggestion of incurable human sin and divine wrath. Instead, many Christian ministers and popular writers in the 1860s and '70s emphasized the personally and socially meliorative possibilities of "Christian" behavior: they spoke of Jesus's masculinity and urged believers to improve their souls, and the world, by improving their bodies. Sin was something to be overcome by sustained exertion, and the human being, like the human world, perfected through concerted action. Theologians also downplayed human depravity and stressed instead the person's altruistic capacities. It was the age of theological liberalism in America, another engine of cultural dissensus, and though Teedie's family members were hardly disciples, their faith and the new, muscular Christianity could sound a lot alike.

By the late 1860s established Northeastern churches had been drifting from Christian orthodoxy for some time. The heterodox creed common to Teedie's youth was Unitarianism, a faith that denied the divinity of Jesus of Nazareth and emphasized instead his moral example and teachings. Thomas Jefferson numbered himself in the Unitarian ranks toward the end of his life, as did a number of other prominent Eastern deists by the 1830s, including Ralph Waldo Emerson. Unitarianism shared a philosophical mooring with Emerson's burgeoning Transcendentalist movement, a North American cultural-literary-philosophical phenomenon that glorified the human spirit and human reason. Both Unitarianism and Transcendentalism challenged the traditional structures of orthodox Christianity, particularly the Protestant evangelical emphasis on the Bible as the revealed and incontrovertible word of God. By the 1830s and '40s, even those

Northeastern denominations with roots in Puritan and Lutheran theologies had begun to feel the Unitarian influence. Episcopalian, Disciples of Christ, Methodist, and Northern Presbyterian denominations were all placing rather less emphasis on the Bible and the person of Christ and more on the importance of moral behavior and Christ's general moral teachings. Talk of the exclusive nature of salvation—a merciful act of God effective only for those who accepted Christ as savior—was increasingly spare.[38]

Then came the new theology from the European continent. As a doctrinal school it originated in Germany, in the divinity faculties of that country's vaunted university system and the writings of Friedrich Daniel Ernst Schleiermacher. Schleiermacher wanted to adapt the Christian gospel to modern culture, to rescue religion from the ethical idealism of Kant and the speculative metaphysics of Fichte. Religious faith is not dependent on ethical systems or contemporary philosophy, he contended, but on a raw feeling of dependence on the infinite—the Great, the Beyond—a religious intuition common to all people. By the mid-1800s German theologians were pioneering a new method of biblical criticism consonant with the latest developments in natural science and philosophy. This "uniformitarian" approach treated the Bible like any other historical text. Miracles and other supernatural interventions it rejected as mythical in light of modern science. Instructed by German historicist philosophy, and with influences as far back as Benedict Spinoza, members of the uniformitarian school interpreted canonical books as products of particular time periods and reflections of the historically rooted consciousness of specific groups.[39]

If, as this higher criticism taught, the Bible was not the historical record of God's supernatural dealings with his people, liberals tended to regard it instead as a record of man's moral growth. From the severity and even barbarism of Old Testament sacrificial law to the emphasis on compassion and service in the New, liberals discerned real moral progress. Jesus's teachings, in particular, they took as the highest expression of human altruism, the product of several millennia of moral development. Liberals found that treating Jesus of Nazareth as the literal Son of God was understandably problematic, having ruled out supernatural interventions in human affairs. But they were eager to embrace him as an ethical role model, and the bolder among them claimed that Jesus's moral excellence was precisely why the evangelists called him the messiah, or Christ, in the first place. He embodied the full ethical potential of the human person, and his example would "save" others by encouraging them to realize their potentials. Jesus's divinity, then, was something akin to a metaphor—an expression of the highest human capacities within all people.[40]

Having reconceived sin and savior, liberals described a different road to salvation as well. Not saving faith in a divine Christ but rather ethical action in the example of Jesus is what the Bible demanded. The gospel message of the Christian Scriptures was that humans were inherently moral agents capable of genuine goodness. The universality of the gospel was not that salvation was available to all who believed in Christ but, rather, that Christ's ethical example was imitable by every person. Consequently, individuals' particular "dogmatic" confessions, their personal religious preferences, did not matter nearly as much as their behavior. Or to put it another way, religion's content was not nearly so important as its results. To be a Christian meant to live morally, as Christ did, or at least to try. In a word, the ethical and the religious were virtually synonymous. As theological populizer Walter Rauschenbusch put it, "[R]eligion and ethics are inseparable . . . ethical conduct is the supreme and sufficient religious act."[41]

Many ministers and laymen of mainline Protestant denominations regarded the new theology with approval. The Roosevelts' pastor, Dr. William Adams of Madison Square Presbyterian, counted himself a leader of "new Presbyterianism" and later took up the presidency of Union Theological Seminary in New York, citadel of American religious liberalism. What tended to worry these Protestants about the eclipse of theological orthodoxy were the consequences. Whether related to theological liberalism or not, in the years following the Civil War male church attendance plummeted. By the turn of the century, American church membership was two-thirds female, and active participation ratios more lopsided still. Popular writers like Carl Case worried that "in overcoming the norms and constraining elements" of the past—by which he meant Calvinist doctrine—Protestant churches had become "passive," overly concerned with appearance, and "feminine." Liberated from the sterner orthodoxy of an earlier age, modern American Christianity, or at least certain brands of it, stood in serious danger of becoming little more than a sentimental celebration of human goodness.[42]

Of course, a return to strict orthodoxy was out of the question—the way barred by the new theology and the scientific, materialistic ethos of the age. Instead, concerned parties took to emphasizing the virility of Jesus as an antidote to their loss of masculinity. In reaction against the "feminization" and theological shift of the period, they embraced a doctrine of religious physicality. At the core of this dogma was an idea strikingly similar to the one held by theorists of neurasthenia. In the words of the Young Men's Christian Association, founded in 1844 to evangelize the lost and by the 1870s devoted almost entirely to physical fitness, there was "a close relation . . . between good muscles and good health, and between good health and good morals." One's physical body reflected one's personal character and, in fact, the extent of one's religious commitment; muscular weakness, flabbiness, and general physical underdevelopment often betrayed sinful habits. Jesus, a carpenter, had been a strong and vigorous man and not, incidentally, a man who was without sin. Advocates of this "muscular Christianity" believed the link between health and holiness was apparent from Christ's own example.[43]

The case for muscular Christianity made sense only if one accepted a series of implicit theological premises. Acquiring ethical character traits could be a step toward salvation only if one believed ethical behavior and salvation were virtually synonymous. Muscle training and physical conditioning could advance the war against sin only if sin was conceived as failure to imitate Christ's manly, ethical model. Behind the mid-century embrace of religious physicality stood the liberal, humanist theology increasingly prevalent in the seminaries and churches of the American Northeast.

Insofar as this theology revised previous conceptions of sin and salvation, divinity and grace, it changed the social and even political landscape of the United States. An appreciable difference separated the idea that humans are naturally depraved and wicked apart from the saving grace of God, from the notion that individuals can, with the proper education and character development, realize their latent ethical potential. The first conception was common to the early American political tradition, with its emphasis on controlling humans' hunger for power and tendency toward corruption. The mature Teedie Roosevelt, by contrast, believed the latter. Personal character was indeed crucial, medicine and religion both told him. But happily, human nature was also improvable. The person could build his body, master his wickedness, and save his soul all at the same time, a teaching whose consequences would reach deep into Roosevelt's political career.

Morals and manliness went together in the Roosevelt world. Weaklings and cowards could not be true Christians because they were not true men. Theodore Roosevelt's example to his son was an inspiring one, but also perhaps intimidating. The senior Roosevelt appeared to find comfort, ultimately, in the divine grace of his savior, in the action of a personal God who completed what he could not, who accomplished what Theodore left undone. But his family knew no such solace. Paradoxically, removing the traditional teachings of human depravity and divine initiative could make the Christian message more demanding, not less. The righteousness of works, like the mantle of the Roosevelt legacy of which it was a part, made a heavy yoke, and Teedie felt the weight. After losing his father in the winter of 1878, young Theodore confessed to his journal, "I often feel so badly that such a wonderful man as father should have had a son of so little worth as I am." Attending a church service reminded him of "how little use I am, or ever shall be in the world. . . . I realize more and more every day that I am as much inferior to Father morally and mentally as physically." Yet Teedie soldiered on, labored on, struggled on, to make himself a man worthy of his father's approval.[44]

Not all members of the family fared so well. Martha Roosevelt would plead with her husband "not to be so hard on me," but it was Teedie's younger brother Elliott who suffered most. Harboring profound feelings of inferiority and personal worthlessness, Elliott never felt adequate to be his father's son. Once the more socially confident and robust of the Roosevelt boys, he would decline into indolence, debilitating depression, and an alcoholic death at the age of thirty-four.[45]

Not even the elder Theodore could always meet his own high expectations. In the fall of 1861, as war burst upon the Union, he hired a substitute to fight and die in his place. It was a decision he long regretted. Unable to live with his choice, or sit in the company of his Southern wife and her mother while thousands of his countrymen sacrificed their lives, Theodore did everything he could to reverse his shame in a blaze of righteous activity. He drafted a bill for the appointment of nationwide allotment commissioners, who without pay would serve the War Department and arrange to send home to needy families portions of soldiers' salaries. For three months he lobbied Congress to secure the bill's passage, and gladly accepted appointment as a commissioner for the State of New York when the act became law. He was away from his city for months at a time, in the depth of winter, riding from camp to camp, often in the saddle six to eight hours a day, standing in the cold and mud, trying to convince soldiers to send home what bit of their paycheck they could spare for the benefit of their wives and children.[46]

His letters to Mittie while away are studded with allusions to duty, honor, and service, and though he did not enjoy the physical hardship, he clearly took grim satisfaction in being without the comforts of home and apart from his wife and children, not unlike the soldiers whom he thought he should have joined. "Give a great many kisses to the dear little children from me," he wrote to her in the winter of 1861. "[I]t seems such a pity to be away from them so much and still I cannot help feeling that it would be my duty unless this had turned up to be away from them altogether by joining the army." But politics and public service were no substitute for martial duty, and that was a lesson Teedie learned as well. Theodore's failure to fight was the one demerit Teedie assigned to his father, and perhaps even this he blamed partially on his mother—she had been the one to insist Theodore not go to war against her Southern family, her brothers. But the failure was a great one nonetheless. In time, the younger Roosevelt not only would take up his father's yoke, he would attempt extravagantly to compensate for this single blemish on an otherwise awesome legacy.[47]

2

A SMALL, ORNITHOLOGICAL BOY

Jake had caught six fish, all before breakfast, and his father maybe two dozen, maybe more, but he hadn't caught any and now the flies were bothering him. Ellie and West were whipping the rapids just downstream, throwing their bodies up against the current and splashing. The flies were a bitter nuisance. Teedie Roosevelt, age twelve, abandoned his rock on the river's shore and, grasping a fishing pole, started down into the current. The water surged powerful and foamy, stronger than he expected, and after a few initial steps the current grabbed his feet and jerked him under. He fought to regain the surface and let go of his pole to use both hands. He was a passenger of the torrent now, swept along where it willed, the riverbed too deep below him to put down his feet, the current too strong to resist. Maybe if he had been stockier or taller—or better able to see. Things tended to go blurry at the edges and at distances, and he couldn't always make out what his brother and cousin did. Or maybe if he had just been a better judge of the river.[1]

The truth was, he didn't have much experience with rivers—none, actually—not much experience with the outdoors at all. He'd read about them a great deal and he saw himself there, out in the wild: riding, camping, fishing, shooting. He went there, to the untamed, often—at night or in idle moments or in his books. There *he* was untamed, and mighty. But the great outdoors were rather more violent in the first person; nature was unpredictable and dangerous at strange moments, even in the relatively civilized Adirondacks, hard by Lake St. Regis, a favorite summer resort of the well-to-do, where Teedie and his family and assorted relatives had come this August for a holiday near nature. Teedie saw his pole stuck along the bank ahead and recovered it as he floated by. The torrent had calmed now. He got to his feet, water gushing from his clothes, and assessed his condition. It wasn't long after lunch. The sun was still high. He decided he'd do a bit of fishing after all. He went half-wading, half-tumbling downstream for the better part of the afternoon, but did not manage to catch any fish.[2]

Teedie had never been camping before the senior Theodore planned the family excursion in August of 1871. He had swum and foraged on the country estate of Roosevelt friend John Aspinwall in previous summers, and had written of being chased there by wild dogs. But this August, Theodore had something more substantial in mind—an opportunity for his wife and daughters to relax at a high-altitude spa and for Teedie to encounter in the flesh the sort of place he was constantly reading about. Quite possibly the first book that had truly interested the boy was a volume by Christian missionary and explorer David Livingstone, describing the Scotsman's journeys through the Dark Continent. It was published the year Teedie was born, and Theodore acquired a copy for the family library. Little Teedie, too young to decipher much of the text, was fascinated by the book's lavish illustrations of the wild and exotic African bush, and frequently dragged the tome around asking to be read to. Perhaps not coincidentally, he titled his journal entries for the Adirondack camping trip, "In the bush."[3] Then there were those adventure stories by Mayne Reid that Teedie had been reading—consuming, really—from his sixth and seventh years. Reid wrote natural histories as well, and the younger Roosevelt later remembered that the "natural history part" of Reid's novels "enthralled me."[4]

One of Reid's characters in one of Teedie's favorite stories, *The Boy Hunters*, carried a small notebook at all times to record his observations of the world outdoors. His name was Lucien and he was a naturalist. Teedie wanted to be a naturalist too. One morning, scampering up Broadway on an errand to fetch strawberries from the nearby market, seven-year-old Teedie suddenly spied a dead seal from the harbor laid out on a slab of wood. That seal "filled me with every possible feeling of romance and adventure," he remembered, as if he had entered the stories he was constantly reading. He studied the seal at length, pondering its origin and wondering what would happen to it next. He wanted to have it, for observation. As a next-best alternative, he ran home and retrieved a small notebook, in which he made a series of notations about the seal's measurements, all devised in his mind. Teedie's career as a naturalist had begun.[5]

The "Roosevelt Museum of Natural History" soon followed, a collection of dead and living animals of all varieties—frogs, field mice, snapping turtles, even a woodchuck—located nominally in the young boy's bedroom, but tending to stray all over the house. More natural history reading followed as well. Noting his son's interest, Theodore gave the boy an illustrated natural history for children by English biologist J. G. Wood. Wood wrote a series of small picture books for boys and girls in which color drawings of various animals—a lion, wolf, and baboon, or "dog-headed monkey," in one edition—were typically accompanied by descriptions of each animal's habitation and physical attributes. Significantly, Wood took care with each animal featured to discuss its personality and character. The lion of Wood's *Animal Picture Book*, for instance, is described as indolent and even cowardly, which accounts, Wood suggested, for his method of stalking prey. For his part, Teedie devoured his father's gift and quickly moved on to Wood's longer work for older children.[6]

Soon he was keeping zoological notebooks, lots of notebooks. Besides the natural history of the seal, which he wrote up following his investigation near the harbor, Teedie filled pages with drawings and descriptions of the birds and other small animals he observed on the Aspinwall estate. The first journal entry Teedie ever penned began with his impressions of the fauna on Aspinwall's country property. When the older Theodore gave him a twelve-gauge, double-barreled shotgun the summer following the adventure in the Adirondacks, a whole new vista opened. Teedie found he could acquire specimens by shooting them. These trophies he would then skin, clean, and stuff. That same summer, 1872, he started lessons in taxidermy with one John Bell, former taxidermist to the great John James Audubon himself and now conveniently situated and for hire in New York City.[7]

He got a pair of spectacles, too, and suddenly the world seemed sharper, more vivid, fuller. By the time Theodore took the family for another year-long excursion abroad in the autumn of 1872, this time to England, the Middle East, and then back to Europe, Teedie's hunting and skinning and mounting mania was in full flower. "Requiring to buy a pound of Arsenic (for skinning purposes)," he noted in Liverpool on October 26, a day before his fourteenth birthday, "I was informed that I must bring a witness to prove that I was not going to commit murder, suicide or any such dreadfull thing, before I could have it!" His entries from Paris, then Cairo, Thebes, and Bellianeh, read like the musings of a man obsessed. November 15, 1872, Paris: "I bought and skinned a bunting in the morning." November 16: "Rainy. I skinned some birds in the morning." November 18: "I skinned some birds in the morning. Rainy in the afternoon." In Cairo, December 13: "In the morning Father and I went out shooting and procured two small warblers and blew a chat to pieces in a walk of a hundred yards. One of these was the first bird I had ever shot and I was proportionately delighted." In Bellianeh, Egypt, in February of the new year, he was still at it: "Saw the temple of Abydis which was quite interesting. Killed 16 pigeons." The entry for that day in February, the seventh, fell on a Friday. In the week preceding Teedie had shot multiple ringed plover, a crane, several snipe, three dozen pigeons, a sand chat, a bat, and three dunlins. Observers remembered young Teedie traipsing about with gun slung over his shoulder, impervious to the safety of others, his hands stained blue with arsenic from the stuffing.[8]

He was a peculiar lad, this Teedie, small, skinny, and bespectacled, looking far younger than his age. His mother had worried some years before that he was too often alone, off in his own world, too withdrawn, and, well, peculiar. "[S]trange child! I am going to try to wake him up to observe what is going on and *make him observe*," she vowed. He was, in reality, quite observant and, as his journal entries indicate, self-consciously precocious. On this second overseas tour, from the fall of 1872 through the summer of 1873, the adolescent Theodore was decidedly restrained in his descriptions, careful not to betray much enthusiasm or express excitement—other than about blasting a rare bird, perhaps—or sound otherwise too childish. But his preciousness and growing talents of observation set him somehow more apart, not less. There was a fierceness about him, tied to his enormous imaginative capacity. Teedie used his imagination not to retreat, but to project, to call forth a new reality and compel himself toward it. He imagined life as an adventurer, an explorer—a naturalist, and he began to make himself one. He imagined himself a stronger, bigger boy, and worked to become that, too. With his imagination he crafted a destiny for himself, pursuing interests no one else in the family shared and building a store of knowledge no one else around him had. But those interests and that knowledge were by no means unconnected to his given identity as a man, a white, Anglo-Saxon Protestant, a Roosevelt. He learned from his childhood stories and certainly from his more serious zoological studies that he was a member of a particular race, characterized by shared physical characteristics, language, religion, and even personal character, engaged in a great evolutionary drama of which his life was a part.[9]

James Fenimore Cooper, R. M. Ballantyne, and Mayne Reid all preached a similar moral, if subtly: a sermon about physical attributes and their link to character, to racial group, to history. These authors frequently described their fictional characters according to "racial type," and made their personalities embody particular racial ideals. In Reid's *Afloat in the Forest*, to take one example, characters are variously introduced as "Saxon," European of "the Milesian type," and "Negro." Their physical and personality descriptions closely match the stereotype associated with each particular "race." The Saxon is fair-haired, blue-eyed, and, not surprisingly, the protagonist. The European Milesian has a "pure pug nose, a shock of curled hair of the clearest carrot colour, an eternal twinkle in the eye, and a volume of fun lying open at each angle of his mouth." Similarly, the book's black character is said to be "nothing special" but personally affable, with "enormously thick lips, flattened nose," and bright white teeth always set in "a good-humoured grin." Irishmen and American Indians feature in Reid's story as well, and behave predictably like their stereotypes—the Native Americans usually depicted as fierce, elemental, and frequently dangerous.[10]

The point made implicitly by Ballantyne, Reid, and Cooper, the latter famous for his celebration of the American frontiersmen's courage and daring in struggles against American Indians, was that physical attributes and personal character were linked—and in fact, shared among people groups. Individuals had particular physical characteristics that betrayed particular personality traits, and so apparently did whole groups of people united by bloodline—races. Teedie encountered this idea at every turn in his childhood ramblings among the scientific literature of his day and explicitly affirmed it as an adult, when he wrote, for instance, that the French Creoles were "an indolent, pleasure loving race, fond of dancing and merriment," while descendants of Scotch-Irish stock tended to be fierce and not a little brutal. Qualities of character were, it seems, transmittable, part of a process of growth and development known as evolution.[11]

The keystone of the scientific world Roosevelt discovered in his youth was Charles Darwin's theory of evolution. Published just after Teedie was born, Darwin's *The Origin of Species* was an instant sensation that transformed the study of the natural world. Though its reception in the United States was somewhat delayed due to the crisis of civil war, when Darwinism did cross the Atlantic, it stormed ashore at hurricane strength. Before *Origin of Species*, Anglo-American scientists dueled over the plausibility of special creationism, whose advocates, like the colorful Louis Agassiz, argued for a plural origin of mankind—the divine creation of different races called polygenism. Other scientists, many of them equally inspired by the book of Genesis, argued instead for monogenism, the idea that all humans shared a single common ancestry. Their stance committed the monogenists to a form of evolutionary development in order to explain the observable difference in human groups, though they stopped far short of claiming that evolutionary adaptation fueled species transformation. The polygenists, on the other hand, explained the existence of multiple "races" by positing the independent creation of each race, either all at once, alongside the Adamite family of Genesis, chapter 1, or in stages across history. Darwin radically and permanently changed the terms of the debate.[12]

Darwin's leading insight was the doctrine of natural selection, which he claimed could explain the origin of all species. Evolutionary change did not simply lead to organism adaptation—it led to organism mutation, transformation, *creation*. The idea, inspired partly by Thomas Malthus's studies on population growth and scarcity, was that living organisms struggled constantly against one another for survival in an often hostile environment. Intense rivalry for scarce food and other essential resources guaranteed that only those organisms best adapted to their surroundings would survive. The weak and inefficient would die out or be killed by competitors in the struggle for life. Nature "selected" the fittest to live, and by this process of struggle and competition evolutionary development pressed forward, organisms becoming ever more complex through ongoing adaptation and, occasionally, successful mutation. The straightforward, even commonsensical logic of Darwin's theory was gripping, its power to explain the origins of the biological world beguiling.[13]

Darwinism's arrival in America may have been late, but it was triumphant, and by the 1870s the Englishman was perhaps more popular, better regarded, and more influential across the Atlantic than he was even in his native country. The American Philosophical Society made him an honorary member in 1869, ten years before his own university, Cambridge, awarded him an honorary degree. His theories of species transmutation and natural selection dominated the outlook of American scientists. At the twenty-fifth meeting of the American Association for the Advancement of Science in 1874, Association vice-president Edward Morse devoted an entire lecture to detailing the contributions of American biologists to the new study of evolution. Darwin's work had captured the field. Some polygenists continued to hold out against the rising Darwinist tide, but the question now was how to integrate his theory of natural selection into polygenism's broader claims. Talk of divine creation—special or otherwise—receded sharply. Indeed, part of what made Darwin seem so fresh and so shocking was the implication that with natural selection, "creation" as an explanatory concept was not needed at all. In this way, Darwin accelerated the trend toward liberal theology, further disrupting an older cultural consensus. Clergymen and scientists would fight vociferously over evolution's moral and religious meaning as the century wore on.[14]

For some, the meaning was perfectly clear. Darwinism offered a new religion, a religion of race. Francis Galton, Darwin's English half-cousin and polymath, anthropologist, geographer, and inventor, believed the doctrine of evolution destroyed the Christian claim of original sin. Instead of falling from grace, human beings were rapidly rising to new states of ever-increasing perfection. Galton conducted his own empirical study using the biographical encyclopedias *Dictionary of Men and of the Time*. He was pleased to discover from a sample of distinguished statesmen, lawyers, military commanders, scientists, and artists—spanning two centuries altogether—that a disproportionately large fraction were blood relatives. He concluded from this evidence that families of reputation were appreciably more likely to produce offspring of high ability. In other words, natural selection operated not only between humans and other animals, but within the human species itself.[15]

Some people, some peoples, were far superior to others. The challenge of the future, as Galton saw it, was to ensure that the right people prospered, for the good of the species. He intended "to produce a highly gifted race of men by judicious marriages during several consecutive generations." Fitness he equated with strong physique and intellectual ability, and assumed it was centered in the middle, upper-middle and professional classes. Like the disciples of neurasthenic theory, Galton's attention centered on these classes, on their preservation, reproduction, and social ascendancy. He saw no reason to trust to the inscrutable workings of a divine providence or submit the human fate to a thing beyond human control. Quite the contrary. With the guidance of advanced science, humans would master their fortune; the species—or its more enlightened members, anyway—would make its own dispensation.[16]

Galton's grand vision wouldn't gain traction until closer to the turn of the century, in what became the eugenics movement. But in the meantime, he was not the only man of science who sensed the new possibility, the new depth, the new power Darwin's theory lent to the category "race." The existence of distinct human races was not a feature of Darwinism per se, of course. The idea far predated *The Origin of Species*. Europeans had toyed with racial groups, some supposedly more advanced or superior than others, as early as the 1700s—a means to explain the seemingly breathtaking difference between the peoples they conquered and themselves. Fascination with human difference and the effort to explain it were fixtures of the Enlightenment. Carolus Linnaeus had used skin color in the eighteenth century to differentiate the varieties of *Homo sapiens*. Johann Friedrich Blumenbach opted for hair pile, skin color, skull and facial features to reach his conclusions. He found five distinct human races in his *Natural Variety of Mankind*.[17]

In the nineteenth century, naturalists developed more sophisticated measurements. Paul Broca invented the occipital crochet, goniometer, and stereograph for the study of crania; Samuel G. Morton and his student Josiah Nott studied skull circumference; Peter Browne, a Philadelphia lawyer, invented the trichometer for the analysis of human hair. For all their technology, none of these racial enthusiasts could agree on the correct number of human races, however. Linnaeus identified four, Blumenbach five, Geoffroy St.-Hilaire eleven. Henry Burke thought he had found sixty-three different racial types. What they did agree on was the existence, the centrality, of race. Darwin's theories lent potent new life to convictions already deeply held.[18]

Race talk composed the intellectual white noise of Teedie Roosevelt's youth. The editors at *Our Young Folks* gave tips on good posture to develop good physiques because health and vitality were thought to be synonymous with racial strength. When they admonished their small readers that soon the fate of the nation would depend on them, on "their manhood and womanhood," notions of physical fitness and strength were in the foreground. Liberal Christians and other purveyors of religious physicality associated bodily fitness with moral well-being partly because they believed morality was itself an evolutionary phenomenon, an attribute of the highly developed human. Developing one's body led to moral betterment precisely because evolution had, over the years, wrought in man a moral sense, an intuition stemming from and still intimately connected with his biological struggle for life.[19]

Teedie had read *The Origin of Species* for himself at age fourteen before the family left for Egypt in 1872. Others may have agonized over the implications of evolution for ethics and religion, but the teenage Teedie seemed to possess no such qualms. He accepted evolution without cavil. In 1873 Theodore arranged for Teedie, Elliott, and Corinne to spend the summer in Dresden, Germany, following the family's tour, and Teedie's letters during his stay demonstrate a casual familiarity with the basics of Darwinian theory. In one missive to his older sister Anna, Teedie illustrates Darwin's doctrine by drawing himself evolving into a stork over four stages. Elliott he depicts evolving into a bull, while cousin Johnny is drawn as (or evolves into—unclear which) a monkey. Teedie considered himself a man of science, and any man of science knew Darwin and knew he was right.[20]

Just as surely as Teedie knew about natural selection and racial competition, he knew that one race especially had distinguished itself above others. His reading made that clear. The Teutonic race, of which the English-speakers were supposedly the latest representatives in a mighty bloodline running back to the early Germanic tribes, exhibited the physical virility, intellectual acumen, and unparalleled moral refinement necessary to master the world. And they had. Teedie did not need Francis Galton to tell him that. His childhood authors made it obvious enough. Reid and Ballantyne's protagonists were Caucasian Anglo-Saxons because the Teutonic or pan-Nordic race of which they were a part was, the authors firmly believed, biologically superior. James Fenimore Cooper's frontier novels told the story of white men's triumph over the native, American Indian "savages" who proved ultimately unable to resist the wholesome courage of the frontiersmen. These fictional stories from Roosevelt's childhood were just the tip of the iceberg. Fiction and scientific literature was drenched with racial narratives that exalted the so-called Germanic races.[21]

Roosevelt came into intimate contact with the indigenous German tradition of racial pride while spending the summer in Dresden. His hosts were the Minckwitz family, upper-middle-class Germans who were friendly with prominent Americans in the city. Dr. Minckwitz was a city counselor, member of the Reichstag, a lawyer and liberal who had taken a leading part in the revolutionary movement of 1848 only to suffer imprisonment afterward. His two sons proudly attended the University of Leipzig, where they were members of the dueling corps. Teedie found the family endlessly fascinating. In the Minckwitz household he learned German and began to read the Romantic "German classics" in the native tongue. Chief among these was the *Nibelungenlied*, a thirteenth century piece of German mythology that told the exploits of the Teutonic hero Siegfried. By the late nineteenth century it had been rediscovered as a text exemplifying the racial prowess of the Teutonic people. This theme of Teutonic, or sometimes Nordic, racial superiority was reprised by scientists, anthropologists, and social theorists of the period, men like Arthur Gobineau, Charles Hughes, and Thomas Kingsley (whose novels of English public school life Roosevelt may well have read), John Burgess, and Nathaniel Southgate Shaler, who would teach Roosevelt at Harvard. These men and others like them argued that what had become the English-speaking race stood head and shoulders above any other in its physical purity, its political and artistic achievements, its religion. All of these were evolutionary developments, and all of them, to the mind of racialists, betokened Teutonic supremacy.[22]

   This constellation of racial ideas was hardly a purely scientific hypothesis, despite its empirical pretensions. Part theology, part ethics and social theory, Teutonic racialism had significant political implications as well. Some of these Roosevelt encountered in the stories of his mother. Mittie Roosevelt saw Bulloch Hall for the last time in 1855, before Union armies destroyed it along with much of Georgia: Bulloch Hall had been only thirteen miles from Atlanta. But the South held a stronghold in her mind always, and that included the Southern commitment to slavery. The Bulloch family owned scores of slaves, and, as Mittie recounted to her children, each Bulloch child was given a "little black shadow" one or two years older to run errands and be a personal help-meet. The slaves slept on the floor in the children's rooms, in case they were needed in the night. For that matter, Mittie's mother, Martha Stewart Bulloch, kept a small slave child herself to sleep under her four-poster bed and fetch things as she wanted. One might speculate that frequent contact with black children close in age might have softened the Bulloch children's racial prejudices. But apparently not. Teedie's Uncle Stewart shot his "little shadow" in a fit of temper. Mittie assured her children Uncle Stewart felt the "deepest remorse."[23]

   The Bullochs regarded their black slaves as labor and entertainment and not much more. While overseers drove the adult slaves in the Bulloch's plantation fields, the Bulloch and Elliott children—the latter from Martha Bulloch's first marriage—amused themselves by secretly placing their small black counterparts on a treadmill, leaving them to walk for hours on end until they collapsed or were discovered by the overseer. Mittie told the story to her children without reservation, and apparently without remorse, just as she gleefully imitated the dialect of the family slave "Old Bess," entertaining dinner guests at the Roosevelt Brownstone with her impersonations. Her husband, who opposed slavery, grew so furious with her carryings-on that he once removed her bodily from the table by throwing her over his shoulder.[24]

Theodore Senior was absent for much of the time between 1861 and 1865, however, and during these years Mittie's Southern influence was strongest. In Mittie and her mother, Grandma Bulloch, Teedie found unabashed defenders of the South and its racial politics. Older sister Anna later remembered that her mother's stories served only to make her and Teedie hate slavery all the more. And Teedie's loudly offered prayers for the defeat of the Confederate armies were, to the chagrin of his mother, the stuff of family legend. Yet while Teedie's boyhood diaries mention his mother's romanticized recollections of Bulloch Hall, they never comment negatively on her racial or political sympathies. And even Anna, while purporting to find her mother's stories revolting, described them in the retelling as "fascinating" and "really very amusing."[25]

Though Teedie never developed a close sympathy for his mother's political outlook, he was a Bulloch as well as a Roosevelt, an heir to the military and racial pride of his ancestors. If nothing else, his mother's influence acclimated the young boy to the idea of a master race and a politics centered on racial difference. Race as statecraft hardly vanished after the South's defeat. The racial narrative was too enticing, the idea of inherent racial differences too popular, to fade suddenly away as a political doctrine. Instead, race found a new political guise in the biological and economic dialogue of the day, as exemplified by the work of the foremost social theorist of Roosevelt's youth, Herbert Spencer.

Spencer's famous defense of laissez-faire political economy was a racial statecraft in its own way, an "evolutionary individualism," as one scholar has called it.[26] Spencer drew his conclusions from the application of evolutionary theory to political life. In 1858, as Darwin readied to publish his groundbreaking work, Spencer was already drawing up plans for a multivolume sociological treatise, applying the principles of biology, as he understood them, to human society. As the foundation, he formulated an evolutionary "law" of his own. "Evolution is an integration of matter and concomitant dissipation of motion; during which the matter passes from a relatively indefinite, incoherent homogeneity to a relatively definite, coherent homogeneity." Evolution, in other words, is a progression from relative incoherence to coherence, combined with a movement toward greater differentiation. The result of this evolutionary process, according to Spencer, was the achievement of a state of equilibrium. Progressive differentiation could not go on forever. The system would run down as matter's energy dissipates and come to a pause, a stasis, a moment of balance. This law described the development of the human organism and also, Spencer maintained, the development of human political society.[27]

The state, Spencer said, was like a superorganism. It was a system of its own. And like every system, it developed from incoherence to coherence, moving from homogeneity to specificity and differentiation. Or to put it another way, society progressed from lesser to greater individualism. In Spencer's grand scheme, the body politic climbs from its beginnings in primitive human associations to what he called a militant regime, where individual conduct is heavily regulated and the individual himself subordinated to the existence of the state.[28]

But eventually the world of military regimes reaches a point of equilibrium. Civilization displaces war and nations no longer fear for their territorial security. At this historical juncture, Spencer believed, the military state becomes an anachronism. States continue to compete, no doubt, but no longer for security. They compete economically, for goods and trade. They compete for prosperity. And from this competition the industrial state is born. While the militant state suppressed individuality, the industrial state lives by it, Spencer said. Economic progress was the child of individual initiative, and to survive in the industrial age—which was also, conveniently, the age of stasis, the end of history—states must free the individual to develop his fullest potential. With this history in mind, the growth of the regulatory powers of the state was an anachronism, Spencer warned, not an advancement. Progress lay in individual liberty and freedom of contract. The business of the state was to keep social order, protect individual liberty and economic freedom, and otherwise let well enough alone.[29]

Spencer strenuously opposed state-supported education and social welfare assistance, as well as tariffs and state banking institutions. It wasn't that he wanted to preserve the status quo. While he has been called a conservative, he would not have thought so. His philosophy left little room for tradition. Poor relief and protective tariffs were venerable public policies in Britain. He wanted to uproot them. He prescribed instead a statecraft of laissez-faire, of let-alone, to advance the human person and, ultimately, the English race.[30]

For him, that race was the vanguard of civilization. Protecting it from nervous disorders and moral decline was an urgent need. Proper breeding was a pressing concern. Individual liberty was a political imperative. The early Americans sought in their republican politics to preserve an independent, moral citizenry capable of ordered self-government. Spencer and other late nineteenth century racialists, in a subtle but significant contrast, wanted to reinvigorate the English-speaking peoples and safeguard the boldness and virility that had characterized them in earlier centuries. The applications of this notion of racial superiority and its similarities to America's older republican political tradition Roosevelt would work out for himself as he grew and matured, beginning while at Harvard. The categories of racialism that he learned as a youth, however—the assertion that races were real, empirically verifiable entities—Roosevelt never questioned. Nor did he ever doubt Darwin's central importance for any attempt at comprehending human life and history. "He who would fully treat of man must know at least something of biology . . . and especially of that science of evolution that is inseparably connected with the great name of Darwin," Roosevelt insisted in his maturity.[31]

Teedie Roosevelt aspired to be a zoologist, a man of science in an age of science. And though he abandoned zoology as an undergraduate, he never abandoned his scientific quest. The history of the human race, Roosevelt told an assembly of Oxford students in 1910, must be considered, "especially in its early stages, in connection with what biology shows to be the history of life." For that matter, history itself should be "treated as a science." Roosevelt spent the better part of his life trying to bring the realities of the natural world, as he understood them, to bear on the study of history and preeminently, to the practice of politics.[32]

Teedie returned to New York with the rest of his family in the autumn of 1873, his father having gone on before them. Theodore was building a new house. Cornelius Van Schaack Roosevelt, patriarch and man of fortune, had died two years earlier and left his sons over $3 million. Each. Theodore decided it was time to move his family uptown. His season of apprenticeship was finished. With his father gone, he now represented the oldest living generation of Roosevelt men. The legacy belonged to him.[33]

Theodore's elder son was coming of age as well. Teedie would be fifteen in October and very soon too old to be called "Teedie." It was near time for him to take his full name and assume its responsibilities. Teedie was passing slowly from his father's trusteeship, bound for young adulthood. In the end, the transition would come more abruptly, more painfully, than either father or son imagined. As it was, in the first fall days of 1873, Theodore envisioned one more stage of education for his eldest son. He wanted him to attend Harvard College. Teedie came back in late October ready to take up the challenge, to put his mind and his body to the test.

3

RACE AND DESTINY

At first the three boys studied together—Teedie, Elliott, and cousin West Roosevelt. Theodore saw to the arrangements. He thought about enrolling them in a nearby secondary school, but there was Teedie to consider. The boy was growing and becoming increasingly sociable, confident, occasionally warm. The asthma was better, too. But he had continued to suffer attacks in Dresden over the summer, one or two of them severe, and Theodore wouldn't risk it. This was too important. They would all benefit, those boys, from the sustained attention of a professional tutor. But Teedie especially needed the instruction. He was the only one contemplating a berth at Harvard, and, if he was going to surmount the entrance examinations, he could no longer afford interrupted study schedules and great swaths of lost time. He needed personal attention, someone to design a teaching program for his unique circumstances and see it through. Theodore chose Arthur Hamilton Cutler, later founder of the Cutler School for Boys. Teedie and his cohorts were to begin with him immediately, in the fall of 1873.[1]

Despite the haphazard character of Teedie's academic instruction up to the time of his fifteenth birthday, he was by no means ill-educated. Anna Bulloch Gracie, Mittie's sister, taught the children rudimentary reading and writing when she lived in the Twentieth Street brownstone during the war years. Teedie's older sister Anna took up the task when Auntie Gracie moved away. Teedie received a few lessons from John McMullen, his father's old tutor, and of course learned taxidermy, to the regret of many family members. The senior Theodore took it upon himself to foster the children's constructive reading and, in addition to the Bible, guided them toward Plutarch, Browning, Irving, Wordsworth, Meredith, and Longfellow. Then there were the Minckwitzes, who hardly allowed the Roosevelt brood to slack. The Dresden family drilled the

Roosevelt children with Prussian efficiency: up at half past six, breakfast at half past seven, eight and a half hours of studying a day. Teedie learned German and studied French and math under the Minckwitzes' dutiful instruction.[2]

But perhaps most importantly, Teedie was a dazzling autodidact. Sister Anna admitted in retrospect that though she was charged with the duties of governess on the family's second European venture, young "Theodore knew a great deal more than I did on almost all the subjects I taught." His reading in the natural sciences was prodigious, and his ingestion of military and European history not far behind. By the age of fifteen, he had spent two full years abroad; besides the summer in Dresden, he had traveled to Britain four times and had spent fourteen weeks in France, ten in Switzerland, and five in Austria, plus four whole months in Italy. He had journeyed the Nile and surveyed the great monuments of ancient Egypt. He lived for over a month in Syria. For any American of any period, this was a remarkable travelogue. No American president before him had traveled so extensively as a child, and none has since.[3]

Still, though he was unusually well-traveled, highly literate, and well ahead of his age group in some subjects—science, history, and German—he was behind pace in math, grammar, spelling, Latin, and Greek. Cutler devised a crash course to prepare Teedie for Harvard's entrance requirements. Elliott and West, by contrast, did not expect to attend Harvard or any other college, and, after the summer of 1874, they stopped attending lessons. Cutler focused his energies on Teedie. He decided to forgo advanced Greek and stick to the minimum requirements there, in order to invest more time in mathematics, elementary science, Latin, and history. Teedie would have to cover three years' material in two, but with eight-hour days three seasons out of the year, and three hours per diem in the summer, Cutler believed he could do it. Teedie had enjoyed the rigor of his studies in Dresden, where he discovered for the first time an area in which he had greater stamina and all-around natural ability than Elliott: schoolwork. Teedie proudly asked for more lessons, writing his father that he didn't feel the Minckwitzes were covering enough ground. Elliott struggled to keep up. Arthur Cutler hoped to tap that pride, that smoldering determination and unmined source of self-worth to drive Teedie to achieve. In the summer of 1874, Cutler ignited a blaze of academic intensity that would stretch unbroken until the spring of 1880, when young Theodore graduated from Harvard College. These years marked the zenith of Roosevelt's education, the height and conclusion of his adolescence. When they finished, he would be no longer a boy, but a man, no longer "Teedie," but Theodore.[4]

The elder son of Theodore Roosevelt sat for the Harvard entrance exams in the spring of 1876. He passed. Cambridge beckoned in the fall.

The town drew its name from the famed university city in the green pasture of the English countryside. The American version was something less pastoral. Cambridge, Massachusetts, was a village, really—small, provincial, and muddy, when it wasn't frozen. The streets near Harvard Square were paved, sparingly, with cobblestone; elsewhere mud and straw sufficed. Horsecar was still the primary form of transportation into nearby Boston, and in the winter months, which were many, coachmen packed the all-purpose straw into the coaches' floors to keep passengers' feet warm. Theodore Roosevelt's New York was the burgeoning capital of America's commercial republic; Boston, the country's self-proclaimed cultural center. And Cambridge? Cambridge was a work in progress. But then, so too was Harvard. Already in 1876 the oldest institution of higher learning in the United States, Harvard College was at the time a private school for wealthy young gentlemen like Theodore Roosevelt, a Brahmin finishing school struggling to transform itself into a world-class center for research and learning. Town and college were perfect reflections of one another: half-made, half-finished, caught in a moment of unsightly transition that may or may not be leading to something more promising.[5]

A great many years later Roosevelt wrote rather uncharitably that "there was very little in my actual studies [at Harvard] which helped me in after life." In fact, Roosevelt's tenure in Cambridge coincided with reformist President Charles William Eliot's determined attempts to overhaul the college's traditional curriculum in favor of a broader, more elective-based system, from which Roosevelt benefited demonstrably. A chemist himself, Eliot fought to win the sciences equal place alongside Harvard's long-standing liberal arts courses. His model was the German university system, where natural and applied sciences were studied in depth as disciplines distinct from the humanities. As a staunch believer in the promise of scientific inquiry and, indeed, as an early convert to Darwinian evolutionary theory, Eliot pioneered the teaching of physiology, chemistry, physics, and, significantly for Theodore Roosevelt, natural history. He wanted to build a modern, scientific university in America, one committed to free inquiry and serious, methodological investigation in every field, liberated from the dictates of a particular theology or other systematic worldview. The sciences were both the tools with which Eliot hoped to remake Harvard and the prototypes for the renovation.[6]

Eliot expanded the faculty to match his ambitions, from thirteen full-fledged professors at the beginning of his presidency to twenty by the Roosevelt years. He also introduced the now-familiar hierarchy of faculty rank: professor, assistant professor, instructor, tutor, and, finally, assistant. Harvard employed twenty-four faculty of one variety or another when Eliot came. There were fifty-one when

Roosevelt arrived. Eliot was professionalizing the Harvard faculty, making the professoriate permanent, hierarchical, and careerist. The upshot was more courses, offered by highly qualified instructors. Seniors who could select from only six electives in 1869, at the beginning of Eliot's premiership, had twice as many options by Roosevelt's fourth year. The would-be naturalist from New York used his electives to take natural history classes, opting for six over his undergraduate career. And thanks to Eliot's recruitment of promising young academics, Roosevelt studied with a series of scholars who were either well known at the time or soon would be, including geologist Nathaniel Shaler and medical-doctor-turned-psychologist-turned-philosopher William James, from whom he took anatomy.[7]

Whatever his later protests, Roosevelt's studies, his natural history and German classes in particular, left an imprint on his thought that proved an important contribution to his developing intellectual topography. He concentrated at Harvard on the fields that had captivated him as a youth. And he found new interests along the way. He looked to natural history first but also took a number of electives in German history, German literature, and the German language. One consequential discovery Roosevelt made relatively early on was also a result of Eliot's renovating. In an effort to stiffen curricular rigor, the Harvard president introduced compulsory laboratory classes into all science and science-related disciplines. Roosevelt found he detested laboratory work and quickly ruled out a career in chemistry or the biological sciences.[8]

He did not abandon his passion for the natural world, however, turning instead to the gauzy area between science and the humanities that came later in his lifetime to be called the social sciences. For all intents and purposes, this area is what Roosevelt had enjoyed as a boy — his natural history reading was, as he admitted when an adult, "wholly unscientific" for the most part, and often just as concerned with explaining the course of human history as it was with any empirical, biological investigation. Then, too, many of Roosevelt's supposedly historical texts, including those in European history read with his tutors, presumed as an explanatory tool racial categories ostensibly drawn from biology and related fields. Roosevelt's decision to abandon a career in biology was, in this light, not so much a departure from his earlier education as a fulfillment of it. He later claimed his choice not to become a naturalist was also, really, Eliot's fault. Harvard, he alleged, "utterly ignored the possibilities of the faunal naturalist, the outdoor naturalist and observer of nature." This allegation was both unfair and inaccurate. Harvard had a first-rate field naturalist on its faculty, and Roosevelt took his class. In fact, Theodore accompanied him in the field, including one trip — to observe glacially caused land formations — that particularly delighted the young undergraduate. Moreover, it was probably in this classroom Roosevelt first encountered a theory designed specifically to reconcile human moral agency and natural selection, a potent blend of Darwin, Christian humanism, and Jean Lamarck that would exert a profound influence on Roosevelt's thinking for the rest of his life. It was eventually called neo-Lamarckianism, and its chief exponent at Harvard was a professor of paleontology, Nathaniel Southgate Shaler.[9]

Nathaniel Shaler came to Harvard as a student at age eighteen. He returned two years after his graduation as a lecturer in geology and natural science. Charles Eliot made him a professor at twenty-seven, and he stayed for the rest of his life. A Kentuckian by birth, bred in a slaveholding community, he nonetheless served the two years after his graduation in the Union army. If there was a theme to Shaler's life and long career it was accommodation: between the South of his youth and the North of his adulthood; between the polygenism of Louis Agassiz and the teachings of Darwin; between Lamarck and Francis Galton–style hereditarianism; between the religion of Christ and the claims of science. His colleagues on the Harvard faculty noted upon his death in 1906, "He never limited his attention closely to one line of inquiry, but was always keenly interested in a wide variety of natural and human phenomena. . . . He was especially fond of tracing the connections which bind together the various regions of knowledge, showing at once the naturalist's love of detail and the philosopher's fondness for large problems." Which is to say he was a generalist, a reconciler, an intellectual accommodator who possessed the accommodator's gift for synthesizing disparate claims and the accommodator's ambition to make those claims whole.[10]

To be sure, Shaler's own thought, developed most fully in the last decade of the nineteenth century, was more holistic than precise. The entrée to his synthesis can be found in his attempted reconciliation of polygenism, the idea that humans had not one but multiple origins, and Darwin's more monogenistic claims of human evolution—from one common source to current, observable states of differentiation. Shaler attempted to accommodate the opposing views by introducing a new metric of racial difference. Following Darwin's one-time competitor Arthur Wallace, Shaler believed humans were in fact evolved from a single common ancestor—monogenism—but at such a remote point in the past as to make the shared origin immaterial. That is to say, humans were hardly human when they emerged, together, from the primal sump. They acquired their humanity—and here was the key contention—as they acquired their moral and spiritual capacities. These higher faculties defined *Homo sapiens* and made them truly distinct, the crown of the animal kingdom. Yet between the distant point of common ancestry and the present day, Shaler held that natural selection had produced radical distinctions among human beings in the development of these higher characteristics. The human species, then, was physically mono- genistic, but morally polygenic. Races existed for Shaler, certainly. Indeed, with his teacher Louis Agassiz and other polygenists, Shaler regarded separate races as separate human species, not to be intermixed or bred. A species, Shaler said, was "an aggregate of kindred creatures in which the sympathies bind the individuals together so as to form a common mind." Common minds, not common origins, explained the nature and the difference of mankind. These races were not so much physical artifacts as cultural ones, with culture itself as a biological pro- duction. But how could "mind" be a product of biology, a consequence of evo- lutionary law? For that, Shaler turned from Darwin to Jean Lamarck.[11]

Lamarck made his most famous claim half a century before Charles Darwin, but the two men's theories have been frequently confused and interchanged. Lamarck argued that changes in an organism's environment led to changes or behavioral adaptations by that organism in order to survive. These behavioral modifications in turn prompted changes in an organism's physical shape and perhaps its size. Lamarck's major assertion followed—the new characteristics ac- quired by organisms through behavioral change could be passed to their prog- eny. In other words, acquired characteristics were hereditary. Fifty years before Darwin, the Lamarckian theory of evolution envisioned biological adaptations, caused by environmental changes, leading over time to changes in lineage and development of new species.[12]

Darwin viewed Lamarck's theory of acquired characteristics with skepticism and built his own account of evolution on the mechanism of natural selection. Species evolved not by transmitting developed traits across generations, but through the survival of those organisms already biologically better suited to their natural environment. Still, Darwin was unable to disprove Lamarck's thesis and admitted that transmission of acquired characteristics might supplement natural selection in the evolutionary process. Lamarck's theory was not finally aban- doned until the turn of the twentieth century, when the rediscovery of Gregor Mendel's laws of heredity cast doubt on the ability of species to transmit individ- ual adaptations to their offspring. Until then, Lamarckianism remained a popu- lar alternative to Darwin's theory of evolution, and even those who considered themselves Darwinists, like Nathaniel Shaler or Theodore Roosevelt, sometimes meshed the two theory's different explanatory mechanisms.[13]

Careful meshing could yield significant theoretical payoffs, as Shaler demon- strated. If in fact personal habits, emotional dispositions, and even particular casts of mind could be transmitted from parents to children, those with common blood would be bound by cords far stronger than mere physical similarity. Cultural particularities—language, religious belief, and tradition—might have their source in shared bloodlines. Further, behavioral stereotypes often assigned to cultures or people groups—short tempers to the Irish, ferocity to the Germans, for example—might be biologically grounded. In sum, cultures and people-groupings might actually be different races, subsets of the human species, or completely separate species altogether, differentiated by their blood lineage and the character traits that lineage conveyed.[14]

If this were so, the Lamarckian thesis would help explain why some races were superior to others. Some groups of people, like some individuals, adapted better to the challenges of their natural environment and developed more of the character qualities needed to survive and flourish. The development of higher faculties came to distinguish the races. Working with this idea, Shaler posited a revised account of man's development: first came the stage of savagery, a Hobbesian state of nature where physiology and Darwinian natural selection reigned supreme. The savage "must slay when he can and propitiate when he cannot slay, and all with hatred in his heart," Shaler wrote. Then came the tribal phase, where humans felt the first glimmerings of shared sympathy and began to foster their social and moral capacities. Hatred was now directed selectively toward those outside the group. Only one tribe—one race—had managed to climb above the tribal stage to the final station of human development, the upland of civilization: the Teutonic race. Only the Teutons boasted subtle, sophisticated written languages. Only the Teutons had embraced an ethic of universal benevolence. Just as importantly, only they had rejected finally the competitive hatreds inspired by savage natural selection in favor of the highest expression of human altruism, the spiritual love of Christ.[15]

If all these Teutonic accomplishments were the result of the race's acquired characteristics, Shaler was willing to admit that environmental adaptation wasn't everything. He carefully preserved space in his theory for a hereditarianism closer to Francis Galton than to Jean Lamarck. Shaler held out the possibility that once Darwinian natural selection predicated on physical differences gave way to the biocultural stage of intellectual and spiritual development, that is, once the species passed from the stage of savagery into tribalism and civilization, the distinctions between the races might permanently ossify. Environmental adaptation would then come to count for relatively little in the ongoing progress of humanity. The great challenge at that juncture would be to preserve the ascendancy of the Teutonic race, that bearer of humanity's greatest potential, through targeted immigration restrictions and selective breeding and planned marriages—eugenics, in a word.[16]

So Shaler's Lamarckianism, his benevolent, humanist evolutionism, culminated in a paradox. The era of civilization inaugurated by the supremacy of the Teutonic race was supposedly characterized by an ethic of universal brotherhood, enunciated most clearly in the teachings of Christ. Like Herbert Spencer, Shaler foresaw a day when war and national conflict would die away, when the hatred nursed in the human heart by the competition to survive would dissolve into charity. But this proud future was also to be characterized by impermeable racial divisions and enforced social segregation. The dawn of civilization worldwide depended on the preeminence of the Teutonic race, yet that race could apparently be kept strong only by keeping its bloodline pure. Shaler's vision, then, called for both Christian brotherhood and virulent racial hatred, at one and the same time, indeed, the one predicated on the other. This was truly a millennial harmony built on the tears of countless thousands. And Shaler did not flinch from the sordid implications. A firm believer in white superiority, he suggested blacks were racially immoral and temperamentally unsuited to participatory democracy. He thought they deserved their subordinate status in America and were acceptable as citizens only if they acknowledged the fact of white supremacy and agreed to submit to the tutelage of white, European civilization. Intermarriage with whites was, of course, flatly out of the question. As for the American Indians, Shaler wrote that they had failed to progress beyond the lowest levels of barbarism—no language, no literature, no legal system. Their eclipse seemed all but inevitable.[17]

Not much in Shaler's thought was particularly unique. It was the mixture that mattered, the way it made room in a materialist theory—evolution—for moral choice and spirituality. On Shaler's account, neither the behavior of individuals nor racial groups was entirely predetermined by their genetic makeup. They could choose their response to their environment. Human choice was an authentic, consequential possibility. Racial superiority was, in this light, a moral condition. Those races that had developed the necessary character to succeed deserved praise and respect, while those that had not could blame only themselves. Theodore Roosevelt could not have failed to notice the striking similarity to his father's preachments, the emphasis on duty, character, *action*. Here was a racial theory in the cadences of the senior Theodore.[18]

The younger Roosevelt encountered such racialism in Shaler's course and numerous other Harvard classrooms, from the natural history classes he initially favored to the German studies and political science courses he began to gravitate toward as his studies progressed. American savant Henry Adams had given a seminar at the college in 1873–74, before Roosevelt's arrival, on the Teutonic origins of American society. The idea was in the air. Roosevelt did not have to be a brilliant student to absorb it. And he was not.[19]

Roosevelt made good use of his time at college and seemed to enjoy his studies, though he confessed to doing relatively little work his senior year. His academic showing was stronger in his first two. Fifty percent counted as a passing grade at Harvard, with 70 good enough for honors in a required course and 75 the honors standard for an elective. At the conclusion of his freshman year, Roosevelt boasted a grade average of 75, and at the end of his sophomore year, 82. He finished his tenure in the top tenth of his class, a showing sufficient to qualify him for Phi Beta Kappa. He did not show much of the competitive fire with his classmates that had flashed between him and brother Elliott in the Dresden summer of 1873. But then this was partly because virtually no one showed competitive fire—for grades. Roosevelt's social class strongly discouraged it. Harvard was still predominantly a gentlemen's school, and gentlemen did not openly compete with one another for academic honors. Why would they? Their futures hardly depended on any intellectual achievement beyond that demonstrated by gaining admittance to Harvard College. The late 1870s was the era of indifference at Harvard, immortalized by 1880 class poet George Pellew in his smug "Ode to Indifference": "[W]e call the man fanatic who applies / His life to one grand purpose till he dies." Roosevelt may not have been indifferent, exactly, but he was still quite self-consciously a member of the social elite. His friends were drawn predominantly from families of standing equivalent to his; he dressed well, sometimes spent lavishly, and belonged to the most pretentious of the famed Harvard clubs. Let others compete for grades. He bragged that he stood "nineteenth in the class, which began with 230 fellows. Only one gentleman stands ahead of me."[20]

His adequate but uninspired academic performance may also have reflected a growing contentment with his intellectual abilities, a sense that he had little to prove. This was not the case physically. Roosevelt continued the frenetic physical activity of his adolescence—tramping through the woods, shooting, climbing, sleighing; he took up boxing and competed for the Harvard lightweight title. He lost. In reality, he was still fairly small, standing at five feet eight inches and about one hundred and thirty-five pounds. With his shirt off, his narrow shoulders and shallow chest were apparent. But he was developing physical hardihood—overcoming his dearth of athleticism with sheer willpower. He would never be a particularly good athlete, but he would never back off, either, and he pushed himself to outlast many a stronger, more naturally gifted man. Harvard classmate Richard Welling remembered ice-skating with Roosevelt for hours on Fresh Pond in the blustery cold, praying the skinny lad from New York would give in first and decide he had suffered enough. Roosevelt kept Welling skating for three hours until nightfall rescued him.[21]

Roosevelt's academic life was undoubtedly affected by social expectations and a competitive focus directed elsewhere, but there is at least one other salient fact: he wasn't sure what he wanted to do with his Harvard degree or, for that matter, what it was he really wanted to learn. The laboratory left him cold. And though his father had promised that if he wanted to make a career in natural science, the Roosevelt fortune would support him, Theodore was less and less sure that science was his calling. He maintained an abiding interest in history, particularly military history, and in his last months at Harvard began researching with some intensity the naval battles fought between the British and Americans in the War of 1812. Mastering the minutiae of naval historiography required determined mental effort, and Roosevelt loved it. He loved writing history, he found; he loved narrative with vibrant characters and epic story lines. He loved the analysis—of ships, of men and their motivations—the discipline required. Perhaps he would be a historian. On the other hand, Uncle Robert, one of his father's brothers, was an attorney, and the possibility of a career in the law crept into his mind. But first, there was the matter of a major at Harvard. In the winter of 1878, Theodore met with his academic adviser, a Professor Laughlin. Given the young man's shifting interests, Laughlin advised against a major in natural history. Political science was his proposal.[22]

Politics and public service, as a major and as a career, started to seem attractive. As a course of study, it combined history—including racial history—with sociology, literature, and law. Public service offered the chance to *do* rather than merely to observe, to act. To matter. And after all, politics is what his father was doing in the last great undertaking of his life.

The trade that passed through the Port of New York, taxed and tariffed and launched into the stream of commerce, brought in revenues that exceeded those of all other American customhouses combined, and represented well over fifty percent of the annual income of the federal government. The Port was the United States' tax revenue turbine engine. It was also the seat of Roscoe Conkling's political power and, in 1877, the site of a ferocious battle for the future of the Republican Party.[23]

Roscoe Conkling was a United States senator from New York City with flowing, curly white hair and a full beard. He looked a little like Michelangelo's God and aspired to play the part for the state of New York, if not the Republican Party. He had served in Congress, in the House, during the Civil War, before the New York state legislature chose him for the Senate in 1866. There he proved a loyal ally of the frequently embattled Ulysses S. Grant, defending the president against a growing faction of Republicans in the 1870s who called themselves "liberals." These Liberal Republicans, led by Senator Carl Schurz of Missouri, former Congressman and Ambassador Charles Francis Adams of the famed Massachusetts Adams dynasty, and Horace Greeley, the mercurial editor of the *New York Tribune*, longed to end the military occupation of the South. They also wanted to draw down the protective tariff and, perhaps above all, make the federal civil service a nonpartisan, well-trained staff of professionals. These goals placed them in regular conflict with President Grant, who was staunchly committed to Reconstruction and otherwise indifferent to government reform. Conkling was not himself especially passionate about remaking the South or improving the plight of African-Americans. But he was passionate about Republican electoral dominance and about his own political future. He formed around himself in the Senate a group of so-called Stalwarts, dedicated to preserving a viable Republican presence in the former Confederacy by guaranteeing freed slaves the right to vote. The Civil War was the Stalwarts' political issue par excellence. Their Republican Party was the party of the Union blue, reform be damned.[24]

The secret to Conkling's political brawn was his disciplined control of the New York Republican machine, the engine of which was the New York Port Authority. The customhouse did an annual business that, if measured in dollar volume, registered at roughly five times that of the largest private enterprise in the country. It employed over a thousand workers in nonelection periods, all political appointees. That made them Conkling's appointees, effectively, and the customhouse his personal property. Cleverly dispensing patronage and playing on his relationship with President Grant, Conkling gradually built a phalanx of loyal supporters from the ward level to the state legislature. For jobs, for favors, for social services, New York Republicans depended on him—all New York depended on him. It was an era when, for all intents and purposes, the party was the state, and the state, the party. That suited Conkling just fine. In fact, he was an architect of the arrangement.[25]

What's more, power in New York brought power in the nation. Allied with three other similarly dominant state bosses—Pennsylvania's Simon and James Cameron and Illinois's John Logan—Conkling controlled the national party convention. These Northern Stalwarts' ambition to maintain Republican strength in the South coincided with Southern delegates' desire to continue Reconstruction and safeguard black civil rights. Together, their votes composed a commanding convention bloc, which prevailed in 1872 to renominate Ulysses Grant. Having vanquished the Liberal Republicans, who left the party to run a joint, losing ticket with the Democrats, Conkling's Stalwart alliance appeared impregnable. But the embarrassing scandals of the second Grant term and the calamitous panic of 1873 opened new fissures in the party and stirred fresh demand for civil service reform. Under assault in New York for patronage practices that bore a striking resemblance to the Democrats' Boss Tweed of Tammany Hall, Conkling failed in 1874 to prevent the election of a reform-minded Democratic governor, Samuel Tilden. He only just managed to avoid the nomination of his hated political rival James G. Blaine as the Republican presidential nominee in 1876, the man who once needled Conkling on the floor of the Senate for his "haughty disdain, his grandiloquent swell, his majestic, super-eminent, overpowering, turkey-gobbler strut."[26]

Stalwart forces finally accepted Rutherford B. Hayes from Ohio, a compromise candidate. But Conkling couldn't hold his home state of New York, which went to Governor Tilden, whom the Democrats, adding insult to injury, had made their presidential nominee. Southern Republicans failed to deliver as well. The electoral college deadlocked. With 185 votes needed to win, Tilden had 184 and Hayes 165. The votes from Louisiana, South Carolina, and Florida remained in doubt. When it convened to certify the result in 1877, Congress faced two competing electoral slates from each of the three states outstanding: one set of votes for Hayes, the other for Tilden. As inauguration day loomed without a president, congressional Democrats sought concessions in exchange for their acquiescence in a Hayes presidency. They wanted railroad subsidies. They wanted an end to Reconstruction. Hayes consented. On March 4, 1877, he became the nineteenth president of the United States. Conkling, meanwhile, his Southern strategy discredited and heavy-handed tactics in New York under scrutiny, found himself seriously weakened.[27]

Theodore Roosevelt of West Fifty-Seventh Street had been a delegate to the 1876 Republican convention, where he had eventually supported Hayes and afterward become a Hayes elector for the state of New York. He was delighted to see his candidate finally prevail. Hayes's endorsement of civil service reform and his choice of reformer John Sherman as treasury secretary pleased Roosevelt even more. Horrified at the excesses of Boss Tweed's patronage graft in New York, and what he, like many in his class, perceived as the general coarsening of American political life, the elder Theodore had become in recent years a dedicated member of the New York Reform Club and an avid proponent of civil service reform. The reformers' idea was to dry up the party bosses' source of political patronage and thereby break their hold on American politics. The bosses' demise, as the ever-supercilious Reform Club founder Henry Adams said, would allow "that class of men who had gradually been driven from politics" to return to power. Reform would rid the country "once and for all of [these] dangerous and noxious counterfeits of statesmen, and thus make room for the genuine article." Reform meant restoration, the restoration of an "intellectual nobility": the restoration of the Roosevelt class to government.[28]

On May 14, 1877, Theodore attended a lavish Chamber of Commerce banquet at Delmonico's restaurant in honor of the visiting President Hayes: it was the president's birthday. The next morning, Theodore and Albert Bickmore gave Hayes a personal tour of one of the senior Roosevelt's favorite projects, the American Museum of Natural History, slated to open to the public shortly. Later that evening, he and Mittie joined Hayes for a private reception at the Fifth Avenue home of former governor Edward D. Morgan. While Theodore socialized with the president, the city buzzed with political gossip. Hayes had ordered Treasury Secretary Sherman to open a massive investigation of the nation's customhouses, and Conkling's New York port was target number one. Following the disputed election and his loss of the South, Hayes had decided to throw in his lot with Republican reformers, or at least to make peace. The state bosses, Conkling especially, were a menace to his control of the party, and he wanted them brought to heel.[29]

The man appointed to head the customhouse investigation was John Jay, an old friend of the senior Theodore. In late May, the so-called Jay Commission called for a twenty percent reduction in customhouse personnel, an end to political assessments on employees, and the removal of customhouse staffers from the appointments process. Hayes went further. The customhouse was headed by a collector, along with a chief naval officer as second-in-command. These were plum political posts—the collector was paid as much as $55,000 a year—more than $1 million in 2005 dollars—and wielded more authority than most Cabinet secretaries. In 1877, both offices were occupied by Conkling men, naturally. Hayes called the collector, Chester A. Arthur, to Washington and made him an offer: Arthur could resign and have the consulship in Paris instead, or be fired. Either way, his days as New York Customhouse collector were over. Hayes's choice to replace him: New York's most respected citizen, Theodore Roosevelt.[30]

The senior Roosevelt now found himself in the middle of a political grudge match unlike anything he had ever encountered. Arthur refused to resign, and Conkling, who had been abroad for much of the summer, returned in September, fists flying. He denounced Hayes to the New York state Republican conven-

American nation, American political institutions, mores, and liberty. Their consistent theme was character—the character necessary for greatness, for achievement in the community of men: political character and political righteousness. This had been his theme in Albany as well. In the West, he broadened its application. Whether he saw a future for himself in politics after 1884 or not, he was developing the mind of a political thinker, spurred by an ambition to make himself a leader of men and also, perhaps, by a despondent search for meaning.

Theodore Roosevelt announced his engagement to Alice Hathaway Lee on Valentine's Day, 1880. They were to be married in October. "I shall study law next year," he wrote on March 25, 1880, "and must there do my best, and work hard for my own little wife." When the time came, Roosevelt found the law boring. Though he had been serious about his decision to enter Columbia Law School, he never seriously considered the practice of law as a vocational pursuit. He discussed the matter with his uncle Robert, a lawyer, on at least one occasion, possibly more, and worked for a while in Robert Roosevelt's law offices. But on the whole, his uncle's political activities were more interesting. Robert, a Democrat, was an active member of the Anti-Tweed Citizens' Association. For much of Theodore's childhood he had been actively involved in trying to curb the power of the notorious Democratic boss. Robert owned, edited, and wrote for the Anti-Tweed Association's newspaper, the *New York Citizen*. He had also served a term in Congress as an independent, anti-Tammany Democrat, from 1871 to 1873. This was just the sort of political engagement, the sort of high-minded crusade for better government, that Theodore had in mind, and he envisioned a law degree as his portal.[3]

Another one opened first. Joseph Murray, a disaffected Tammany Democrat lately converted to the Republican Party, was looking in the fall of 1881 to mount a coup in the Twenty-First Republican District of New York, and he needed a candidate. Roosevelt had joined the district association the year before. Though uncle Robert was a Democrat, every other male member of the Roosevelt clan was a Republican. The Republicans were the party of Lincoln, the Union, and national development. In New York City, they were the party that stood against Boss Tweed. Maybe most importantly for Roosevelt, they were the party of his father. He had already demonstrated in favor of the Republican Rutherford B. Hayes in the election of 1876; Roosevelt would later explain his decision to join the Republican Twenty-First as practically preordained: "[A] young man of my upbringing and convictions could join only the Republican party, and join it I accordingly did." Murray saw the young Knickerbocker from the brownstone district as a perfect weapon with which to topple the local ward boss. Murray would make Roosevelt his candidate and beat the local boss's own anointed in the primary, thereby securing for Murray control of the district.[4]

For Roosevelt, the race was nominally about garbage. The district representative, William Tremble, had voted for a bill awarding street-cleaning contracts to partisan Republicans, which Roosevelt opposed. Shades of his father, he wanted nonpartisan administration of city services as a step toward draining the clout of local bosses. Defeating Trimble, as Murray pointed out, was one way to make the point. But really, Roosevelt appears not to have needed any encouragement. Uninterested by his legal studies, the state assembly race offered a sterling opportunity to abandon the law and jump immediately into active politics. The law degree had never been much more than a credential anyway. If now the credential was not required, why wait? Murray's schemes and Roosevelt's ambition aligned.[5]

Their designs were not the only forces at work in the portentous election cycle of 1881, however. Roosevelt's rise was facilitated by the shocking implosion of his father's former nemesis, Roscoe Conkling. When President James Garfield, a Republican, attempted to make good the threats of his predecessor and wrest control of the party from the Stalwart state bosses, Conkling took the field. Garfield's play for control was a familiar one: he chose an anti-Conkling man to head the New York Customhouse. Conkling again made his stand in the Senate, but this time was forced to a desperation move. He resigned. His stratagem was to dramatize the gravity of Garfield's transgression and then be safely and swiftly returned to the Senate by loyal supporters in the New York state legislature. Under heavy pressure from the Garfield administration, however, New York assemblymen declined to support Conkling's ploy, and the one-time master of New York, the chief of the Stalwarts, was finished. His collapse reverberated from Washington to the New York City wards. Stalwart ward heelers, including Jacob Hess in the Twenty-First, got the message: the reign of Conkling was over. Reform was the order of the day. Though Theodore Roosevelt was not Hess's first choice for the New York Assembly, Roosevelt's candidacy began to look far less problematic in the light of Conkling's demise, especially when the young blueblood won the endorsements of the city's reform-minded, wealthy elite.[6]

"Mr. Roosevelt," the *New York Evening Post* trumpeted, "has hereditary claims to the confidence and hopefulness of the voters of this city for his father was in his day one of the most useful and public-spirited men in the community." Most citizens in Roosevelt's district agreed. Roosevelt beat the Republican incumbent and then beat his Democratic challenger, a discredited former manager of an insane asylum, to become a New York state assemblyman at the age of twenty-three. He set out for Albany without any definable legislative agenda or, truth be told, any particular political goals. He had a credo instead, one preached to him as a youth that he now set in a political key: politics needed to be cleansed of corruption. Politicians—like every real man—needed to observe the highest moral standards. This conviction was, initially, a purely procedural one. It tended to merge with his other favorite mantra that better, more able and honest men ought to run for political office. But in Roosevelt's brief time at Albany, his fixation on righteousness showed signs of becoming something more.[7]

Whatever Roosevelt was expecting, the New York State Assembly was not it. "Work both stupid and monotonous," he wrote in his diary when the new session opened in January 1882. He had no better opinion of his colleagues. "A number of Republicans, including most of their leaders, are bad enough, but over half the democrats, including almost all of the City Irish, are vicious, stupid looking scoundrels with apparently not a redeeming trait, beyond the capacity for making exceeding ludicrous bills." More than a third of the members he estimated were "thoroughly corrupt." Many of them—in 1881, "them" being thirty-five farmers, thirty-five lawyers, six liquor sellers, six carpenters and machinists, two bricklayers, a cooper, a butcher, a typesetter, and a pawnbroker—did not think much more highly of their new colleague. The *New York Sun* mocked him as a "blonde young man with eyeglasses, English side whiskers and a Dundreary drawl in his speech." He pitched his speaking voice at a high octave and chopped his words with loud clacks of his teeth, as if he were biting the sentences off a stick of taffy. Nor was he a particularly impressive parliamentarian. One friend told an early biographer that Roosevelt would sometimes offer such convoluted motions that even his own party could not follow him.[8]

Still, he was earnest and zealously committed to high moral standards, though some found irritating his tendency to sermonize. Said one Democratic newspaper: "It is evident from his talk that he has no idea why he is a Republican." Worse, his lofty pronouncements indicated "a comfortable estimate of himself as a political providence which is extremely earnest and equally amateur. There is an increasing suspicion that Mr. Roosevelt keeps a pulpit concealed on his person." When Roosevelt proposed a bill to institute public whipping for any male convicted of harming a woman or boy under the age of fourteen, the newspapers howled with laughter. His penchant for appearing on the floor of the assembly in tails and a satin waistcoat didn't help. With his aristocratic airs, dandified dress, and holier-than-thou moral assertions, Roosevelt could be something of a self-parody. Certainly there was no mistaking him as the representative from the wealthiest district of the wealthiest city in the state of New York.[9]

Probably none of his critics would have been in the slightest surprised to read

in the *New York Times* October 13, 1882, that Roosevelt had hosted a meeting of
"young men of the most prominent families of the city" in the Roosevelt manse
on West Fifty-Seventh Street, for the purpose of organizing a city reform club.
Roosevelt told the *New York Tribune* that the impetus for the group "was the deplorable lack of interest in the political questions of the day among respectable,
well-educated, young men especially." He put his aim bluntly. "The respectable,
educated, refined young men of this city should have more weight in public matters than they do." Perhaps predictably, the Harvard-trained New York Brahmin
who lampooned his colleagues' grammar and vocabulary—"there was a laboring man's advocate in the last Legislature . . . whose efforts attracted a good deal
of attention from his magnificent heedlessness of technical accuracy in the use
of similes"—took as his great political prescription the need to increase the representation of his own class. Get the right men in politics, Roosevelt seemed to
think, men like himself, and every other pressing public problem would resolve
on its own.[10]

And yet, if Roosevelt's first firm political convictions were both naïve and con-
descending, largely imported from the reformist rhetoric of his father's class, they
deepened quickly into more nuanced and perspicuous analysis. Roosevelt found
he distrusted many of the lower-class legislators and the machine politicians for
the same reason. "They are usually foreigners, of little or no education, with exceedingly misty ideas as to morality." The last was the key point. Politicians from
the city and the party machine routinely confused their own selfish wants with
the needs of the public at large. And that, to Roosevelt, was an unforgivable sin.
"Working men," he came to believe, "whose lives are passed in one unceasing
round of narrow and monotonous toil, not unnaturally are inclined to pay heed
to the demagogues and professional labor advocates who promise if elected to try
to pass laws to better their condition." Roosevelt saw nothing wrong with trying to
improve the conditions of the working poor, necessarily; the danger came in the
laborers' temptation to ask government to do their work for them. "They are
hardly prepared to understand or approve the American doctrine of government, which is that the state has no business whatever to attempt to better the
condition of a man or a set of men, but has merely to see that no wrong is done
him or them by any one else." Lower-class politicians and party bosses were all
too likely to promise what Roosevelt regarded as handouts to the working poor in
order to secure their votes, to promise them something for nothing.[11]

In March of 1882, Roosevelt voted against labor union–supported bills to increase the pay of policemen and firefighters in New York City. He opposed a similar proposal to establish a minimum wage for laborers employed by any city with
a population of more than one hundred thousand. These measures offended his

sense of political propriety. The job of government was not to satisfy every want of the working class nor to remove every hardship, but only to see that "all alike are to have a fair chance in the struggle for life." Roosevelt believed the laboring classes and their representatives shared a stunted political morality partly because they focused too much on material goods — on getting ahead and on getting government to help them get ahead, as if the whole purpose of political life was to improve one's own economic fortunes. This was a deplorable, if understandable, frame of mind for those "struggling for the necessaries of existence." What scandalized the young Knickerbocker was the degree to which the middle and upper classes embraced the same mentality.[12]

Tipped off by a friendly reporter that financier Jay Gould was attempting to bribe Judge Thomas R. Westbrook of the New York Supreme Court in order to facilitate Gould's acquisition of the Manhattan Elevated Railway Company, Roosevelt swung into action. He conducted his own investigation, pouring over reams of private correspondence and other information about the pending railway deal collected by the *New York Times*. Convinced Gould had broken the law, and Westbrook with him, Roosevelt took to the floor of the Assembly and demanded impeachment. "The men who were mainly concerned in this fraud are known throughout New York as men whose financial dishonesty is a matter of common notoriety," Roosevelt alleged. He added, lest his listeners miss the force of the accusation: "I make that statement deliberately." Gould was no day laborer; he did not struggle for the necessaries of existence. Yet he, too, and numerous men like him, Roosevelt concluded, saw politics no differently from the average union boss. "A merchant or manufacturer works his business, as a rule, purely for his own benefit, without any regard whatever for the community at large." The wealthy man, like the poor one, used his influence to secure benefit for himself. "Each views a political question . . . from the standpoint of how it will affect him personally; and private business is managed still less with a view to the well-being of the people at large."[13]

The root of the illness Roosevelt diagnosed as a disjunction between political virtue and private morality. "Many a machine politician who is to-day a most unwholesome influence in our politics is in private life quite as respectable as any one else." The problem was that the rich manufacturer no less than the machine politician "has forgotten that his business affects the state at large, and, regarding it as merely his own private concern, he has carried into it the same selfish spirit that actuates the majority of the mercantile community." The trick was to get wage laborers and railway owners both to assess their political demands in light of their obligations, and to think of their duties to the body politic as a whole. In private life, an individual considered his family members' needs before acting.

Politics should be no different, Roosevelt insisted. Personal morality and political duty were not separate spheres. The man who had an obligation in one had an obligation in the other. Expedience was not justified as a rule for public life. Only duty. The public good. Service. Implicit in Roosevelt's critique was a rejection of Benthamite political utilitarianism, the notion that politics consisted of maximizing the interests of the greatest number of people, with "interest" defined as whatever made individuals happy. Nor did he accept the Adam Smith–inspired celebration of individual selfishness. For that matter, it is not clear he would have thought much of James Madison's argument, in *Federalist* Number Ten, that the American republic could make do without public virtue by setting competing interests against each other, if he had paused to consider it. Roosevelt didn't believe politics had much to do with interests at all. Politics for him was about right and wrong, duty and obligation: righteousness.

Roosevelt's conception of public virtue as private morality writ large depended on some account of political obligation—some story of why citizens owed each other respect and service in a way similar to what they owed their families. How exactly factory workers and financiers were related to one another, what it was that obligated them to consider each other's needs and the health of the country as a whole, Roosevelt could not yet say. But he was certain that a strong, morally relevant relationship bound them together, one more robust than mere economic convenience. He was not prepared to do without public righteousness—virtue, character, concern for the common good—in citizens or statesmen. He wanted more of it, in both.[14]

But he was also increasingly certain, as time wore on, that his own class was making matters worse. They were treating the poor as grist for the mill of money-making. He was sickened by a tour of city tenements where thousands of New Yorkers manufactured cigars right in their own homes. He saw small children —six, seven, eight years of age—working alongside their parents in filthy conditions, often suffering from contagious diseases. The small ones sometimes collapsed in exhaustion and, having nowhere else to sleep, sprawled on the stinking tobacco heaps. Mortality rates for children employed in the cigar trade were twenty percent higher than for other children of their age group, he learned, at a time when the general child mortality rate was already swollen from widespread child labor. Though he distrusted trade unions, Roosevelt supported the Cigar International's crusade to end tenement labor. And when Jay Gould's acquisition of the Manhattan Elevated won through despite Roosevelt's aborted efforts to impeach Judge Westbrook, Roosevelt called for an antitrust suit against the new company. These incidents were linked by a common political imperative. If government did not act here, Roosevelt feared further alienation of the upper

wumps, Blaine and his shady real estate ventures were anathema, and, when he won the Republican presidential nomination in 1884, they broke with the Republican Party. Roosevelt refused to go with them. He detested Blaine personally and was wary of the Maine senator's grand schemes to secure a lasting Republican majority with a national economic plan centered on the protective tariff. But Roosevelt by that time had decided he was a party man. He was a politician, not a social gadfly or amateur reformer, or even a well-meaning philanthropist like his father. He respected the Mugwumps' position and shared their moralistic, reformist aspirations. But he thought they were making a foolish, even sophomoric, mistake. Politics was a rough business; the political man must, to do any good, be willing to work with the less-than-ideal. And Theodore Roosevelt in 1884 had chosen a vocation in politics. He had become a man of the republic. But a regime man in America needed a party, and the Republicans were his. He might have gone on to be a state party leader or seek statewide office. But in the summer of 1884, tragedy intervened.[19]

On the thirteenth of February, 1884, Roosevelt received a telegram while on the floor of the Assembly. His first child, a girl, had arrived. This was his moment of triumph. The legislature was hours away from approving his bill, drafted in the committee he chaired, to strip the New York City aldermen of their power to confirm the mayor's appointments. This was the measure Roosevelt believed would bring new accountability to city administration. This was his most promising bid to help the cause of good government in New York. But there would be no celebrating. A second telegram found Roosevelt before the bill could be voted. He must come home, it read. He must come home at once.[20]

In the family mansion on West Fifty-Seventh Street his wife was dying, and his mother was dying, too. Roosevelt arrived just in time to say goodbye to Martha Bulloch Roosevelt, the first woman in his life, the source of his wit and storytelling charm, his "darling motherling," and then climbed to the third floor to hold his dying wife in his arms. She stopped breathing at two in the afternoon on Valentine's Day, four years exactly since the announcement of their engagement. Roosevelt's one-line diary entry that night bespoke his grief. "The light," he wrote, "has gone out of my life." The cries of his day-old baby girl, named Alice for her mother, echoed through an empty house. He would not seek reelection.[21]

He did go back to the state capital a mere three days after his wife's funeral, and worked tirelessly through the spring. At the end of April, New York Republicans elected him to serve as a delegate-at-large to the national convention in June. Roosevelt went there as well and campaigned for Senator George Edmunds. But his fellow delegates nominated James G. Blaine to be the next Republican presidential candidate, and Roosevelt, his tenure in Albany completed, his child safely in the hands of her Aunt Anna, turned his eyes to the West. There he would go, to a small Dakota outpost called Medora, to ranch and raise cattle and bury his grief.

"The cowboys form a class by themselves. . . . They are mostly of native birth, and although there are among them wild spirits from every land, yet the latter soon become undistinguishable from their American companions, for these plainsmen are far from being so heterogeneous as is commonly supposed. On the contrary, all have a curious similarity to each other; existence in the West seems to put the same stamp upon each and every one of them. Sinewy, hardy, self-reliant, their life forces them to be both daring and adventurous, and the passing over their heads of a few years leaves printed on their faces certain lines which tell of dangers quietly fronted and hardships uncomplainingly endured."[22]

He wanted to be one of them. He had wanted it all his life, in one way or another, and he wanted it especially now. Their life was simple, uncomplicated. It was also virile and rugged and beautifully, mercifully unreflective. They rode for hours, sometimes days, without stopping, herded cattle, roped steers, braved the snow and the heat, built homes, cleared brush — made their lives, literally, with their hands. These men didn't observe nature. They lived in it, with it, made by it. The land formed their character. Roosevelt was twenty-six in the autumn of 1884, when he turned his back on Albany politics and went West to remake his life. Or to finish the making he had begun as a boy. He had pushed and punished his body but never succeeded in transforming his frame: he was still thin and somewhat delicate as a young adult, given to fits of asthma and bouts of diarrhea, even after his marriage and his season in the Albany legislature. He had spent some time in nature but never became a true outdoorsman. He had been on a hunting trip with Elliott once, back in 1880, but his little brother had spent more time than him in the West. Elliott knew more about life on the trail and hunting big game. He had not yet managed the metamorphosis he had so earnestly imagined as an adolescent. Dakota was his chance.[23]

The work of the cattle roundup was the most physically demanding he had known. Forty or fifty cowboys rode together to assemble the cattle from the grazing land. They began at sunrise, scoured the open pasture for miles in a designated radius, then drove the cattle to a nighttime meeting point. Day after day it continued, mile after mile, sunup to sundown, the herd growing, the toil exhausting. This wasn't just ranch work. This was competition. This was a test of manliness. "Clumsiness and, still more, the slightest approach to timidity expose a man to the roughest and most merciless raillery," Roosevelt remembered, "and the unfit are weeded out by a very rapid process of natural selection." Natural selection was what he wanted — to be proved and to be made worthy. The conditions out there were harsh, even unforgiving, but so was life. Roosevelt had written after his father's death that "nothing but my faith in the Lord Jesus Christ could have carried me through this, my terrible time of trial and sorrow." No such professions grace his notes or correspondence while in the Dakotas. He sought now a redemption through strife; new life — his life — won by his hardship. The Badlands were his proving ground.[24]

Meaning through strife, wrought by human hands: this was the theme that occupied his thoughts during his months in Medora and those that followed. Were not the cowboys much like the frontier settlers, the mighty men of the race he had read about as a boy? Dakota was their frontier, and it shaped them as surely as the Western wilderness shaped an earlier generation of American pioneers. Roosevelt had spent years reading about the Anglo-Saxon people and their triumphs, about nature and its power to kill and renew, make and reform. On the ranch in Dakota his ideas and his experience began to draw slowly together. As a politician at Albany he had learned about practical politics and the need for reform. Now he lifted his gaze higher, to tell the history of the race that had made those politics, to find the history of America. He may have turned away from the New York legislature, but if his writing was any indication, he had not turned away from political life. The intellectual task he set for himself in Dakota and the years that followed suggest a man preparing, not retreating; a would-be statesman limning first principles in training to lead.

His thinking led to writing and then to books. The historical works he produced in the years following his stay in the West were grand tales, captivating yarns of adventure, conquest, and daring. They were also investigations into the beginnings and the development, into the very nature, of the American republic. They were in this sense works of political theory. And the secret of the story once told, the heart of his analysis, turned out to be the same as his core conviction in politics: character. Righteousness.

Before his thirty-eighth birthday, Roosevelt completed five major volumes on American history, beginning with his *Naval War of 1812*, published in 1882, the year he entered the New York legislature, and running through his fourth and final installment of *The Winning of the West*. It was brought to press fourteen years later in 1896, the year Roosevelt debuted in national politics. In all five books, Roosevelt addressed himself to explaining what he regarded as the central historical fact of the modern period, the dominance of the Aryan, Teutonic, Anglo-

Saxon, English-speaking race. He pursued the idea in other venues as well, from essays and book reviews to a collection of stories for children. The need to account for the historical fact of Anglo-Saxon racial preeminence was pressing to Roosevelt's mind, as it was to many of his contemporaries. For him, the reason was political. Only by understanding how the English-speaking peoples achieved their current ascendancy could wise leaders hope to preserve it. Even more to the point, only by accounting for the rise of America could Americans prepare to take their place among the great powers of history.[25]

For Roosevelt, a man steeped in social Darwinism and racial theory from his earliest youth, the English-speakers' success was obvious. The merest glance at a map told as much. When he cast his eye over the Western Hemisphere in the 1880s, he saw the English-speakers triumphant, ready to finish "the work begun over a century before by the backwoodsman, and dr[ive] the Spanish outright from the western world." Not that he held a grudge against Spain. Spain had once been a great power. It had won great triumphs for civilization in its day. But the Spanish merely did "as countless other strong young races had done in the long contest carried on for so many thousands of years between the fit and the unfit": they conquered militarily weaker peoples. This feat in itself was no telling accomplishment. Many nations had claimed foreign shores as their own. But the English-speakers had achieved something greater. "England alone, because of a combination of causes, was able to use aright the chances given her for the conquest and settlement of the world's waste spaces." England, not Spain, spread itself across the globe and became the world's leading power. Consequently, "the English-speaking peoples now have before them a future more important than that of all the continental European peoples combined."[26]

Roosevelt's historical method keyed on race, which hardly made him unique. A bevy of "new school" historians in the 1870s and '80s set out to explain the splendor of the Anglo-American peoples by tracing their racial development from Aryan antecedents. Inspired by Herbert Spencer's application of evolutionary law to social development, these new historians sought a scientific history based on biological facts. Edward Augustus Freeman led the way, linking England's social and political institutions to Aryan, specifically Teutonic, forerunners. He imagined the Teutonic peoples, based first in Germany and then England, were descendants of an earlier, pan-Nordic race. The Teutons then birthed the Anglo-Saxons, who carried the banner of civilization. Freeman's chief disciple in the United States, Herbert Baxter Adams, introduced American institutional history, really the study of race-based political development, as a distinct discipline at Johns Hopkins in 1880. Not long after, Roosevelt's one-time professor at Columbia Law School, John W. Burgess, recommended historians pursue such institutional studies comparatively to explain the racial origins of different nations and their politics. John Fiske did just that, arguing that the history of the United States began with the fall of the Roman Empire and the triumph of Teutonic principles of personal liberty over Roman despotism. This "Teutonic idea," nourished for centuries in the Black Woods of Germany, eventually made its way to England, where it became the almost-exclusive domain of the Anglo-Saxons. From there the disaffected Puritans carried it to the New World, and the Teutonic race was reborn in the self-governing New England township.[27]

Roosevelt, then, was not the only one mining Anglo-American racial history. But the historiographical tradition he came to proved highly ambivalent on the meaning of the word "race." In the novels Roosevelt loved as a child, "race" was often identified with particular linguistic groups, such as the French, the Irish, or the Germans. Roosevelt himself seemed at times to adopt this approach, referring to the Spanish and Portuguese as discrete races, or to the French as distinct from the French-Creoles. For Herbert Spencer and Nathaniel Shaler and the new school historians, race could mean "nation" or ethnic group. It denoted sometimes biological constitution, sometimes cultural heritage or social identity, or all of the above, all at the same time. Then there were more strict, genetic racialists like Joseph Gobineau and soon Houston Stewart Chamberlain, who downplayed the role of culture and language in constructing identity and emphasized almost exclusively common bloodline. In all cases, sweeping references to the "Teutonic race" were undergirded by a (mistaken) belief that the great majority of racial group members shared a common ancestry and further, that this ancestry was in some way determinative of group members' behavior. According to this reasoning, English-speakers could be classed with their German-speaking brethren as joint members of the Teutonic race, itself a descendent of the Aryan peoples.[28]

Predictably, given the prevalence of such ambiguous race talk, Roosevelt's own use of the category was far from consistent. In *The Winning of the West*, Roosevelt identified each group of historical actors as a separate race, calling Irish Calvinists, for example, "sturdy . . . enterprising and intelligent" settlers who displaced "Indians, French and Spaniards alike," each of the latter represented as a distinct racial group. Yet in reviewing Francis Parkman's history of the American frontier in 1892, Roosevelt referred simply to one homogenous "white race," including all the European peoples. He scoffed in 1910 at those who "spoke of the Aryan and Teuton with reverential admiration," as if those terms denoted "something definite," while he had reverently invoked precisely that terminology in both his *Naval War of 1812* and *The Winning of the West*. Yet Roosevelt was not merely parroting, in all its confusion, the racial terminology of his time. Rather, his ambiguous, shifting use of "race" revealed an ongoing effort, conscious or not, to express a political view of human identity in racial grammar, an assimilationist effort that hints at an interpretation of English power different from mere social evolution.[29]

Following those anthropologists who equated race with ethnicity, Roosevelt thought of race less as a strict biological category than as a shorthand for nationality or, even more fundamentally, for cultural similarity. But Roosevelt went yet a step further. He regarded a people's form of government as indicative of their racial character, both cause and consequence of their identity. In some imprecise way, national character and political community were related. For example, "the backwoods Presbyterians," he said, were "fitted to be Americans from the very start," because for generations "their whole ecclesiastic and scholastic systems had been fundamentally democratic."[30] Social practice determined racial identity. That idea, of course, was not unique either. In fact, its lineage reached farther back than the conjectures of Herbert Spencer. The ancient Greeks had believed a people were characterized by a shared polis, speech, and history. They regarded the polis—city—as the natural human social grouping. Their politics was based on it. The city's organization or *politeia*, its "regime," gave the individual citizens of the city their particular character. Prior to any ethnic division, a people were characterized by their regime, by the way they lived together. And in fact ethnic distinctions in the ancient world tended to coalesce around regime types, as evidenced by the Greeks' distinction between their self-governing communities and the "lawless barbarians."[31]

The Romans shared a similar conception of politics and identity, and Roosevelt would have encountered both versions in his Greek and Latin studies, not to mention his recreational reading of ancient history. Then, too, the American founders were heirs to this school of thought, and something of the ancients' politics echoed in the nineteenth century American political tradition, in its concern for moral health and vigor and manly independence. In his own thought, Roosevelt retained the idea that forms of government and cultural tradition divided one group of people from another. He continued to believe that regime type and citizens' character were related. But onto these older understandings of group identity Roosevelt superimposed the notion of inherent biological difference. The two explanations of community, one political and linguistic, the other biological, coexisted uneasily in Roosevelt's mind, denoted by his ambivalent use of "race." The English-speaking race had grown mighty partly due to the mixture of its blood, Roosevelt believed—the biological explanation. But just as he did not accept a purely biological account for the composition of various peoples, neither did Roosevelt accept genetics as the determination of "racial" greatness. Rather, drawing on the neo-Lamarckianism discovered in his undergraduate career and the moral lessons of his childhood, Roosevelt concluded that the strength of a race or a people depended ultimately on the makeup of its character. "If a race is weak, if it is lacking in the physical and moral traits which go to the makeup of a conquering people, it cannot succeed." For Roosevelt, perhaps more than for most other theorists influenced by Lamarckian ideas, moral virtue was at the heart of the human evolutionary story. The ancients and the early Americans related regime and virtue. Roosevelt linked virtue and race.[32]

The English race had succeeded, he wrote, rising to rule a quarter of the earth, because it possessed the physical and, above all, moral traits of greatness. Individuals and nations proved these traits, they tested the quality of their inner resources, in the forge of conflict and battle. Fourteen hundred years before the founding of America, "the Saxon and Angle had overcome and displaced the Cymric and Gaelic Celts" in the fight for control of the British Isles. The Saxons and Angles proved their virility and their moral vigor in the key test of conquest. Americans on the Western frontier had done the same. In fact, if conquest were the test of virility, the English-speaking settlers scattered along North America's Eastern seaboard in the late eighteenth century found themselves with a singular opportunity. An entire continent lay open before them. Englishmen had emerged as a united race in the Celtic wars centuries before the age of exploration. By the time the first Puritan colonists sighted the Massachusetts coast, Britain had been settled for several hundred years. North America, however, was not. And North America was no mere island. The scope of possible conquest circa 1770 was enormous.[33]

Races were like branches of a vine, Roosevelt thought; they gained new life when grafted onto a new host. Old racial "stock" that had existed relatively unchanged for generations might suddenly acquire new virtues and develop new attributes if brought into contact with a different race or, better still, if transplanted to a foreign environment. Nathaniel Shaler spoke of the race "stock which was nurtured in north-west Europe," "invaluable seeds" brought to America and nourished, by the new surroundings, into new life. Roosevelt applied the theory. Great changes are produced, he summarized in a lecture at Oxford in 1910, when "the old civilized race is suddenly placed in surroundings where it has again to go through the work of taming the wilderness, a work finished many centuries before in the original home of the race." American history was a case in point. Following Shaler, Fiske, Adams, and the new historians, Roosevelt believed the migration of the long-established English race to North American shores brought fresh life to the aging English stock. To a far greater degree than his contemporaries, however, Roosevelt leaned on the importance of hardship for the acquisition of character. Geographic factors revived the Anglo-Saxon seed by providing new opportunities to develop the conquering character traits that made a race great. Races that did not move or migrate following their original settlement ran the risk of degenerating into physical and moral weakness. If the environment did not provide occasions to use the fighting character traits, they would be first abandoned, then forgotten, and would finally disappear from the race's character.[34]

Such was the fate of most races. "The nationality and culture of the wonderful city-builders of the lower Mesopotamian Plain have completely disappeared," Roosevelt pointed out. Similarly, the Roman Empire declined from its global supremacy and vanished forever. Other races gave way in the face of external threat—namely, harder, rougher conquerors, as the American Indians did to the white settlers. "[I]n but a few years these Indian tribes [of Oklahoma] will have disappeared as completely as those that have actually died out," as the remaining members of the Indian "races" fast melted "into the mass of the American population," Roosevelt thought. The winning of the West was historically decisive because it signaled that the English race, which Roosevelt regarded as the bearer of civilization, had avoided this fate. On the Western frontier, the English stock was rejuvenated. English-speaking settlers acquired in their struggles the fighting, virile character traits that made races great, and in the process of subduing their new environment, became a new people themselves.[35]

The site of the settlers' struggles was the frontier, and Roosevelt considered it the defining attribute of the American nation. The challenges of the natural environment and the battles Americans fought there formed the country's national identity, binding together in the crucible of conflict an otherwise disparate people. "A single generation, passed under the hard conditions of life in the wilderness, was enough to weld together into one people the representatives of these numerous and widely different races," Roosevelt wrote.[36]

Frederick Jackson Turner would suggest something quite similar in his famous 1893 thesis, *The Significance of the Frontier in American History*. Generations of schoolchildren would learn his claim: that "the existence of an area of free land, its continuous recession, and the advancement of American settlement westward explain American development." But, in fact, Roosevelt pioneered the idea. For one thing, he wrote first. The opening two volumes of *The Winning of the West* appeared in 1889, four years before Turner's thesis. Turner read them. He reviewed them and used the occasion to preview his own frontier-based analysis. In the West, he wrote, recapitulating Roosevelt, "a new composite nation is being produced, a distinct American people, speaking the English language, but not English." Turner's genius lay partly in his impressive ability to grasp the implications of Roosevelt's arguments, drawing together themes and ideas only hinted at in Roosevelt's volumes, and express their consequences with greater clarity and precision than did Roosevelt himself. The New Yorker acknowledged as much when he wrote Turner after reading his thesis, "I think you have struck some first class ideas, and have put into definite shape a good deal of thought that has been floating around rather loosely."[37]

A good deal of thought indeed. The effect of environment on racial stock was a well-worn topic by the time Roosevelt put pen to paper in the late 1880s. German Friedrich Ratzel had published the first of his two-volume opus, *Anthropogeographie*, seven years earlier, in 1882, arguing a refined version of the Roosevelt thesis, that environment acted directly upon geographically isolated groups to shape their racial characteristics and way of life. Ratzel's was only the latest, most scholarly incarnation of the environmentalist idea. The masterly adaptation of the Anglo-Saxons to their new home in North America was a standard trope of the Teutonic myth. The contribution of Roosevelt and Turner to this well-established body of thought was their emphasis on the West, the frontier specifically, as a crucible. But it was Roosevelt only who stressed the seminal importance of battle and warrior struggle—violence—for the development of American character. He reveled in it. "It was a war waged by savages against armed settlers, whose families followed them into the wilderness. Such a war is inevitably bloody and cruel." Or: "The war was never-ending, for even the times of so-called peace were broken by forays and murders." And again: "[A] man might grow from babyhood to middle age on the border; and yet never remember a year in which some one of his neighbors did not fall victim to the Indians."[38]

The violence Roosevelt recounted, even celebrated, flared between white settlers and Native Americans. He was dismissive of the latter, which he regarded as a lesser race. "The Appalachians were in the barbarous, rather than in the merely savage state," Roosevelt opined in his first volume, appropriating Shaler's stages of racial development. Elsewhere his pointed references to "red savages" were quite deliberate. He meant to say that American Indians had hardly progressed beyond the first, primal stages of race advancement. They were backward, underdeveloped peoples who had to give way before the march of civilization. What Roosevelt did admire was their courage and physical hardihood, and, in a way, their violence. One of the most striking features of the Cherokees, he wrote, was their "tests of tremendous physical endurance." They had the physical gifts of warriors. The native tribes may have practiced, in Roosevelt's judgment, "hideous, unnamable, unthinkable tortures" on their victims—foremost among

them, supposedly, the rape of white women — but this made them fitting foes for
the English-stock settlers. The Native Americans were battlers and warriors, and,
on Roosevelt's retelling, they taught the settlers to conquer, passing to the white
men their virility and violence even as the whites triumphed over them. It was as
if one race drew strength, drew power, from the other. This was racial regeneration through violence.[39]

Among his contemporary historians, it was Roosevelt, the sickly child once diagnosed with effeminacy, the Eastern dandy come West to make himself a cowboy, who saw the frontier drama as a violent morality play. Western conquest was
about more than environmental influences. "It has often been said we owe all
our success to our surroundings," Roosevelt acknowledged in the first installment of his Western history. But other nations had once possessed similar opportunities and failed to use them. On Roosevelt's interpretation, Americans showed
themselves a hardier, sterner, stronger race than either their European contemporaries or their Indian enemies, and this moral strength precipitated American
success. Character equaled destiny.[40]

Even when settlers were brutal, oppressing native inhabitants and otherwise
failing to observe the ethical standards of their supposedly advanced civilization,
Roosevelt still praised their virtue. This was because for him, battle was more
than the primary fact of history. It was the foundation of morality. Others looked
to natural law or the commands of a righteous God as the sources of moral imperatives. Roosevelt looked to battle. In battle, individuals proved their worth,
and nations refined their character. In battle, humans wrestled with their destinies and found meaning for their existence. It was a dark vision. Theodore Roosevelt made it his personal code.

Roosevelt placed men who lived strenuously and embraced conflict, men like
the first border settlers and the Dakota cowboys, at the front of his personal pantheon. Maybe it was because he was trying to make himself into one. The first
time Roosevelt met William Merrifield, his long-time ranch hand and hunting
guide, a man most other men in the region couldn't stomach for his insufferable
arrogance and overbearing attitude, Roosevelt was taken. He described him as "a
good-looking fellow who shoots and rides beautifully; a reckless, self-confident
man." When he recounted his Western adventures for East Coast audiences,
Roosevelt portrayed himself in much the same way. "I have two double-barrelled
shotguns: a No. 10 choke-bore for ducks and geese, made by Thomas of Chicago;
and a No. 16 hammerless, built for me by Kennedy of St. Paul, for grouse and
plover." Better than all the rest was a "half-magazine Winchester. The Winchester, which is stocked and sighted to suit myself, is by all odds the best weapon I

ever had, and I now use it almost exclusively, having killed every kind of game with it, from a grizzly bear to a bighorn." Of course, every ranchman carried a revolver and hunting knife in addition to his other weapons, and that included Roosevelt. As for clothing, "the ordinary ranchman's dress is good enough: flannel shirt and overalls tucked into alligator boots, the latter being of service against brambles, cacti, and rattlesnakes." No more satin waistcoats or walking sticks, no more silk or smoking jackets or gold pocket watches. Roosevelt was one of the cowboys. He hunted like them, worked like them, ate and lived with them.[41]

To the reading public, and to himself, he had become a rancher, one of the Western men. In his ranching books he helped Easterners see inside this life, but he never identified himself in print as an Easterner, only as a ranchman, a man of the prairie and the frontier. A man of physical courage and hardihood, as well—those two things above all—and of some physical skill in roping, shooting, and riding. He was a literate rancher, hunting by day and reading by night. In short, he portrayed himself as something of a Western Thomas Jefferson, though given his low opinion of the Virginian, he would have hated the comparison. Even when he described his blunders, his hunting mishaps and mistakes, he described them as committed by one who was, on the whole, well-practiced and competent, as the blunders not of a small, somewhat sickly, nearsighted East Coast Brahmin struggling to be someone else, but the blunders of an old ranch hand who knew better. He did not lead the reader to the edge of some circle of cowboys, to observe from afar. He invited the reader to join the circle of which he was already inside.[42]

As Roosevelt knew, one may be "a consummate diplomat, and a born leader," and yet possess "neither the moral nor physical gifts requisite for a warrior." Behind this historiographical concern with conquest lay a distinct moral view of life, one centered on the battlefield and its warriors. If battle was life's core reality, as Roosevelt believed it was, then warriors were the human ideal type, and their moral code the universal guide to behavior in a strife-riven world.[43]

In view of his upbringing, one might have thought religion would supply the substance of Roosevelt's moral code. Roosevelt did embrace his father's Christianity as he understood it, a faith of duty and service and high standards. Yet especially after Alice's death, he thought of God as an impersonal Providence, a being perhaps beyond discursive knowledge. "To appreciate that the great mysteries shall not be known to us, and so living, to face the beyond confident and without fear—that is life," he once told a friend. That was his life, anyway; his peace with the world. He would live for the present moment and for the treasures humans made, for honor and respect, glory. Whether heaven waited or

not, this could be a high calling, one that linked him with generations gone before. He feared to fail them. "Were I sure there were a heaven my one prayer
would be I might never go there, lest I should meet those I loved on earth who
are dead," he confessed in a moment of self-hating despair. The God of the Bible
may have revealed himself in the person of Christ and the written Scripture, but
for Roosevelt, life, like history, remained a swirl of chance and indiscernible fate,
as the realities of the natural world, especially the realities of evolution, attested.
Evolution was more than theory; to Roosevelt's mind, it was fact, and he spoke
confidently of "the establishment of the doctrine of evolution in our time." The
evolutionary facts, as Roosevelt knew them, left little room for orthodox Christianity.[44]

By casting doubt on the biblical explanation of mankind's origins, Darwin's
theory of evolution, and scientific naturalism more broadly, cast doubt on the
god the Bible described. One might reject the book of Genesis as myth and dis-
card later biblically recorded supernatural interventions as apocryphal, but not
without cost to biblical Christianity. Clerics and theologians who warred on
these issues during Roosevelt's adolescence realized the stakes involved, and
while some Americans, typically from more evangelical Protestant denominations, wholly rejected Darwin as incompatible with Scripture, most opted for
some sort of rapprochement along liberal lines. Roosevelt decided that science
quite adequately explained the physical or material realm, but that "beyond the
material world lies a vast series of phenomena which all material knowledge is
powerless to explain." The natural world was a closed system, he thought. It
could be comprehended, or at least described, through empirical study, without
recourse to supernatural explanations. But in the realm of the mind and the soul,
science had little explanatory power. Here, outside of the natural environment,
lay "a wholly different world, a world ordered by religion."[45]

Though religion may provide meaning, however, it was not therefore true in
any strong sense. Roosevelt held that Christianity was "the greatest of the religious creations which humanity has seen," but it was still a human creation. God
did not form man—quite the opposite, although Roosevelt occasionally took
others to task for saying so explicitly. At best, religious systems were edifices of inspiration that expressed humans' attempts to understand the cosmos. These systems naturally had to adjust to accommodate the latest scientific discoveries, for
after all, in the dualistic categorization of knowledge Roosevelt postulated—a
categorization that assumed the primacy of the natural world—religion was confined to the unverifiable category. Religion was not grounded in "reality," if reality was understood, as Roosevelt certainly understood it, as the empirically de-
monstrable.[46]

But however quantifiable, the natural world offered no solace either for the seeker of meaning. Roosevelt the amateur naturalist knew this well enough. He was a son of his age, whose intellectuals expected progress in human affairs through the objective application of scientific knowledge. But science was not, any more than religion, cosmically, really, take-it-to-the-bank true. The idea accepted by the ancients and their early modern counterparts that the universe and each of its components had an appointed purpose or end, a *telos*, late nineteenth century intellectuals dismissed out of hand. Progress came about via random meetings of unknowable forces, which might possibly be explained or at least quantified by artificial, man-made scientific formulas, but nothing more. The universe was not, ultimately, intelligible. Humans could not really explain why it worked as it did, though they could devise formulas useful for categorizing their own recurring perceptions and in that way, paradoxically, assert their mastery over nature.[47]

Roosevelt's cosmos was therefore an uncertain one. Forces beyond human control and even perception dominated the fields in which he acted or studied. He took comfort ultimately neither in religion nor in empiricism, but in battle. In the idea of deliberately chosen struggle, Roosevelt found an arena of moral meaning compatible with his racial, evolutionary world. As the ancient Greeks wrote in their epics Roosevelt so admired, the battlefield was where man could become his own sovereign, master in an otherwise masterless universe. Greek warriors fought sometimes in conflicts of their own making, sometimes in those made by the gods. But whatever precipitated the fight, the warrior battled under his own volition and for his own honor. Though he could not know the outcome or control his ultimate destiny, he fought. The battlefield was a place where his wits, his wisdom, and his will mattered. The choices he made there had real effects. The way in which he fought determined how he was remembered.

Roosevelt appropriated this romantic warrior mentality and folded it into neo-Lamarckian evolutionary theory to create a personal code of conduct. Humans might not be able to alter the laws of nature. They might not be able fully to understand or even describe them. But humans did possess the capacity to adapt to their circumstances, and those adaptations were effected through consciously made decisions. These decisions revealed the individual's personal character, and character, in turn, shaped the unfolding evolutionary drama. Moreover, a person's decisions and choices held some value simply because the individual consciously, deliberately made them. Humans would never master their world or know its meaning, but as reflective beings they could choose the actions they took. They could behave as the warrior who, fate notwithstanding, chose to fight. For Roosevelt, the battlefield was the great moral arena, the place where humans asserted their agency and struggled to make their lives matter. For a select few, like the Greek warrior or American frontiersman, actual physical battle was an experienced event. For most, however, the struggle for meaning took place in the "battle of their own lives," the daily maelstrom of choices and interactions.[48]

Roosevelt invested these commonplace decisions and pedestrian activities with imaginative consequence, as he had since he was a boy. In his mind, a man strove to prove himself each moment by living strenuously and for a worthy cause. Life was a battlefield, and the fundamental virtues were "the fighting virtues." "However the battle may go, the soldier worthy of the name will with utmost vigor do his allotted task, and bear himself as valiantly in defeat as in victory," Roosevelt believed. In the end, it was the character the battle tested and revealed that mattered most. "The chief factor in any man's success or failure must be his own character—that is, the sum of his common sense, his courage, his virile energy and capacity."[49]

These sentiments inspired his most famous and oft-quoted speech, his address to the Sorbonne in the spring of 1910, which was, in a certain sense, an oblique response to the snide languor of George Pellew's 1880 class day poem. "It is not the critic who counts," Roosevelt insisted. "The credit belongs to him who is actually in the arena"—to the warrior, the mighty fighter—"whose face is marred by dust and sweat and blood," the man who "knows the great enthusiasms, the great devotions; who spends himself in a worthy cause." The man who struggled deserved credit, whatever the outcome, because in struggling he proved himself fully human. He was no mindless organism to be buffeted about by animalistic impulses; he was a man who could think and reflect and attempt to control his own fate, even if he proved ultimately unsuccessful.[50]

His view of life as an ongoing struggle, where "the strife is well-nigh unceasing and the breathing spots are few," provided Roosevelt both an account of personal virtue and a set of general ethical imperatives. The virtues of the warrior praised by Roosevelt arose from his appreciation for battle's significance—indeed, its sanctity. According to him, humans needed conflict. They needed a sphere of action to assert their agency, however ephemeral, and a place where their choices would matter. Great causes, campaigns, athletic contests, and wars provided space for human agency and were therefore an integral part of human life. Beyond agency, however, humans needed the triumphs that conflict provided. Triumph was a source of meaning humans could create for themselves by choosing to honor those who achieved it. Great deeds marked the hero as worthy of the acclaim of his fellow men. They brought him what the ancients called glory, the earned acclaim of one's peers. The quest for this man-made glory helped shape the person's identity by ordering his ambitions and life goals. It also defined a hierarchy of virtues. Strength, virility, courage, and hardihood were, to Roosevelt's way of thinking, the most praiseworthy of personal character traits because they were the traits that made triumph possible.[51]

In time, no American would be more famous for his exaltation of "primal needs and primal passions" than Theodore Roosevelt. From the way he wrote, it could seem virility was morality, and morality virility. But Roosevelt believed strength was not an end in itself but rather for use in the battle, and the battle implied its own universal moral obligations. "A gentleman," Roosevelt said, appropriating the term used both by the Greeks and contemporary Englishmen to describe the man of high character and excellence—"a gentleman scorns equally to wrong others or to suffer others to wrong him." A gentleman's awareness of the importance of struggle, and his personal quest to become worthy of distinction led him to be jealous for the fairness of the contest, and for the ability of others to struggle as he did. A strong man "will demand liberty for himself, and as a matter of pride he will see to it that others receive the liberty which he thus claims as his own." In other words, the individual who struggled to win and create meaning for himself would want others to be able to do the same. Insisting on a framework of fairness and opportunity that would allow other people to work to make something of their lives was, for the true gentleman as for the true warrior, a point of personal honor. The ethical imperative sprang from the person's self-respect.[52]

Yet Roosevelt's ethics had another foundation, one with an important link to his racial ideas. In private life, Roosevelt noted, many of the "men of strongest character"—which is to say, those most courageous and virile—"are the very men of loftiest and most exalted morality." As the ages went by, he held, this would only become more commonplace. "Rugged strength and courage, rugged capacity to resist wrongful aggression by others, will go hand in hand with a lofty scorn of doing wrong to others." Ethical behavior, as it turned out, was an evolutionary attribute. Struggle lay near the heart of Darwinist doctrine, and Roosevelt's romantic, almost Homeric vision of battle was imaginatively compatible with evolutionary theory. As he had learned from Nathaniel Shaler, races, like species, progressed through conflict and adaptation, and this was another reason the character traits that facilitated victory over other races could be called virtues: they at once enabled the person to perform the tasks that made him human and helped the evolutionary cause of the race. Making certain that members of the race could participate in the struggle of life equally, "fairly," one might say, emerges in this account as another moral, because universal, obligation in that it maximized racial advantage. Thus it was firmly grounded in the race's evolutionary needs as discerned by empirical science.[53]

Roosevelt's evolution-based ethical system had a certain internal consistency. Virtues were the personal qualities that helped the individual or race survive and progress; the needs for fairness and equal treatment of others obligated all persons because without them the battle could not occur, at least not in a manner that tested the true abilities of all contestants. Further, a race whose members did not have the opportunity to develop the conquering character traits was not likely to go forward in the long run, so fair dealing with one's fellows was a race-specific obligation. If it was fairly consistent, this warrior, evolutionary morality had significant problems nonetheless, and tellingly, Roosevelt did not advocate it unalloyed.

For one thing, constructing an ethical system on the edifice of evolution depended on investing the evolutionary process with a moral significance the theory did not support. Evolution was an empirical, and therefore materialist, doctrine. Attempts to make the evolutionary process an end in itself, a sort of moral lodestar, begged questions about the process's moral significance. Why should the evolutionary development of the human race be valued? Because it is inevitable? Yet evolutionary theory, especially in its modern variants, also foretells the eventual extinction of the human race, if not the planet on which humans live. Why should a strictly scientific morality, then, not seek to hasten human extinction? Actually, evolution as an empirical doctrine contains no moral imperatives; they must be imported. Darwin described an ongoing series of events in the natural world that required no special help from human beings or any other species. The notion that natural selection must afford its human subjects a fair, equal chance to compete for survival is one entirely unknown to evolutionary theory as such, and entirely dependent on the extraneous idea that human life is intrinsically valuable.

Roosevelt's moral code included many such extraneous ideas, standards of value outside his warrior worldview that he superimposed on an otherwise evolutionary, racialist intellectual system. "We cannot afford to deviate from the great rule of righteousness which bids us treat each man on his worth as a man," Roosevelt often said in one form or another.[54] Similarly, he praised groups of frontiersmen for their "straight-forward effectiveness [in] right[ing] wrongs," while excoriating various Native American tribes for their "outrages" upon morality. Indeed, the "laws of morality" governing individuals should, Roosevelt concluded, be "just as binding concerning nations." All of this language suggests some morally significant standard or series of standards distinct from human experience and biological necessity, principles that obligated Indian and frontiersmen alike, for example. Yet the origins of these standards is unclear, to say the least. If Roosevelt actually believed the advancement of the race was the first, foundational moral principle, then presumably racial advantage and moral obligation could never clash. His statements above, however, as well as his repeated admonitions to his fellow Americans to live and progress "honorably" as a people—as if the evolutionary process should conform to a moral ideal—suggest he thought a clash was possible.[55]

What happened when moral imperative and racial advantage collided Roosevelt never said. He acknowledged that frontier settlers were, to put it delicately, less morally refined than those who followed after them. But he did not condemn them. So blinded was Roosevelt by the pseudo-science of racial determinism, he argued that war between settlers and Native Americans was just. And he treated natives' Western land claims with utter contempt. "During the past century a good deal of sentimental nonsense has been talked about our taking the Indians' land. . . . The simple truth is that the latter never had any real ownership in it at all," he said. Pressed to defend acts of violence and rapacity on the part of individual settlers, Roosevelt shied away but insisted the behavior of the "red savages" had been far worse.[56]

In fact, Roosevelt's moral system was saved from complete depravity only by importing the Christian ethics of his childhood. His homilies on the need to cultivate a "high standard of character for the average American" pointed to an ethical criterion exterior to his evolutionary ideas, one that Roosevelt did not theoretically account for and to which he was not, strictly speaking, logically entitled. Really, like his teachers at Harvard and the neurasthenic theorists of his youth, Roosevelt regarded certain actions as moral and others as immoral because he embraced a Christian ethical code. His was yet another attempt to account for Christian mores with a scientific theory. And like many of the theories he encountered in his boyhood, Roosevelt's ultimately succeeded in preserving Christian ethics only by predicating them on narrow, intolerant cultural and racial prejudices. As Nathaniel Shaler had done before him, Roosevelt envisioned personal and national evolution—fueled by struggle—toward ever greater moral excellence, culminating in a supposedly glorious day of worldwide peace brought by the triumph of the English-speaking race. This was his moral vision, such as it was.

He was a member of that great English-speaking race, and, like his forebears, he was frontier-tested in the West. "When he departed for the inhospitable wilds of the cowboy last March, he was a pale, slim young man with a thin, piping voice and a general look of dyspepsia about him," the *Dickinson Press* noted in October of 1885. "He is now brown as a berry and has increased 30 pounds in weight." It was true. Though he spent only a portion of his time in Dakota between 1884 and 1886—the high water mark was twenty-five weeks on the ranch in 1885—Roosevelt found new life there and forged new ideas that occupied him for years to come. "Here, the great romance of my life began," he said as president years later. The West was for him an end, and a beginning.[57]

July 4, 1886, was the one hundred and tenth anniversary of independence, and the residents of Dickinson, Dakota Territory, located just to the east of Medora, asked the once and future politician to be their speaker. "We have fallen heirs to the most glorious heritage a people ever received, and each one must do his part if we wish to show that the nation is worthy of its good fortune," Theodore told an assembled crowd on the day. "Here we are not ruled over by others, as in the case of Europe; we rule ourselves. . . . When we thus rule ourselves, we have the responsibilities of sovereigns, not of subjects. We must never exercise our rights either wickedly or thoughtlessly," he concluded; "we can continue to preserve them in but one possible way, by making the proper use of them." This was the politics of duty for the good of the race, the politics of manhood and manly righteousness and national glory. This was the politics of Theodore Roosevelt. On the train to Medora later in the day, Roosevelt sat next to Arthur Packard, editor and proprietor of *The Bad Lands Cow Boy*. As the train steamed along, Roosevelt, perhaps buoyed by his speech or just in a reflective mood, remarked to Packard that he believed he could now do his best work "in a public and political way." "Then, you will become President of the United States," Packard said. Roosevelt made no reply.[58]

5

APOSTLE OF EXPANSION

And then he came home to politics. Benjamin Harrison, twenty-third president of the United States, remembered Roosevelt's loyalty to the party in 1884—after being repeatedly reminded by Roosevelt friends and supporters. The Mugwumps had deserted the Republican side that year and cost the party the election, but Roosevelt stayed, despite his misgivings and despite the furious denunciations from his erstwhile allies in the Mugwump camp. Now he was back in New York, more or less permanently, with a new wife and a new home on Long Island: Sagamore Hill, he was calling it. He needed a job. He was writing books and a few essays and supposedly enjoying his new family—he had a son now, Ted—but he wanted back into politics. When the New York Republicans needed a mayoral candidate in the fall of 1886, for what was sure to be a losing campaign, he had dutifully allowed his name to be submitted. Roosevelt had been a loyal soldier. Harrison decided to reward him, bring him to Washington with a post on the United States Civil Service Commission. What better place for an advocate of administrative reform? The Pendleton Act, passed in the wake of President Garfield's assassination by a disaffected office-seeker—a Stalwart, no less—placed nearly fourteen thousand federal offices under an examination system for future appointments. That was in 1883. The size of the nonpartisan service had grown since then, and the commission was in charge of supervising examinations, investigating allegations of wrongdoing, and recommending rules to govern federal employees under its care, among other things.[1]

For Theodore, the civil service job meant a ticket to Washington, and that was enough. He knew Harrison was not exactly enthusiastic about attacking the spoils system. Only 11 percent or so of federal employees were covered by the Pendleton Act, and the president was hardly pressing for more. But Roosevelt believed the work was worth doing, and, more importantly, he was back in politics, national politics, right in the center of the action. In 1882 Roosevelt had met a young politician from Boston, also from a wealthy patrician family, also a Republican and would-be reformer. His name was Henry Cabot Lodge. He and Lodge both opposed Blaine's nomination as the Republican presidential candidate in 1884, but both decided to stay in the party together when Blaine carried the convention. Now Lodge was in Washington, too, as a congressman from Massachusetts. Theodore looked forward to many an hour together, talking and strategizing about the future of the Republican Party and the nation. He reported for work on May 13, 1889.[2]

Part of the price of remaining a Republican regular included following the party's shifting orthodoxy. In 1889, orthodoxy was economics, and free trade was decidedly and completely out. The protective tariff was in. Inconveniently, Roosevelt had started his political life as an avid free trader. Six years before, in the spring of 1883, he had been giving speeches at the New York Free Trade Club. "He thanked his stars," he told the *New York Times* after one meeting, "that he was not dependent in any way upon politics and as soon as any disagreement upon subjects of public importance"—like free trade—"arose between himself and his constituents, he was prepared to step out of office without reluctance." Times changed. With the ascent of James Blaine and his Half-Breeds, the Republicans forged a new, national alliance with emerging industries, the centerpiece of which was the protective tariff. The tariff, Half-Breeds argued, fostered American manufacturing, safeguarded American workers, helped farmers, and generally fueled the development of the American industrial economy. "Under the Protective system, agriculture, manufacturers and commerce have flourished in equal degree," Blaine contended. This was his alternative to the politics of the Stalwarts, the sectional politics of North and South. A high protective tariff bound the country together, benefiting all sections; it promoted economic nationalism. Growth, nationalism, prosperity, wise economic management: these were the new Republican keynotes. Roosevelt sang along.[3]

Actually, he did feel much more strongly about national development than about free trade. His visions of national expansion were, if anything, grander than those the Half-Breeds and other tariff true believers entertained. Roosevelt saw development of the American interior as only the first step. He wanted a policy to extend American power to the world. The United States, let it not be forgotten, carried the torch of civilization, and he believed it was Americans' mission, it was their destiny, to push civilization forward worldwide. This was as much a moral imperative for him as a geostrategic necessity, a great moral calling the United States was bound to answer. Earlier generations had called this dream manifest destiny, and Roosevelt fashioned his own version with verve, incorporating his racialist theories and history of the American frontier, drawing on earlier Americans' imperial ambitions as well as on the trends of present-day world politics. There was no better place than Washington to gild these grand visions, with fellow schemer Henry Cabot Lodge and his salon of intellectuals. Let economic development be just the beginning. International power, a "continental policy," was the best program for a truly "progressive Republican party," as Senator William E. Chandler (an imperialist) put it in 1893. A progressive policy. That's what Roosevelt was after.[4]

It was clear to Theodore Roosevelt that the human species progressed through the domination of one race over others. "The torch has been handed on from nation to nation, from civilization to civilization, throughout all recorded time," he said in 1910. Leadership of the species passed from race to race as history unfolded, the torch dropping "from the hands of the coward and the sluggard," kept high "by those mighty of heart and cunning of hand." Great races, like great individuals, grew tired and weary. Eventually others succeeded them at the fore, pushing onward the thin line of human progress. This much Roosevelt concluded in the 1880s, if not earlier, and he believed then that a baton pass was in progress. He saw leadership of the species shifting from the English to what had become the American race.[5]

The Americans, Roosevelt wrote in his *Winning of the West,* "began their work of western conquest as a separate and individual people, at the moment they sprang into national life." He was confident that the British and the North Americans shared a common racial heritage. But in Roosevelt's mind the English colonists in North America had encountered a wholly different environment than the subdued and tranquil landscape inhabited by their brethren at home. This radical change in geographic circumstance produced a corresponding change in racial character, a rejuvenation, by Roosevelt's lights—a recovery of the warrior virtues. And so, while the American settlers remained descendants of "English stock," their environment, principally the Western frontier, wrought in them such a change of character that Roosevelt could speak in his *Naval War of 1812* of the "contest between the two branches of the English race." One branch had nearly reached its zenith, as the following years would show, while the other, more "rapidly growing one of these same two branches"—the American branch —was just beginning the work that would make it great.[6]

Though the British Empire would not attain its full splendor until the mid-nineteenth century, Roosevelt believed the rapid population growth and swift western expansion of the American peoples as early as the 1790s clearly foretold their future ascendance over the British. Under the American banner, English civilization had marched across the continent. From Roosevelt's point of view, the irony of that Anglo-American spat known as the War of 1812 was that, in purporting to pursue their national interest, the "English of Britain" were in fact "doing all they could to put off the day when their race would reach to worldwide supremacy." In North America the English race had secured a continental outpost that would ultimately prove more durable and more powerful than the Empire. The American continent, once fully populated, provided a base from which the English-speakers could extend their reach over an entire hemisphere. Great Britain's colonial holdings, meanwhile, unless populated with Britons, offered no comparable advantage. They were administrative entities, not permanent racial outposts. All that was required to activate English ascendancy in the Western Hemisphere was the western expansion of the United States. Britain's eclipse as the leader of the English-speakers was at hand.[7]

The Americans' gathering strength conferred weighty responsibilities, however. As he knew from Shaler and Spencer and Freeman and Burgess, the English represented the most advanced, most progressive civilization yet achieved by humankind. They had developed parliamentary democracy and the common law, written a great national literature, and safeguarded the Christian religion. Their civilization was the hope of the human race; it was the future possible for all peoples, given proper racial and cultural development. Americans now had an obligation to spread that civilization across the globe, to bring it to the world's "waste spaces," as Roosevelt called underdeveloped countries, just as the British had been doing for centuries. Having settled the continent, Americans now needed to turn their attention to the rest of the Western Hemisphere, where there was much work to be done. In 1889, that work began with ejecting the Spanish from Cuba.[8]

The American confrontation with Spain illuminated for Roosevelt the moral nature of expansion. Spanish iniquity threw Anglo-American virtue into sharp relief. The Spaniards' empire was autocratic and backward, Roosevelt charged, hostile to Teutonic self-government. The Americans never could have established their imperium of liberty had they not first driven the Spanish from the continent. Unfortunately, when the expanding United States forced Spain off the North American landmass, the Catholic kingdom retained island holdings in Cuba and the Caribbean, and continued to "misgover[n] the islands as she had misgoverned the continent." This geopolitical state of affairs presented the United States with a dilemma. Liberty and autocracy, Roosevelt believed, could not coexist. Either the Americans would displace Spain's Catholic, monarchical, exploitative system with the democratic liberty and Protestant ethos of English civilization, or the Spanish regime would gradually infect the Americans' own and eviscerate their English heritage. Conflict was certain and unavoidable, ordained by the unfolding of history. The only question was the identity of the victor.[9]

The English-speakers' role as the guardians of civilization and their resulting moral duty to expand were linked, in Roosevelt's mind, with their advocacy of self-government. The Spanish had never practiced free government in any portion of their realm, while the English had virtually invented modern republican democracy. For Roosevelt, the development and exercise of self-rule was another sign of Anglo-American racial superiority, for, tellingly, like the racialist "new historians," he regarded free government as the trapping of a strong, vigorous people, not as a right common to all people everywhere. Liberty was a good thing, to be sure, but only for those racially suited to it, and one burden borne by the English and now the Americans was to bring the gift of liberty to the world through territorial and political expansion. Freedom, as it turned out, depended on conquest.[10]

"Self-government is not an easy thing," Roosevelt judged. "Only those communities are fit for it in which the average individual practices the virtues of self-command, of self-restraint, and of wise disinterestedness." Admittedly, few peoples possessed these qualities. "It is no light task for a nation to achieve the temperamental qualities without which the institutions of free government are but an empty mockery." The American settlers on the frontier "solved the difficult problem of self-government," Roosevelt boasted, by fashioning rough-and-ready democratic institutions like town assemblies, impromptu courts and juries, executive councils, and law-enforcement bodies. Settlers in what is now Tennessee went so far as to form an independent association and write a constitution for themselves as early as 1772, Roosevelt noted proudly, to say nothing of the constitutions and social compacts drafted by the first English comers to North America. "Our people are now successfully governing themselves," Roosevelt concluded, "because for more than a thousand years they have been slowly fitting themselves, sometimes consciously, sometimes unconsciously, toward this end."[11]

If races acquired the capacity for self-rule only over time (if at all), the need for free government sprang from a race's conquering character. Those individuals who won honor and glory, those who pressed forward frontiers or conquered adversaries were invariably "bold, self-reliant, and energetic." Or, as Roosevelt sometimes summarized, virile men and women tended to be "strong individualists." There was more than a faint echo of Herbert Spencer's sociopolitical theory here, his idea that racial advancement led to greater individualism—human history culminating in a society of self-reliant, self-supporting, independent individualists. Roosevelt suggested something very similar. The strong person, living in a political community, "will demand liberty for himself, and as a matter of pride will see to it that others receive the liberty which he thus claims as his own." Virile races, then, full of strong-willed, independent-minded individualists, required a form of self-government in order to accommodate the peculiar virtues of their members. Rather than a right, republican democracy was one expression of a mighty people's moral strength. Freedom and "orderly liberty" were won through centuries of struggle, as races developed the virtues that required self-government and the capacity to sustain it.[12]

What took the Anglo-Americans "thirty generations to achieve, we cannot expect to see another race accomplish out of hand," Roosevelt cautioned, "especially when large portions of that race start very far behind the point which our ancestors had reached even thirty generations before." Liberty should spread around the globe, not because it was a birthright, but because free government had proved to be the highest form of rule developed by the most advanced races—the best of which the human species was yet capable of achieving. Those races who had developed the capacity for freedom, the English and Americans preeminently, advanced the cause of liberty by bringing order and republican institutions to regions of the world where they did not currently exist. The American frontiersmen did precisely this as they pushed westward, Roosevelt maintained. Though they came as conquerors, and as such had a right to "treat the defeated as they wished, yet it was ever their principle to free, not to enslave, the people with whom they came into contact." The settlers brought with them democratic practices and freedom of religion, the great ornaments of their race. When asked by a group of recently subdued French Creoles in the Illinois country whether they might open a Catholic church, George Rogers Clark replied, "[A]n American commander had nothing to do with any church save to defend it from insult, and that by the laws of the Republic [their] religion had as great privileges as any other." The "mercurial creoles [*sic*]" listening to Clark's speech, Roosevelt recorded, "instead of bewailing their fate . . . could not congratulate themselves enough on their good-fortune." Americans were conquerors, yes, but liberators at the same time.[13]

Whether on the Western frontier or in the Caribbean, "our aim is high," Roosevelt asserted. In the case of the Filipinos, for instance, a people oppressed by the Spanish for decades, "we do not desire to do for [those] islanders merely what has elsewhere been done for tropic peoples by even the best foreign governments." The United States would not rob and pillage indigenous societies for its own benefit or leave them benignly neglected. Rather, "we hope to do for them what has never before been done for any people of the tropics—to make them fit for self-government after the fashion of the really free nations." Because self-rule stemmed from racial strength and required for its preservation additional quali- ties of character beyond virility and independence—qualities like restraint and wise disinterest—tutelage by the elder races of those "but recently arisen from the barbarism which our people left behind ages ago" was absolutely essential. The less-advanced, quasi-barbaric races were like a young child, gifted and promising, but desperately in need of a parent's guidance to meet her full poten- tial. And just as the parent cajoled and directed, demanded and exhorted, for the good of his charge, "there can be no justification for one race managing or con- trolling another," Roosevelt held, "unless the management and control are exer- cised in the interest and for the benefit of that other race."[14]

The United States had a unique historical mission, Roosevelt argued. This was his own form of American exceptionalism. That mission was "to bring civi- lization to the waste spaces of the earth," to expand liberty by building a liberal empire. Through territorial enlargement, the United States would help less- advanced races progress, further democracy, and push forward the development of the entire human family. American expansion would, in short, be America's gift to the world. In so arguing, Roosevelt adopted the messianic aspirations of his national forebears even while subtly reshaping them. The first English Puri- tan settlers had intended to build a colony that, governed by the word of God, would act as an inspiration for humans the world over, an emblem of the good life possible when men followed God's will. "Wee shall be as a Citty upon a Hill," John Winthrop wrote in 1630, thinking of the passage from Matthew's gospel. "The eies [sic] of all the people are upon us." The Puritans' sense of mis- sion was an outgrowth of their ecclesiology—their conception of the church and its function in the world. Much like their theological inspiration, John Calvin, the early American Puritans made little if any distinction between the ideal po- litical community and the church, that is, the assembly of believers in a particu- lar place. One had to be a professing Christian to be a member of political soci- ety. This Christian state that Calvin had attempted to found in Geneva, the Puritans aimed to replicate and perfect in Massachusetts.[15]

As the colonial period gave way to the revolutionary years, Americans' sense of purpose became somewhat more secular, less tied to any particular ecclesiology, but still distinctly religious. The agnostic Thomas Jefferson captured this chang- ing sense of national mission elegantly when he announced in the Declaration of Independence that Americans held "these truths to be self-evident, that all men are created equal, and endowed by their Creator with certain unalienable rights, among them life, liberty and the pursuit of happiness," sentiments common across the thirteen colonies and voiced in strikingly similar terms in town assemblies and meetings for months preceding the Declaration's composition. The colonists, the Americans, would fight for these rights, waging a war of principle for their own sakes and for the sake of all humanity, who shared in the Americans' inalienable, God-granted liberties. To enunciate and defend this common, divine grant was America's special purpose.[16]

Roosevelt didn't give much attention to the rights-based component of early American nationalism. "Rights" was not a word often found in his vocabulary. Instead, Roosevelt drew on another, somewhat newer strand in the American tradition, an expansionist strand that emphasized the benevolent possibilities of American empire. Benjamin Franklin, George Washington, and even Thomas Jefferson had all understood the need for a unified, consolidated, well-fortified, and expansionist state able to establish itself in North America. But it was not until the early nineteenth century that Americans took up the dream of a continental empire in earnest. John Quincy Adams was one of the first to foresee that, with the advent of the Monroe Doctrine in 1823, the path was cleared for the American nation to spread from coast to coast. America would occupy an entire continent. Thanks to the Louisiana Purchase and Monroe Doctrine, no European power would be present to halt its progress. As American expansion pushed westward and the country's population grew to match, the United States, he predicted, would become the center of a new global equilibrium. It would stand midway between Europe and Asia, astride two great oceans, a center for trade and commerce at the crossroads of the world. "He who won America," John Quincy's grandson Brooks Adams summarized, "might aspire to that universal empire which had been an ideal since the dawn of civilization."[17]

For this empire to become a reality, internal development was a necessity. Asa Whitney, the man who sold Congress on a transcontinental railroad, captured the imperative. He proposed to link Oregon with the East Coast via steel rail, opening the American interior and facilitating commerce across the continent. The effect would be to blaze a new route to Asia, by connecting American manufacturers in the East and farmers in the Midwest with Pacific ports. And if America was connected, Europe would be connected. The railroad, he said, would "revolutionize the entire commerce of the world; placing us directly in the centre of all." All the earth would be tributary to America, "and, in a moral point of view, it will be the means of civilizing and Christianizing mankind." Mathew Fontaine Maury, United States naval hydrographer, took Whitney's schematic one step further. Cut a canal through Panama, he urged Congress, and European shippers would be forced to reach Asia through territory under the control, direct or indirect, of the United States. To forgo the shortened route would be foolhardy for foreign traders, and bad business. By leveraging American control of the continent into hemispheric dominance, Maury proposed to take manifest destiny global.[18]

Asa Whitney had hinted at the moral case for continental expansion. Expansion's advocates hoped to erect in America a citadel for political liberty and Christian truth, which many, by the 1840s, regarded as more or less the same thing. "We point to the everlasting truth on the first page of our national declaration," journalist John O'Sullivan wrote in his famous 1839 essay, the one that coined the phrase "manifest destiny," "and we proclaim to the millions of other lands, that 'the gates of hell'—the powers of aristocracy and monarchy—'shall not prevail against it.'" America became the church militant on this reading, God's pilgrim people on earth establishing a political kingdom of freedom and justice over which Christ would come one day to reign. It was America's destiny "to establish on earth the noblest temple ever dedicated to the worship of the Most High. . . . Its floor shall be a hemisphere—its roof the firmament of the star-studded heavens, and its congregation . . . hundreds of happy millions, calling, owning no man master, but governed by God's natural and moral law of equality." The 1850s sectional crisis threatened to destroy this noble project and disciples of manifest destiny worked to avert the gathering war with one purpose above all: to save the messianic American state. William Seward, cofounder of the Republican Party and Abraham Lincoln's secretary of state, warned the South that secession would destroy America's global supremacy and, with it, the hopes of Christian civilization.[19]

Foremost among these apostles of expansion was Stephen A. Douglas, a Democrat but a committed opponent of Southern secession. It was Douglas, perhaps more successfully than any other advocate of manifest destiny, who bent America's redemptive identity into a doctrine of conquest, an attractive example for Theodore Roosevelt. Douglas explained how manifest destiny would *work*, and melded it with larger geopolitical considerations. For him, the rationale for expansion rested on a single critical claim: American territorial growth meant the advent of equality and constitutional liberty for the native peoples. "Our federal system is admirably adapted to the whole continent," Douglas said in the 1848 debate over the annexation of Texas, "and while I would not violate the laws of nations, nor treaty stipulations, nor in any manner tarnish the national honor, I would exert all legal and honorable means . . . [to] extend the limits of the republic from ocean to ocean." Douglas wanted to "make the area of liberty as broad as the continent itself." His reasoning was twofold. First, the U.S. Constitution knew no "provincial" designation in the tradition of, say, imperial Rome. Any territory acquired by American expansion was presumably a future state,

destined to be a full and equal member of the American Union, its inhabitants
future citizens—not subjects—to whom would accrue all the constitutional
privileges and protections afforded every American citizen. In brief, American
arms brought American liberty. And for places like Mexico, the site of perpetual
revolution and, in Douglas's view, lawless, crippling anarchy, to come under
American control would be to find true liberation. American rule would bring
the first real promise of self-government ever vouchsafed to the native people.
The Union's expansion was therefore a fundamentally liberating enterprise,
moral in a way no other imperialism before had been. And while Douglas loudly
insisted he desired no territory beyond the North American continent—"I do
not wish to go beyond the great ocean, beyond those boundaries which the God
of nature has marked out"—he pointedly refused to renounce territorial ambitions in Mexico, modern-day Canada, or Central America.[20]

Douglas offered another reason for continental expansion, one that adum-
brated Roosevelt's later logic. "I would," he declared in the debate over Texas,
"exert all legal and honorable means to drive Great Britain and the last vestiges
of royal authority from the continent of North America. . . . I would make this an
ocean-bound republic, and have no more disputes about boundaries or red lines
upon the maps." Identifying Great Britain as the villain in America's morality
play much as Roosevelt would forty years hence identify Spain, Douglas characterized American territorial growth as the antidote to Britain's royal tyranny.
That is, he called American expansion a geopolitical imperative. Douglas was
convinced that Britain was a royal despotism, whatever Whitehall's rhetoric, and
if America hoped ever to emerge from Britain's shadow it would have to grow
strong and large enough to rival Britain's mammoth empire. America would
never be a force for world liberty if it became just one nation among many on the
North American continent. Unless the United States wanted to find itself like
the German states at mid-century, surrounded by potential enemies, disunited,
distracted, and perpetually on the brink of war, it would have to possess the continent entire. Preventing the re-creation of European political chaos and, not incidentally, despotism was what made manifest destiny politically important. A
strong, united, continental America might conceivably challenge the British
Empire and its reactionary allies in their attempts to crush republican revolu-
tions in central Europe, India, Africa, and elsewhere.[21]

Roosevelt's reasoning ran remarkably parallel to these advocates of American
continentalism, though with important variations. Roosevelt wanted the United
States to bring the cultural habits and mores of free government—or what for
Roosevelt was the same thing, the racial characteristics—to the people it ruled,

with the intention of eventually rendering them self-governing nations (or races), rather than political members of the American Union. In this way, Roosevelt's scheme was more truly imperial than, say, Douglas's version. Roosevelt envisioned not the enlargement of the nation proper, but enlargement of the nation's political power and influence over other, admittedly and permanently foreign peoples. Nevertheless, Roosevelt still conceived his imperial project as a moral one, for much the same reason Douglas had, though here again there is an important distinction. Douglas understood self-government as humans' God-given right, which the United States, in extending its territory and concomitant system of civil and political rights, was helping to secure. Roosevelt, by contrast, regarded the self-government brought by American power as an opportunity for backward peoples to join the progress of the human race, to become "civilized" and show themselves worthy of obtaining a form of government their betters had already attained.[22]

If the indigenous peoples resisted America's gift of political freedom, conveniently disguised as conquest, their wishes were to be ignored and, if necessary, forcibly thwarted. For after all, the first and greatest imperative was the progress of the human species, and America represented that progress. The frontiersmen's encounter with the native American peoples offered a case in point. Roosevelt readily admitted that the white settlers on America's western border were not the most refined personages. "One who in an Eastern city is merely a backbiter and slanderer, in the western woods lies in wait for his foe with rifle; sharp practice in the east becomes highway robbery in the west." The decades-long war between settlers and Native Americans along the Western frontier was "bloody and cruel," and the settlers stood guilty of much bloodshed. However, in the final analysis, Roosevelt acquitted them entirely of any noteworthy wrongdoing. Bloody, even tragic, though the struggle was, Roosevelt concluded, "we are bound to admit" that it "was really one that could not possibly have been avoided." For unless the Americans were willing "that the whole continent west of the Alleghanies [*sic*] should remain unpeopled waste . . . war was inevitable."[23]

The Anglo-American settlers represented the vanguard of civilization, the most highly evolved of the human species, and, as such, it was their duty as well as their right to expand their regime of freedom and self-government, for the uplift of the whole human race. The frontiersman and the American Indian "represented two stages of progress, ages apart; and it would have needed many centuries to bring the lower to the level of the higher." For Roosevelt, the inescapable reality of America's imperial duty was simple: when the interests of the American race and those of the indigenous peoples conflicted irreconcilably, their clash had to be "settled by the strong hand." The war that came was "in its essence just and righteous on the part of the borderers."[24]

Whether Douglas or Adams or Maury or any other advocate of 1840s manifest destiny would have sanctioned an imperial ethic on this order is doubtful. But then those earlier proponents of American expansion did not harbor a conquest-based, warrior morality, which Roosevelt fused with his expansionist logic to produce a strange imperialism—liberal in aspiration, yet illiberal in practice and racist as well. Roosevelt may have embraced a basically Christian ethical system for his preachments on politics and public life. But in his interpretation of history, he was far more willing to hue to his own cold, evolutionary logic and treat moral standards as biological products, created and refined by humans over the millennia of their development. He sometimes talked as if morality was an essentially utilitarian construct of the human experience, useful for helping humans evolve. Taken to its logical conclusion, this train of thought cast moral systems as products of force. "It is indeed a warped, perverse, and silly morality which would forbid a course of conquest that has turned whole continents into the seats of mighty and flourishing civilized nations," he wrote in *Winning of the West*. "It is as idle to apply to savages the rules of international morality which obtain between stable and cultured communities, as it would be to judge the fifth-century English conquest of Britain by the standards of today." This was moral historicism on a Machiavellian scale. Though he never said so outright, Roosevelt's reasoning strongly implied, as Machiavelli's *Prince* said bluntly, that moral systems came into being when the conquering power imposed its value preferences on the conquered. And while Roosevelt spoke of the "great rule of righteousness, which bids us treat each man on his worth as a man," if one follows strictly his logic, rather than his glittering moral conclusions, one sees that his moral universe is, in the end, a desolate place founded on force, violence, and raw power. His doctrine of imperialism and its consequences for the American Indians revealed as much. "[I]t is of incalculable importance that America, Australia, and Siberia should pass out of the hands of their red, black, and yellow aboriginal owners, and become the heritage of the dominant world races." What the strong could take belonged to the strong. It is difficult to imagine a more thorough or repugnant apology for oppressive exploitation.[25]

Of course, by "dominant world races" Roosevelt meant the Teutons and their progeny, whom he believed had invented self-government. But why, ultimately, free government should be prized and extended, Roosevelt was hard pressed to say. Self-rule both begat and sustained mighty races, in his understanding, but surely Americans did not intend to make every other race under its influence strong.

6

THE FATE OF COMING YEARS

How to return was another matter. The leading cause of Theodore Roosevelt's discontent as his thirty-eighth birthday loomed was a fact about which he did not write or speak openly, but a fact no less real for being unarticulated. His political career had stalled. Six years at the civil service commission followed by eighteen months on the New York City police board was not the materiel with which to build a national political following. That's not to say he didn't enjoy the job of police commissioner. He did. Or he did at first. Mayor William Strong had rescued him from the increasingly mundane and obscure civil service commission. That was cause enough for thanks. But Roosevelt shared his new post in New York with three other commissioners, also political appointees, and though his colleagues had elected him president of the board, his powers were nominal. The commissioners made all decisions on a consensual basis, which meant Roosevelt's vote counted no more than anyone else's. What's more, the other three commissioners soon tired of his antics. He forced out the chief of police within three weeks of his arrival in May 1895 and soon thereafter took to walking the streets at night, in disguise, on the lookout for police misbehavior and often with reporters in tow. The man was a publicity hound. And that wasn't all. He insisted on enforcing the Sunday antiliquor law, which happened, not coincidentally, to strike at the nexus between saloon owners and the Tammany Hall Democratic machine. He introduced civil service exams for hiring policemen. And when friend, reporter, and social activist Jacob Riis recounted his own harrowing experiences as a recent immigrant living in a police lodging house—a cheap hostel where a lodger might get a room for ten cents a night or less—Roosevelt shut down every police lodging facility in the city. After twelve months of this one-man crusade for righteousness, the other board members dug in their heels. Besides speaking up for social reform on the city's health board, on which he sat as police commission president, there was not much more for him to do. Roosevelt had exhausted the possibilities of his power.[1]

Henry Cabot Lodge, now Senator Lodge—and the man who had pressured Strong to put Roosevelt on the police commission in the first place—kept urging his younger friend to look upon the police board as a stepping-stone to statewide office. But Roosevelt was impatient, and uncertain. He suspected that his police stint in New York was bogged down beyond salvation. He needed another opportunity, a new field in which to work and earn political attention. He needed, in short, a break. For Roosevelt, the summer of 1896 was a time of reckoning. Either he must jolt his career suddenly forward or resign himself to mid-level administrative positions in perpetuity, perhaps settle down to finish the last two volumes of his Western opus. Roosevelt looked for the jolt. He had spent too long searching the lessons of history, strategizing about America's future and pushing reform, too long preparing to lead the way, to shrink away now into political limbo. He sensed that the moment of American destiny was near at hand, the time when his countrymen would rise to assume the world prominence for which their history had fitted them . . . or be forgotten and left behind. Now more than ever the country needed wise, long-sighted leadership, skillful statesmen who knew how to call a great people to do the best in them and direct their energies to the common good. Roosevelt was ready. But he lacked the opportunity.[2]

He wasn't the only one who felt restless in the spring of 1896. A financial panic touched off three years earlier by the failure of the Reading Railroad and a run on the nation's banks had spiraled into the worst depression in American history. Fifteen thousand businesses failed. Unemployment in the nonagricultural labor force hit 30 percent. In the early months of 1894, as many as half those seeking work in manufacturing and construction had no jobs. Poverty in America's cities had never been worse, the plight of the workingman never more bleak. The farm economy was suffering, too, and, after three years of depression, feeling among farmers against the great corporate industries—emblems of the new age—ran high. It was a season of discontent in America, for Roosevelt, for the whole country. By luck of the calendar, a presidential election waited in the fall, and the campaign was going to reflect Americans' mood: urgent, anxious, vicious, historic.

The contest provoked some of the most strident rhetoric of Theodore Roosevelt's career and put his classist social conservatism on full display. Not that his positions were atypical. In fact, they were widely shared by the conservative political establishment. But the targets of Roosevelt's vitriol were sometimes surprising, revealing that he was more than a conservative reactionary. On the contrary, he was ready to take bold steps to transform American society. He was not content with the status quo. Not in the least.[3]

Given his own ambitions, the political clamor in 1896 focused Roosevelt's mind with a sense of urgency accented by hysteria. He insisted the nation that year was threatened "by evils greater than those of any war." All that the American founders and frontier generations had won now hung precariously in the balance. "It was the greatest crisis in our national fate," Roosevelt told his sister soon after the voting, "save only for the Civil War." Other members of his social and political class, including Henry Cabot Lodge and the Republican episcopacy, shared his assessment. Indeed, 1896 was arguably the most class-conscious election in American history, a wild riot of a campaign featuring multiple political parties, flamboyant characters, stinging rhetoric, and three decades of burning industrial discontent that erupted, finally, with the force of a tectonic shift. It *was* a tectonic shift, politically. The election produced a new national political alignment that held securely for over a dozen years and remained more or less intact for thirty-five. When the tumult died down, Republicans emerged with majority status, breaking two decades of political stalemate and fierce party competition.[4]

The result was far from foreordained. The American electoral map was a scramble of shifting alliances and changing coalitions forming and reforming, each alignment sensitive to the slightest shock, like a weather radar in the middle of a low-pressure storm system. It had been that way for twenty years. Democrats controlled the White House in 1896 and looked, until recently, to be on the verge of majority power. Grover Cleveland, president once before, from 1885 to 1889, led the Democrats back to the White House in 1892, becoming the only chief executive to serve nonconsecutive terms. He presided over a party nearly obliterated by the Civil War but one that made a swift comeback soon after, thanks to a combination of careful repositioning and voter disenfranchisement. A key turning point proved to be the compromise of 1877, when Republicans abandoned Reconstruction in the South in exchange for a Rutherford B. Hayes presidency. The beginning of the end for Roscoe Conkling's Stalwarts—who had wanted to continue Reconstruction in some guise and maintain a viable Republican Party in the former Confederacy—was the beginning of a major Democratic resurgence. With black voters frequently denied the ballot, Democrats established an electoral lock on the South, while simultaneously recasting the Northern wing of the party as the champion of government "retrenchment" and fiscal conservatism. The combination worked well, and the political contests of the 1870s, '80s, and '90s were among the hardest fought and most closely watched elections ever held in America. Control of one or both houses of Congress changed nine times in twenty years, and voter participation regularly topped eighty percent.[5]

Cleveland came back to the White House in 1893 with sizable Democratic majorities in both the House and Senate. But astute political observers saw reason to postpone celebration. The political radar was registering a disturbance in the West, the effects of which were hard to gauge. While Cleveland racked up healthy margins in the electoral college over his opponent, Republican incumbent Benjamin Harrison, he managed to assemble less than 50 percent of the popular vote. Intriguingly, nearly 9 percent of that vote—over one million ballots—went to a newly minted third party, the Populists, organized in Omaha, Nebraska, in the spring of 1892. For such a new organization, Populists showed surprising political muscle. They carried five states in the 1892 presidential canvass, all in the middle and far West, and elected numerous state and local candidates. The party's supporters were mostly farmers—grain farmers, to be specific—and their disaffection was hardly new. This Populist disturbance was only the latest manifestation of a long building, long powerful political force.[6]

The storm of agrarian anger Roosevelt witnessed in 1896 had first gathered in the Midwest some thirty years earlier, stirred by farmers furious at the railroad rates they paid to ship their grain. By 1863 huge grain surpluses were moving from the rail hub in Chicago to Eastern markets and eventually overseas. Railroad operators set their rates based on distance, however, meaning that the price farmers paid bore no particular relation to the value of the commodities they shipped. The farmers found this fact outrageous, and all too typical. For them, the railroads were both blessing and curse. As Asa Whitney and other prophets of American expansion predicted, the transcontinental rail lines opened the country's interior to vast new markets and new technologies, making for new prices and profits. But opportunity came at a cost for farmers. As the steel links between East, West, and Midwest transformed the larger farm market, grain growers were forced to rely on the railroads for their livelihood. The power to set shipping rates was the power to control the farmer's future. For some, the dawning of the industrial age—the railroad age—looked like a Faustian bargain: prosperity in exchange for control. That was a bargain many were unwilling to make, if they could help it.[7]

From this malaise the Grangers were born in 1867, originally a loose-knit society of cattle farmers and ranchers—the National Grange of the Patrons of Animal Husbandry—set up around local chapters, or "granges," meant to function basically as social clubs. They rapidly became quasi-political groups instead. Grangers fought the lordship of the railroad by promoting local cooperatives that brought farmers together to purchase and market their goods. But soon they took aim squarely at the railroads, demanding lower through-rates to the East. Railroads, they complained, were monopolies, artificially massive business establishments that controlled the market and sustained their size by preventing competition. They ought to be regulated. The Grangers became America's first anti-monopoly movement, pressing for shipping rates to be set by statute or, alternatively, public commission. They also wanted laws banning discriminatory rate pricing. With the onset of an economic downturn in the early 1870s, small merchants and shippers joined their coalition, and the Grangers' political heft in the upper Mississippi Valley grew formidable. They won an early victory with the Illinois Railroad and Warehouse Commission in 1873 and worried Congress enough to launch the first national investigation of the railroads, the so-called Windom Committee, in the U.S. Senate. By the mid-1870s, the movement had the makings of a multiregional phenomenon. Grangers were joined in their rate agitation by the National Farmers' Alliance, based in Texas and with influence extending throughout the South. The Granger and Alliance forces together secured state legislation across the Midwest and South regulating both railroad rates and services. Farmers' Alliance pressure was partly responsible for the Interstate Commerce Act of 1887 — an attempt, if halting, at national railroad regulation — and the Sherman antitrust statute of 1890. This was a political force that left its mark.[8]

Over time, the nebulous, unseen pressures of the market dissipated Granger discontent, as the railroads acquired or constructed new through routes between Eastern ports and interior cities and fought one another in a raging price war. After 1877, the absolute level of shipping rates fell steadily. Granger clubs returned to performing their original social functions. But the Southern Farmers' Alliance lived on, turning its attention to general anti-monopoly laws. And Midwestern farmers continued to resent alleged rate discrimination as well as rate instability. Paradoxically, as some economists have pointed out, preventing the rate discrimination farmers so abhorred would actually have worked to their detriment. After the mid-1870s, railroads typically charged more for a short haul on their lines than for a long one, a classic instance of price differentiation based on consumer demand that actually facilitated the low long-haul rates Western farmers and merchants enjoyed. Indeed, a number of economists have wondered why Grangers bothered to attack the railroads at all, noting that "the utmost regulation of railroad rates compatible with survival of the railroads would have made an almost negligible addition to farm incomes." The answer is easy enough: rail-

roads symbolized the emerging economic order that threatened farmers' autonomy. They were, in the Grangers' experience, the most direct cause of farmers'
economic distress or, in any event, the cause most easily reached. And before the
rate wars of the 1870s, prices were in fact quite high.[9]

Rates declined in the 1880s, but the railroads did not shed their iconic status,
and a severe downturn in agricultural prices in the early 1890s revived the farmers' ire. This time the beneficiary was the newly formed Populist Party. Its Omaha
platform soldered the old railroad initiatives of the Grangers with the more radical vision of the Farmers' Alliance. Since the last major round of agrarian agitation, the U.S. Supreme Court had declared the state-enacted railroad regulation
laws unconstitutional, a violation of the "dormant" commerce clause. If Congress alone had the authority to regulate interstate commerce under the Constitution, the Court majority reasoned in its 1896 decision *Wabash v. Illinois*, then
state regulations that affected interstate commerce trenched on Congress's
power. The fact that Congress had not adopted any railroad regulations of its
own was beside the point. States could not be allowed to disrupt the "right of continuous transportation." With state regulation denied them, Populists called for
a bolder approach: national ownership of railroads, federal support for crop
prices, federal credits to farmers, and a graduated income tax.[10]

When the illness infecting the farm economy metastasized into a nationwide
depression in 1893, Democrats, fresh from their electoral triumph, found themselves suddenly imperiled. The weather map had changed again. Voters returned a Republican majority in the House of Representatives in the 1894
midterm elections, the largest single Republican seat gain in party history. President Cleveland's mercantilist economic conservatism appeared discredited, and
party regulars feared repercussions in 1896. To stem the tide of defeat, they opted
for a bold stroke. Facing widespread discontent in the industrial Northeast and a
Populist insurgency in the West and South, Democrats threw overboard the fiscal conservatism that had been the national party's hallmark since Reconstruction and hoisted the flag of Populist-inspired economic radicalism. In the summer of 1896, the Democratic convention nominated William Jennings Bryan of
Nebraska, the so-called Boy Orator of the Platte, from the geographic heart of
Populist power, thirty-six years old and already famous for his rolling, resonant,
mellifluous cadences, for his humble beginnings, his belief in the common
man, for his ardent, impassioned evangelical Christianity. Bryan favored a lower
tariff and national regulation—but not ownership—of the railroads. He also advocated the monetization of silver in a sixteen-to-one, silver-to-gold ratio, an effective devaluation of the currency aimed at relieving debtor farmers and cash-

strapped consumers. That was good enough for the Populists, who nominated Bryan themselves on a joint Democrat-Populist ticket.[11]

Republicans knew their opponents were fighting from a position of weakness, but still the Democrat-Populist merger caused them tremendous discomfort. The Populists galvanized the Democratic base in the South and put the middle and far West in play. To counter, Republicans united firmly behind the protective tariff and tried to finesse the "free silver" issue as much as possible, signaling their opposition to devaluation to business allies in the Northeast while emphasizing the benefits of tariff protection and promotion of enterprise to audiences west of the Mississippi. Bryan was a formidable campaigner, however, and he looked to be the early favorite. William McKinley, lately governor of Ohio, had been chosen as the Republican presidential nominee on the first ballot in St. Louis, and while he remained in his home state pursuant to campaign tradition, his campaign manager was looking for Republican officials willing to make the party's case in the West, people willing to brave the storm. Theodore Roosevelt volunteered.[12]

No one was more aware of the Republicans' electoral situation than Theodore Roosevelt, if only because he was quite certain that his fate and the party's were tethered. This conviction may have inspired much of his white-hot rhetoric in 1896. But personal ambition aside, Bryan's candidacy troubled him, profoundly, for other reasons. Roosevelt believed Bryan was an agent of disorder, a demagogue willing to whip up the nation's unsavory elements as a means of gaining political power. In so doing, Roosevelt believed Bryan threatened the future of the race. Roosevelt initially read the agrarian discontent in the West and South and the labor unrest back East as an ill omen of impending anarchy or, worse, socialism. This is not to suggest Roosevelt was a proponent of laissez-faire economics. He believed in state action to improve society, and his racial ideas in fact carried distinctly collectivist implications. But Roosevelt saw European-style socialism as the opposite of true national solidarity. Socialism destroyed the private property on which economic progress was built. Worse, it thrived on class hatred; it encouraged envy. And it deprecated the importance of individual righteousness. Socialists blamed an impersonal capitalist "system" for society's ills. Their doctrine deemphasized individuals' moral agency and with it individuals' moral responsibility. To Roosevelt, that made socialism synonymous with license. It was immoral. Before genuine reform could take place, the socialist threat had to be thwarted.[13]

Edward Bellamy had predicted in his best-selling 1888 novel, *Looking Back-*

wards, that widespread social turmoil provoked by abused laborers would give rise to a new socialist state. His book inspired an instant "nationalist movement" that attacked private property and criticized competition as the basis of the American economy. Roosevelt didn't like Bellamy's scenario or his ideas. Unfortunately, given the course of events, Bellamy's prophecy seemed all too realistic. By 1896, Roosevelt genuinely feared a social revolution, if not quite perhaps the mass upheaval socialists forecast. For proof of his concerns, he pointed to the labor strikes of the past decade.[14]

"During the summer of 1894, every American capable of thinking must at times have pondered very gravely over certain features of the national character which were brought into unpleasant prominence by the course of events," Roosevelt thought. "[T]he attitude of many of our public men at the time of the great strike in July, 1894, was such as to call down on their heads the hearty condemnation of every American who wishes well to his country." He was referring to the spectacular labor unrest that erupted in Pullman, Illinois, in that year, eventually implicating one hundred and fifty thousand workers in twenty-seven states. Pullman—just outside Chicago—was named for George Pullman, founder of the Pullman Palace Car Company, one of the largest producers of railway cars in the world. In the panic of 1893, George Pullman slashed company wages by a quarter but refused to lower the rent payments he charged his workers for the housing he provided. Pullman workers went on strike in early May of 1894, forcing the closure of the plant. Members of the newly formed American Railway Union (ARU) joined the effort in July. The effect was devastating. ARU switchmen around the country refused to switch trains pulling Pullman cars, paralyzing scores of rail lines. Illinois governor John Peter Altgeld, a Democrat, refused to deploy the state militia to break the strike, by now the largest in American history, and, when the railway stoppage threatened to impede the flow of U.S. mail, President Grover Cleveland lost his patience. Ignoring Altgeld's strenuous protests, Cleveland ordered federal troops to Chicago with instructions to end the strike by force. But instead of order, the troops brought chaos. Striking workers overturned railway cars and attempted to blockade city streets as soldiers entered the city on July 4. Rioting and looting broke out, and on July 7 fire set by some of the six thousand rioters consumed a cluster of buildings in the city's Columbian Exposition, a monument built for the previous year's World's Fair that celebrated the progress wrought by Europeans' discovery of the New World. Now progress, it seemed, had dissolved into anarchy.[15]

Roosevelt was appalled. The number of labor strikes nationwide had increased noticeably since the early 1880s, but the Pullman incident was on a scale hitherto unseen in the United States. "Had it not been for the admirable action of the Federal Government," Roosevelt concluded in retrospect, "Chicago would have seen a repetition of what occurred during the Paris Commune, while Illinois would have been torn by a fierce social war." Roosevelt spied a menace to social stability in the gathering and progressively more violent labor disquiet of the late 1880s and early 1890s. The average number of strikes per year tripled between 1880 and 1886; this was to him an ominous portent of social decline. The violence of these strikes fed his fears. The 1886 Haymarket strike, located, like the Pullman incident, in Chicago, ended with a bomb blast that killed innocent bystanders. In 1892, disgruntled workers seized Andrew Carnegie's Homestead, Pennsylvania, steel mill and battled for days with Carnegie's hired Pinkerton forces. And then came the Pullman strike in Chicago, this one far larger, causing far more damage than any before.[16]

These incidents rang in Roosevelt's mind like fire bells and, taken in conjunction with agrarian demands, warned of imminent danger. Progress was not a given. He shared none of the serene confidence in automatic social advancement espoused by many of his contemporaries. "The old nations of the earth creep on at a snail's pace; the Republic thunders past with the rush of the express," Andrew Carnegie exclaimed in 1886. Roosevelt's vision of life was too dark, his view of the cosmos too chaotic for such triumphalism. He knew full well that what progress in human affairs men of earlier generations had achieved was won by struggle or, to be perfectly frank, violence. Forces of disorder lurked forever just beneath the surface of civilized society, an element of humans' barbaric past ready to reassert itself should social control slip too badly. Anarchy was a state of nature humans left only with great effort and much evolutionary refinement, which was why less-advanced races were beset by the anarchic curse. Indeed, the violent disorder characteristic of less-evolved races was one of Roosevelt's leading justifications for civilized conquest. Social order, in the final analysis, had to be imposed.[17]

Yet any race or nation, no matter how advanced, was a composite of various individuals and groups. Watching the mayhem unfold in Chicago and remembering the violence of Haymarket and Homestead, Roosevelt worried that the United States harbored a vicious, lawless underclass eager to break the cords of social civility. "The completeness of the victory of the Federal authorities [in Chicago], representing the cause of law and order" should not obscure the fact, Roosevelt insisted, that "we were on the brink of an almost terrific explosion." Farmers' agitation in 1896 for devaluation of the currency and other debt relief was of a piece. Roosevelt regarded these demands as immoral, just as he had regarded labor's press for higher wages when he was a member of the Albany assembly. The farmers were trying to shirk their legitimate financial obligations, he thought. And their shiftlessness threatened economic security. If debts were not paid and loans honored, credit would collapse. Private property would be endangered. These "free silver" advocates, Roosevelt concluded, had forgotten the Eighth Commandment, "Thou shalt not steal." That was all there was to it. They were materialists, vulgarians. They would throw aside moral commands and take what was not theirs simply to ameliorate their economic condition. Once this started, Roosevelt could hardly imagine a way station short of total revolution.[18]

Though he viciously attacked the rural Populists, most of these "lawless classes" Roosevelt associated with the urban, immigrant poor he had observed from a distance as a child. They were the new strains in America's racial stock, most of them "utterly unused to self-government of any kind" and, for the most part, "even yet not assimilated." A few of these immigrants were professed anarchists, philosophical followers of Proudhon or other instructors in the German anarchist school flourishing on the European continent at the time. Roosevelt as president would propose to exclude such people from American citizenship. But he thought that most immigrants were simply poor, uneducated, underdeveloped newcomers who needed to be raised racially to the high American average. This project would take time. Meanwhile, "the anarchic violence of the vicious and ignorant poor [is an] ever-threatening dange[r]," and countermeasures of some sort might be required. Besides immigrants and debtor farmers, Roosevelt identified underprivileged rural whites, mostly Southerners, as the other members of the lawless set. These were the sort of people who "distrust anything they cannot understand" and were often "emotionally religious." Refined tastes "and a tendency to bathe frequently, cause them the deepest suspicion." Narrow-minded and judgmental, they were, above all, jealous. "If they cannot be well-to-do themselves, at least they hope to make matters uncomfortable for those who are." These types, though undeniably full-fledged Americans, were a warning of the regression possible within even the best races.[19]

The worst thing one could do, whether dealing with the urban lower classes or the uneducated "cracker, the poor white" of the South who so fervently remonstrated for free silver, was to flatter them. But flattering as a means to win electoral support was exactly what Roosevelt believed a number of prominent politicians were doing—the large majority of them, conveniently, Populists and Democrats. "It would be difficult to overestimate the damage done by the example and action of a man like Governor Altgeld of Illinois," Roosevelt fumed, recalling Altgeld's refusal to end the Pullman strike by force. In a time of great social crisis, Altgeld "act[ed] as the foe of the law-abiding and the friend of the lawless classes, and endeavor[ed], in company with the lowest and most abandoned office-seeking politicians, to prevent proper measures being taken to prevent riot and punish the rioters." Had President Cleveland not ordered federal soldiers to Chicago, "Governor Altgeld would have been primarily responsible" for "the horrible waste of life" that would undoubtedly have come.[20]

However, the Populist governors in the Western states, and a handful of Republican governors as well, were just as much at fault. By refusing to take stronger stands against the strikers, they "shared the shame with [Altgeld]," shared his "blatant demagogism which, more than any other, jeopardizes the existence of free institutions." Their demagoguery might win short-term political gain, but it would also stir up class antagonisms, incite law-breaking, and ultimately threaten the peace and stability of the American nation. Altgeld and men like him were accomplices, Roosevelt charged, in an assault on the American race. They were as much a danger to the future of that race as the lawless classes themselves or the previous inhabitants of the American continent, for that matter. Such people had to be defeated.[21]

To Roosevelt it came as no surprise that when the Democrats convened in July of 1896, Altgeld led the battle for free silver, securing it a prominent place in the party platform. And the acceptance speech of the Democrats' eventual presidential nominee, William Jennings Bryan, he found particularly repulsive. "You shall not press down upon the brow of labor this crown of thorns," Bryan thundered from the floor of the Democratic convention. "You shall not crucify mankind upon a cross of gold." Despite his bimetallist fervor, Bryan was not the convention's first choice. Altgeld's forces held out over five ballots before endorsing Bryan. That made the Boy Orator, in Roosevelt's mind, precisely the sort of public flatterer the country could ill afford, willing to say and do anything to advance his political career. As the summer wore on and Bryan launched a whirlwind whistle-stop speaking tour in the West and South, Roosevelt's low opinion of the Democratic nominee sagged further. Roosevelt concluded Bryan was a foolish man given to schoolgirl hysterics, "a well-meaning demagogue" who had his head "turned by the applause of men of little intelligence."[22]

Convinced of the danger confronting the nation, Roosevelt took up his pen and then took to the hustings, hammering Bryan and the Populists mercilessly throughout the summer and fall. "Thrift, industry, and business energy are qualities which are quite incompatible with true Populist feeling," Roosevelt inveighed. "Payment of debts, like suppression of riots, is abhorrent to the Populist as immoral." Bryan was a hypocritical flatterer who would do anything to get elected, and his Populist running mate, Thomas Watson, born in Georgia, "an embodied retribution on the South for having failed to educate the cracker." While Bryan was really a "sham and a compromise," Watson represented "the real thing," Roosevelt told his readers. Watson, "with his sincerity, his frankness,

his extreme suspiciousness of anything he cannot understand," was a barbaric id-
iot, a savage just out of the cave. On Nathaniel Shaler's chart of human progression, it was unclear he and his supporters would even appear.[23]

Roosevelt's searing attacks on Bryan and his running mates may have been
personally cruel and ferociously hyperbolic, but the inspiration for his invective
was real. The country was at a historical turning point, just as Roosevelt thought.
Forces of economic, social, and intellectual change were transforming the nation at a remarkable pace. Participants in the election of 1896 felt this upheaval
personally, sensed it in the strident tone and sheer intensity of the public debate
that season. Roosevelt perceived an impending class war; William McKinley
and his political captains, the genesis of a new electoral configuration. But actually, no one was sure how the landscape would appear when the winds of change
lessened. The nation was suspended again in that uneasy place between past and
future, plagued by uncertainties created, in some measure, by the resolution of
an earlier crisis.[24]

The North's victory in the Civil War, the conflict that had hung over the country like a Damocles sword at Roosevelt's birth, set America's course into the future. The United States would not splinter into smaller, warring nations. Slavery
would not be allowed to spread into the territories. In fact, the war doomed chattel slavery in North America and, with it, the South's vision of republican
government and political economy. Union arms consigned to oblivion John C.
Calhoun's "concurrent majority" theory of government—actually a form of minority rule that postulated government was legitimate only if approved by the nation's key minority groups, meaning, not coincidentally, the Southern slave
states—and ensured that the constitutional rule of the majority as devised in
Philadelphia and defended by Abraham Lincoln would prevail. Northern victory also guaranteed, as Calhoun had suspected, the triumph of industrial capitalism over Southern rural agrarianism. The leisured, landed gentleman would
be no more; not that the Southern planter aristocracy had counted many members anyway. More than anything else, it was a social ideal that perished with the
Confederacy, a death that had serious consequences nonetheless.[25]

Americans had long identified a link between financial independence and
suitability for self-government. He who would deliberate with other free men
about the future of the whole political community needed himself to be disin-
terested and free from selfish ambitions. That meant, when it came right to it,
that citizens needed to own property. James Harrington and other English revolutionaries of the seventeenth century—the "commonwealthmen" who opposed
monarchy and reset the republican thought of ancient Greece and Machiavelli's

Italy to Christian England—taught Americans that property ownership prevented covetous ambition by removing its primary source: economic need. In this way, property holding guaranteed personal independence, a critical requisite for republican liberty. If a person were going to participate in self-government, he would have to be able to make his own decisions on his own volition. If others made his choices for him, he would hardly be free in any meaningful sense. Americans before and after 1776 believed a person's socioeconomic situation determined his political identity. Slaves were the leading example. Totally subject to the will of the master, without property of any kind to call their own, they were denied political personhood altogether. Children were a less extreme instance of the same logic. They did not vote because they were dependents, and many revolutionary leaders justified the exclusion of women from the franchise on the same grounds: they were dependent on their husbands. It followed from there that otherwise free men, nonslaves, who did not own property and work for themselves, should nonetheless be denied the ballot, because they were dependent on their employers for a wage.[26]

Wage workers were not economically independent, and that made them dangerous in a republic. "Dependence," Thomas Jefferson counseled, he one of the great republican spokesmen of the founding generation, "begets subservience and venality, suffocates the germ of virtue, and prepares fit tools for the designs of ambition." Jefferson denied that men who depended for their livelihood on other people, who lived at close quarters in cramped and dirty conditions, who owned no personal property but lived from wage to wage, spending all they earned on basic necessities—Jefferson denied these people had the independence necessary for self-government. "Cultivators of the earth are the most valuable citizens," he held instead, for they "are the most vigorous, the most independent, the most virtuous." The life of the independent farmer called forth the character traits needed for democratic freedom, which is why landowners large and small were, more than any other group, "tied to their country and wedded to its liberty." Roosevelt's arguments against the Populist political program—indeed much of his analysis of the urban working class—sounded a good deal like Jefferson, right down to fear of the demagoguery to which the working classes might be susceptible. The working poor, Jefferson had concluded, were "instruments by which the liberties of a country are generally overturned." Roosevelt in 1896 seemed to agree.[27]

Property was valuable for another, related reason. It served as a bulwark against the coercive power of the state. Whether owned by individuals or families or clubs or churches, property provided a sphere of privacy into which the state had difficulty reaching, thanks to the protections of the English common law. By cabining the power of government, property allowed "the people" to protect their rights and privileges, where "the people" is understood as a group essentially separate from the political ruling class. But this was just another way of saying that property guaranteed independence—economic, personal, and political.[28]

Appealing to this intellectual constellation, this republican political philosophy, the South argued in the run-up to the Civil War that its plantation system and strict social hierarchy yielded the independent, well-educated aristocracy critical for free government, while the North's citified, wage-paying brand of capitalism manifestly did not. Free labor advocates like William Seward and Abraham Lincoln tried to blunt the South's intellectual offensive by arguing that the source of a laborer's politically necessary independence was his ability to choose his work freely and keep the products of his labor. Land ownership was, technically, unnecessary. But even free laborites made the landowning Western homesteader their sociopolitical ideal, and they did not challenge the connection between financial independence and suitability for self-rule. On the contrary, most Americans in the late nineteenth century remained committed to an economy of small, independent, local producers operating in a competitive market. They distrusted large concentrations of power, including mammoth industries based in distant cities; they suspected employers who apparently intended to keep their workers laboring for a wage indefinitely. This preference for a certain kind of economy was actually a preference for republican *political* economy, an economic arrangement that affirmed the virtues of independence, autonomy, and self-direction that Americans still treated as synonymous with liberty. But how republican economy could survive in the industrial tempest was yet to be worked out. And that made the survival of republican liberty an open question as well. The United States was no longer a collection of seaboard states or even a frontier nation. It was a continental, industrializing behemoth. Roosevelt's childhood New York had, as it turned out, been a portent for the country's future.[29]

Wage labor was one central feature of that future. Still an aberration in the 1850s, when the labor ideal remained that of a man working for himself on his own land or at his own craft, wage-paying industries accounted for the major growth in the American economy by the 1890s. Between 1870 and 1910, the proportion of middle-class men who were self-employed dropped from 67 percent to 37 percent. Work under the direction of another person and for which one received an hourly payment was to become the norm. Production on a mass scale was a new norm as well. For the next three generations, the factory would be a permanent part of the American economic terrain. While the percentage of

American workers involved in manufacturing remained relatively constant at 19 percent, manufacturing output surged from 33 percent of all commodities produced in the United States in 1869 to 53 percent twenty-five years later.[30]

The American economy in this period was undergoing a dramatic structural transformation. The size, the shape—the very nature of the beast was changing. From the conclusion of the Civil War until the panic of 1893, real per capita gross national product grew at an annual rate of 2 percent. Already by 1896, the average per capita income in America was climbing to regions higher than those reached by any other country, and it would hit $227 in 1900. Higher incomes meant higher levels of savings and investment. Americans of means, "capitalists," invested in industry. The growth of tangible capital stock far outpaced the growth in population, with significant consequences. Over three decades, the capital stock per worker grew by 80 percent, leading to breathtaking gains in efficiency and rapidly escalating production. To manage their growth, firms adopted hierarchical, multidivision management structures, a design pioneered by the railroads. And they expanded with abandon, merging and reorganizing into larger units to realize greater economies of scale. When at all possible, they integrated vertically, drawing in suppliers of raw materials and former wholesalers in an effort to internalize transactions that once took place in markets.[31]

Railroads, meanwhile, fed the production boom and, along the way, worked a revolution in the American interior. The railways' need for steel drove the production of iron from statistically zero in the early 1860s to 27 million tons a year by 1910. Railroads also opened hundreds of thousands of acres of land for cultivation, which, along with new machines for planting and harvesting, transformed the agricultural sector. As a result, American agricultural production multiplied many times over in the latter part of the nineteenth century. Between 1850 and 1870 wheat production in the United States rocketed from 15.2 million bushels per year to 104 million, while corn production grew from 68.3 million to 218.6 million bushels yearly. A middling agrarian economy at the time of the Civil War, the United States would rank as the world's largest, most powerful economic producer within a decade of the century's turn.[32]

The industrial expansion rewrote demographic patterns and produced new social conditions in its wake. Rural Americans suddenly found themselves involved in a vast, intricate, and often impenetrable network of continental interdependence, linking together wage laborers, farmers, railways, and corporations. The appearance of a large-scale corporate economy sustained by rail and telegraph forced the integration of formerly local markets, and small, rural communities often experienced this integration, like the Grangers, as a loss of autonomy. The rural population grew at the outset of the industrial period—doubled, in fact—from twenty-five to fifty million between 1860 and 1910. But tellingly, the urban population grew even faster, bursting from six million to forty-two million in just fifty years. A rapid urbanization trend was under way. In 1860, one-sixth of Americans lived in cities. By 1900, the proportion was closer to one-third.[33]

Displaced rural workers sought jobs in the new wage-paying industries, but the urban population explosion was due mainly to increased immigration, and this created serious problems of its own. Fourteen million immigrants flooded into the United States between 1860 and 1900, encouraged by the booming American economy and reductions in the cost of ocean transportation. Another nine million, mostly from eastern and southern Europe, came between 1900 and 1910. New York City's population increased four times over between 1860 and 1920, while Boston's and Philadelphia's increased by almost as much. The Midwestern cities grew more rapidly still: Chicago, St. Louis, Detroit, and Cleveland posted a ten- to twentyfold population growth in forty years' time. In America's eight largest cities in 1910, more than one-third of the population was foreign born, and most of them, especially in the East, were living in filthy tenements or other ramshackle housing and working in the factories. The immigration swell placed severe downward pressure on wages and badly overburdened cities' social infrastructure. New York's lower east side housed 330,000 inhabitants per square mile, the densest living space in the world. The squalor was indescribable: Jacob Riis made his name telling the story, with photographs, of the tenement dwellers' conditions.[34]

The gale force of economic change brought social stress and dislocation with its other wonders, and Americans responded with a kaleidoscope of reform initiatives and countermeasures. The Grangers and Farmers' Alliance backed legislation to regulate railroads and prevent corporate consolidation, measures animated by a republican preference for local autonomy. These groups sought to preserve the competitive economy of small, independent producers—and to help farmers, Jefferson's most virtuous class, along the way. In the cities, laborers hard-pressed by the deflationary trend in wages organized under the leadership of Samuel Gompers and agitated for better pay, as well as for better working conditions. The labor strikes Roosevelt deplored were part of a broader effort to win unskilled laborers a voice in the corporate-dominated economy. It was a need workers felt urgently. The American Federation of Labor increased its membership from 250,000 in 1897 to 1,562,000 in 1910, and doubled it again by the eve of the First World War. Other, better-off urbanites worked to improve the plight of the poor. Jane Addams brought the settlement house movement from England to the United States to provide basic social services to neighborhood poor, founding Hull House in Chicago in 1889. House directors, like Addams, lived on location, among the people they served. A new wave of municipal reformers, horrified at the opportunities for political corruption stimulated by the latest immigration boom and immigrants' desperate need for welfare services, promoted the expansion of mayoral power and nonpartisan administration to clean up city politics.[35]

Corporations were usually identified as the wizards of the industrial age, but corporate chieftains could feel just as powerless as the man earning ten dollars a week in the factory, just as subject to nameless economic forces beyond anyone's control. The panic of 1893 caught heavy industry in the midst of a tremendous expansion in production, underwritten by the prodigious capital investment of the foregoing decade. When the panic became a depression, demand fell off steeply and industrial profits turned to losses. Suddenly confronted with a glut of excess capacity, many firms' first move was to trim prices in an effort to rekindle sales. But the sales failed to materialize, and instead corporate managers found themselves trapped in a retaliatory price war. A new imperative quickly took shape: survive. Manage competition, dampen it, curb it—if necessary, stifle it, but by all means survive. The mid-1890s saw firms experimenting with trade associations and gentlemen's price agreements—otherwise known as price fixing—but without much success. With the election of 1896 underway, they had not yet found a solution to their predicament. The greatest merger movement in American history was just over the horizon.[36]

Roosevelt faced the economic transformation that vexed so many of his contemporaries with the same sanguine detachment he had shown writing about the displacement of the ranchman by the Western farmer. "For we ourselves and the life that we lead will shortly pass away from the plains as completely as the red and white hunters who have vanished from before our herds," he wrote of the Dakota ranchers. The free, open-air life of the ranchman was "by its very nature" ephemeral. The same could be said of almost any economic arrangement. Roosevelt believed in evolutionary progress. He was not wedded to any particular status quo. He was a social conservative but no arch traditionalist. What worried him in the fall of 1896 was not the corporations or the fact of industrial growth. Roosevelt worried about Americans' response. The Populists he castigated as dangerous, socially retrogressive boors and Bryan as their willing fool. He feared social disorder and the destruction of private property. These concerns placed him squarely in the conservative mainstream, alongside Republicans from William McKinley to William Howard Taft. They marked him as a member in good standing of the conservative political elite, which worked throughout the 1890s to dissipate labor's growing clout. While the Republicans (and moderate

Democrats) campaigned against free silver, another arm of the conservative establishment, the United States Supreme Court, busily expanded the power of the federal judiciary to enjoin strikes, declaring "freedom of contract" and private property to be the Constitution's definitive guarantees.[37]

What set Roosevelt apart from his establishment compatriots as early as 1896 was not his dismay in the face of labor unrest or his defense of private property and the gold standard. All that was typical of his class and party. What made Roosevelt intriguing were the unconventional ideas partly obscured by his social conservatism. His rhetoric contained another strand, one that echoed and developed his Albany themes, a reformist and vaguely collectivist line of thought that might reach beyond 1896 to a broader, more positive agenda. That line of thought represented Roosevelt's future. It began, as did most of Roosevelt's ideas, with a moral judgment.[38]

Bryan and "the men who stand at his right and his left hands," Roosevelt thundered from the campaign trail as the fall wore on, represent "those forces that simmer beneath the surface of every civilized community," forces that would destroy "property and civilization" and finally "themselves, leaving after them a mere burnt-out waste."[39] But the agents of disorder were not the only ones to blame for the country's suddenly precarious position. The "old-stock Americans" descended from the original western European settlers, whose families had lived in the United States for a century or more and had risen to stations of social prominence, had largely abandoned their responsibility to provide social and political guidance. They were the leaders of the race, but they were refusing to lead, distracted instead by the quest for greater wealth and material comfort. Their selfish behavior made them complicit in the destructive actions of the seething underclass. "There are . . . plenty of wrong-doers besides those who commit the overt act. Too much cannot be said against the men of wealth who sacrifice everything to getting wealth."[40]

Roosevelt was surely thinking here of his own socioeconomic stratum. He equated "Native Americans," as he sometimes called those of "the old stock," with the wealthy, well-educated families of the Northeast and especially of New England. These Americans had won their place in society through generations of hard work and thrift. Their wealth and refinement were the products of their virtues, and their trajectory the one he hoped all Americans—more than that, all the world—would follow. But economic prosperity held dangers of its own. Having gained material riches, the prosperous might all too easily come to think of wealth as an end in itself. They might forget that character signaled the true worth of a man, and that material goods were, at best, character's by-products.

"There is not in the world a more ignoble [person] than the mere money-getting American, insensible to every duty, regardless of every principle, bent only on amassing a fortune." A fixation on accumulating wealth clouded the individual's vision and moral judgment, turning his attention away from the interests of the race toward the gratification of his immediate, increasingly selfish desires for comfort and leisure.[41]

Men corrupted like this soon proved only too willing to defer the responsibilities of government, community life, and social welfare to others. Any obligation that interfered with money-making would be shunted aside. "The man who is content . . . to see the maladministration of justice without an immediate and resolute effort to reform it, is shirking his duty and is preparing the way for infinite woe in the future." Rich men would not have a society in which to make money if they did not see to their social duties, Roosevelt believed. Their indifference was, in the long run, tragically self-destructive. "Hard, brutal indifference to the right, and an equally brutal shortsightedness as to the inevitable results of corruption and injustice, are baleful beyond measure." And yet Roosevelt saw this self-absorbed, materialistic myopia as increasingly characteristic of a great many moneyed Americans.[42]

Observing what he took to be the cool apathy of the urban elite amid the den of populist unrest, the exhortations of the elder Theodore came burning into Roosevelt's mind, and he applied his father's instruction to the political situation as he found it. "No man is worth much to the commonwealth if he is not capable of feeling righteous wrath and just indignation, if he is not stirred to hot anger by misdoing," he said. "No man is worth much anywhere if he does not possess both moral and physical courage." Apparently a great many of his own class no longer did. They were too busy "speculat[ing] in stocks and wreck[ing] railroads," while allowing their sons "to lead [lives] of foolish and expensive idleness and gross debauchery." Not only did they fail to administer justice and preserve American political institutions, their money-obsessed activities actually incited the underclass to greater unrest and violence.[43]

Roosevelt's judgment was a reprise of his Albany theme, a moral critique of his own class for its shortsighted self-absorption and rampant materialism. But sounded here, in 1896, the critique took on new resonance. It opened intellectual space within his conservative defense of property and the gold standard for a constructive, proactive attempt to address the causes of the social anomie he condemned. The police commissioner from New York may not have sounded much interested in reform on the campaign trail for McKinley in 1896, but in fact he believed social reforms were necessary, even pressing. The gist of his criticism of his own class was that they didn't share his realization. They did nothing.

The wealthy capitalists were the worst of the lot, in Roosevelt's judgment. Many of them were better characterized as members of the "wealthy criminal class." They looked only to protect their bottom line, treating their workers as so much chattel. Roosevelt was not for nationalizing railroads or coining more silver, but neither was he for doing nothing. His upbraiding of the wealthy for their impotence hinted at a possible program of reform and possible coalitions to support it.

He was well beyond calling for more "refined" and "educated" young men in politics now. Instead, he wondered in print about measures to improve city life by fostering a "system of mixed individualism and collectivism." Specifically, he endorsed city planning and professional fire forces, advocated the construction of playgrounds and parks, and supported public transit and new regulation to make city housing both safer and more affordable. This made him a natural ally of the burgeoning city reform movement, led in New York by Mayor Strong. Municipal reformers, sometimes called "good government" reformers, were businessmen and middle-class professionals who wanted to improve the efficiency of city administration and break the power of political bosses. Actually, they could sound a lot like the old Mugwumps, and many of their favored administrative reforms Roosevelt had himself proposed more than a decade before in the Albany legislature: enlarge the powers of the mayor, elect councilmen from the city at large rather than by wards, make administrative appointments according to civil service rules.[44]

Other urban reform advocates sought not only to make administration more efficient in a time of economic depression, but also to expand social welfare services. Mayor Hazen S. Pingree of Detroit, first elected in 1890, pushed for public regulation of utility and trolley companies, and a redistribution of Detroit's tax burden. Roosevelt's proposed regulation of city housing and public transport was not far from Pingree's program, and, as Roosevelt knew from experience, the advantage to administering social welfare services at the city level, in addition to helping the underprivileged, was the blow it dealt to the boss-run machines. They thrived by integrating the widely dispersed services of city government and making them available to the immigrant poor. Replace machine welfare with city welfare, and the bosses' clout might diminish, and corruption along with it. Of course, not every urban reformer blamed political bosses, graft, or the depression for urban ills. Temperance advocates blamed excessive drink. Roosevelt had not insubstantial ties to that group as well, having advocated steep saloon-licensing fees and liquor taxes while a state legislator, and having fought to enforce the Sunday closing laws as police commissioner. While he opposed an outright ban on alcohol, he ceded nothing to temperance proponents when it came to moral tone, and, unlike many of them, he directed his anti-vice sermons to members of the upper classes and not just the immigrant, largely Catholic, urban poor.[45]

Roosevelt had not in 1896 assembled a coherent reform program, but he was trying new ideas on for size, even as new reformist groups sprang up around the country. The common element in his experimental reform concoction was an element shared by the good government reformers and temperance advocates, the same element that connected Roosevelt to an older republican political economy. That element was righteousness. Roosevelt, as ever, believed in righteousness, believed that character—or virtue, as an earlier generation might have called it—sustained the republic and republican liberty. In the political theory of the English liberals and the American revolutionaries, property was central because property guaranteed independence and disinterestedness. But independence and disinterestedness were in turn really about character. They were virtues, civic virtues necessary to live responsibly in a free republic, to share in democratic life—to be a free person. Roosevelt didn't share the earlier republicans' fixation on property or necessarily their preference for a property-based economy of small, independent producers. But he was worried about character traits and the conditions necessary to get them.

In the measures he advocated, Roosevelt blended his Albany calls for social responsibility with a fresh emphasis on collective action. Subtly, in his effort to get the conditions that produced the warrior virtues, he was reversing the political teaching of Herbert Spencer that he knew as a youth. Roosevelt's proposals suggested individualism was not the highest stage of human evolutionary development. Instead, democratic collectivism was, the capacity for coordinated political action that brought together society's members for a common purpose while yet preserving the integrity and strength of the individual. In his *Winning of the West*, Roosevelt criticized the disorganization and political impotence of territorial governments, arguing that settlers would have enjoyed greater safety, "and incidentally greater liberty—had the central authority been stronger." But this analysis—and the general thrust of his new proposals—called into question the worth and very legitimacy of laissez-faire politics. Perhaps there was a role for the state beyond merely keeping order and protecting freedom of contract. He had already abandoned laissez-faire free trade and embraced the Half-Breed Republican program of tariff protection and promotion of enterprise. Additional forms of economic regulation could hardly be called out of the question.[46]

Was Roosevelt in 1896 a budding reformer or merely a conservative opportunist tempering the wind to the shorn lamb? For the time being, Roosevelt denounced as lawless the only major reform proposals on the table—namely, the

Populist proposals: extensive regulation of railroads and government support for farmers. Though he was pushing beyond his Albany refrains toward a broader political platform, his ideas were still distinctly Eastern and unmistakably urban in focus. He had very little to say about the agrarian rumblings in the South and West, beyond denunciation. But his commitment to reform was genuine, rooted in his evolutionist view of history and his Christian liberalism. He criticized those who ignored the plight of the poor. He was impatient with what he regarded as capitalism's ethic of selfish individualism. He was alive to the structural banes of the industrial economy—the exploitation of workers and children, the social inequality, the political corruption. Roosevelt was no socialist, but he believed in collective action for the good of the whole. He believed in collective action to improve society. And as early as 1896, he was imagining a society no longer riven by class distinctions, one based, instead, on a shared national purpose, where the only relevant differences were ones of moral character.

The industrial age would not make itself, he concluded. No age did. The opportunities awaiting the American race would not become something on their own. Wise, constructive regulation was going to be necessary to raise the race to its righteous potential. And that called for wise, flexible, and creative leadership.

William McKinley won the election by 601,854 votes. The Republicans had captured 271 electoral votes out of a possible 447, managing to carry California, Oregon, North Dakota, and seven states in the Midwest, despite Bryan's purported regional strength. This showing was partly a testament to Roosevelt's earnest efforts in the region and partly to the prowess of the local Republican machines. The Republican campaign there, generously financed by Eastern business, targeted upper Midwestern farmers and members of the middle class who benefited from the rapid mechanization and increasing land values brought by the railroads. These voters worried about free silver's long-term consequences for the struggling economy. They voted Republican. But the real story was in the East, which voted solidly Republican, from Maine to Maryland. The party's embrace of the tariff and economic nationalism was finally paying major dividends. Eastern capitalists, alarmed at Bryan's anti-industrial rhetoric, lined up behind McKinley. The strength of local Democratic machines and their close ties to laborers and immigrants notwithstanding, a majority of industrial workers voted Republican, too, motivated by the fear that a deflationary coinage of silver would make it harder to buy food and pay rent. Middle- and upper-middle-class urban residents supported Republicans for similar reasons—fear of deflation and economic decline. But they also voted Republican in protest against the sordid Democratic machines that had risen to prominence in the depression years. In short, Democrats' bold endorsement of the Populist program, even a somewhat diluted version, proved to be a long-term political disaster. Between the depression and their perceived acquiescence to agrarian radicals, Democrats had wrecked their reputation for economic stewardship. It would take almost twenty years to recover.[47]

As the storms cleared, a new, stable electoral configuration emerged, one unlikely to be upset by isolated shocks, especially as the economy recovered following McKinley's inauguration. For Roosevelt, that meant new possibilities greater than he could yet imagine. McKinley offered him the post of assistant secretary of the navy—with some prodding from Henry Cabot Lodge—and Roosevelt gladly accepted. He was thinking again about America's international position and hoping for a war with Spain. But he was also musing about what it would take to lead a broad-based reform movement. The fright of 1896, if partly self-inflicted, nevertheless convinced Roosevelt that the challenges facing the American race required political solutions. The nation's greatest challenge, were the United States to take its proper place in the world, would be to recover the warrior virtues that won the West. "Thrift and industry are indispensable virtues; but they are not all-sufficient. We must base our appeals for civic and national betterment on nobler grounds than those of mere business expediency," Roosevelt concluded. Good citizens required "the rougher, manlier virtues, and above all the virtue of personal courage, physical as well as moral."[48]

In the months following the election of 1896, Roosevelt began speaking of these virtues as more than personal or even social, more than applications of good morality, as he had characterized them earlier. The warrior qualities were *civic* virtues, he declared; they were indispensable to the health of the American polity, to republican liberty. "In the last analysis a healthy state can exist only when the men and women who make it up can lead clean, vigorous, healthy lives," Roosevelt told the Hamilton Club; "when the children are so trained that they shall endeavor, not to shirk difficulties, but to overcome them; not to seek ease, but to know how to wrest triumph from toil and risk." As the new leader of the English race, the United States held "in its hands the fate of coming years." America needed the political virtues of courage and strength in order to meet the requirements of liberty at home and champion liberty's cause in the increasingly unstable international system.[49]

On February 15, 1898, the USS *Maine* exploded in Havana harbor. Two hundred and sixty-six Americans were killed. Be prepared, Assistant Secretary of the Navy Roosevelt cabled the commander of the Pacific fleet ten days later, to begin "offensive operations in the Philippine islands." The reckoning was at hand. Under intense public pressure, President McKinley asked Congress on April 11 for authority to intervene in Cuba, and Theodore Roosevelt, with a sick wife, a new baby, and five other children at home, resigned a post he had held barely a year to volunteer for the cavalry. His wife and friends, including Henry Cabot Lodge, advised against it. But he didn't entertain a moment of second thoughts. What had he been as a man? A naturalist, a writer, a historian, a rancher after a fashion—a politician. Always a politician. But never a soldier. He had written about the warrior virtues, lauded them and preached them; he had tried to win them for himself in the West. But the battle of life was still for him just another metaphor. Like his father, he had never fought. He had never put himself to that ultimate trial. The men he admired most in history, however, had been soldiers. Even Abraham Lincoln had served briefly in a border war. He was not going to miss this opportunity to show the stuff that was in him and to fight with his country in its moment of truth. He was not going to miss the chance to redeem his father's legacy. Not for wife, not for children or for friends. Not for the world. This was the jolt he had been seeking these last years and his whole life. It may or may not launch his career to a new level. He didn't count on that. But it would give him the chance to do something unequivocal, to make his manhood mean something for all time. He would be part of history. "Are me a soldier laddie?" he asked his aunt Anna as a child in 1861. Now he was.[50]

In the first week of May, his wife Edith joined him in the army camp at Tampa, Florida, where he and his brigade—the Rough Riders—had been training. "Our camp is on a great flat," he wrote his children, "on sandy soil without a tree, though round about are pines and palmettos. It is very hot, indeed, but there are no mosquitoes." There were only soldiers, hosts of them, thirty thousand, waiting to be dispatched to Cuba. Roosevelt was in mighty company. "At night the corridors and piazzas are thronged with officers of the army and navy; the older ones fought in the great Civil War, a third of a century ago, and now they are all going to Cuba to war against the Spaniards." And then he went with them—to the brutal heat and the cannons and gunfire and a charge up Kettle Hill.[51]

7

MASTER-SPIRIT

Roosevelt went on charging right into the governor's mansion. The Cuban campaign was a spectacular success, and when reports of his military heroics reached the press, the conquerer of Kettle and San Juan Hills became a household name. Roosevelt wasted no time converting his newfound popularity into political advantage. Almost as soon as he returned from Cuba, Roosevelt pushed himself into the New York gubernatorial campaign. In the autumn of 1898, New York voters chose their new favorite son to lead the state. Roosevelt was back in elected office, back in a big way. Intriguingly, the new responsibility prompted him not just to do, but to philosophize. Soon after taking office, Roosevelt began work on a biography of Oliver Cromwell, a volume which turned out to have far less to say about Cromwell than it did about Theodore Roosevelt. As the Rough Rider navigated the uncertain currents of New York politics, *Oliver Cromwell* became his journal, the place where he recorded his insights and reflected on his experiences. The *Winning of the West* had been his analysis of the American political character; *Oliver Cromwell* became his homily on political leadership.

Leading a democracy was no simple task. Just as free government required certain qualities in its practitioners, so it demanded certain virtues from its leaders. A republican leader had to understand his countrymen. He had to know their capacities and their calling, grasp their possibilities. A responsible democratic ruler must be willing to risk the people's wrath, to tell them no and stand firm for right as he understood it. "[I]t is very essential that a man should have in him the capacity to defy his fellows if he thinks that they are doing the work of the Devil, and not the work of the Lord." But even then, perhaps especially then, circumspection was in order. "[H]e must be most cautious about mistaking his own views for those of the Lord; and also remember that as the Lord's work is accomplished through human instruments . . . and therefore, imperfect, in the long run a man can do nothing of permanence, save by joining his zeal to sound judgment, moderation, and the desire to accomplish practical results." Sound judgment, moderation, courage with practicality. The more Roosevelt thought about it, the more he concluded that these were the qualities the free regime demanded of the free leader, the leader of great men. "The truth is, that a strong nation can only be saved by itself, and not by a strong man." Though he quickly added, "it can be greatly aided and guided by a strong man."[1]

Like Oliver Cromwell. No English leader had surpassed him, Roosevelt thought. Cromwell was a master of men, strong, stern, noble-minded, and bold. When the English attempted in the middle seventeenth century to wrench themselves free from the "degrading superstition" of monarchy and the divine right of kings, Cromwell saved their faltering efforts. He united the splintered advocates of freedom into a single, mighty movement, the first modern movement of history.[2]

Roosevelt interpreted the English civil war as a reform effort, aiming to secure popular self-government and religious freedom. Indeed, at his hands, Cromwell's commonwealthmen became the forebears of Roosevelt's central convictions. This was historical presentism of the worst kind, but revealing. The revolution, Roosevelt said, "was the first great stride toward the practical achievement of civil rights and individual liberty as we now understand them." Roosevelt saw Cromwell as a proponent of religious toleration, even liberalism — "it was the era in which the old theological theory of the all-importance of dogma came into sharp conflict with the now healthily general religious belief in the superior importance of conduct." Roosevelt understood Cromwell to advocate a wide franchise, a protectionist, nationalist economic program — "like the system of protective tariffs" — and an aggressive foreign policy. Above all, Cromwell was vigilant for the character of the English people. For several generations their national fiber had rotted in ignoble peace. Cromwell led the people through "the fiery ordeal of Civil War" to reverse their decline and call them up toward liberty.[3]

Yet his signal achievement, Roosevelt thought, the real measure of his greatness, made him sound like a politician of the late nineteenth century. According to Roosevelt, Cromwell had brought under a common banner the disparate, and sometimes competing, supporters of reform. "A very considerable portion [of the population] avowed extreme republican theories," Roosevelt noted. Some of the extremists were in advance of their age, but many others were "not in advance at all, but simply to one side or other of a great movement" or "lagging behind it, or trying to pilot it in the wrong direction." Roosevelt saw a moral. "If the movement is not checked at the right moment by the good-sense and moderation of the people themselves, or if some master-spirit does not appear, the extremists carry it even farther forward until it provokes the most violent reaction." Cromwell stopped the revolution at the right moment, at the place where it was sustainable and the coalition in support broadest. He brought the stragglers and the enthusiasts to common ground. And this was at the very heart of foresighted, progressive democratic leadership. Leadership was adjustment, wise balancing.[4]

Roosevelt was trying to do a bit of balancing of his own, between the cautious political bosses who ruled his party and the needs of the state as he was coming to see them. "It has become more and more evident of late years that the state will have to act in its collective capacity as regards certain subjects which we have been accustomed to treat as matters affecting the private citizen only," he told the New York Assembly in 1900, the summer *Oliver Cromwell* went to press. "And that furthermore, it must exercise an increasing and more rigorous control over other matters which it is not desirable that it should directly manage." In particular, he was increasingly convinced that the "relations of the state to corporate wealth" merited close attention and, quite possibly, legislative action. He proposed, and won, a new eight-hour workday law for laborers on public contracts; new consumer protection laws; and an anti–sweat shop act to end the sort of tenement labor he had observed as an assemblyman.[5]

Roosevelt was also attempting to formulate some sort of policy to address the sudden mass of corporate mergers. He secured higher corporate taxes as a start and a fixed duration for state-granted monopolies. He toyed with the idea of investigating in-state corporations and releasing the details to the public, using publicity to keep these new "trusts" honest. This regulatory agenda was modest and more or less in step with the emerging Republican position nationally. Still, key observers noticed a change in tone. The anti-regulatory invective so prominent in his tirades against William Jennings Bryan had died down as Roosevelt's latent, pro-reform sympathies pushed to the fore. His attention to antitrust publicity and corporate taxes, in fact, sounded ever so faintly like the Great Commoner himself. Senator Thomas Platt, the New York state Republican boss, detected a political shift and disliked it. He wanted Roosevelt out of New York before the colonel became too difficult to manage. In the summer of 1900, Platt pondered the feasibility of burying the colonel in the shadow of William McKinley, in the vice presidency.[6]

Roosevelt had his sights set on national office as well, though for once he was willing to bide his time. If Oliver Cromwell had exhibited a fault, he decided, it was an obsession with power. The great Englishman became fixated on controlling the revolution. Consequently, Cromwell was not sufficiently dexterous politically at the right moments. He became inflexible. He tried to accomplish too much. He ultimately ignored the lesson of his own experience, that the master-spirit must forsake personal ambition for the good of the movement. Roosevelt didn't want to make the same mistake. If there was a movement to be led—a movement to be made—he would do so carefully, skillfully; not risking too much too fast; waiting for the tide to reach its flood. He hoped only that he could lead with the greatness of Cromwell. "He will be recognized," Roosevelt predicted, "as a man who, in times that tried men's souls, dealt with vast questions and solved tremendous problems; a man who erred, who was guilty of many shortcomings, but who strove mightily toward the light . . . who sought to make the great laws of righteousness living forces in the government of the world." A force for righteousness. In praising Cromwell, Roosevelt offered the epitaph he hoped for himself.[7]

At three o'clock in the afternoon on September 6, 1901, Leon Czolgosz wrapped a handkerchief about his right hand and walked into the Temple of Music in Buffalo, New York. Inside, President McKinley, resoundingly reelected with a new vice president little less than a year earlier, stood shaking hands with guests as an organ played in the background. Czolgosz pressed through the crowd toward the president, his handkerchief slipping too late to reveal a pistol. Before McKinley could withdraw his outstretched hand, the young anarchist thrust the muzzle to the president's stomach and, to the strains of the organ, pulled the trigger. Several hundred miles to the east, in Vermont, Vice President Roosevelt sat lunching under a late summer sun on the Isle La Motte. Within an hour, an urgent telephone call brought him news of McKinley's wound. Eight days later the man from Ohio was dead, and Theodore Roosevelt was the twenty-sixth president of the United States.

At long last, Roosevelt's time had arrived. Years of striving and struggle, self-mastery, self-assertion, and self-doubt ended now in a flush of power. The small, ornithological boy of Number 28 East Twentieth Street, the son of Theodore and Martha Bulloch Roosevelt, the asthmatic child of fierce imagination who made himself first a naturalist, then an assemblyman, a rancher, a writer-historian, the hero of Kettle and San Juan Hills—each iteration more daring than the last, always reaching for something more—this boy, this man, was now president of the United States. "How strange," he said during his first night in the White House when, according to custom, a yellow rose boutonniere was passed to him after dinner. "That is the flower we always associated with my father." He was the father now.[8]

Roosevelt might have celebrated more if the moment of his ascent were not marred by the crime of a madman. "It is a dreadful thing to come into the Presidency in this way," Roosevelt wrote to Henry Cabot Lodge some days after taking the oath of office. "But," he went on, resolutely putting the circumstances to one side, "it would be a far worse thing to be morbid about it." The moment of fulfillment was at hand. If the dark and "evil human passion[s]" that lurked in every human soul and threatened every political community, the very passions of disorder Roosevelt so fiercely decried in the campaign of 1896, were now, ironically, responsible for his advancement, so be it. Roosevelt was not one to dwell on historical ironies or the mysterious ways of Providence. He was a man of action, and for the next seven and a half years he forged ahead, capturing the national imagination with his policies, his pronouncements, and his genius for self-promotion. He attacked trusts and settled strikes, built a canal, stared down one foreign power and helped two others end a war, sent the fleet around the world, reformed the nation's spelling—or attempted to—and hunted bear, with press contingent in tow, of course. And he enjoyed every minute. So successful was Roosevelt at conveying his enthusiasm to the public in the image of a fearless, vigorous chief executive that Americans decades after he left office would remember him as the "trust buster" who brought dynamism back to the presidency.[9]

At the first, though, Roosevelt remembered the lesson of Oliver Cromwell and moved with caution. Within seconds of reciting the oath of office in a stuffy parlor in Buffalo, he pledged to continue "unbroken the policy of President McKinley for the peace, the prosperity, and the honor of our beloved country." No radical announcements here. Roosevelt was too astute for that, and, besides, he wasn't a radical. He harbored no ambitious agenda to spring upon the country. As governor of New York he had pursued a modest program, whatever Tom Platt said. He was most outspoken when it came to imperial policy, but since the Spanish-American War and the McKinley administration's successful acquisition of the Philippines, his ardor on that front had somewhat abated. Roosevelt was still pressing for a larger navy, but a buildup under McKinley was under way. In 1901, Republican orthodoxy was Roosevelt's creed. Detractors in the party establishment who doubted his dependability weren't wholly mistaken, however. Roosevelt was indeed unpredictable and had long relished the role of rabble-rouser. More to the point, some aspects of the party creed had begun to trouble him. He was content, in the fall of 1901, to wait before striking out on a new course. He wanted to get the lay of the land before acting too boldly. But he would not be content to wait for long. He had three years before facing the voters as a presidential candidate himself, three years to build a record and make his case to the people. In retrospect, nothing he did in that time appears particularly noteworthy in its own right, or particularly outlandish, with the exception of two foreign policy ventures—the Venezuela incident and the Panama Canal. Domestic concerns dominated, however, and Roosevelt addressed them cautiously. Yet when his actions are viewed together, it becomes apparent that each step took him further from the Republican orthodoxy of the 1890s and toward a new orthodoxy of his own.[10]

The starting point of Roosevelt's long policy evolution was a dustup over that pillar of Republican dogma, the tariff. Before McKinley's death, his State Department had negotiated a series of reciprocity treaties lowering the custom duties on particular goods, in return for favorable treatment in the signatory's own market. McKinley hoped by this method to achieve targeted reductions in the protective tariff in areas where American producers held a competitive advantage, as well as to deflect growing consumer complaints about higher prices. Makers of heavy machinery and farm equipment in the Midwest wanted access to European and Latin American markets; they liked the treaties. Some industries also welcomed the prospect of cheaper raw materials once duties were reduced. Coming from William McKinley, the reciprocity proposal carried a certain moral authority. No Republican had been a firmer supporter than he of the protective tariff. In his first term, McKinley had secured new duties on wool, textiles, cattle hides, silk, and numerous industrial products. The changes he sought at the outset of his second term were adjustments, relatively minor revisions at the margins. Still, Republicans in Congress balked. Party leaders prevented a vote on the treaties in the summer of 1901, and McKinley's assassination in September had no visible effect on their opposition.[11]

Roosevelt felt no special connection to the reciprocity policy. Since his decision to remain a party regular in 1884, the tariff had been to him a matter of political expediency. Following McKinley's policy, Roosevelt included supportive language for the treaties in the early draft of his first message to Congress in the fall of 1901. Senate majority leader Nelson Aldrich objected. Strongly. He worried the treaties would undermine a manufacturing sector still recovering from the 1890s depression. Roosevelt obliged him and struck the offending text from his message. With no objections from the White House, the Senate shelved tariff revision indefinitely. The run-in was minor and easily resolved, but not without consequences. Thanks to the structure of the congressional calendar, tariff revision could not feasibly be taken up again any time before the presidential election of 1904. The second congressional session scheduled for early 1903 was too short, and the first full session of the new Congress in 1904 preceded a general election. More potentially worrisome to Roosevelt than any opposition to tariff change, however, was the stand-pat attitude of the congressional Republicans and their close association with Northeastern industrial interests. Beginning in 1894, congressional elections through the end of the century produced remarkably homogenous party caucuses in Congress. Republicans represented largely industrial and urban constituents, Democrats rural and Southern ones. In the 55th Senate, for example, sitting from 1897 to 1899, Republicans represented states with an average of $286 million in value added by manufacture, while Democrats hailed from states posting only $121.2 million in value added by industry. The population density of states with Republican senators was, on average, 66.1 residents per square mile, while the population density in states with Democratic senators was about 35.2 residents per square mile.[12]

This homogeneity in congressional party membership resulted in a rigid leadership hierarchy, especially on the Republican side. In that age of pendulum congressional majorities, most members were not careerists. The few that were exercised control disproportionate to their numbers. Northeastern senators, from the heart of Republican power, were appreciably overrepresented on the four major committees in 1901: finance, rules, appropriations, and commerce. Moreover, after Republicans took back Congress in 1894, the party leadership seized control of committee appointment authority. Nelson Aldrich in the Senate and eventually Speaker Joseph Cannon in the House determined which members would sit on which committees, merging Congress's committee system with party hierarchy. The result was lockstep voting. Republicans voted cohesively for tariff protection, the gold standard, and U.S. expansion. In over half the votes in the 55th and 56th Senates, 90 percent of one party opposed 90 percent of the other party. Ninety percent of the time, a majority of Republicans opposed a majority of Democrats. Never before had congressional leadership exerted such influence over committee structure, with such prolonged success. Roosevelt faced a highly disciplined, extremely homogenous congressional caucus, dominated by party leaders from the industrial Northeast acutely sensitive to the effect of any policy change, in virtually any area, on Northeastern manufacturing.[13]

Once these party leaders had been members of the vanguard, rejecting the Stalwart politics of mid-century in favor of a forward-looking economic nationalism. But the political success of the 1890s and the Bryan scare—Democrats nominated him again in 1900—solidified their pro-tariff, pro-business dogma and dampened any enthusiasm for policy experiments. Republicans had found a winning combination. Why fiddle with it? But the political scene was far from static, as Roosevelt recognized; a winning combination in one election might be a calamity in the next. He had his own fortune as president to worry about. McKinley had explored select tariff reductions partly as a response to building consumer concern over price inflation and the amazing, unprecedented consolidation of American industry. Roosevelt watched these trends with equal unease in the opening months of his tenure. If tariff reform was out of the question, he would have to find some other way to address the mounting public pressure for a response to what was coming to be called, simply, the trust question.[14]

The U.S. Supreme Court struggled for years with the Sherman Antitrust Act. Passed in 1890 with the strong support of the Farmers' Alliance, the country's first nationwide anti-monopoly measure seemed potentially radical. "Every contract, combination in the form of trust or otherwise, or conspiracy, in restraint of trade or commerce among the several States, or with foreign nations, is declared to be illegal," the text read. But just how radical was it? Did "every contract . . . in restraint of trade" mean literally each and every agreement that hindered commerce in any fashion whatsoever? The common law, the uncodified, judge-announced law fashioned case by case over time, contained prohibitions on restraints of trade, running back to the English *Case of Monopolies* in 1603. However, the common law never barred all restraints, in England or the United States. After approximately 1700, the general rule of thumb was this: a geographically limited, contractual restraint of trade was legal provided the restraint was reasonable and the contract fair. For instance, an English common law court held in 1711 that a baker who wanted to purchase another man's bakery was perfectly entitled to require, as a term of sale, that the seller not open another, competing bakery in the same area for a term of years. Yet the Sherman Act on its face appeared to disallow even such circumscribed restraints of trade, calling into question the day-to-day business operations of the industrial economy. The act seemed to require as a matter of law an economy of small, independent, local producers, in keeping with the republican agrarian vision. On the other hand, the text might just mean to adopt the prevailing common law rule. Or it might be an implicit instruction to the Court to develop a common law rule. In fact, the language of the act was both spare and opaque, and the Court vacillated as to its meaning. One set of justices opted for a relatively strict interpretation, construing "commerce" and "restraint of trade" broadly to encompass many corporate activities. Another group wanted narrower definitions of the same terms in order to cabin the law's reach.[15]

In 1897, the strict interpretation won—only temporarily, as it turned out, but long enough to inaugurate a new chapter in the industrial age. In *United States v. Trans-Missouri Freight Association*, a bare five-to-four majority ruled that railroad association agreements which coordinated shipping rates and traffic levels between members restrained trade, diminished competition, and therefore violated the antitrust statute. Regardless of the decision's merits as statutory interpretation, the Court majority was unquestionably right about one thing: association agreements were indeed an attempt to curtail competition, an effort by railroads and industry to stay afloat when the depression of the 1890s caught them burdened with excess capacity and plunging profit margins. Now, denied this avenue of escape, industry took the one road prior court decisions appeared to leave open: consolidation. Between 1897 and 1904, American companies combined and merged at a terrific pace: 4,227 firms joined to create 257 new combinations in just over six years. A bare 1 percent of the nation's companies came to control 45 percent of the country's total manufacturing output. It was a merger movement on a mass scale, pulling railroads, manufacturers, banks, investment houses, and raw material suppliers into its transformative whirl.[16]

Only a few of the industry combines actually achieved their goal of long-term price stability, but the immediate effect, when joined to a secular inflationary trend already at work, was to push up consumer prices. In particular, railroad consolidation stimulated a noticeable increase in freight rates, much to the consternation of Western farmers, shippers, and small merchants, the very constellation responsible for the so-called Granger laws of the 1870s. Some economists feared that systematic rate discrimination was conferring monopoly power on railroads in other portions of the economy and in both West and East, in North, South, and Middle, monopolies were becoming a proxy for the industrial era and its dislocations. Populists, with their Western and Southern agrarian constituency, weren't the only ones who wanted action. Alarmed by the merger typhoon and alive to voters' concerns in their region, Midwestern Republicans began to wonder about the link between the protective tariff and monopoly. The Iowa state Republican platform in August 1901 called for "any modification of the tariff schedules that may be required to prevent their affording a shelter to monopoly." Urban reformers fretted about the effects of monopoly and "cutthroat" competition on city life, like the slums manufacturing was creating and the immigration it attracted. An increasing number of "good government" reformers interpreted corporate power as a corrupting influence: monopoly and municipal corruption were cousins, they thought. All of these various groups called for action to curtail the influence of the trusts.[17]

To their ranks in 1901 and 1902 came a group of investigative journalists Roosevelt would later label "muckrakers." These reporters wrote for magazines mostly—*Arena*, *Ladies' Home Journal*, *Munsey's*, and *Cosmopolitan* constituted the field in the late 1890s, though *Arena* was the only one of the group attempting to sell copies by making investigative reporting and advocacy writing its exclusive content. Topics for analysis and comment included biblical higher criticism, Darwinism, academic freedom, psychic research, and spiritualism. But the investigative journalists' real bread-and-butter was the exposé, a motif they pioneered. The reporting in these pieces tended to shade into advocacy, and the advocacy into sensationalism, but, after all, there were magazines to sell. As the new century began, the corporations presented a rich target. A journalist named Ida Tarbell began a multipart series on the Standard Oil corporation in 1902 for newcomer *McClure's* magazine, her reports a harbinger of things to come. The muckrakers considered themselves reporters but reformers first, and they hoped with their writing to change American society and politics. Disciplining corporations would soon go to the top of their list.[18]

Theodore Roosevelt thought business combinations were natural products of an evolutionary process. "We do not wish to discourage enterprise. We do not wish to destroy corporations," he told the New York legislature as governor in 1900. The Populist's agrarian ideal, the republican vision of small, independent producers, failed to move him. He had been a child in the country's greatest industrial city, after all. He felt no personal commitment to a small-scale economy and not much sympathy for the Sherman Act's (to his mind) misguided attempt to turn back the march of industrial progress. "Very many of the antitrust laws which have made their appearance on the statute-books of recent years have been almost or absolutely ineffective because they have blinked the all-important fact that much of what they thought to do away with was incidental to modern industrial conditions," he believed. Corporate bigness could not be eliminated "unless we were willing to turn back the wheels of modern progress." He was considerably more disturbed, however, by the rapacity with which a number of corporate titans behaved, taking the fact of competition as an excuse to mistreat their workers, lie to competitors, and mislead consumers. They reminded him of railroad developer and speculator Jay Gould from his days in the Albany legislature.[19]

Back then, he had urged an antitrust suit against Gould's holdings as a form of punishment, a sort of moral discipline. As governor, he called for state investigations into corporate activities followed by publicity to expose wrongdoing. Now in the White House, he explored the idea of implementing these measures nationally. In his December 1901 message to Congress he called for greater publicity of corporate activities, and, at his direction, Attorney General Philander Knox began preparations to file an antitrust suit against one of mogul J. P. Morgan's conglomerations. The economic side of these questions did not really engage the president. "He had no economics," journalist Lincoln Steffens later commented. These were moral matters to him, questions about what kind of people Americans would be, what kind of character they had. If the nation could not find a way to preserve its virtue in the new era by matching right behavior with the competitive demands of the industrial age, and if it could not make the conditions of the twentieth century conducive to the qualities of character that sustained free government, then the American experiment in liberty would not go forward. This was the problem at the heart of Roosevelt's statecraft. He understood it to be the signature problem of all republican statecraft in all times. "Free government is only for nations that deserve it," he wrote in *Oliver Cromwell*. "They lose all right to it by licentiousness, no less than by servility." If a race lost the capacity to govern itself, "it makes comparatively little difference whether its inability springs from a slavish and craven distrust of its own powers, or from sheer incapacity on the part of its citizens to exercise self-control and to act together."[20]

Roosevelt was searching for a method to bring Americans to act together. "Every group," he believed, "must show the necessary subordination of its particular interests to the interests of the community as a whole." The question was how to convince his countrymen, with their diverse needs, interests, and circumstances, their various complaints about the emerging social order and distinct remedies for it, to join a common agenda for reform. Soon Roosevelt would offer the country his own brand of righteous reform, a warrior republicanism to preserve American democracy in the new century. His leadership would create an atmosphere of policy experimentation and change that came to be called the progressive era. More than any other single public figure, Roosevelt was that era's godfather, the maker of a moment that lasted nearly twenty years. National progressivism began with his preaching and his creative politics of regulation and presidential power. This politics would not come fully into view until the fight for railroad rate regulation in 1905 and 1906, but already many of the intellectual elements were in place, assembled over the years: the political moralism of his tenure in the Albany legislature; the racialism of his ranching days; and the critique of his class and concern for social order. Now, in the first years of his presidency, two more critical components shifted into focus, two sets of ideas that would lend his politics its unique righteous and activist character. The first was a gospel of heaven on earth; the second, an economic program of righteous regulation.[21]

Roosevelt learned at a tender age that the business of life was to perform God's will. Numerous other members of his generation, particularly those from his socioeconomic stratum, absorbed the same lesson. Like Roosevelt, they also absorbed a certain distaste for Christian orthodoxy, and the paradoxical result was a fervent commitment to moral reform divorced from any particular attachment to the person of Christ or to the concept of spiritual salvation. Instead, these believers embraced a salvation worked out on earth, in the present life, through self- and social improvement. They embraced what came to be called a social gospel. This doctrine—really, a theological *disposition* as much as anything else—had been fermenting for several decades, as Roosevelt and the children of the post–Civil War generation came of age. Then, at the turn of the century, the movement found its most articulate spokesman, just as Roosevelt's presidency opened. His name was Washington Gladden.

Gladden believed in social salvation. That was how he put it, and he said it best. Many Christian ministers in the years following the Civil War believed that improving social conditions and spreading the good news went hand in hand. "The question of food and clothes," said Charles Ferguson, "is inextricably bound up with the interests of arts and letters, and all together are meshed and woven in with the grand eternal issues." Which was to say, conversion had a fundamentally social aspect, and the way to change society at large was to change individuals' behavior. If some Christian divines, particularly in the Northeast, understood conversion to mean rather less than their Puritan forebears had, if they emphasized humans' innate altruistic capacities rather more, to the detriment of all that talk about depravity and sin, still their prescription sounded in orthodox Christianity, or orthodox evangelicalism at least: change the sinner to change society. Gladden, speaking for a new type of American Christian, reversed the equation. There would be no progress on the "grand eternal issues," he maintained, until there was progress on the economic ones. Salvation was a corporate affair. It was a matter of societywide uplift, of realizing humans' highest potentials for social cooperation and ordered liberty.[22]

This was the social gospel, and Gladden became its leading intellectual evangelist. He won many converts throughout the late nineteenth century, chiefly in Eastern cities, though the movement counted adherents in other urban areas as well. His message skillfully fused the new liberal theology from the European continent with the evolutionary cult of progress rampant in the United States, joining both to the crusading mentality of mid-century Protestantism, the latter typified by the abolitionist campaign. The social gospel offered an attractive doctrine for the educated middle and upper classes, often—like Theodore Roosevelt—children of devout parents who could not quite come to believe in orthodox Christianity themselves. Gladden's teaching presented a biblically inspired rationale for this worldly action, Christian righteousness without the dogma. It was political theology and a sort of spiritual Darwinism combined that just managed to avoid slipping into materialism. Its promise captured clergymen, writers, social workers, sociologists, ethicists, even economists. And politicians. It had roots in British Christian socialism, but the social gospel was really a uniquely American phenomenon, which helped give birth to a uniquely American moment. Already sympathetic to its major tenets, Roosevelt became a full-fledged believer, adopting gospel rhetoric and most of its social program. Not surprisingly, the movement helped organize progressive ambitions for the next twenty years.[23]

Gladden's gospel began, appropriately, with a social claim. "It springs from some dim recognition," he wrote, "of the solidarity of society — of the fact that we are members of one another." That meant "the ills which the community is heir to are matters of concern to all of us." Right at the outset, Gladden replaced a biblical doctrine of solidarity with a different one, and this move was both the beginning and the culmination of his theology. "Members of one another" was an oblique reference to Ephesians 4:25, in which the apostle Paul admonished Ephesian Christians to refrain from lying to their fellow believers, because Christians were "members of one another." The church was a single corporate body, the body of Christ, chosen by him and called out of the world. Gladden's teaching referred to the unity of society as a whole, however, not just to believers. His moral imperative was a universal one, founded not on a shared life in Christ but on a shared humanity. "When the fundamental fact of theology is the fact of fatherhood, the fact of brotherhood cannot be ignored in any phase of religious experience," he said. The fatherhood of God, the brotherhood of man: this was the lodestar of Gladden's theology. He erased the distinction between church and society, the elect and the damned. All people were equally children of God because all shared God's capacity for altruistic love.[24]

Sin to Gladden had little or nothing to do with offense against God and his perfect law. The narrative of the New Testament — as interpreted by earlier generations of American Protestants anyway — turned on the irremediable permanence of evil in the human soul. Humans needed a savior to rescue them. Gladden interpreted sin differently. "The essence of sin is the defect of love," he taught. Sin was the failure to live up to one's potential and to realize the divine altruism of which all were capable. It was fundamentally social, not personal, and could be remedied by a change in character. No savior necessary here, or not a savior of the same kind. Christ became for Gladden a grand moral example, a model of love and self-sacrifice to imitate. And no distinction between believers and nonbelievers either, because not belief but behavior is what mattered. True conversion meant a dawning acceptance of one's social responsibilities, the inherent dignity of one's fellow man, and the obligation to help him.[25]

God was working out his salvation upon earth, in human history, by bringing human beings to a greater knowledge of their common brotherhood. The scientific record of evolutionary development confirmed as much to Gladden's mind. He appropriated Darwinian theory for the purpose of verifying a spiritual progression, rather than a material one. The advancement of the human race was beyond mere biology. "The fact for you and me to keep steadily before us is that human society is under the sway of spiritual motives," Gladden held. According to him, science's seminal contribution in the last century was to prove the malleability of human nature or, to put it another way, the perfectibility of the human person. Thus did science, Gladden believed, prove gospel truth. Biology revealed that human beings *could* become like God, through hard work and reformation. Salvation was a process that occurred over time, extending from one generation to the next. "This is not mere sentiment; it is the scientific fact, the historic fact . . . and we are to take our stand upon it, and insist upon interpreting the phenomena of society in the light of the spiritual laws." The similarity to Nathaniel Shaler and the neo-Lamarckians was unmistakable, and Gladden all but acknowledged his debt. "The one lesson that the social reformer as well as the theological reformer needs to learn is the lesson of evolution," he admitted. For therein lay the hope of mankind.[26]

Gladden and his followers didn't give up on heaven, they just relocated it. They preached millennialism of a new variety. Human society, with its waxing altruistie awareness and growing mutual sympathy, with its firmer and firmer belief in universal brotherhood—this was the kingdom of God. An apocalypse to usher in the ultimate, completed rule of the messiah was unnecessary. A final judgment of the unrighteous was superfluous, metaphoric. The brotherhood of man and fellowship with one's neighbors was realized in the present world or not at all. The person was saved in the current age, by improving his character, or never. Gladden's millennialism was the kingdom of God already come, or the kingdom of God now coming, all without Christ. No apocalypse, no judgment, no heavenly afterlife. Just the steady outworking of God's divine love in human society, to be advanced or hindered one generation at a time. "Translate the evolutionary theories into religious faith, and you have the doctrine of the Kingdom of God," Gladden's fellow traveler Walter Rauschenbusch helpfully summarized. This was theology custom-made to appeal to Theodore Roosevelt, a salvation of struggle and effort. What he had already resolved to do personally—earn his hope, his purpose, in the here and now—the social gospel urged as a prescription for social regeneration.[27]

Social amelioration, in turn, issued in the development of sound personal character, manliness even. That was its goal. Christians of all walks—charity workers and politicians no less than ministers—were called to save souls by saving character. "To save a soul from ruin is simply to save a man or woman from ruin; and the character is the thing to be saved." Drunkenness, prostitution, gambling, and the like—these vices which hindered the kingdom of God, which disrupted social life and tore at the fabric of the community—they could all be

sum of individual interests, as Bentham and his disciples would have it. No, the social interest was categorically different, another thing altogether, achievable only when individuals adjusted their short-term wants to the needs of the whole. Adams rejected unfettered individualism and its economic cousin, laissez-faire, as destructive of the public good. But he was not a statist. Instead, he called for limited government intervention to promote what he regarded as the common, long-term interest of every individual: a well-functioning, property-based civil society. "Society is the organic entity about which all our reasoning should center," he argued.[32]

Adams identified himself as an "economic mugwump," a label which made some sense considering his diagnosis of the ills caused by unregulated industrial competition. Above all, the ills were moral. "First, the free play of individual interests tends to force the moral sentiment pervading any trade down to the level of that which characterizes the worst man who can maintain it himself." Thus, so far as ethics were concerned, "it is the character of the worst man and not of the best men that gives color to business society." Secondly, the laissez-faire rule of noninterference made it impossible to realize the benefits of natural monopolies. Some enterprises, like utilities, for example, required such massive capital investment and suffered from such high barriers to market entry that vigorous competition was virtually impossible. It would be better, Adams theorized, if the state were able to grant monopolies in these industries and regulate them for the public good. Finally, restricting public regulatory powers within the narrowest limits possible rendered the government "weak and inefficient," and a weak government was easy to capture by powerful private interests.[33]

Adams proposed two solutions. The first was the more important: the state should intervene to determine the rules of market competition. Cutthroat competition produced moral confusion. In language echoing the young Theodore Roosevelt, Adams lamented that citizens observed one code of conduct in private life and another in public, one for peace and another for war, "one code for the family, the social circle, and the church, and a different one for mercantile man." But make no mistake, in an impersonal and increasingly consumer-oriented society, the effect of moral pluralism was moral decline and the triumph of the market's lowest common denominator. "The fact upon which we insist at this point is that an isolated man is powerless to stem the tide of prevalent custom," Adams argued. State action was required. The state could set a moral standard via regulation, set terms of competition that rewarded righteous behavior. In so doing, the state would resolve—or if nothing else, mitigate—the moral confusion stimulated by competing codes of ethics in different spheres of life.

State regulation was an instrument with which the political community might reaffirm its moral priorities and thus exert mastery over the forces of economic life. The state, in short, could act to promote moral community.[34]

With this idea, Adams handed the social gospel a mode of action and Roosevelt a means of reform. State regulation properly applied could make honesty, safe working conditions, higher wages, and nondiscrimination in the best interests of individual businessmen. Government could make the free market work for character, make it productive of civic virtue. Legislation could be a moral undertaking. "Surely religious teachers should be interested in the opportunity which such thought opens," Adams believed. Opportunity indeed. Regulation to promote a moral standard might lend the otherwise separate items of a political agenda an overarching rationale. It might provide a common philosophical ground for reformers, a unifying vision of what the new industrial order could be. It could join the energies of Eastern urban reformers to Western agrarians, of social gospel believers to Midwestern merchants. The state as moral agent. That was a powerful idea.[35]

Adams's second proposal was a bit less theoretical and more pragmatic. State regulation, he suggested, could realize the benefits of monopoly for the public good. Naturally occurring monopolies should be allowed to exist, but their prices and output regulated to replicate the market as nearly as possible. In sum, regulate these monopolies and eliminate all others by means of the antitrust laws. "Such monopolies as exist should rest on law and be established in the interests of the public; a well-organized society will include no extra-legal monopolies of any sort."[36]

Adams looked forward to a day of cooperation between the state and private entrepreneurs to develop the economy as a whole. But in the near future, the state had to gain a measure of independence, he believed, in order to prevent laissez-faire individualism from going "to seed" and wrecking civil society along the way. The doctrine of economic noninterference, by relying entirely on individual action and unregulated markets to manage the economy, was an "obstacle to the restoration of harmony in social relations." It pitted one class against another in business, one group against another in the race to capture control of a weak government. By contrast, Adams's approach would chart a middle way between Spencerian laissez-faire and German-style statism, for the purpose of conserving true democracy over the "commercial democracy which now rules the minds of men." Here was one final connection to both the social gospel and Roosevelt's earlier thought. Money-making was not enough. A healthy political society would never regard it as the goal of political life. The profit motive was rather the means to a larger purpose. That larger purpose was true democracy—a society of individuals prosperous enough, secure enough, equal enough, to share in self-rule. An economy of independent local producers may no longer be possible, but the republican dream need not die. Adams's ideas were a bid, in essence, to marry the social gospel with republican political economy, and make both work for the industrial age. Theodore Roosevelt followed his lead.[37]

With change-wary majorities in Congress, Roosevelt acted first on his own. It would become a habit. He began where political mugwumps, economic mugwumps, social gospel supporters, urban reformers, and Western Populists all more or less agreed: civil service reform. The first step in getting an independent state able to master the swelling corporate interests, he believed, was to guarantee that state a professional, nonpartisan administrative arm. Merit employees, free from the shifting winds of political majorities, could be specialists in their fields, appointed for their training and specific skill sets rather than for their partisan connections. Thus civil service reform achieved multiple goods at once. It struck at partisan corruption and bossism by curtailing the spoils system and, happily for Roosevelt, augmented the administrative capacities of the executive branch. Roosevelt certainly did not intend to rely on congressional oversight to address the problems of industry, particularly with a Congress so closely identified with industrial interests. He wanted a stronger executive, a president with a large and professional career administrative staff at his disposal. "The stronger the executive and judicial departments of our government," Henry Carter Adams had said in 1886, "the less opportunity will there be for particular legislation, and the more likely it will be that such laws as are passed will conform to the just requirements of general laws." Civil service reform was a step in the right direction.[38]

Beginning in the autumn of 1901, Roosevelt helped rewrite civil service rules to expand substantially the supervisory authority of the civil service commission over merit employees. Remembering his own frustrating years on the commission, Roosevelt worked to plug holes in the merit system. He directed the comptroller of the Treasury to withhold the salary of any merit employee whose appointment violated the commission rules, and then ordered employees to verify the circumstances of their employment. No verification, no paycheck. In 1903 he won increased funding from Congress for commission activities and continued to place additional government staffers under the merit rules.[39]

Civil service reform pleased urban reform advocates, particularly members of the new professional middle class, who wanted greater efficiency in government administration. Enlarging the civil service was something he could do on his own, with a little extra funding from Congress. Roosevelt confronted a more del-

icate situation, however, with the rising demands for regulation of railroads and
the giant corporations. In his second annual message to Congress in December
1902 he tried an Adamsite approach. "We are not hostile to them," he said of the
corporations. "We are merely determined that they shall be so handled as to sub-
serve the public good. We draw the line against misconduct, not wealth." To prevent corporate misconduct, Roosevelt proposed a Bureau of Corporations—a
national extension of his New York program—to be housed in the executive
branch. The Bureau would possess authority to investigate corporate activities
and make reports directly to the president. Should the Bureau uncover corporate
wrongdoing, Roosevelt could decide to release the information to the public and
also to order criminal prosecution. "The capitalist who, alone or in conjunction
with his fellows, performs some great industrial feat by which he wins money is a
well-doer, not a wrong-doer, provided only he works in proper and legitimate
lines." The federal government would help preserve the integrity of those legitimate lines by exposing the capitalists who violated them. This was no radical,
anti-business proposal, Roosevelt insisted. "Publicity can do no harm to the honest corporation." This was merely enforcement of the law as it existed. This was
about efficiency and good government.[40]

Roosevelt in fact killed a harsher version of his proposal. In debate over the
Bureau bill in January 1903, Congressman Charles Littlefield of Maine introduced a resolution calling for corporations to file reports directly with the Interstate Commerce Commission. The punishment for failure to comply was stiff.
Noncompliant corporations would be banned from the channels of interstate
commerce. Roosevelt ordered attorney general Philander Knox to express White
House disapproval. Exclusion from interstate trade was too much, Roosevelt
thought, too hard on the corporations. Moreover, the Littlefield resolution had
businesses reporting to a commission. But Roosevelt was quite clear that he
wanted a Bureau of Corporations to report to him, giving him the discretion to
publicize or withhold derogatory information about corporate activities as he
saw fit. The Littlefield resolution failed, and, on February 11, 1903, Congress
created a Bureau of Corporations and a new Department of Commerce to go
along with it. "The enactment of this law is one of the most significant contributions which have been made in our time to the proper solution of the problem of the relations to the people of the great corporations," Roosevelt trumpeted in April.[41]

In reality, the Bureau bill was a modest measure, more about publicity than direct regulation. In 1902 and 1903, Roosevelt still believed the combination of
publicity and criminal prosecution might provide all the discipline corporations
required and calm public clamor for government action. Publicity would rein-

fresh thinking and new ideas. President Roosevelt "assisted all good causes and hindered all bad causes" muckraking publisher S. S. McClure exulted. The American people apparently agreed. They returned Roosevelt to power in the autumn of 1904 with a prodigious, 56-percent share of the popular vote.[46]

In the 1880s, social and municipal reformers in Britain had seized on the term "progressive" to distinguish themselves from the ruling Liberal Party. With Theodore Roosevelt's resounding election in November 1904, the progressive moment in America was at hand.[47]

8

Warrior Republicanism

According to the civic liturgy as then prescribed by the U.S. Constitution, Theodore Roosevelt swore the oath of office at twelve noon, March 4, 1905, on the east steps of the Capitol. Thousands of well-wishers turned out to witness the Rough Rider president, the colorful, quotable, indefatigable steam-engine-in-trousers-president, take the oath in his own right. No longer the accident of an assassin's bullet, he belonged now in the company of the chosen, the latest in a distinguished line of American statesmen. And he intended to claim his republican heritage. While the Constitution makes no provision for an inaugural address, every president since Washington had made one, and Roosevelt had Washington on his mind this day. In uncharacteristically brief remarks, fewer than a thousand words, Roosevelt cast himself as the revered founder's intellectual and moral successor. He placed himself in the company of the framing generation and Abraham Lincoln, as the man at the hinge of a historical moment as critical as theirs. Roosevelt's inaugural address announced his arrival as a mature political leader by staking his claim as a serious political thinker. The rhetoric was skillful, even subtle. He invoked the mystic chords of memory to justify a new departure, offering a vision of the future forged from the influences of his past: the neurasthenic theories, the racialism, the works-righteousness and social gospel—they were all there. Claiming the founders' mantle as well as that of Lincoln, he articulated a politics tellingly different from their own. His statecraft as it came into view in the months and years following his election in 1904 was less concerned with rights or the dangers of political power; it was more activist, more nationalist, more statist than that of his predecessors. This was the direction in which he would try to take the country. More than that, it was the character of the era he was helping to create, a *kairos* of reform and change.[1]

"No people on earth," Roosevelt began in the tones of his battle-centric life philosophy, "have more cause to be thankful than ours, and this is said reverently, in no spirit of boastfulness." The great "Giver of Good" had blessed the nation with bountiful opportunities, and, to their credit, Americans had turned opportunity to achievement and wrested "well-being and happiness" from the melee of historical circumstance. "Under such conditions," Roosevelt warned, "it would be our own fault if we failed." Surely Roosevelt knew George Washington's strikingly similar admonition, issued in the form of a circular to the states at the close of the Revolutionary War. "At this auspicious period, the United States came into existence as a Nation," Washington wrote in 1783, "and if their Citizens should not be completely free and happy, the fault will be intirely [*sic*] their own." Roosevelt imitated Washington's warning in thought as well as form; both statements summarized an earlier list of national blessings and culminated in exhortations to continued good behavior. Yet though their function is rhetorically parallel, the two men's summaries of America's blessings and beginnings—Washington's "auspicious period," and Roosevelt's "such conditions"—are revealingly dissimilar.[2]

When Washington spoke of the "auspicious period," in which the United States was founded, he referred to a particular moment in the history of ideas. "The foundation of our Empire was not laid in the gloomy age of Ignorance and Superstition," he wrote, but rather at a time "when the rights of mankind were better understood and more clearly defined, than at any former period." Americans had been favored by Providence insofar as they had been given greater knowledge than those who had tried the republican experiment before them. Thanks to the "labours of Philosophers, Sages and Legislatures, through a long succession of years," and preeminently to "the pure and benign light of Revelation," the men who founded the American republic understood human nature better than any other comparable group of statesmen in the whole of recorded history. The ancient Greeks founded great republics, and the Romans, too, but not a single one of those states endured. Americans' ancient counterparts failed, Washington suggested, because they could not control faction and similar abuses of political power, a systemic defect stemming from the ancients' lack of appreciation for the rights belonging to all people by nature.[3]

Roosevelt saw America's providential endowments rather differently, which led him to picture a different vista for America's future. "To us as a people it has been given to lay the foundations of our national life in a new continent," he told the throngs assembled for the administration of the oath. "We have not been obliged to fight for our existence against any alien race; and yet our life has called for the vigor and effort without which the manlier and hardier virtues wither away." Washington pictured America's blessings in terms of ideas. Roosevelt, by contrast, celebrated the Americans' vast opportunity for conquest. He located the source of American singularity in open land that was available for settlement and yet stern enough to call forth the hardy, heroic virtues that made for greatness.[4]

Strength of character defined the American experiment, according to Roosevelt. Under conditions so promising for cultivating the warrior virtues, "it would be our own fault if we failed." Earlier generations of Americans had proved themselves worthy of their blessings. They developed conquering character and subdued a continent, advancing civilization in the process. Considering their countrymen's success in the past, it now fell to the current generation of Americans to renew the pioneering spirit and show "that under a free government a mighty people can thrive best."[5]

The intellectual contrast between Roosevelt and his predecessor was sharp and consequential. Washington believed his country's blessings consisted of wisdom and historically fresh insight into human nature, by which he meant a historically fresh appreciation for the doctrine of natural rights. Washington pleaded with Americans to live with "a sacred regard to public justice," to remember, for the sake of self-government, the rights of their fellow men and the limits of political power. The truth of humans' equal moral worth was more than an intellectual proposition, it was the ground for free civic life and the source of shared civic identity. Washington wondered whether a republican government could sustain the moral understandings that led to liberty. Never before in history had the experiment been tried. No regime had ever been founded on the inalienable rights of humankind. Whether Americans would preserve their moral commitment to the equal rights of all citizens would determine the fate of republican liberalism. With their actions, Washington told his readers in closing, "will the destiny of Millions yet unborn be involved."[6]

Roosevelt, too, was profoundly concerned with citizens' conduct as it implicated the fate of free government, but in a different way. His concern ran not to inalienable rights and their moral predicates, but to virility. Roosevelt worried that self-government might breed weakness and mediocrity by gradually undermining the warrior virtues. A prosperous commercial republic might breed effeminacy. The challenge facing his generation was to prove otherwise. American settlers demonstrated the virtues of personal and national heroism when they subdued the expansive West, Roosevelt thought. Thanks to their valor, the nation now stood as the balance of power in the world, the country with the potential to direct the course of the international system for decades to come. But the moment was fraught with peril.[7]

Crafting his own historical narrative of challenge and response, Roosevelt noted that the country had undergone "extraordinary industrial development" in recent decades. That development produced an explosion in "wealth, in population, and in power," which in turn stimulated tremendous social change, including a plethora of new social and political problems "complex and intense" in nature. To overcome these developments, America needed to cultivate anew the moral virtues of greatness. Amid the material wealth economic expansion had brought the country, Americans needed to recover the hardihood and sheer manliness that drove their forebears to conquer the West. They needed to prove that free government could provide for "the things of the soul," as well as "the things of the body." In sum, the nation needed to demonstrate that a democracy could spur humans to their highest moral potentials. This was the American challenge. The whole of his agenda would be geared to meeting it.[8]

He was finished with the politics of prosperity for its own sake. Today he announced to the country a politics of virtue. He was going to back bold measures to combat the moral chaos of the business world. He was going to fight the forces that undermined Americans' control over their own lives. He would call his countrymen to leave behind class loyalties and realize the noble, national life together for which their history of racial and spiritual development fitted them. These were his priorities, and he hoped by his preaching to make them the priorities of his generation.

Roosevelt intended his clarion call for the country at large, but he wanted his fellow Republicans to pay particular attention. If congressional leaders thought the president's smashing election victory would buy them breathing space, they were wrong. On the contrary, Roosevelt read the election returns as validation of his reformist initiatives and a mandate to do more. In November 1904, Republican electoral strength achieved new feats. Roosevelt won 336 electoral votes and over 7.5 million popular votes—56 percent of the total number cast—to form a solid band of Republican states from Delaware to California. Thirty-three of the forty-five states in the Union voted the Republican ticket, every state outside the old Confederacy with the lone exception of Kentucky. The 1904 election was an unqualified Roosevelt landslide. The Republican coalition in the Northeast of industrialists, urban workers, and middle-class professionals more than held. Roosevelt racked up commanding majorities in Pennsylvania, Ohio, Maine, and Vermont. But these were Republican states anyway. Roosevelt's real strides came in the West, in the land of the Populists and William Jennings Bryan. Colorado, Idaho, Nevada, and Montana, states that had voted for Bryan in both 1896 and 1900, now moved to the Republican column. Roosevelt's antitrust prosecutions,

lowed, forcefully: the time had come for the federal government "to act directly."
It was absurd to expect states to eliminate corporate abuses on their own, especially—though he did not say this—given the Supreme Court's rediscovery of
the dormant commerce clause. No, the "National Government alone can deal
adequately with these great corporations." And the national government *should*
intervene, Roosevelt declared, to subject the interests of the corporate economy
to the public good. Proper regulation would help to promote "responsibility and
forbearance among capitalists and wage workers alike." Wise legislation could
foster "a feeling of respect on the part of each man for the rights of others; a feeling of broad community of interest." National regulation, in short, could promote civic virtues and help forge moral community. Here was Roosevelt the economic mugwump, offering a program of national regulation as a partial antidote
to the social anomie infecting the modern era. Here was the state as moral
agent.[14]

The rhetoric was grander than the proposed regulation. After calling in his
message for strict enforcement of the Elkins Act, outlawing all railroad rebates,
Roosevelt urged Congress to vest the Interstate Commerce Commission with
the authority to set a "reasonable rate" in but one specific instance—where a
given rate had been challenged by a shipper and found to be unreasonable by
the commission after a full hearing. The new rate would remain in effect indefinitely, unless and until reversed by a reviewing court. Roosevelt also backed
measures to strengthen the commission's control over railroad finances and accounts. "The government must in increasing degree supervise and regulate the
workings of the railways engaged in interstate commerce," he admonished congressmen. Actually, he was proposing to give the commission roughly the same
amount of regulatory authority it had claimed and briefly exercised under its
original charter in 1887, before federal courts intervened.[15]

Roosevelt considered his proposal politically moderate and strategically astute. Cries for rate regulation came loudest from shippers in the South and Midwest, both regions increasingly critical of the tariff and the latter, of course, crucial for Republicans' long-term electoral prospects. Shippers were far from
unified as an interest group, but they tended to support administrative discretion
on the part of the commerce commission to hear disputes and set rates without
extensive review by courts, which they rightly considered hostile to commission
oversight. A freshly empowered commerce commission would therefore help
tamp down potentially damaging discontent over the high tariff Roosevelt had
decided not to revise, by winning plains state citizens' approval on an equally
contentious and, to them, equally important, issue. For that matter, the railroads
were not wholly opposed to a revival of the national regulatory project. Rail own-

ers were interested in regulation to legalize pooling (which allows rival companies to combine resources and divide customers by agreement, effectively agreeing not to compete), guarantee their financial solvency, and generally keep shipping prices stable. Roosevelt's December proposals failed to offer much to the railroads' liking, but, importantly, they did not regard federal regulation as out of the question, to be defeated at all costs.[16]

Despite his impressive electoral showing and the imminent arrival of new Republican congressmen from the West and Midwest more favorably disposed than the congressional leadership to regulatory reform, Roosevelt still found Congress reluctant to act. With considerable cajoling from the White House, the House of Representatives passed a compromise bill in the second week of February 1905. The margin of approval was, in the end, quite impressive, due partly to the president's whispered threat to throw open the tariff debate should Republican congressmen not stand with him. "There is no use objecting. You've got to take it," an irritated Speaker Cannon reportedly told his caucus on the eve of the vote. "If you don't, there will be tariff reform." Roosevelt really had no serious intention of revisiting the tariff issue, but he was not above using the prospect as a political maneuver. Unfortunately, the Senate proved less susceptible to his ploys. Majority leader Nelson Aldrich played to run out the clock. He regarded Roosevelt's latest regulatory ideas as improvident and his rhetoric alarming. The 58th Congress expired on March 4, inauguration day, and Aldrich stacked the Senate's legislative calendar with the president's own arbitration treaties to prevent the compromise railroad bill from coming up for debate. In a sop to the president of his party, Aldrich promised to hold hearings on an interstate commerce bill sometime in May.[17]

Congress adjourned for Roosevelt's inauguration without a single debate on a joint railroad bill, exposing at the height of Theodore Roosevelt's political power his weakness within his own party. Though Republicans commanded a twenty-four seat majority in the Senate, the president could not compel action on his leading domestic priority. Congressional leaders were irredeemably intransigent, he decided. They had become an "old guard" unwilling to face the realities of the industrial age. If he hoped to enact any additional regulatory measures in the coming four years, he would have to go around them. And he would. Roosevelt decided to fight. As spring arrived, he settled on a new approach to secure rate reform. He intended to leverage his public popularity against the congressional leadership in his own version of asymmetrical warfare. Roosevelt would speak to the public directly, traveling the country to tell the people his views on government regulation, all in an effort to build public pressure on Congress to act. The Senate could stall all it wanted. Roosevelt was taking his case to the people.

This decision to break openly with his party's congressional leadership, at least in the Senate, held enormous political and institutional consequences. For one thing, Roosevelt's strategy flouted past tradition that discouraged presidential pronouncements on policy matters, especially bills under consideration by Congress. His public speaking tours would end up helping to foster a new and lasting set of institutional mores and a new set of public expectations for American presidents. The break with Congress also pushed Roosevelt further toward an open embrace of administrative regulation, which would become a staple of progressive reform. An administrative state, run from the executive branch, was his model for bringing order to the industrial economy. More immediately, his conflict with the Senate forced Roosevelt to articulate clearly and publicly his ideas about government's proper role. It forced him to continue the task he had started at his inauguration: to exert political leadership through rhetoric, to attempt coalition building by speech making, which in turn led him into a discussion about the true interests of citizens, the meaning of rights and duties, and the nature of self-government.[18]

After a test run or two in March of 1905, Roosevelt's undeclared campaign for rate legislation began two months later in Denver, on the return from one of those bear hunting expeditions his wife loathed and the press loved. Not coincidentally, the Senate Commerce committee opened hearings on rate legislation that same month. For the rest of the year, Roosevelt timed his speaking schedule to match the inflection points in the congressional calendar. When progress on a bill stalled in the autumn, Roosevelt launched another speaking tour in the Midwest and South. Everywhere he spoke, his message was the same, a political sermon founded on the doctrine of economic mugwumpery. "Actual experience has shown that it is not possible to leave the railroads uncontrolled," he told crowds in Raleigh, North Carolina. "Such a system . . . is fertile in abuses of every kind, and puts a premium upon unscrupulous and ruthless cunning in railroad management." Unregulated competition forced down the ethical plane to the lowest common denominator. It pressed those shippers who wanted "to do the right," whether large or small, into "acts of wrong and injustice, under penalty of being left behind in the race for success." Henry Carter Adams had made precisely this argument, in almost exactly these terms, eighteen years earlier. Now Roosevelt deployed Adams's logic to justify rate regulation. Government intervention was essential to bringing fairness to the competition between small and large shippers, Roosevelt argued, by ending secret rebating and discriminatory rates. Only then could shippers behave justly without economic penalty. Moreover, prudent regulation by a body of administrative experts should help stabilize shipping prices and curtail the brutal competition of which railroad executives so often complained. "What we need is some administrative body with ample power," Roosevelt said, able to "prevent favoritism to one individual at the expense of another."[19]

In another message to Congress at the conclusion of his speaking campaign, he put the matter directly. "We desire to set up a moral standard," he said. "There can be no delusion more fatal to the nation than the delusion that the standard of profits, of business prosperity, is sufficient in judging any business or political question." Financial success and economic growth were "good thing[s]" insofar as they were "accompanied by and develop a high standard of conduct—honor, integrity, civic courage." The social reformer Jane Addams would later summarize Roosevelt's position with a syllogism. "As the very existence of the state depends upon the character of its citizens, therefore if certain industrial conditions are forcing [down] the standard of decency, it becomes possible to deduce the right of state regulation." American statecraft, Roosevelt insisted, must stand "for manhood first, and for business only as an adjunct to manhood." In short, the national state could act to preserve the qualities of character necessary for democratic government by adjusting the legal boundaries of the marketplace. Careful, limited government action could make the market work for civic character, make it a force again for orderly liberty and a morally wholesome prosperity. The industrial economy had become a threat to the rule of the people, Roosevelt implied, partly because its sheer size swallowed individual agency, but also because it rewarded the wrong things. Use regulation to make it reward honesty, thrift, and initiative, and the market would become a prop rather than a menace to republican freedom.[20]

Roosevelt had nothing against free enterprise. He believed in private property as much as ever, and he was anxious for his audiences to understand that. "Most emphatically we do not wish to see the man of great talents refused the reward for his talents. Still less do we wish to see him penalized." It was just that he refused to regard the market as an independent entity, as if it existed somehow apart from civil society and the state. Like Henry Carter Adams, Roosevelt saw the market as one division of society as a whole, one facet of social life. Accordingly, he found it perfectly reasonable to regulate that facet in order to preserve the health of the larger organism. Roosevelt might have made his case in more explicitly economic terms. He might have promised lower freight rates, an end to discriminatory charging, regulation to put money in the pocket of every American—or every farmer, or shipper, or small merchant. But he said little in this vein, even to sympathetic audiences. He was aiming for something more than a pocketbook coalition. He was striving to achieve moral resonance. He was forging an argument and, by extension, a politics, that would appeal beyond narrow segments of the economically affected to an entire nation disconcerted by the modern market, if not modern life. His was a politics of reclamation, a politics of renewed moral order and refound decency, made possible by a collective political life of moral purpose.[21]

But the federal government could not bring moral order to the market unless its development kept pace with that of society at large. Modern life required a modern state. Regrettably, America did not have one. Government would have to change, Roosevelt told audiences. The federalist system was not adequate to the tasks of the modern day. Given his proposals, Roosevelt needed only to elaborate a rationale for fairly modest national regulation. Nothing more was politically necessary. But his theoretical justifications implied a much broader, organic, and even unitary conception of American nationalism than any previously embraced by American popular culture. His rhetoric reached beyond his immediate proposals for rate regulation to imply a critique of earlier Americans' wariness of political power and to suggest a newfound eagerness to use it. Roosevelt would pursue that train of thought long after the rate debate ended, taking his generation with him.

It started with an evolutionary story. In the second half of the nineteenth century, according to Roosevelt, "the power of the mighty industrial overlords of the country increased with great strides," while the means of the federal government to regulate and control them "remained archaic and therefore practically impotent." Now railways stretched from one edge of the country to the other, crisscrossing the continent in a bewildering maze of lines and routes. They had become a national enterprise. "When such is the case," Roosevelt said in Denver, "it is absolutely necessary that the Nation, for the State could not possibly do it, should assume a supervisory and regulatory function over the great corporations." Consolidation of power in the commercial and financial spheres was an evolutionary, and therefore natural, phenomenon—"this is an age of combination," Roosevelt said repeatedly. Many people, including the railroad senators, accepted that. Roosevelt argued that consolidation of political power was natural as well. If the environmental circumstances had prompted businesses to combine on a national scale in order to survive, government too would need to grow in order to match the swelling power of enterprise and protect the interests of the race. Failure to adjust politically to the fresh realities of the industrial age would carry the same consequences of failure to adapt biologically—chaos, followed by decline and, finally, extinction.[22]

Roosevelt thought America's federal system of government with its "sharp division of authority between the nation and the several States" had served the country well in the past. The Constitution's framers designed a state that met the needs of a young, rural frontier nation splendidly. But he also thought the Constitution's decentralized structure and dispersal of political power was proving to be something of an obstacle to the changes the new era of combination required. The federal arrangement was now "undoubtedly responsible for much of the difficulty of meeting with adequate legislation the new problems presented by the total change in industrial conditions during the last half-century," Roosevelt concluded. It needed to be updated, modernized. Fortunately, Roosevelt believed the framers had wisely provided for just the sort of political mutation the new circumstances demanded. The interstate commerce clause of Article I, Section 8 of the Constitution, conferred the right to regulate commerce between the states exclusively on the national government. Roosevelt located the constitutional sanction for his regulatory proposals there. "The power of Congress to regulate interstate commerce is an absolute and unqualified grant, and without limitations other than those prescribed by the Constitution." Echoing faintly the cadences of Chief Justice John Marshall in *McCullough v. Maryland*, Roosevelt declared himself confident that "Congress has constitutional authority to make all laws necessary and proper for executing this power." The Constitution provided the means for the national government's evolutionary expansion.[23]

Roosevelt saw the commerce clause as much more than a convenient excuse for the growth of national power, though, as if it were some sort of constitutional loophole. He took the commerce clause to be the linchpin of the whole Constitution and national expansion as the inner logic of the constitutional scheme. According to him, the nation's leading statesmen journeyed to Philadelphia for the purpose of forging a new political system able to regulate interstate trade. "The makers of our National Constitution," Roosevelt told Congress, "provided especially that the regulation of interstate commerce should come within the sphere of the general government." The arguments in favor "of their taking this stand were even then overwhelming," because with this power over economic relations between the states, the central government would be able to function effectively as a sovereign and bind together the separate states into one nation.[24]

Where others saw the effective protection of minorities or an inspired model of limited government, Roosevelt identified the genius of the Constitution in what he took to be its proto-nationalism. The constitutional text was sufficiently explicit in its conferral of authority as to leave no doubt, at least in Roosevelt's mind, as to its intent. "It seems to me clear without possibility of dispute not only that the vital need of governing all interstate and foreign commerce of the Nation was the prime cause of calling the Constitutional Convention," he wrote in private correspondence a few years later, "but that the framers of the Constitution explicitly and emphatically . . . conferred upon the Federal Government in this respect a power meant to include everything relative to its subject; and this excluded all power in the States." Happily, the framers designed the Constitution to be sufficiently broad that, equipped with its "necessary and proper" clause, federal officers could exercise wide discretion in the use of their powers. "The Constitution cannot be made a straightjacket," Roosevelt insisted. The framers meant it to be interpreted so as "to permit us properly to manage our insular affairs."[25]

The extension of the state was vitally important now because only through it could the American people, the American race, hope to exercise mastery over the corporations. As was true during the frontier days, it remained so now that the achievements of the mighty few had to be turned to the advantage of the whole. One part of the body politic depended on another. The "less fortunate and less able" benefited immensely from the jobs and general prosperity the corporatist created. Conversely, the corporatist could create nothing without his workers. The challenge was to get the economy to work for all segments of the populace. The race would never move forward if only one portion of its members prospered, or if only one segment possessed the virile virtues. Practically, this meant that corporate "combination and concentration should be, not prohibited, but supervised and within reasonable limits controlled." Government regulation was the means through which the race or the public would regain direction of its fate. That "there have been aristocracies which have played a great and beneficent part at stages in the growth of mankind," Roosevelt did not doubt. "But we had come to the stage where for our people what was needed was real democracy; and of all forms of tyranny the least attractive and the most vulgar is the tyranny of mere wealth, the tyranny of a plutocracy." The people would reclaim their agency through the state.[26]

Underlying Roosevelt's advocacy of a progressive state able to master and direct the energies of business was his identification of the people with the government. The American public could regain control over the corporate economy by national regulation of business because the government and the people, Roosevelt believed, were essentially one and the same. And by government Roosevelt meant not just any level of government or the constitutional system as a whole, but the federal or, as he tellingly preferred, "national" government. Sometimes he spoke as if the national government was merely a stand-in for the American public, a sort of proxy, as if the two were synonymous. He told Philadelphia's Union League in January 1905 that "neither this people nor any other free people will permanently tolerate the use of the vast power conferred by wealth, without lodging somewhere in the Government the still higher power" of directing corporate wealth for "the interests of the people as a whole." He said much the same in his fourth annual message to Congress, claiming that "[w]ith-in the Nation, the individual has now delegated [his interests] to the State; that is, to the representative of all individuals." Even here, however, while referring in passing to the government as the representative of multiple individuals, Roosevelt subtly conflated the nation and the state, treating the two—the body politic and the national government—as identical.[27]

On other occasions Roosevelt was even more direct. "It is right to remember the interests of the individual," he told a group of attorneys in 1905, "but it is right also to remember the interests of that great mass of individuals embodied in the public, in the Government." The Supreme Court's decision in *U.S. v. E. C. Knight*, limiting the scope of the Sherman Antitrust Act, Roosevelt believed had "left the National Government, that is, the people of the Nation, practically helpless to deal with the large combinations of modern business." Roosevelt conceived the national state as nothing other than the people acting in concert, a theory helped along by his evolutionist reading of history and displaced millennialism. He recognized no consequential distinction between government and civil society, as if the people of the nation arrived at their common, civic identity apart from the apparatus of the state. Instead, individuals came to know themselves as a unified body politic—they became a people, an *ethnos*, in the full political sense of the term—when they participated in the joint exercise of political power. A common political identity rooted in a common state made separate individuals one political person, with one set of shared political interests. Roosevelt described political agency as a collective phenomenon, not an individual one—something to be found in combined action through the state rather than exercised by private persons or classes. He made no effort to argue for a recovery of individual economic independence as the basis for authentic political agency. He was willing to let that aspect of the republican dream die. Instead he offered a collectivist theory for a collectivist age.[28]

Roosevelt spoke for a progressive state, one fully resident in the modern age of combination. Indeed, he regarded a more powerful, more centralized national government as merely the latest chapter in the race's evolutionary story, the latest foothold on the climb toward greater democracy realized and practiced in a shared national state. This brand of what might be called corporate nationalism, in which the nation and the state are held to shape and even create one another, was not uncommon on the European continent during Roosevelt's day. The origins of the corporate nationalist formulation ran back to the French Revolution, and the Germans had adopted something very much like it as their national philosophy after national unification in 1871. If Roosevelt's nationalism and conception of the state had a home in Europe, however, it was largely foreign to America.

Roosevelt's portrayal of the national government as the sovereign of the American political system, based on his conflation of state and populace, was an idea distinctly not a part of the earlier American political tradition. The Constitution's drafters and ratifiers dispersed political power among various levels of government to ensure that sovereignty remained always and finally with the people themselves, not collected in any particular institution or office able to be dominated by corrupt men. The difference is more than one of emphasis. Roosevelt's conception of the nation-state departed substantially from early Americans' understanding of political power as contractual, and suggested that they and Roosevelt held divergent ideas about the origins of the state and its uses.

"The origin of all civil government, justly established, must be a voluntary compact, between the rulers and ruled," Alexander Hamilton wrote in 1777 in a statement typical of the United States' first generation of statesmen. A contract was needed to establish the civil authority of government because those persons who would be governed were each of them bearers of inalienable rights. The American framers rejected the Greek republicans' subordination of the individual good to the interests of the polis much as John Adams did when he condemned the political economies of Sparta, Lacedae, and Athens as "frigid system[s] of national and family pride," totally disrespectful of the individual and faintly authoritarian.[29]

Instead, early American thought from the Puritan colonists to the framers held that the state existed for the good of the person in society. Individuals were not solitary beings; they required and were meant for social company, the family first of all. Civil society and even the state were natural and necessary extensions of humans' social nature and without them the individual could not exist. In that sense, the political community was prior to the person, the irreplaceable context in which humans' nature was fully realized and protected. Yet the state still existed by compact, called forth by rights-bearing individuals equal in their moral worth. Ontologically, the political community came before the person, but chronologically the individual in society was first. Government was not an automatic outgrowth of society. It required the consent of the persons who lived together in community in order to exist justly. A state that possessed the power of coercion and physical force meant in practice that some persons would exercise power over others. If humans were in fact equal in all essential respects, this situation could be legitimate only if approved by the consent of its members. Political power undoubtedly had its uses. The state brought order, provided stability, and protected liberty. But political power could be easily abused. It needed to be cabined and its uses carefully codified so that rights were safe and civil society could flourish. Thus, Hamilton concluded, "certain great first principles [must] be settled and established, determining and bounding the power . . . of the ruler," so to secure "the rights and liberties of the subject."[30]

The first American statesmen—or most of them—were nationalists, to be sure, and American nationalism had a long history before Theodore Roosevelt. But earlier, more traditional American nationalism preserved a distinction between government and civil society. Though he would never have admitted he was breaking from the founders' school of thought, Roosevelt did seem to acknowledge these earlier American understandings of government that were different from his own by characterizing them as products of an age of "individualism." "The men who first applied the extreme Democratic theory in American life," by which he meant the idea that the people themselves, rather than an elite, should rule, "were, like Jefferson, ultra-individualists, for at that time what was demanded by our people was the largest liberty for the individual." In the days of the early republic, the United States was without a fully formed national consciousness. Moreover, Americans had much expanding to do that could not be directed from a central authority, and the very people responsible for that expansion—the frontiersmen—were far too independent and strong-willed to submit to the heavy hand of government. They were "rugged individuals" in an era of individualism, an age necessary for the country to traverse if it were to become a continental nation.[31]

Be that as it may, "during the century that had elapsed since Jefferson became president the need had exactly reversed. There had been a riot of individualistic materialism, under which complete freedom for the individual . . . turned out in practice to mean perfect freedom for the strong to wrong the weak." The age of individualism was past, the era of combination at hand. According to Roosevelt, as the race became stronger and more highly developed, it shook off individualism with all its attendant theoretical constructs about individual rights and the dangers of centralized power, and realized its shared destiny in collective action. On this evolutionary account, a sort of Herbert Spencerism read backward, government emerged not so much by common consent as by common need. The state was pictured as one further stage in an unfolding evolutionary process which humans did not, finally, control. So the state was not a product of human rationality or deliberate choice. It was an evolutionary imperative rooted in humans' need for stability and physical safety in order to progress beyond other animals.[32]

That meant the social contract was a theoretical mistake. The state was not, strictly speaking, the result of any particular contract, a view visible in Roosevelt's thought as early as his first volumes of *The Winning of the West*. Roosevelt stressed the Teutonic racial origins of the American people and their government. In his account, peoples or races may indeed consciously design a government for themselves, as the Americans did. But this was not the same as establishing "certain first principles" that called the state into existence, as Hamilton had it. Rather, to write or reform a constitution was merely to alter the administration of a political community that already existed, before any act of deliberative consent. This is why, for Roosevelt, the order of society was ultimately predicated on force. An advanced race brought structure to its surroundings by imposing its will on everything within its domain, including other, weaker races. This is what Roosevelt believed the Western settlers had (rightly) done with the indigenous American tribal peoples. According to his logic, government did not originate in the considered consent of rights-bearing individuals; rather, all political agreements for protection of rights and other interests—agreements that could be quite profitable for the race and even necessary for its success—came after the fact. Government existed by evolutionary necessity, realized by force.[33]

The consequences of this idea of government's beginnings reverberated in every other aspect of Roosevelt's political thought, affecting his understanding of the Constitution, citizenship, rights, and the connection between personal character and self-government. Nowhere was the influence of his evolutionary idea more apparent than on the subject of political power. The framers sought to disperse it, distribute it, and prevent it from concentrating in any one place. State power, to them, was dangerous. Should the balance between state and society be upset, and the coercive power of the state grow too strong, the rights of citizens could be jeopardized. Roosevelt, on the other hand, was far more willing—even eager—to use the power of the national government. If some national good could be achieved through vigorous state action, then he was for it, especially when he was the one running the state.[34]

But if Roosevelt in his writing and his rhetoric imagined the state as the ultimate embodiment of the nation, rejecting the founders' contractual account of government, and if he cast the Constitution as a basically nationalist document in contrast to the framers' emphasis on dispersal of power and balance of interests, he by no means discarded the American republican tradition wholesale. Like these earlier Americans, Roosevelt believed self-government was a difficult task, requiring specific character traits in its practitioners. He too was concerned with the problem of civic virtue. But even here, in echoing a great theme of American political thought past, Roosevelt offered his generation a different path.

"Self-government is not an easy thing," the president reminded his listeners in North Carolina. "Only those communities are fit for it in which the average individual practices the virtues of self-command, of self-restraint, and of wise disinterestedness." Free government, in sum, depended on good character, a claim Roosevelt made repeatedly in one variation after another throughout his presidency, and especially during the six months of his pro–rate regulation speaking blitz. Roosevelt, however, was not interested in civic virtue because it promoted the ability of citizens to share in self-government and experience freedom. Rather, his interest in self-government and the virtues which sustained it stemmed from his passion for racial mightiness, national greatness. It was not that self-government was valuable because it made men free. Self-government was worth preserving because it was necessary for "a mighty people." Roosevelt sought the warrior virtues that would allow the race to triumph—to restore moral order at home, to spread Anglo-American civilization around the globe and bring the United States to world power. Roosevelt believed in the importance of civic virtue but changed the definition of virtue.[35]

The late colonials and early Americans had worried that wage work could not produce good citizenship because republican citizenship was so difficult and the qualities needed for it were comparatively rare. Wage work had become a commonplace before Roosevelt's presidency, however, and earlier controversialists had tried to meet the challenge of developing a republican model of citizenship workable for the modern age. The leaders of this revisionist effort were the first members of Roosevelt's party. Republican partisans in the 1850s redefined independent laborers to be "working white men," as distinguished from enslaved black men, and not necessarily self-subsisting farmers or property owners. They addressed Jefferson's worry about the servile quality of wage labor by maintaining that unforced labor was independent labor, whether performed for a wage or not. In other words, free labor advocates argued that republican citizenship was not so difficult after all. Independent labor or, at least, labor that allowed an independence of mind was far more common than Thomas Jefferson and other founders thought. Theodore Roosevelt built on the free labor logic and added his own twist. Virtue, he said, was not so difficult to attain either.[36]

Roosevelt, unlike both Jefferson and most free labor advocates, was not wedded to an account of self-government as the culmination of man's rational, rights-bearing nature. He did not justify republican politics based on rights or rationality. His case for democracy was practical and almost utilitarian. He believed that self-government was best because it best accommodated the strength and vigor of a great, warrior people. Consequently, his political theory did not require that citizens cultivate the (perhaps rare) character traits that would be needed to protect rights and participate in the institutions that preserved and embodied them. Moderation and patience, moral refinement and political learning, did not particularly interest Roosevelt as civic qualities. He believed that individual hardihood, vigor, and physical courage were the really desirable virtues. "The man's moral quality . . . his cleanliness of life, his power to do his duty toward himself and toward others [are what] really count," Roosevelt told Congress while president, gently reiterating the neurasthenic language of his youth. These virile virtues were the character traits that resulted in achievement and racial progress. And these virtues were accessible to almost any person, at any socioeconomic station, who cared to cultivate them. The man "who in driving an engine or erecting a building or handling deep-sea fishing-craft shows the necessary moral, intellectual, and physical qualities demanded by his task ought to be instantly accepted as standing upon as high a plane of citizenship as any human being in the community." What sort of work a person performed did not matter. It only mattered that the work he did, he did well, evidencing the warrior qualities of character.[37]

Roosevelt solved the problem of republican political economy by racializing traditional republican virtues. Wage workers or anyone else could develop individual initiative and personal strength of character if given a fair opportunity, Roosevelt argued. Thus his focus became securing that opportunity for workers in their existing circumstances, rather than trying substantially to change those circumstances. In Roosevelt's political science, the conditions of industrial progress were also industrialism's peril—unprecedented combinations of business power and size increased productivity but threatened to crowd out opportunities for achievement by individuals just beginning in life, or by those without wealth or inherited social standing. Such a situation would seriously weaken the race over the long run, Roosevelt feared, by depriving the nation of the energies and achievements of its vast majority while removing the wealthy few from challenge and competition. Roosevelt thought he detected those very conditions already in much of the corporate world. The federal government needed to intervene to ensure that every American had a chance to make something of him- or herself. Reforming the Interstate Commerce Commission was just the beginning, more important for the principle than the actual effect it might have: righteousness and equality, those were the watchwords. "Equality of opportunity," Roosevelt said in 1910, "means that the commonwealth will get from every citizen the highest service of which he is capable."[38]

Roosevelt's fixation on the warrior virtues, and his drive to secure conditions where they could flourish at times, made him sound more virtue-centric than the founders. To consider their different attempts at fostering virtue is to realize they and Roosevelt had very different priorities. John Adams thought that virtues in the citizenry were a result, rather than a prerequisite, of a system of government whose divisions among multiple sovereigns promoted the flourishing of local communities and civic associations. "The best republics will be virtuous," Adams mused, "but we may hazard a conjecture that the virtues have been the effect of the well ordered constitution, rather than the cause." James Madison followed Adams's line of reasoning in his attempt, outlined in *Federalist* Number Ten, to use the extensive population and geographic size of the Union as tools to neutralize groups of self-interested citizens who would trample the rights of others in pursuit of their own agendas. If the republic's size were matched with a representative form of government where elected officials made decisions rather than the people themselves, violently self-interested collections of citizens, or factions, would be hard-pressed to seize the reins of power.[39]

Madison was not contending that virtue was unimportant. It certainly did matter. Like Adams, he wanted to encourage good character by encouraging the institutions that stood between the individual and government, especially religious institutions. Meanwhile, he thought a written constitution could provide mechanical protections for rights independent of the virtues of statesmen or citizens, and he sought to multiply those provisions as much as possible. Constitutional protections of rights would also act as educators, reminding the populace of the ground of their civic identities and of their obligations to their fellow citizens. Lincoln later cast the Declaration of Independence in this role, claiming that it contained the essential principles of American government, and of all free government. For him, as for Adams and Madison, the virtuous behavior that would preserve free government flowed from an appreciation for rights and their need for protection.[40]

The founders and Lincoln appeared far more hesitant than Roosevelt to rely on virtue for the sustenance of the republic, and far more likely to lean on civil society and private institutions to craft the character traits they did find essential. But had Roosevelt recognized these divergences, and there is no sign he did, they likely would have only confirmed for him the profoundly different circumstances between his day and theirs. That is, they would have returned Roosevelt to the basic tenets of his economic mugwumpery: the state needed to intervene in order to redress the imbalance in civil society created by the era of combination. Private associations, like private individuals, were being swamped by the economic and political might of the giant corporations and the men who ran them. Only the national state was strong enough to set the scales aright. For Roosevelt, rate legislation represented just the sort of constructive intervention the country required, a means to the end of remoralizing American society and reconnecting the interests of major businessmen with the interests of the nation as a whole. "What is needed is not sweeping prohibition of every arrangement, good or bad, which may tend to restrict competition," he said, "but such adequate supervision and regulation as will prevent any restriction of competition from being to the detriment of the public."[41]

Aldrich and company did not find the president's public sermons particularly inspiring. But the tide of opinion ran with Roosevelt. In the summer of 1905, a New York state investigation spearheaded by young attorney Charles Evans Hughes uncovered a sordid alliance between Republican politicians and life-insurance company executives. The details shocked the public. State assembly members had drafted legislation protecting the insurance companies in return for campaign contributions and outright bribes. The muckrakers couldn't have dreamed up a more salacious story if they had tried. News of the investigation spread quickly around the country, and that wasn't all. In Pittsburgh and San Francisco, graft trials of city officials exposed municipal networks of corruption similar to those in New York. The newspapers had a field day. Just a few years earlier, investigative journalists had struggled to keep reformers' hopes alive by printing long lists of prominent reform advocates. Now corporate politics and the influence of railroads were on the tip of every tongue. Kansas journalist and Roosevelt ally William Allen White captured the restive national mood that season when he wrote that "our senators went to Washington obligated to the large corporate interests of their states." The public was in an increasingly anti-corporation frame of mind.[42]

The big beneficiary of the public outcry was Theodore Roosevelt. His rhetoric was perfectly timed to take advantage of the shifting popular mood, and, in this context, his ideas resonated. A powerful reform coalition was coming together under his guidance, a popular groundswell of support from shippers, small merchants, and farmers in the Midwest and West, good government reformers in the cities, social gospel advocates, middle-class professionals, and readers of the new periodicals, their general, often inchoate and sometimes conflicting calls for action shaped and organized by Roosevelt's public rhetoric. He didn't create the elements of the coalition any more than he dreamed up ex nihilo the regulatory measures he forwarded. The various groups that backed his efforts at national regulation existed before 1905—some had been around for decades, the sources of their convictions rooted in various circumstances and events unrelated to him. Similarly, the independent commission he proposed to strengthen was the brainchild of an earlier generation, just like the Sherman Antitrust Act he used and the anti-monopoly laws in twenty-five states, all adopted before Roosevelt came to the White House. Neither the measures nor the reformers were new, but Roosevelt creatively invested preexisting ideas with fresh significance, drawing on traditional republican themes and Christian ethics, folding in racial theories of progress and a belief in the potential of science, administration, and expertise. In an age of rapid change and upheaval, Roosevelt offered the state as an agent of order and restoration. A broad array of Americans responded to his call, invigorated by his preaching and his will to act. Like him, they came to see the relation of public to private power and the preservation of free government as the central issues of the age.[43]

Historians have argued over which component group in the gathering pro-regulation coalition was most responsible for reform, which represented the real progressive constituency. Some have argued the agrarian element was dominant, fueled by the Granger remnant, the Populists, and small shippers in the South and West. Others traced the national drive for reform to a fading urban upper-middle class, the mugwump type, whose social status as keepers of the nation's literary, cultural, and religious mores withered in the explosion of industrial wealth and mass immigration, boss-oriented politics, and new media forms. Still others believed regulatory reform originated with the emerging professional middle-class exponents of science and technology, eager to assert their newfound social influence. Or perhaps it was the apostles of the social gospel, or the good government reformers, or the temperance movement, or any one of a dozen other groups hawking reform in the industrial age. In fact, no one group dominated because there was no one reform movement. The rate debate introduced a reform moment, or perhaps a series of moments stretching over two decades. The rate debate was the first act of the progressive era, a nationwide season of reform when Americans tried to preserve their democracy in the threatening circumstances of the early twentieth century. Roosevelt's genius was to bring the generalized reform impulse that had been building for almost thirty years to the national stage, to create a moment when concerted action was possible. He did it chiefly by propounding a public philosophy of self-government through reform and renewal, a warrior republicanism.[44]

The moment, as 1905 gave way to 1906, belonged to him. After a strongly worded annual message in December 1905, in which the president also endorsed an employers' liability law for the District of Columbia, pure-food-and-drug legislation, and a Commerce Department inquiry into child labor practices, the Senate finally reported a rate bill out of committee on February 26, 1906. As its chief sponsor, Republican Senator Jonathan Dolliver, had drafted it, the bill conferred on the Interstate Commerce Commission an additional two members and, among other things, the authority to set a maximum rate in the event of a dispute between railroad and shipper. Dolliver's version said nothing about court review, however, leaving the distinct impression that commission decisions may not be open to review at all. Aldrich had failed to keep the bill off the Senate floor, but he gathered enough Republican votes to prevent passage in its current form. Roosevelt would have to rely on an impromptu assemblage of Republican moderates and Democrats, or else find some way to compromise with the Aldrich forces. Initially he ignored the Senate leader and worked to build a majority of moderates from both parties in support of a slightly rewritten bill that allowed only narrow court review. But when Democrats proved unable to deliver enough votes to pass that version, Roosevelt backtracked. In April, he returned to Aldrich and struck another bargain. Senator William Allison, a member of the Aldrich camp, had drafted an amendment that provided for judicial review of commission decisions, but without specifying any particular standard. Aldrich and supporters believed it would guarantee the widest review possible. Roosevelt decided to hope for the best, and, with his assent, the Hepburn rate bill and Allison amendment became law in June 1906. The Hepburn Act expanded the Interstate Commerce Commission from five members to seven and authorized commissioners to appoint examiners and agents. It enlarged the commission's jurisdiction to cover sleeping cars, express companies, and oil pipelines. In an effort to prevent expansion of railroad monopoly power, the act prohibited railroads from owning the goods they transported. It explicitly delegated maximum rate-making authority to the commission, which could be suspended only by court injunction. Roosevelt believed it was the greatest domestic achievement of his presidency.[45]

Before the summer was out, Roosevelt scored two more victories with the Pure Food and Drug Act and the meat inspection law. He had the investigative journalists especially to thank for these. Legislation providing for national standards and labels for food shipped in interstate commerce had been a hardy Washington perennial since the 1890s. Roosevelt recommended food regulation again in December 1905, but prospects looked dim with Congress and the White House fixated on rate reform. Then, in early 1906, Upton Sinclair published *The Jungle*, a fictionalized exposé of Chicago meat-packing plants. For a year it was the best-selling book in the United States. Roosevelt read it himself, as did several members of Congress, and in the wake of the book's startling revelations popular opinion swung solidly behind food regulations for consumer safety. The president capitalized on the turn of events by launching a federal investigation of the Chicago stockyards. Then he released the stomach-turning results to the public. For his timing and finesse, Roosevelt got two bills that together mandated inspection of all meat products, gave the Department of Agriculture authority to oversee packing house operations directly, and forbade the sale, manufacture, or transport of adulterated food stuffs in interstate commerce.[46]

The Democratic *New York World* moaned that Roosevelt's railroad and food-inspection bills together constituted "the most amazing program of centralization that any President of the United States has ever recommended." This was an exaggeration, but there was no denying Roosevelt had achieved a decisive break with the past. His initiatives shifted political power away from Congress and toward the executive branch. More accurately, they generated a new locus of power in administrative bodies like the Interstate Commerce Commission, nominally independent of both legislature and executive. Indeed, the Roosevelt legislation of 1906 marked the genesis of a professionalized, bureaucratic administrative state, a state in theory at least beyond the control of private interests or party machinery, though the reality was more ambiguous. Roosevelt believed in expert, independent administration, and given his political experience from Albany to Washington, he identified party participation in the execution of laws as corrupt, or corrupting. But it would be a mistake to believe he wanted the professional state to be strictly independent. He had little authority over the Interstate Commerce Commission, but then it predated his arrival in Washington. In practice, his own administrative creations—the Bureau of Corporations, the Department of Commerce—reported to the president. The administrative state was, for him, the presidential state.[47]

Just as significant as his actual legislative accomplishments was the rhetoric he used to win them. It too marked a historical departure. Roosevelt invoked the founders' statecraft but abandoned its priorities. He appealed to an earlier tradition of republicanism but rewrote its themes. He offered the country a new intellectual synthesis, an activist, nationalist state in pursuit of moral community, stability, prosperity and uplift. The administrative state Roosevelt helped midwife would grow to a size and shape beyond his intentions, into a bureaucratic behemoth of alphabet agencies directly accountable to neither the president nor Congress, nor any elected official. In a similar way, his rhetoric swept beyond the immediate political context in which he formed it to justify state action on a much grander scale, to open theoretical avenues for the creation of a national social welfare state. In 1906, Roosevelt's ideas—his warrior republicanism—were helping to transform the American political scene, and he was transformed by them in the process. In the years to come, he would follow their logic to bolder proposals for larger reforms, while trying to hold together the coalition that had brought him this moment of triumph. But time waits for no man, and it would not wait for him. His ideas and their consequences and the new reform era hurtled forward together, developing, changing, reverberating in the vortex of history. Roosevelt would spend the rest of his career trying to get back to this moment, trying to return to this place of victory and political consensus, when he, of all people, should have known that a return to the past is never possible.

9

THE PROGRESS OF A PROGRESSIVE

Almost at once the coalition began to splinter. Or perhaps the moment was just passing beyond Roosevelt's command. Much of the public saw the president's railroad bill and his food and drug and meat inspection acts as great victories. Not all White House allies were equally celebratory, though. Roosevelt's legislative maneuvers at the end of the congressional session exposed tensions within the pro-regulation camp, which proved to be portentous. A klatch of Western and Southern senators, some Republicans, some Democrats, bristled at Roosevelt's decision to make peace with Aldrich and accept potentially extensive court review of the Interstate Commerce Commission's rate-making decisions. They regarded the president's compromise as a betrayal. Part of the disagreement was purely tactical. The White House needed twenty-six or twenty-seven votes from Democratic moderates in order to pass a rate bill without Aldrich's support. Late in the session, Democratic floor sponsor Ben Tillman—"Pitchfork" Ben Tillman from South Carolina—could muster only twenty-five. Members of the bipartisan breakaway group would have preferred the president wait a bit longer or try a more subtle adjustment in the bill's language before tracking back to the Aldrich gang. Roosevelt calculated otherwise. But at its core, the latent tension between the White House and segments of the new reform coalition was a matter of ideas.[1]

One of Roosevelt's chief critics within the pro-regulation party was Republican Senator Robert La Follette. Robert Marion La Follette had been elected to the Senate as a reformer—a "progressive," he called himself—in 1905, after serving for four years as governor of Wisconsin. He arrived just in time for the last act of the rate debate. La Follette represented a new sort of Western Republican: pro-regulation, skeptical of the high tariff, stridently anti-monopoly. This brand of Republican was not entirely sui generis, of course, as the "Iowa Idea" from earlier in Roosevelt's presidency attested. But influential though they were, this sort had never before been part of the party establishment. Beginning in 1905, that changed. Progressive Republicans used the direct primary, referendum, initiative, and recall to wrest control from party bosses and catapult themselves to power. They captured the South Dakota statehouse in 1906 and launched bitter factional fights for control of the state parties in California, Oregon, Kansas, Iowa, and Wisconsin. Their influence spread as far east as New Hampshire and New Jersey, but the Republican insurgents were concentrated west of the Mississippi, and while they warmed to Roosevelt's reformist rhetoric and backed his drive for regulation of railroads, meat packers and food producers, their own reform ideas carried a distinctly Granger-ite ring. They preferred to cut corporations down to size through aggressive prosecution of the antitrust laws and heavier regulation to prevent monopolies from forming in the first place. La Follette's arrival in Washington in January 1906 signaled the newfound electoral success of progressive reformers and the broadening of the national reform coalition. La Follette was among the first to use the "progressive" label routinely to describe himself and like-minded politicians. Ironically, his emergence as a national figure raised questions as to what the word "progressive" exactly meant, and who counted as one.[2]

Watching Roosevelt's performance in securing the Hepburn bill, La Follette began to have his doubts about the president's status as a genuine reformer. He suspected Roosevelt's willingness to compromise with Aldrich betrayed a hidden fondness for big business. Roosevelt, he decided eventually, was more interested in the appearance of change than in change itself. The president's "most savage assault upon special interest," La Follette noted tartly in his 1913 autobiography, "was invariably offset with an equally drastic attack upon those seeking to reform abuses. These were indiscriminately classed as demagogues and dangerous persons." There was more than the compromise with Aldrich to fuel his qualms. La Follette was particularly disturbed at Roosevelt's swipe at the investigative journalists at the height of the railroad battle. No single group was more consistently supportive, even clamorous, for reform. Yet Roosevelt had attacked them. The incident was actually more complex than La Follette may have imagined, but the Wisconsin senator was certainly right to find it revealing.[3]

Investigative writer Lincoln Steffens of *McClure's* sought Roosevelt's help as early as 1905 with an investigation of the federal government aiming to expose the squalid workings of the party machines. *McClure's* had already printed exposés of state and municipal corruption. Now it intended to turn the light of public scrutiny on the federal government. What was the most outrageous patronage appointment Roosevelt had been forced to make to appease senators, Steffens wanted to know. Roosevelt declined to cooperate. At first. When progress on the Hepburn bill ground to a halt in early 1906 over the problem of court review, however, Roosevelt gave Steffens carte blanche. He had reason almost immediately to regret his decision. In March, David Graham Phillips published in *Cosmopolitan* the first installment of a series "exposing" the U.S. Senate. He called it "The Treason of the Senate." The charges were explosive. "Treason is a strong word, but not too strong," Phillips exclaimed, "rather too weak, to characterize the situation in which the Senate is the eager, resourceful, indefatigable agent of interests as hostile to the American people as any invading army could be, and vastly more dangerous." Phillips selected for particular condemnation Nelson Aldrich and Roosevelt family friend Chauncey Depew. He called Henry Cabot Lodge "the familiar coarse type of machine politician, disguised by the robe of the 'Gentleman Scholar.'" Roosevelt was furious.[4]

The president certainly had his own frustrations with the Senate leadership, and his own suspicions about their integrity. He may well have confided as much to Lincoln Steffens, though almost certainly not to Phillips. But he had to work with the senators all the same, and the attacks on Depew and Lodge he took as personal affronts. He considered them both completely out of bounds. In January at the private Gridiron Club dinner, Roosevelt had gently reproved investigative journalists for their occasionally sensational reporting. Now in April, he took the opportunity at the dedication of the new executive office building to mount a sharp, public counterattack on the salacious reports he feared were threatening his chances to get a railroad bill. He called the investigative journalists "muckrakers," a term lifted from John Bunyan's *Pilgrim's Progress*. It had been one of Roosevelt's favorite childhood novels. "In Bunyan's *Pilgrim's Progress* you may recall the description of the Man with a Muck-rake, the man who could look no way but downward, with the muck-rake in his hand," Roosevelt told his audience. Reporters who attacked business indiscriminately fit the profile. The muckraker "typifies the man who in this life consistently refuses to see aught that is lofty, and fixes his eyes with solemn intentness only on that which is vile and debasing." There were great evils in the nation's political and economic life that required remedy, to be sure, but "crude and sweeping generalizations [that] include decent men in the general condemnation means the searing of the public conscience," Roosevelt lectured. "Hysterical sensationalism is the very poorest weapon wherewith to fight for lasting righteousness." Summarizing his approach to reform, Roosevelt argued that "the reform which counts is that which comes through steady, continuous growth; violent emotionalism tends to exhaustion."[5]

Roosevelt privately assured Steffens he did not have him in mind as a muckraker. He said the same thing to journalist Ray Stannard Baker. And in truth, his April remarks did contain a few qualifications. He praised as "a benefactor" every journalist who exposed concrete malfeasance, provided the reporter refrained from sensationalism and "indiscriminate assault upon character." In reporting the president's attack, however, the mainstream press lumped all the investigative journalists together, Steffens and Baker alongside David Graham Phillips. Strategically, Roosevelt had timed his remarks to function as an olive branch to the Aldrich senators, to whom he was making renewed overtures by mid-April. As a result, he did not do overmuch to correct the mainstream press's misimpression of his meaning, if there was a misimpression. Baker, for one, never quite forgave Roosevelt. He later accused him of "short-circuit[ing] a fine and vigorous current of aroused opinion." Listening just to the president's rhetoric, private assurances aside, reformers in the mold of La Follette could legitimately wonder whether Roosevelt had meant to attack them as well. "The only public servant who can be trusted honestly to protect the rights of the public against the misdeed of a corporation is that public man who will just as surely protect the corporation itself from wrongful aggression," the president said. To La Follette, it sounded rather pointed.[6]

The Wisconsin senator concluded that Roosevelt was quietly sympathetic to the corporations, perhaps even a closet conservative. In his judgment, the president was a pretender, a rhetorician. He was a compromiser. He was forever willing "to accept half a loaf," La Follette later protested, adding, "I believe that half a loaf is fatal whenever it is accepted at the sacrifice of the basic principle sought to be attained." That was the bottom line: La Follette believed he and Roosevelt adhered to different principles. He wasn't necessarily wrong. Between 1905 and 1908, progressive reform was all the rage, and most of it bore a decidedly Rooseveltian impress. Fifteen states established railroad commissions, and fifteen more buttressed existing regulatory structures. Reform governors talking like Roosevelt swept to power across the West and South, including reform-minded Democrats in Alabama, Georgia, and Mississippi. But the arrival of the insurgent Republicans and the split with the muckrakers underscored twin aspects of Roosevelt's evolving political thought that set him apart from some constituents of his own coalition and bespoke the breadth of the progressive moment. Roosevelt was in fact a conservative, of a type, and a corporatist, too.[7]

For one thing, Roosevelt was no great fan of the initiative, referendum, and recall, not in 1906 and 1907. He was even cooler to much of the insurgents' anti-corporation rhetoric. Their talk reminded him of William Jennings Bryan, that obnoxious, evangelical rabble-rouser whom Roosevelt continued to denounce in private even after appropriating many of the Boy Orator's themes and ideas. The Bryan types refused to recognize that business combinations were products of an "imperative economic law," a natural economic evolution that could not be gainsaid. This refusal made them at once retrogrades and radicals, to Roosevelt's mind, utopian reformers who wanted to return the world to some halcyon past rather than face reality as it was. He cast himself by contrast as a Cromwellian movement leader, trying to balance between the "old guard" stragglers, the Bryanite crackpots, and those, like La Follette, who rushed ahead. Rushing, Roosevelt still thought in the latter years of his presidency, was almost always a bad idea. The first need was to get in mind the right type of reform, and then to pursue it moderately. To try to deal with the corporate problem "in an intemperate, destructive, or demagogic spirit would, in all probability, mean that nothing whatever would be accomplished," he told Congress in 1904. What the country needed most was "the quiet determination to proceed, step by step, without halt and without hurry." Roosevelt was more than temperamentally conservative, however. He believed in property rights, and that included capitalists' right to *their* property and to a fair return on their investments. "We must stand heartily for the rights of every decent man," he wrote in 1908, "whether he be a man of great wealth or a man who earns his livelihood as a wage worker or a tiller of the soil." Roosevelt continued to fear the social disorder he believed lurked just beyond so-called radicals' plans for leveling corporate wealth. Maybe he sounded somewhat like Oliver Cromwell, but maybe more like Edmund Burke.[8]

Roosevelt's abiding fear of social revolution separated him from the progressive insurgents and lent even his bolder reform initiatives a cautious, conservative cast. Commitment to tradition, social custom, and gradual change are philosophical conservatism's best-known principles, articulated most forcefully in the modern age by Burke, the Irishman-cum-British-politician. In his seminal 1790 *Reflections on the Revolution in France*, modern conservatism's founding text, Burke blasted the French revolutionaries for their abandonment of tradition, their speculative "rights of man," their attack on Christianity and subsequent attempts to perfect society. Burke believed humans did not have it in their power to start the world anew. Statesmen and would-be reformers had to work with the materials granted them, with the circumstances of their country as they found them, in order to make any real progress. Rapid, sweeping change was never a wise idea. It ruptured the circle of events that gave individuals a sense of personal identity and continuity with earlier generations. Those earlier generations were important on Burke's account. He maintained that tradition embodied the "wisdom of the species," an idea that appealed to Roosevelt's historicist racialism.

Tradition should not be lightly shoved aside in the name of the "rights of man" or some utopian scheme. Burke purported to endorse "the *real* rights of man" which arose from humans' social nature and responsibilities, including the right to property and to the products of one's labor, a right to protection from harm, and, significantly, a right to "sufficient restraint upon [one's] passions." Though humans were social creatures, Burke held, they could live in political society only if their selfish and destructive tendencies were tamed—controlled. This thought supplied the deeper logic of Roosevelt's economic mugwumpery. Government must erect moral restraints in law because "the restraints on men, as well as their liberties, are to be reckoned among their rights." Restraints made self-government possible.[9]

Roosevelt readily claimed Burke's influence in explaining his formative politics, his ambition to shape citizens' characters through state regulation of the market and civil society. Those who desired to practice and pass on self-government to their children, Roosevelt wrote to Congress, "should ever bear in mind the thought so finely expressed by Burke: 'Men are qualified for civil liberty in exact proportion to their disposition to put moral chains upon their own appetites; in proportion as they are disposed to listen to the counsel of the wise and good in preference to the flattery of knaves.'" And then the coup de grace: "'Society cannot exist unless a controlling power upon will and appetite be placed somewhere, and the less of it there be within the more without.'" When Burke called for a "controlling power" on men's passion, Roosevelt undoubtedly envisioned the national state. He presented his regulatory policies in almost precisely these terms, casting the state as a controlling interest directing the energy and output of the nation's great businesses toward the public good. Indeed, the state would direct all elements of society to the public good, unifying the nation as a steward of the public welfare.[10]

Roosevelt frankly acknowledged that his goal was to avert class-based radicalism and social turmoil through state-sponsored reform. As historian Samuel Hays has noted, Roosevelt was ultimately uninterested in balancing the demands of capital and labor. His aim was to transcend class conflict and supplant class loyalties with a common commitment to the national collective. The state was for him an agent of social unity and preservation. His efforts were essentially conservative, then, to the extent they sought to preserve the basic order of the American capitalist system and social hierarchy. But they were revisionist to the degree they attempted to render that order irrelevant.[11]

"The proper antidote to the dangerous and wicked agitation against the men of wealth as such," Roosevelt said in his sixth annual message, "is to secure by proper legislation and executive action the abolition of the grave abuses which actually do obtain in connection with the business use of wealth under our present system." Roosevelt did not seek a social revolution. Quite the contrary. He sought to prevent one. Burke had said, "A state without the means of some change is without the means of its conservation." Roosevelt reiterated the theme in 1902, telling Congress that "wise evolution is the sure safeguard against revolution." The reforms that he proposed were bold but not radical, Roosevelt maintained, at least not in the sense of introducing social dislocation.[12]

Through the final years of his White House tenure, Roosevelt expressed no interest in strategies to redistribute wealth. Some of his pronouncements, actually, sounded like apologies for inequality. No "help of a permanently beneficial character can be given to the less able and less fortunate, save as the results of a policy which shall inure to the advantage of all industrious and efficient people who act decently." Therefore, "any benefit which comes to the less able and less fortunate must of necessity come even more to the more able and more fortunate." Private property was the fundamental base of civilization, and some individuals would naturally possess more property than others. Social inequality was perfectly normal, even desirable, insofar as "the man of small means . . . [is] helped by making conditions such that the man of exceptional business ability receives an exceptional reward for his ability." Roosevelt had little sympathy and even less patience for silly dreamers like "[Edward] Bellamy and Henry George . . . Carl [*sic*] Marx and Proudhon," who believed that "at this stage it is possible to make every one happy by an immense social revolution." They were foolish, for "in the hideous welter of social revolution it is the brutal, the reckless, and the criminal who prosper, not the hard-working, sober, and thrifty." Roosevelt found socialism "deadening and degrading," especially in its communist form. It destroyed the "individual initiative . . . energy, character, and foresight" upon which the republic—the race—depended.[13]

As La Follette and other insurgents perhaps intuitively suspected, a good part of Roosevelt's frustration with the congressional leadership stemmed from his inability to make them understand that his reforms were attempts to protect the corporate economic order and reinforce social stability. Roosevelt was at pains to convince Aldrich and Cannon and the congressional caucus that only moderate government interference could preserve the rights of contract and property they so prized. "As a matter of fact," Roosevelt warned, "socialism, and especially its extreme form, communism, and the destruction of individual character which they would bring about, are in part achieved by the wholly unregulated competition which results in a single individual or corporation rising at the expense of all others." The best means to banish the socialist specter that menaced so much of Europe was to introduce regulatory and labor reform steadily, but calmly. "We shall not act hastily or recklessly," Roosevelt assured. But he would act—to conserve.[14]

Roosevelt's conservative dread of social instability along with his attachment to private property and the profit motive led him to distrust Western insurgents' programs for preventing monopoly and attacking corporate wealth. His social Darwinism helped convince him that corporate bigness was simply inevitable. None of this meant that the status quo capitalist economy should go unregulated. Paradoxically, his Burkean, republican commitment to restraining men's worst passions merged with his evolutionist affirmation of the corporate order and unbridled enthusiasm for expanding state power to push him in 1907 and 1908 along a path of reform both distinct from the insurgents and distinctly unconservative. In contrast to those progressives who wanted to augment the antitrust laws and expand Sherman Act prosecutions beyond the administration's forty-three ongoing cases, Roosevelt proposed instead to use the federal government to direct the corporate economy's evolution and stimulate a unifying surge of national feeling. "I strongly advocate that instead of an unwise effort to prohibit all combinations there shall be substituted a law which shall expressly permit combinations which are in the interest of the public, but shall at the same time give to some agency of the National Government full power of control and supervision over them." Burke's *Reflections* crackled with energetic diatribes against the French revolutionaries' use of coercive state power. Wariness of coercive authority, especially centralized coercive authority, might be called one of Burkean conservatism's founding commitments. For all his other conservative credentials, this was not one Roosevelt shared.[15]

When he called for national control and supervision of corporations, Roosevelt had in mind a licensing arrangement, to be administered by the Bureau of Corporations. Any corporation doing business in interstate commerce would require bureau approval before merging with another corporation. Further, the bureau would take on new power to compel the publication of corporate accounts and inspect corporate records. Roosevelt effectively proposed to transform the bureau from an investigative body into a full-fledged administrative agency. Along the way he intended to abandon the Sherman antitrust law. In 1907 he explicitly called for an amendment to the Sherman law "to forbid only the kind of combination which does harm to the general public." Everything else would be regulated by the Bureau of Corporations. "I believe that it is worse than folly to attempt to prohibit all combinations as is done by the Sherman antitrust law," he said again in 1908. "Such a law can be enforced only imperfectly and unequally, and its enforcement works almost as much hardship as good." He recommended removing railroads completely from the domain of antitrust laws, giving them over instead to supervision by a larger, more powerful Interstate Commerce Commission. "The power of the commission should be made thoroughgoing," the president maintained. He wanted to give the commission new authority both to raise and to lower rates, without court review. To the delight of the railroads, he also proposed to legalize pooling and permit its practice under commission supervision. He advised that telegraph and telephone companies also be made subject to commission oversight.[16]

To the Western progressives' vision of free market competition guaranteed by the state, Roosevelt juxtaposed a corporatist nationalism. The conclusion of his administration brought him to the end of his patience with the Sherman Act and similarly inspired attempts at restoring a competitive market of independent producers. That was the past. He now advocated using the state to guide the economy toward a productive, equitable future, an extension of his economic mugwumpery from intervention to management. If neither Edmund Burke in 1796 nor Henry Carter Adams in 1886 anticipated quite this level of state involvement in civil society—state direction of the economy—it seemed natural enough to Roosevelt given the logic of his rate campaign a year or two before. "I believe that under the interstate clause of the Constitution the United States has complete and paramount right to control all agencies of interstate commerce," he reiterated in 1908, his tone betraying impatience. He had already made the argument many times. The corporations were "the most important factors in modern business." It would be economic suicide to destroy them. Control, not destruction, was the right policy.[17]

Was Roosevelt fundamentally a corporate conservative? Some historians, Gabriel Kolko chief among them, have speculated that the major legislative enactments of the Roosevelt presidency—including especially the Hepburn railroad rate bill—were thinly veiled gifts to business, regulation for the benefit of the regulated. Roosevelt's well-known skepticism of antitrust laws and his growing corporatism as his presidency wore on might lend some credence to that assertion, but in fact there is little evidence to support it. The railroads were indeed advocates of state intervention between 1877 and 1917, but not usually the sort of intervention they got. Railroad executives generally disliked the Hepburn bill, as it contained no provision to legalize pooling, and were downright hostile to the Interstate Commerce Commission's rate-making authority without judicial review. They launched a public-relations campaign in late 1905 to try and counter Roosevelt's blitz and defeat rate reform. When Roosevelt finally did propose to legalize pooling in 1907, railroad chiefs were pleased. But the proposal failed. And while the president himself was sympathetic to corporations' complaints about cutthroat competition, his emerging corporatism followed from his nationalism and his willingness to use state power rather than from any deep-seated belief in the goodness of industry. In fact, part of the reason he proposed national regulation was because he regarded corporations as beneficial in theory, but often malign in effect. He saw the federal government as a means to bend corporations to their beneficent potential.[18]

As for his conservatism, Roosevelt was never a radical at any point in his political career. He firmly believed in reform by degrees, step by step. And various substantive conservative ideas studded Roosevelt's political thought. He abhorred class conflict. The racialism he learned as a youth from Nathaniel Shaler and others reflected a certain reverence for history and tradition, though the Teutonic tradition Roosevelt venerated ultimately proved to be mostly ersatz. Then there was Roosevelt's unwavering commitment to the traditional family, private property, and historically revealed moral absolutes, all of which marked him as a conservative.

Nonetheless, Roosevelt shared virtually none of the Burkean conservatives' fear of centralized power—or their hesitance to use it. If he showed spare enthusiasm for reconfiguring class hierarchies, that was because he hoped ultimately to make them obsolete. His social conservatism actually concealed an ambitious project to forge a new national unity through state action. According to him, the body politic was essentially one political person, with one set of common interests: Americans were one race. Particular loyalties, whether class-based, religious, or ethnic, whether held by the immigrant or native born, distracted from commitment to the collective as a whole. They obscured the common good. Roosevelt hoped to use the national government to redirect the energies of the American people back to an overarching, unitary public interest. The national state, and specifically the executive, would act as the "steward of the public welfare," the fixed point around which all Americans could rally, knowing they would be treated equally and as individuals, regardless of their social standing. The government would "judge each man not as a part of a class," Roosevelt promised, "but upon his individual merits." He would be judged on his conduct and character, on whether he possessed the virtues of "courage, honor, justice, truth, sincerity, and hardihood—the virtues that made America great" and the race strong. The central government would, in this way, help build a national sense of community. The state was the place where Americans would rediscover their common racial interest and exercise their corporate agency—their sovereignty.[19]

Unlike traditional conservatives, then, Roosevelt demonstrated little concern for the private institutions that historically stood between the public and the state, protecting citizens' rights from government coercion. He rarely spoke of rights at all, and harbored a very different conception of their nature than did the Burkeans or American framers, as his policy proposals in 1907 and 1908 revealed. His conservatism was more a Christianized Darwinism than anything else, a celebration of evolution, struggle, and effort giving birth to moral character and national unity. He prized the family as an evolutionary achievement, and private property too. Both were necessary, he thought, for the development of the modern nation-state. This same racialist evolutionism justified his corporatist proposals as well, including those he made in the final years of his presidency. He realized that in pressing for government management of the evolving corporate economy he was breaking with both the congressional leadership and many progressives. "The truth is that we who believe in this movement of asserting and exercising a genuine control . . . over these great corporations have to contend against two sets of enemies." The first were the railroad senators who believed no regulation was necessary at all. The second were "the men who, being blind to the economic movements of the day, believe in a movement of repression rather than of regulation of corporations." Neither understood that federal supervision alone could really control the corporations. In typical Roosevelt fashion, he convinced himself that his way was the only viable option.[20]

If the president and certain cadres of progressives had their differences of opinion by the end of 1908, the distance between Roosevelt and the congressional leadership had opened into a yawning chasm. Roosevelt once described Speaker Joe Cannon to his son Kermit as "an exceedingly solemn, elderly gentleman with chin whiskers, who certainly does not look to be of playful nature." That was in 1903, when the president could still call Cannon "a great friend of mine." By 1908 the Speaker was neither playful nor friendly. Hostility between Capitol Hill and the White House began to simmer well before the last months of Roosevelt's term, though the president's bold new regulatory proposals did not help. By 1908, the congressional leadership saw them as of a piece with Roosevelt's—from their point of view—dangerous, boisterous love affair with power. But really, the Rough Rider president made the congressional leadership nervous almost from the first with his adventures in executive authority. In his first term, these were confined to an isolated labor strike and foreign policy, and Republicans were publicly supportive in all instances. That didn't make Roosevelt's executive forays any less alarming, however.[21]

The first demonstration of Roosevelt's intention to use presidential power to its fullest came in the fall of 1902, when anthracite coal miners in Pennsylvania walked off the job. Winter was on the horizon, and the strike created the potential for a severe coal shortage in the Northeast. Roosevelt intervened. For the first time in American history, he assembled labor leaders and mine owners at the White House and shepherded negotiations. Privately, he readied a more ambitious plan. Should negotiations fail, the president intended to seize the mines by military force and employ the miners as government workers until a permanent settlement could be reached. As it happened, owners and strikers reached an accord without further presidential action, and a good thing, too—Roosevelt's takeover designs were almost certainly unconstitutional. The commander-in-chief clause of the Constitution's Article II gave the president plenary power over the armed forces, but other constitutional provisions set bounds to that authority. Article I, Section 8 gives Congress the power to "raise and support Armies," not the President. The Fifth Amendment, for example, prohibits government from taking private property without compensation or due process of law. The Third Amendment bars the federal government from quartering soldiers in private homes, effectively a ban on government commandeering of private property, even for emergency purposes short of war—and then, only with congressional approval. Tellingly, when President Harry Truman tried to seize steel companies to prevent a work stoppage during the Korean war, a Supreme Court more sympathetic to executive action than the one Roosevelt faced still condemned Truman's actions.[22]

The anthracite coal strike was only the start. Early in 1901, Cipriano Castro, dictator of Venezuela, sparked an international crisis by announcing that his country would not pay back millions of dollars it owed to European nations, principally Germany. Venezuela owed Britain as well, and Germany and Britain together began a blockade in late 1902 off the Venezuelan coast, twelve months after Roosevelt came to office. Roosevelt had considered Germany a danger to U.S. interests since the 1890s, and in November and December of 1902 he moved to counter what he perceived as a German threat to the Monroe Doctrine. Roosevelt named Admiral George Dewey commander of the U.S. fleet, the same Dewey he had directed, while assistant secretary of the navy, to take the Philippines. On Roosevelt's orders, Dewey moved the battle fleet to Trinidad, five hundred miles closer to Venezuela, and began the fleet's first-ever naval maneuvers in the Caribbean. This saber-rattling caught the attention of London and Berlin. Roosevelt later insisted he had issued Kaiser Wilhelm an ultimatum in December 1902: if Germany did not agree to settle the dispute by international arbitration, "I would be obliged to order Dewey to take his fleet to the Venezuelan coast and see that the German forces did not take possession of any territory." Whether Roosevelt actually made such a threat remains a matter of historical dispute, but either way the Germans did eventually agree to arbitration, and Britain did as well. As in the case of the coal strike, Roosevelt's more aggressive plans were not ultimately put into action. Perhaps he would have hesitated to do so. But then, he didn't hesitate in Panama.[23]

At about the same time the Venezuelan crisis cooled, Secretary of State John Hay concluded a treaty with the government of Colombia, masters of Panama. The treaty provided finally for Roosevelt's long-held dream of an American-owned canal through the Panamanian isthmus. Under the terms of the Hay-Herran treaty, named for the secretary and his Colombian counterpart, the United States would acquire the rights of the French New Canal Company to build a canal zone six miles in width across Panama. Colombia would retain nominal sovereignty, but the United States would have full power to create courts, make regulations, and police all activity within the zone. The whole transaction cost the American government $10 million in gold, with an annual rent of $250,000 to follow for one hundred years. Roosevelt was delighted; the Colombian senate less so. Apparently believing they had been underpaid, and in a show of resistance to the faltering dictatorship of José Marroquín, Colombian senators unanimously rejected the treaty in August 1903. Rather than abandon the Colombian route and purchase canal rights in Nicaragua, another workable site, Roosevelt schemed to build a Panamanian canal without the approval of Colombia and without further consulting Congress. He got his chance in November, when the latest of periodic rebellions erupted in Panama. A treaty negotiated with Colombia's predecessor state in 1846 guaranteed to the American government the right to land military forces on the isthmus in the event of a rebellion—to protect American goods and travelers—provided U.S. forces respected the sovereignty of Colombia. In the past the United States had landed troops multiple times—six times, by Roosevelt's count, and as recently as 1902—but, on five of those six occasions, with the express permission of the Colombian government. In November 1903, Roosevelt refused to ask permission. He ordered U.S. military personnel to Panama on his own authority, nominally to protect American citizens but really to prevent Colombia from sending its own troops to put down the rebellion and to ward off any interference from European powers. The result was the new Republic of Panama, which the Roosevelt administration promptly recognized. The president would get his canal after all.[24]

The Panama incident ignited a firestorm of public controversy in the United States. Newspapers criticized the president's actions as a flagrant violation of international law. Roosevelt felt compelled to defend himself at length in his December message to Congress, and when that failed to quell the uproar in the press, he sent another, special message in January 1904. Complicating matters, newspapers accurately reported that Roosevelt had met with the French proprietor of the New Canal Company, Philippe Bunau-Varilla, in October, before the uprising began. Bunau-Varilla later attested that he told Roosevelt then of plans to foment a rebellion and secured an implicit promise from the president to support Panamanian independence. Roosevelt does not appear to have made any such promises, and his decision to order troops to the isthmus was valid both constitutionally, pursuant to the Article II commander-in-chief clause, and legally under the 1846 Bidlack-Mallarino Treaty with New Granada, Colombia's predecessor-in-interest. However, Roosevelt's refusal to seek Colombian permission to land troops was questionable, and his strategic use of American forces to prevent any Colombian effort to put down the rebellion may well have violated the 1846 treaty terms requiring the United States to respect and support the sovereignty of Colombia.[25]

The president's fiercest critics came from the Democratic side of the aisle, but congressional Republicans had reason to be concerned at the pattern that was developing, and not just in foreign affairs. Roosevelt was an unabashed devotee of executive discretion and presidential power. His domestic initiatives, from the Elkins Act and Bureau of Corporations in 1903 to the railroad rate bill three years later, all shifted authority toward administrative agencies within the executive branch. The trend accelerated in 1907 and 1908. Roosevelt's new proposals to convert the Bureau of Corporations into a full-fledged administrative agency and to extend the jurisdiction of the Interstate Commerce Commission represented a major expansion of administrative-executive regulatory power, beyond the immediate control of Congress. Congressional Republicans killed these initiatives, but Roosevelt took others on his own. In 1905, he created the Commission on Department Methods and made Assistant Treasury Secretary Charles Keep its chairman. The commission's purpose was to investigate how to improve the administrative operations of the federal government. As a result of its probe, the committee recommended a major reorganization of the executive branch: reclassification of civil service positions, creation of a general supply committee to centralize federal purchasing under executive order, a national archives to gather and classify government documents, and a new interdepartmental statistics committee to coordinate information. Its boldest recommendation was to remake the Department of the Interior by consolidating the department's four divisions into one, directly under the authority of the secretary of the interior. Roosevelt implemented all the commission's plans by executive order, to the fury of the congressional leadership.[26]

Roosevelt's belief in the benevolent power of executive action found particularly vivid expression in his mature conservation program. The ruinous overharvesting of the country's timberlands, severe water shortages in the arid West, the rapid deterioration of the famed open ranges, and the more gradual but steady disappearance of suitable wildlife habitat nationwide—all these developments convinced Roosevelt as president that the United States needed a rational, unified policy to manage the nation's natural resources. As in the field of economic regulation, Roosevelt concluded here as well that, when it came to conservation policy, Congress was not up to the task. The issues were too complex, the competing demands of resource protection and rational development too politically charged to be entrusted to a group of partisan legislators. Roosevelt believed conservation policy should be set scientifically and administered by experts, not politicians. His conservation narrative sounded in the grand themes of his broader regulatory vision: nonpartisan executive action could quell the chaos and curb the physical destruction wrought by runaway individualism. The trusts threatened to exhaust the country's natural wealth with no thought for the future, but government would check the trusts. Government intervention would bank the fires of selfish, special interest exploitation and redirect public policy toward the long-term good of the whole.[27]

Roosevelt made the goal of his conservation program efficient development. The idea was to match the use of natural resources to the needs of the industrial economy in the immediate term, while preserving those resources as much as possible for future use. That meant developing them rationally, efficiently, at a pace that was sustainable. The administration experimented with water management and public land use measures in Roosevelt's first term, but not until the final year of his presidency did he settle on a unified conservation agenda. Like so many other Roosevelt initiatives, this one was the brainchild of a presidential commission, appointed without the approval of Congress. In December 1908, Roosevelt's National Conservation Commission recommended a raft of regulatory policies to promote efficient development. These included classifying all existing government lands according to highest use, as well as leasing public grazing and coal lands; the commission recommended the creation of additional national forests in the East, development of flood waters, anti–soil erosion measures, and repeal of antiquated land laws. The Roosevelt administration sought congressional action to implement these initiatives, but the president did not want Congress actually to set policy. Instead, Roosevelt and his conservationists wanted Congress to adopt general authorizing statutes and leave the policy design to the executive. The logic of the conservation commission's proposals mimicked that of Roosevelt's corporate regulatory agenda. Public policy in the industrial age should be devised by expert civil servants under the direction of the executive branch. Conservation matters were profoundly technical, and resource management was not about politics; it was about science. So scientists ought to do the managing.[28]

But Congress had heard quite enough of this refrain. Roosevelt had already stretched his powers under the Forest Management Act, Reclamation Act, and General Dams Act—he had set aside hundreds of thousands of acres of public lands as wildlife preserves and expanded federal authority over navigable waters, all without congressional authorization. In early 1907, Congress tried to rein in Roosevelt's conservation-by-executive-order policy. Republican Senator Charles Fulton of Oregon added an amendment to an appropriations bill barring the creation of new forest reserves in Oregon and five other western states except by act of Congress. Both houses approved the measure and the bill went to the president at the end of February. Roosevelt dared not veto an entire appropriations bill over this one provision, so before signing it he directed forestry chief Gifford Pinchot to draw up proclamations creating twenty-one new conservation reserves in the very states the Fulton amendment covered. He signed the proclamations on March 2 and the appropriations bill on March 4, 1907. When Roosevelt forwarded the National Conservation Commission's proposals to the legislature just over eighteen months later, and requested an additional $25,000 for commission work, Congress turned a deaf ear. The president, congressional leaders concluded, was out of control.[29]

More was at issue between President Roosevelt and Congress than the proper uses of executive orders or the shape of conservation policy. By 1908, Roosevelt and the congressional leadership had developed serious differences over the proper uses of executive power. "I declined to adopt the view that what was imperatively necessary for the Nation could not be done by the President unless he could find some specific authorization to do it," Roosevelt wrote in 1913. Instead, he believed the president could do "anything that the needs of the Nation demanded unless such action was forbidden by the Constitution or by the laws." This assertion sounded blithely lawless at first, a perfect inversion of the early Americans' purpose in drafting and ratifying a written constitution to restrain political authority. Certainly the president's critics thought so. But in actuality Roosevelt meant to offer not unbounded presidential discretion above and beyond the law, but a principled neo-Hamiltonianism. He characterized himself as a practitioner of the "Jackson-Lincoln school" of presidential leadership, by which he meant the vigorous assertion of executive prerogatives for the national good, in the tradition of Alexander Hamilton. Roosevelt openly admired his fellow New Yorker preeminently among the founders, and for one overriding reason: Hamilton was "a strong believer in a powerful National government," and a powerful national executive to go with it.[30]

Alexander Hamilton's constitutional science laid great stress on administration, which led him to champion a strong national government. State governments, in Hamilton's experience, were inefficient, ineffective, self-regarding things, and often foolish. He judged the states-oriented Articles of Confederation to be a disaster and arrived at the Constitutional Convention in Philadelphia determined to provide for the long-term security of the United States by strengthening the national state. To Hamilton, the executive was the single most vital component of any political system, and he sought in his proposals as a convention delegate and later as George Washington's secretary of the treasury to carve out as much constitutional leeway for America's executive as possible. It would do no good to have a president institutionally dependent on Congress and unable to act apart from congressional bidding. The president, Hamilton told Washington in his opinion on the constitutionality of a national bank, had "a right to employ all the means requisite, and fairly applicable to the attainment of the ends of [his constitutional] power," so long as the means were "not precluded by restrictions and exceptions specified in the constitution, or not immoral, or not contrary to the essential ends of political society."[31]

Roosevelt gleefully embraced Hamilton's advocacy of executive power and mimicked Hamilton's phrasing in propounding his own theories of executive discretion. After decades of congressional dominance of the federal political system, Roosevelt sought to return the presidency to center stage by shattering the alliance between congressmen, state and local party officials, and government administrators that dated to the Jacksonian period. His weapon was an administrative state independent of both Congress and party, to be directed by the executive branch. He fought on two fronts. First, he marshaled (and perhaps exceeded) the constitutional powers of his office to set precedents for executive action without the authorization or oversight of Congress. And second, he forged a new alliance of executive-administrative elites to run the federal government, rebuilding the executive's institutional capacities along the way. In sum, Roosevelt worked to build an executive bureaucracy to exert the sort of institutional energy Hamilton wrote about in *The Federalist*. Roosevelt, however, claimed presidential discretion far beyond Hamilton, and for a reason that reveals their different political philosophies.[32]

When Roosevelt wrote that he believed it was his right and duty as president to "do anything that the needs of the Nation demanded unless such action was forbidden by the Constitution," he omitted Hamilton's crucial qualifier that the executive action taken be "applicable to the attainment of the ends" of the president's constitutional power or, in other words, in pursuit of an objective clearly sanctioned by the Constitution. Roosevelt appeared to believe that the president held general powers apart from those granted the federal government in the nation's fundamental law. But this was not a Hamiltonian idea. Hamilton never argued that the president could take any action not strictly prohibited by the Constitution. He argued that presidents must have the ability to fulfill their constitutional obligations by doing things, if necessary, not explicitly mentioned in the Constitution. In short, Hamilton thought that presidents retained residual powers—thanks to Article III's "vesting clause"—that they might exercise consistent with the constitutional limits placed on the national government as a whole. Executive discretion was important to Hamilton because, when it came right down to it, he was not so sure that the republican political experiment would work in America. It had been tried in Britain only after a fashion. "The idea of a perfect equality of political rights among the citizens, exclusive of all permanent hereditary distinctions" was a bold and daring premise for a government, Hamilton confided to George Washington.[33]

Without a monarch or hereditary landed class to take a more circumspect view of the best interests of the state, and without the need to reach agreement between the differing social estates, the fate of the nation would be entirely dependent on the behavior of the average citizen. Or to recur to traditional republican language, the state would depend entirely on civic virtue. Hamilton thought the selfish and parochial behavior of the state governments under the Articles regime did not bode well for the republican experiment as the Americans had conceived it. The system had a chance of success only if talented leaders came to office and enjoyed the maximum discretion compatible with liberty in using their power. Granting that discretion, in fact, was the best hope Americans had of preserving their liberty at all.[34]

Roosevelt also had his doubts about America's republican venture, and he too prescribed the executive as an antidote. Not state interests but special interests worried Roosevelt as president: railroads, manufacturers, investment tycoons. They had grown so large in wealth and economic power, they could all too easily influence, if not dominate, the party system of government by co-opting its chief actors—individual congressmen or senators or party officials. The best way to break the power of the interests and return government to the people was to put government administration in the hands of nonpartisan elites, under charge of an executive elected by the people as a whole. A professional administrative state under the supervision of the president captured every constitutional virtue of Article II—it could act with dispatch, and secrecy when necessary; it could initiate the legislative agenda and prevent self-interested factions from gaining control of national affairs—while also augmenting the power of the people. To Roosevelt's way of thinking, power concentrated in one set of hands or under the authority of one man was not less democratic, but more so, because it promoted popular accountability. "Democracy is in peril wherever the administration of political power is scattered among a variety of men who work in secret," he told Congress. "It is not in peril from any man who derives authority from the people, who exercises it in sight of the people, and who is from time to time compelled to give an account of its exercise to the people."[35]

Of course, for concentration of power to increase popular accountability, the concentrated powers had to be answerable to an elected official. And though Roosevelt spoke of a nonpartisan, independent bureaucracy, in practice he wanted one strictly accountable to *him*. In the end, it was not so much an administrative state but a presidential state he advocated. The Hamiltonian case for executive discretion and the case for concentration of power were one and the same in Roosevelt's mind, in a way they never were for Hamilton. But this was largely because Roosevelt associated the state and the populace, treating them as a unity. He cast the president as the steward of the people. Every power the people possessed as sovereign he thought was available to the president, unless the Constitution said explicitly otherwise. By his interpretation, the powers of the executive were no longer residual and limited but general and expansive. Perhaps Congress was a body possessing specific, enumerated powers, but not the president, not according to Roosevelt. Hamilton's opponents accused him of being a closet monarchist, but he never encouraged concentration of political power to the extent, and with the justifications, that Roosevelt did. He never argued that the president wielded general powers outside the bounds of the Constitution. It is virtually impossible to imagine him concluding, as Roosevelt did, "In the great days of the Roman Republic no harm whatever came from the dictatorship."[36]

Roosevelt's neo-Hamiltonian philosophy of the executive was more new than it was Hamilton, and more Roosevelt than it was anything else. As always, he was politically creative: the implements of the administrative state—the independent commissions and nonpartisan civil service—predated his presidency by decades. They were not new ideas. But he put them to new uses, wedding them to a professional bureaucracy and an expansive theory of executive power. He made them part of a broader project in state-building and republican virtue politics.

Besides the fact that he imagined the president as the steward of the sovereign people and trustee of their authority, Roosevelt promoted national power for another reason. He was a rights-positivist. Rights were things as often secured by government as threatened by it, he believed. Indeed, rights were in important respects the creations of the state. He had suggested as much in his public sermons in 1905, when he spoke of getting via government regulation equality between big and small shipper, between capitalist and farmer. But if the state could achieve the conditions necessary for democratic politics by adjusting the terms of market competition, and that was Roosevelt's argument in 1905, why couldn't the state intervene more proactively to help groups disadvantaged by the industrial economy—laborers and farmers, for example—stand on the same plane as the wealthy capitalists? If competition was important to develop the warrior virtues, why shouldn't the state make certain that competition was fair and orderly? Slowly this logic, itself sounding in Whiggish republican themes, overcame Roosevelt's earlier convictions about the "American doctrine" of government, "which is," he once believed, "that the state has no business whatever to attempt to better the condition of a man or a set of men, but has merely to see that no wrong is done him or them by any one else, and that all alike are to have a fair chance in the struggle of life." By the end of his presidency, Roosevelt began to believe that Americans of small means and little influence would be protected from wrong and given a fair chance only if the state actively intervened on their behalf. His earlier conviction became a rationale for state action, not forbearance.

Between December 1907 and the inauguration of his successor a year and three months later, Roosevelt proposed a workmen's compensation system for all laborers on federal projects, a complete ban on child labor nationwide, an eight-hour workday, new rights for female workers, federal support for farmers, and a progressive inheritance tax for large fortunes. As he had in 1905, Roosevelt explained these measures by reference to the social virtues they would encourage. One of the "first stages in the battle" for industrial justice, he said, was the "fight for the rights of the workingman." He had not always thought so. As late as 1896 he castigated labor unions and their members as agents of social chaos. But the imperatives of his economic mugwumpery, his virtue politics, gradually changed his mind. Laborers needed to possess equality in bargaining position when it came to securing better wages from their employers. They needed, wherever feasible, an eight-hour workday and protection from injury on the job. These "human rights" Roosevelt cast as the modern translations of the "life, liberty, and pursuit of happiness" that the Declaration of Independence deemed inalienable. Workers deserved such "rights," Roosevelt thought, so that they might contribute to the good of the nation. Social justice in the industrial age demanded new guarantees for material well-being because, as things stood, ordinary individuals, and especially wage workers, were in danger of being dwarfed beside those "artificial individuals called corporations." The total domination of corporate power over individual workers meant whole segments of the population would be unable to develop the warrior virtues, unable to strive and make something of their lives.[37]

In the first instance, then, the need for new "human rights" grew from Roosevelt's republican formative ambition. Providing workers with state-backed guarantees for work safety, bargaining power, and injury compensation was part of the institutional rearrangement necessary to harness the circumstances of modern industrial life to the common or racial good. The rights problem for his time, as Roosevelt saw it, was that "individualism" could no longer meet the needs of most members of society. The "property rights" of the large coal operators and railroad owners conflicted with the "human rights" of wage workers and farmers. That is, the employers' massive acquisitions won by self-effort threatened to crush others' ability to win the same. Theoretically, there was nothing wrong with the capitalists' buildup of wealth and financial power. "These men were not weak men," Roosevelt reflected. Instead, they were in many cases admirable men with admirable talent for business innovation and management. But the age was "an age of combination," as Roosevelt said repeatedly, and it required a new set of rights appropriate for a new scale of life.[38]

Rights were useful. They were instrumental to encouraging the conquering qualities of character. But they also possessed moral significance in Roosevelt's thinking, albeit an evolutionary one. Roosevelt believed that humans, especially Americans, owed one another fair and equal treatment because of their highly evolved status, and this meant two things. For starters, strong men insisted on the same liberty for others that they demanded for themselves. It was part of their character as virile, honorable people to do so. Secondly, the strong treated their peers fairly as a show of respect, as an acknowledgement of the other's evolutionary achievement. Strength respected strength. Roosevelt seemed to regard rights in a similar way. He thought of them as the products of the race's advance. When the West beckoned to be settled, Americans required especially individual rights that protected them from government interference, rights that allowed them wide latitude of action and individual initiative. In addition, they needed protection for the land they acquired and the products they made and grew from it. Businessmen needed guarantees of their financial property so they would be free to develop the economy in a way beneficial to the race. Now, in the early twentieth century, the circumstances of the race had changed. So too had the people's rights. The one constant was the goal of racial greatness. Rights arose, then, not primarily from the nature of the individual, but from the nature and needs of the race. Rights were teleological—derived from a collective goal and oriented to-

ward a particular, communal end outside the individual. Rights were also conventional. They could be, and indeed needed to be, adjusted regularly to bring
maximum benefit to the race.

Roosevelt's assertion that government could create rights tailored to contemporary situations points up the theoretical distance between his notion of rights
and the founders' "inalienable" version. Life, liberty, and the pursuit of happiness Thomas Jefferson used as proxies for the natural rights belonging to all people by virtue of their existence. More than anything else, the Declaration of Independence and later the U.S. Constitution were meant to defend, one by
announcement and the other by institutional arrangement, the way of life where
human rights were exercised. Rights were not lists of economic privileges or
claims to material provision by the state. They were an expression of where man
stood in the cosmos, as an independent creature endowed by the Creator with
unique worth and purpose. This is not to say government might not provide different institutional guarantees in different times as part of an effort to secure the
person's unchanging rights. Free labor advocates, passionate believers in natural
rights, started down the road toward just such an institutional readjustment by
reimagining the civic status of wage workers. However, Roosevelt's quick equation of the Declaration's inalienable rights with guarantees for "a living wage . . .
decent working and living conditions," and "freedom of thought and speech and
industrial representation," was not simply another iteration of a natural rights
doctrine. It was a rejection of the whole concept. There were no natural rights in
Roosevelt's political science. There were racial rights, national rights—rights afforded to individuals as members of the race; positive rights for the good of the
nation.[39]

Roosevelt's rights-positivism reinforced his nationalist leanings in interesting
ways. His thought devalued states, localities, civic associations, and other arenas
of sociopolitical membership where republicans—and Burkeans—traditionally
believed rights were practiced and protected. Nor was there much talk from
Roosevelt of individual conscience as a source of rights or limit on state action.
The social gospel made religion a public, not private, affair. It sanctified the
state, merging the kingdom of God and the body politic. Rather than setting
bounds to state action, if anything, the social gospel fostered a religious nationalism, a righteous republicanism.[40]

Roosevelt's proposals in 1907 and 1908 amounted to national social welfare
policies, if not quite yet a social welfare state. Other Western nations had begun
furnishing work safety guarantees and injury compensation to their citizens. He
urged Congress to do the same. "Since 1895 practically every country of Europe,
together with Great Britain, New Zealand, Australia, British Columbia, and the

Cape of Good Hope has enacted legislation" to protect workers, Roosevelt said in 1908. "I urge upon the Congress the enactment of a law . . . [to] bring Federal legislation up to the standard already established by all the European countries." He knew his plans stood little chance of enactment. That was one reason, perhaps, why he proposed so many of them. He was still trying to provide guidance to the supporters of reform, to indicate by rhetoric and proposal where he believed the progressive effort should focus. In the final eighteen months of his presidency, Roosevelt put forward new regulations for government management of the industrial economy, government-backed social rights for workers, and federal support for farmers and the disadvantaged. Nationalism was the watchword. National regulation and national rights for a better, more virtuous, more righteous national community.[41]

He had hoped to make the Republican Party the "progressive and indeed the fairly radical progressive party of the Nation." And despite mounting opposition from the congressional leadership, Roosevelt moved his party, as he moved the country, decisively in that direction. Historians and commentators later would quarrel over Roosevelt's identity as a progressive, much as they would over the true meaning of progressivism. Most of this quibbling was and is motivated by present-day political preferences: by the standards of the modern left or the benchmark of the New Deal, Roosevelt is said not to have gone far enough. This judgment presumes Roosevelt's political thought lies along some sort of continuum with the later policies of his distant cousin Franklin or with European democratic socialism. It takes for granted that a truly progressive politics, like modernity itself, culminates in a highly developed, centralized, socially liberal welfare state. All these assumptions are questionable, and, anyway, they shed no light on what it meant to be a progressive during the first decade of the twentieth century. Roosevelt's political thought does. He championed national regulation, social reform, and moral betterment. He sought to use the national state as a moral agent, to bring moral order to a chaotic, profit-obsessed economy. He wanted to replace class consciousness with national feeling, local loyalties with devotion to the collective. He advocated a stronger executive branch with a professional, nonpartisan administrative arm to guide government policy toward the public interest and away from influential private actors. He favored the presidency over Congress and the courts, the national government over the states.[42]

Muckraker Lincoln Steffens would later conclude that Roosevelt "was not a reformer in the White House; he was a careerist on the people's side." In a word, Roosevelt was not a movement man. And it is true that Roosevelt was careful not to identify himself too closely with any one group of reformers or sacrifice his po-

litical flexibility for the sake of any one reform cause. He was too skilled a politician for that, and too self-interested. Roosevelt could be an opportunist. He was
not above adjusting his principles or trading his allies in order to score a political
victory—just as he did to secure a railroad rate bill. Across three decades in public life, Roosevelt advocated reform with zeal, but he never lost sight of his own
political fortunes and never ceased to advance them. More than one observer
noted that the preaching president's rigid sense of moral rectitude always conveniently coincided with the course of action he favored—and that benefited him
the most.[43]

But if anyone was a progressive, Roosevelt was. He was also a corporatist, a
racialist, an economic mugwump, an imperialist, and a republican. Progressives
were all of these things, in various degrees and combinations. If Roosevelt did
not exhaust the possibilities of progressivism, he surely represented one iteration
of progressive thought, and he helped define the progressive moment.

Roosevelt's presidency would cast a long shadow over the future of American
politics. His string of accomplishments altered the character of the American
state and reconfigured public expectations for government and reform. His most
noteworthy and longest-lasting institutional achievement was the creation of a
professionalized administrative bureaucracy under the auspices of the executive
branch. Roosevelt left the executive with greater administrative capacities than
at any time in American history. In the years to come, those capacities would
swell larger still—much larger. Roosevelt's model of regulation by independent
agency proved remarkably effective. It facilitated federal oversight of huge industries by relieving Congress of the need to craft highly specific remedial statutes and by relieving the executive of the need to rely on courts to enforce them.
Instead, Congress could adopt broad regulatory laws and then delegate to professional administrators the authority to fill any gaps with new rules. The executive could delegate to the agency the task of implementing those rules in specific
situations. This way, regulation could be flexible and context-specific, yet uniform—a given regulation was interpreted and enforced by a single authorized
agency, not by a variety of fractious and hostile courts.

Uniformity and efficiency came at a price, however. The more authority Congress delegated to administrative agencies, the more its own political standing
deteriorated. By the middle of the twentieth century, with Roosevelt's presiden-
tial-administrative model the modus operandi of the federal government, Congress would cede whole bodies of regulatory law to unelected officials, to be
interpreted, applied, even rewritten, by them. In so doing, Congress came dangerously close to abdicating its constitutional responsibilities to write the laws of
the United States and keep watch over the executive branch.

Though Roosevelt intended the professional bureaucracy to benefit the executive, the rise of the administrative state cost the presidency as well. Proliferating independent agencies proved difficult to monitor or command, and in time career civil servants insulated from political accountability would exercise as much control over public policy as the president and his chosen advisers. These career administrators proved highly susceptible to special interest lobbying, much like the politicians they were supposed to replace, with one alarming difference: administrators could not be removed by election. As one president after another discovered in the second half of the twentieth century, oftentimes career civil servants could not be removed at all.

Thanks in no small part to Theodore Roosevelt, the American state in the twentieth century became one composed of agencies and administrators, a government operated by bureaucratic professionals, not by Congress or the courts or the president. Thus it became, arguably, a state less responsive — or at least, less accountable — to the will of the voting public even as it grew dramatically in size and power. The sort of general, extraconstitutional authority Roosevelt assigned to the president tended in practice to devolve to the agencies that increasingly enforced the law. In the long run, then, Roosevelt's tenure represented not so much the arrival of the imperial presidency as it did the birth of a fourth branch of government whose existence has strained the constitutional order as severely as did the party state Roosevelt sought to destroy.

Roosevelt as president changed American government, and he changed the public's expectations for it too. This would turn out to be another enduring legacy. The Rough Rider president personalized his office as never before, using his frequent speaking tours, colorful pronouncements, conversations with reporters, and carefully crafted stories about his family to generate a public persona for mass consumption. Americans felt as if they knew Roosevelt personally. He was the president as celebrity. In the future, Americans would expect to know all of their presidents this way. They would expect the president to take the public into his confidence, to share his thoughts and his life. They would expect their chief executive to have a clearly defined legislative agenda and to speak to them directly to build support for it. They would expect him to lead Congress and set the tone for national life. Many a president would stumble beneath these giant expectations, and American politics would become a cult of personality to a degree it never had been before. But Roosevelt succeeded, and his success set the standard.[44]

Just as they would expect their presidents to do more and be more, after Roosevelt Americans expected the federal government to do more as well. Roosevelt's success inspired deep confidence in the state's ability to improve the economy and society—to improve the world. That confidence remained intact and pervasive until the early 1930s; when it shattered, it cost a president his career and a political party power for a generation. More broadly, the reforming impulses Roosevelt stirred would remain a force in the political firmament for the duration of the century, sometimes dormant or dammed up, but liable to burst forth once summoned. At times in the years to come, Americans would view the federal government as a barrier to progress rather than its agent. But for all their disillusionment and libertarian leanings, American voters never entirely abandoned their Roosevelt-inspired faith in the capacity of collective action to lift up the lowly, empower the weak, transform personal character, and change the world.

The administrative state, the personal presidency, and new expectations for national action were profound developments, but they were not the only legacies of the Roosevelt era. Roosevelt's presidency brought with it a surge of social reforms notable for their vicious racial inspiration. His politics of virtue may have been well-intentioned, but it could be put to malignant uses. If the state could be a moral agent, it could also be an agent of immorality. New voting rights restrictions on black Americans followed the progressive tide in the South. Until the middle-1890s, the position of Southern African-Americans remained relatively strong. Their political and social position had, of course, deteriorated since the abandonment of Reconstruction, but black citizens remained an important, if distinctly a minority, voice in the region's politics. They remained an important element in the South's economy. During the Roosevelt presidency, however, racism rushed to new heights, pulled in large measures by the racial theories associated with many progressives, including Roosevelt, and their purifying impulses. Some prominent progressive reformers concluded that African-Americans were simply inferior and unsuited to self-government. "It is easy . . . to see," social gospel preacher Lyman Abbott wrote after a tour of the South, "that the men of that generation," the Civil War generation, "blundered egregiously, and brought upon the country, and especially the South, and upon most of the negro race, the tragic disaster of their blundering." Americans of African descent were not ready to participate in self-rule, and needed to be left to the "best whites" of the South to be more properly assimilated into the Teutonic American race. Meanwhile, new anti-immigration measures became commonplace in many American cities. Discrimination against Catholics, Jews, and other disfavored minority religious groups were all part and parcel of the progressive project. Religio-ethnic minorities of this ilk needed to be "Americanized" and taught the requisite racial virtues, the line went, while many progressives proved willing to leave African-Americans out of American society altogether. To nu-

tration's vigorous antitrust prosecutions. When Taft attempted to distance himself from Roosevelt by making changes in the cabinet, however, insurgents were horrified and whispered about an anti-progressive purge in the party. In December 1909, discontent over Taft's cabinet appointments mushroomed into a full-scale political disaster. The new president had unwisely promised Roosevelt—or appeared to have done so—that he would keep on the ex-chief's cabinet for sake of continuity. He soon reneged on this pledge and, among other replacements, installed Richard Ballinger as interior secretary in place of James Garfield. Chief Forrester Gifford Pinchot, keeper of Roosevelt's conservation legacy and something of an egoist, was livid, interpreting Taft's actions as a lack of commitment to the Roosevelt-Pinchot conservation agenda. The bungling Taft failed to persuade Pinchot otherwise. When Congress reconvened, Pinchot violated the legal gag order on federal employees and provided insurgent senator Jonathan Dolliver with information accusing the new interior secretary of fraud and mismanagement. He also leaked the allegations to the press. Faced with an act of rank insubordination, disloyalty, and violation of the law, Taft fired Pinchot in early 1910. Progressives howled and added another count to their lengthening indictment of the president. A congressional investigation eventually cleared both Ballinger and Taft of any wrongdoing, and even Pinchot privately admitted his actions had been less than upright, but the incident was politically damaging. Republicans seemed more interested in attacking one another than in governing the country. And Taft looked increasingly out of touch and incompetent.[6]

After winning four consecutive presidential elections and controlling Congress since 1894, the Republican Party was suffering from a bout of majority fatigue in 1910. Roosevelt as president had helped create a new political climate, but it was less clear that he had succeeded in fitting his party to prevail in the new circumstances. He had never managed to displace the old guard or convert them to his way. His warrior republicanism began as a variation on the stock Republican themes of economic nationalism and territorial expansion, but he had not been able to make it the dominant motif. And he had made other, tactical errors. In retrospect, despite a number of praiseworthy attributes and a commendable performance as secretary of war, Taft was probably a poor choice to succeed Roosevelt as leader of the Republican Party, let alone as president of the United States. Though Roosevelt cleared Taft's path to the nomination, the ex-president made a strangely lackluster effort to persuade progressives that the new party standard bearer could be trusted. The muckraking *American* claimed in 1908 that Taft's strongest supporters were the "great financiers," directly suggesting even then that Taft was the tool of business and the Republican old guard. Roosevelt never convinced the muckrakers, progressive cabinet members, or the congressional insurgents otherwise. The truth was, Roosevelt was selfish. He wanted to be needed. He wanted to remain the de facto leader of the party, the one on whom all factions relied. It would have required a politician of considerable talent to finesse the situation Roosevelt had left. Taft was not that man.[7]

Party strategists feared a bloodletting in the autumn midterm elections, punishment for the Republicans' public squabbles and lack of direction. Egged on by Pinchot and other disaffected progressives, Roosevelt plotted to seize the role he had been styling for himself for almost two years, ever since he fulfilled the promise he privately regretted of not seeking another term. With the party in need and the cause of reform stymied, the colonel would ride to the rescue. In August of 1910, he still planned to support Taft for renomination two years later. His strategy was to make himself the leader of the Republican insurgents and, that accomplished, to heal the party divide by endorsing Taft. Roosevelt would become the agent of unity, party peacemaker, savior of the Taft administration. If all went according to plan, Roosevelt would emerge again as the Republicans' indispensable man and perhaps a presidential candidate himself in 1916. The first step was to gain control of the insurgents. It was imperative, he told Henry Cabot Lodge, to keep them "out of the wrong kind of hands," and that meant he needed to reassert intellectual leadership of the progressive cause. Like a prophet returning to his people, Roosevelt returned to call the progressives and, via them, the nation, back to the path of righteous reform. False teachers had come in among them, men like Robert La Follette; disunity and division prevailed. Progressives needed now to be reminded of the nature of their faith. They needed to be recalled to the task at hand. Roosevelt would remind them. He would call them back. Yet though he came to teach an old gospel, what he called the message of Lincoln and the men of 1776, Roosevelt's sermon sounded somehow new. It was sterner, fiercer, less varnished than what he had said before. It was bolder, too, and more ambitious. This was no program of interstitial change Roosevelt had in mind. This was a call to social transformation.[8]

At the John Brown Memorial Park, thirty thousand spectators waited to see the former president. Some came on bicycles or by horseback, others on foot, their children in tow. They milled about in the late summer heat, scores of them wandering over to purchase sandwiches and drinks from vendors plying their wares in booths set up around the area. The scene might have been mistaken for a county fair. Roosevelt's party entered the park around two in the afternoon to thunderous applause. Event organizers had placed a picnic table on the speakers' platform to serve as a makeshift podium. At a quarter after two, introduced as a man "whose name is synonymous with liberty, justice and righteousness," the eyes of thirty thousand Kansans upon him, the future of his party again at stake, Roosevelt impulsively climbed atop the table to deliver the most famous oration in Kansas history.[9]

From the first sentence it was clear this address was only formally a tribute to John Brown. Roosevelt was going to preach. "We come here today to commemorate one of the epoch-making events of the long struggle for the rights of man—the long struggle for the uplift of humanity," Roosevelt began, chopping the air with his arms as he spoke, slicing it like a human blade with forceful, almost violent motions that reminded some observers of the evangelist Dwight L. Moody, whom Roosevelt had seen as a boy. The colonel was the one evangelizing now. America, he said, required a "New Nationalism, without which we cannot hope to deal with new problems." This was his message to the Republican Party and to the American public. This was his gospel. "The New Nationalism puts the national need before sectional or personal advantage," he went on. "It is impatient of the utter confusion that results from local legislatures attempting to treat national issues as local issues." It was still more impatient with a legalistic attachment to the federalist system, with "the impotence which springs from overdivision of governmental powers." The new nationalism understood the federal government must act to secure the public good. It recognized the need especially for a strong executive. "This New Nationalism regards the executive power as the steward of the public welfare." Further, "it demands of the judiciary that it shall be interested primarily in human welfare rather than in property"—that it shall stop thwarting progressive reforms, in other words; and then a swipe at the congressional leadership—"just as it demands that the representative body shall represent all the people rather than any one class or section of the people."[10]

Roosevelt's paean to nationalism was not new. He had struck these notes before, gently first in 1905 and then with increasing passion through the end of his presidency. The objective at that time had been to galvanize public opinion as a means to assembling a legislative majority. Now Roosevelt was trying to appeal to a movement, not a legislature, to lend guidance to the progressive insurgency by suggesting a political creed progressives might offer the public at large. That creed was nationalism, yes, but democracy also: democracy renewed and reinvigorated through nationalism. "Our country—this great Republic—means nothing unless it means the triumph of a real democracy," he said, "the triumph of popular government." Not only was national action the best way to regulate the market and restore moral order; national action and a powerful national government were means to achieving popular sovereignty. Hamiltonian measures could be leveraged for Jeffersonian ends. For Roosevelt, this democratic angle represented an extension of his earlier thought, a play on his equation of the people with the state and belief in the moral potential of government action. What was new was his self-conscious effort to connect nationalism directly with popular self-rule, to suggest that a sense of national community fostered by the national state somehow actualized the people's sovereignty. It was as if Roosevelt had been reading Jean-Jacques Rousseau.[11]

Actually, the connection may have been suggested to him by Herbert Croly, whose book *The Promise of American Life* Roosevelt read in the spring of 1910. The phrase "new nationalism" was in fact Croly's coinage. Croly lauded Roosevelt's record as president, praising him as an inspired reformer. But he especially admired the colonel's ideas, his attempts to use the state as a tool for moral uplift. With his preaching, Roosevelt had done far more good than he knew, Croly maintained, because he accomplished not only social amelioration but a promising new intellectual synthesis. "I will take the risk of asserting that Mr. Roosevelt's nationalism implies a democracy of individual and social improvement," he wrote, rather than the—to Croly—antiquated doctrine of democracy as individual liberty. Roosevelt's nationalism promoted democracy because democracy essentially meant government for the welfare of the people—government to help them reach their highest potentials and achieve collective self-mastery. Reading an interpretation of his own ideas may have helped Roosevelt clarify his thought and explore avenues for further development. Or it may simply have been that the political circumstances of the hour, the need to appeal to the populist-influenced insurgents, pressed him to extend his earlier conception of nationalism and popular sovereignty. Either way, the doctrine Roosevelt preached under the Kansas sun claimed national unity as the culminating stage and final achievement of democratic government. He didn't go quite so far as Croly to imply that government for the welfare of the people might be divorced or somehow distinct from rule by the people themselves. According to Croly's account, popular participation as a component of political liberty fell almost completely away. Roosevelt by contrast retained the republican emphasis on citizen participation in self-government. But he pictured that participation as synonymous with state action, popular sovereignty as simply state regulation in accordance with the people's will—or for their benefit—all on a national scale. Democracy in short meant the state behaved in obedience to the public will, and, in this way, the people ruled.[12]

So Roosevelt remained a republican, but a nationalist republican with a highly generalized, almost esoteric notion of popular rule. His unitary nationalism sounded more like the French revolutionaries and their intellectual sire, Jean-Jacques Rousseau, than like the English Whigs or American framers. Croly realized the intellectual debt and acknowledged in his opus the influence of the French theorists on his understanding of true democracy, though a brief meditation on the teachings of Rousseau would have proved even more illuminating. Rousseau bent the Whig idea that all legitimate government originated ultimately with the people and was administered for their good into an ontological claim. The people in fact possessed one common or general will, he said, and it was both the wellspring of the state and the ultimate source of man's humanity. The general will was not merely the will of all, however, which "looks to private interest and is only a sum of individual wills." It was not the total of individual interests or desires. The general will had a being all its own: "take away from those [individual] wills the pluses and minuses that cancel each other out, and the general will remains." Reaching beneath the clash of private self-interests, the general will embodied the common nature of humanity, the prerational, purely volitional will for freedom the individual possessed in his solitary condition before any state. Modern man could know this freedom again only through the body politic, Rousseau postulated, where the general will submerged individual desires and so reconstituted solitary liberty on a collective level. There was no strife in a state governed by the general will because there were no factions or differences of opinion. There was scarcely any need for deliberation. The political community was wholly unified, as unified as a presocial individual. No longer aware of any interests distinct from those of anyone else, members of this new political community lived without discord in calm, happy, unitary freedom.[13]

Roosevelt's new nationalism leaned heavily on this unitary notion of democratic community. Popular government advanced when the state acted to secure the common will of the public, the common welfare. "The object of government is the welfare of the people," Roosevelt told his audience. What Rousseau had contributed to liberal theory a century and a half earlier Roosevelt now picked up, the claim that the collective surrender of individual freedom actually broadened political liberty. Rousseau imagined the sovereign as the political community itself, as a collective of individuals. All individuals in the collective surrendered their freedom one to another, and so all ruled together as equals. Precisely because they were each subject to the collective, they were each free, so long as the collective or general will, and not the will of any one individual or group of individuals, was carried out. Roosevelt too forthrightly called for a surrender of "individualist" rights for the general good. To start with, he said, private fortunes, even if honestly earned, should be allowed only if they benefited the community as a whole. "It is not even enough that it should have been gained without doing damage to the community," he said. "We should permit it to be gained only so long as the gaining represents benefit to the community." He rec-

ognized that to implement this policy meant "more active governmental interference with social and economic conditions in this country than we have yet
had." But he believed government had to intervene more aggressively to promote the welfare of the whole. Only by so doing could it forward genuine
democracy. Roosevelt was taking his well-rehearsed, mugwump logic out to a
new, Rousseauesque horizon, casting national regulation as more than just a
market adjustment for the health of civil society; he cast it as an achievement of
popular freedom.[14]

As for what constituted the general will, Roosevelt thought he knew. The general will was the permanent political good, which was identical with the unfolding progress of evolution: the moral uplift of the citizenry. "Just in proportion as
the average man and woman are honest, capable of sound judgment and high
ideals, active in public affairs . . . just so far, and no farther, we may count our
civilization a success," Roosevelt said. In this sense at least, Croly was right.
Roosevelt did believe in democracy as something more than the protection of
individual liberties. He believed in democracy as a communal venture for
the improvement of the person and the race. Renewing American democracy—"genuine democracy"—meant for him fostering a spirit of national feeling, mutual sympathy among the citizenry, and the capacity to act effectively in
concert. "We must have," he preached, "a genuine and permanent moral awakening, without which no wisdom of legislation or administration really means
anything." That was not to say legislation was unnecessary. To his Kansas audience and to the country, he offered a slew of policy proposals to achieve popular
government and the moral awakening that sustained it.[15]

At the top of his list came taxes on inheritance and large incomes. He had
these in mind when admonishing his listeners that only private fortunes productive for the national community should be allowed to exist. A traditional republican concern for equality lurked here, reset to the tune of moral and social uplift.
Massive inheritances only separated citizens from one another, creating an artificial aristocracy of unearned wealth. Better to break that wealth apart, Roosevelt
believed, and distribute a portion to society at large, than to allow huge fortunes
to be perpetuated over time. He renewed his calls for federal oversight of corporations to replace the outmoded Sherman Antitrust law and proposed an extension of his earlier plans for corporate regulation by a federal administrative
agency. "It is my personal belief that the same kind and degree of control and supervision which should be exercised over public-service corporations should be
extended also to combinations which control the necessaries of life." He was
thinking specifically of the meat, oil, and coal industries. Public ownership was
not necessary. Roosevelt did not call for corporate socialism. But he did urge a

major expansion of national regulatory oversight, in the name of curbing special interests and promoting both sustainable economic growth and popular control.[16]

When it came to popular control, Roosevelt balanced the corporatist regulatory ideas that had earlier rankled insurgents with a strong endorsement of the direct primary and recall, insurgent favorites both. Really, corporate regulation and the recall and direct primary reforms were all of a piece, Roosevelt suggested. They all strengthened the average citizen's political influence in relation to the "monied interests." He gave another nod to insurgent sensibilities by calling for tariff revision—but then added a Roosevelt twist: tariff revision by nonpartisan commission. "Such a commission can find the real difference between cost of production, which is mainly the difference of labor cost here and abroad," he maintained. Take the tariff out of politics and give it to experts. As it happened, President Taft was already attempting this solution, and without much success. Taft had claimed authority under an obscure provision of the 1909 Payne-Aldrich tariff to establish a nonpartisan tariff commission of just the sort Roosevelt endorsed. True to form, Roosevelt ignored Taft's effort and put the idea to his own uses. An expert tariff commission appealed to progressives' faith in professional administration while cleverly clearing the deck of the tariff controversy. Roosevelt was careful not to call for the tariff to be lowered or raised, just removed from the political conversation.[17]

Instead of tariff reform, the colonel tried to direct progressives toward a national child-labor ban, workmen's compensation laws, an eight-hour workday, sanitation regulations, currency reform, and perhaps a minimum wage. He justified these measures, all but the last two holdovers from his presidential term, as steps to promote a more active, politically involved citizenry. "No man can be a good citizen unless he has a wage more than sufficient to cover the bare cost of living, and hours of labor short enough so that after his day's work is done he will have time and energy to bear his share in the management of the community." As usual, Roosevelt avoided arguments focused on economic growth or even economic fairness, though there were hints of the latter here and there. He concentrated on civic justifications. His economic mugwumpery was fully intact. But now he fused to it a concern for democratic participation. State action would help enable Americans to act collectively, to bear the burden of self-government.[18]

Roosevelt's new nationalism called for a reinvigorated progressive agenda of national regulation and administrative reform to advance popular government. While some of his phrases that afternoon in Osawatomie suggested an appreciation for democratic participation in local communities, Roosevelt was mainly interested in popular participation and democratic community on a *national* level. It was national unity he wanted, national fellow-feeling. "The betterment which we seek must be accomplished, I believe, mainly through the National Government," he said. This fixation on nationalism rendered the connection between state action and popular government somewhat opaque, despite Roosevelt's best efforts. Besides the direct primary and recall, to which he was a late convert, Roosevelt's proposals promoted popular sovereignty only by inference, and only when popular sovereignty was understood as the outworking of the common good, the esoteric yet supposedly identifiable general will. Not that the general welfare was a notion invented by Roosevelt, or Herbert Croly, or even Jean-Jacques Rousseau. The American founders and English Whigs and the classical Greek philosophers before them all spoke of the common good, arising from the permanent nature of humankind and humans' permanent interests, which included, for the Anglo-Americans, the right to govern oneself. Roosevelt's iteration arose by contrast from the person's improvability, his evolution toward moral perfection in community. The right to govern oneself, like rights generally, was a significantly more malleable concept for him. Popular government and social improvement could be elided.[19]

When Roosevelt finished his hour-and-a-half-long oration, Kansas governor Walter Stubbs leapt up on the table beside the former president and exclaimed, "My friends, we have just heard one of the greatest pronouncements for human welfare ever made." The praise was not uniform. The Eastern Republican establishment reacted to the speech with alarm. Henry Cabot Lodge and Elihu Root both wondered if Roosevelt appreciated the impression his remarks left—the Eastern press made it sound as if he wanted to nationalize practically everything. The conservative *New York Sun* warned voters that "the third greatest crisis in the history of the nation has arrived," calling the ex-president a "new Napoleon" who deemed it his mission to destroy free government "in the name of public opinion and . . . personal advancement." The *New York Tribune* labeled the speech "frankly socialist." Some historians have hailed the Osawatomie address similarly, "the most radical speech ever given by an ex-President," in the words of one biographer. Roosevelt's "concepts of the extent to which a powerful federal government could regulate and use private property in the interest of the whole . . . were nothing short of revolutionary," some have claimed—revolutionary in 1910 at least. But viewed in context, neither Roosevelt's proposals nor his logic was revolutionary. His demand that private property, specifically private fortunes, be used for the benefit of the public was really just his mugwump doctrine restated. Roosevelt was not questioning the legitimacy of private property, and he never would. He was insisting merely that corporate wealth—the source of those swollen fortunes—be regulated for the good of civil society. What lent the speech its radical ring was Roosevelt's new emphasis on popular democracy, on the will of the people. That populism, combined with his many abundant proposals for government regulation, sounded aggressive, especially from the lips of the hard-charging, publicity-seeking, praise-loving patron of executive power.[20]

Aggressive may have been just the impression Roosevelt wanted, however. His business in Osawatomie was to reclaim leadership of the Republican insurgents. For this project, the new nationalism represented a major step forward, both in the policies it advanced and the new amalgam of ideas it put forward. The *Kansas City Star* interpreted Roosevelt's effort best, saying it "marks the progress of the leading progressive." But not all progressives warmed to Roosevelt's evangelical nationalism. Roosevelt may have inaugurated the progressive moment on the national stage, but the assortment of reform impulses that fueled its momentum was susceptible to many interpretations, of which Roosevelt's was only one.[21]

When it came to progressivism, there was no single orthodoxy, only a series of political doctrines to be arranged and exposited by those who hoped to claim progressivism's mantle. While the colonel preached his new nationalism through the autumn of 1910, another would-be progressive leader tested a reform synthesis of his own, in New Jersey. He was a Democrat, and his aim was grand. Inspired partly by Roosevelt's example, he intended nothing less than to remake the Democratic Party, transforming it with new leaders and new ideas. Once freed from the shackles of Bryanism and the radical populists, he believed the Democrats would become "the ruling party of the country for the next generation," able to draw "all the liberal elements of the country" to themselves. Democrats had the opportunity, with the Republicans in disarray, to build a lasting progressive majority on a gospel different from Roosevelt's. He admired Roosevelt's progressive impulses; he admired the colonel's deft use of presidential power. But Roosevelt, Woodrow Wilson believed, had mistaken the true promise of progressivism. Wilson would correct the colonel's doctrine. Where Roosevelt sought to nationalize, the reformed Democrats would look to empower the competitive market economy. Where he trusted discretionary executive power, they would pursue reform by detailed, remedial legislation. In 1910 Wilson's version of progressivism was still in flux, but of one thing he was sure. If he could reform his party, curb its excesses and adapt its postwar priorities to the progressive mood, he could accomplish what "Mr. Roosevelt missed in his folly." He could unite the progressives under one banner—his banner—for good. Let Roosevelt preach. Wilson was going to give the country a message of his own.[22]

In one sense, Wilson had been an ardent reformer most of his adult life. By 1910, he had already been president for eight years—of Princeton University. There he proved to be a zealous advocate for change in the mold of Harvard's Charles Eliot, championing a curricular overhaul, departmental reorganization, new graduate schools, and a dramatically expanded faculty, among other things. He was only lately a political progressive, however, and he came to that stance on his own terms. A lifelong Democrat, Wilson was born in the South, in Staunton, Virginia, December 28, 1856, the third child of a Presbyterian minister. He earned a law degree from the University of Virginia and dabbled briefly in private practice before returning to the Johns Hopkins University in Baltimore, Maryland, to pursue a doctorate in political science. He loved politics and political history—William Gladstone was an early inspiration—and harbored a secret ambition to seek elected office. But he opted for academia as a start, hoping to make a contribution to his country's political life in the realm of ideas. He published eight books between 1884 and 1901, and another one in 1908, treating American politics. In them, he wrestled with America's constitutional system and came to several firm conclusions. He disliked the separation of powers, not unlike Theodore Roosevelt. He loathed congressional domination of the federal government, finding it inefficient and highly susceptible to special interests. He regarded the presidency, especially as the Roosevelt administration played out, as an enormously promising, if potentially dangerous, office. But Wilson was no nationalist. He looked favorably upon the states as central to the preservation of liberty. He forecast their continued relevance in the century ahead.[23]

The Princeton presidency offered Wilson a field in which to exercise his political ambitions, but academic politics did not ultimately satisfy him. In fact, by 1908, Princeton politics was frustrating him badly. With encouragement from a group of supportive journalist friends who believed Wilson had a political future, the professor began after 1908 to consider seriously a fresh turn in public life. When the Princeton board of trustees defied his wishes for the location of a graduate college and blocked his attempt to redesign the university's quadrangle layout, Wilson decided the time had come. He would seek the Democratic nomination for governor of New Jersey in 1910.[24]

He was new to elective politics but far from a political neophyte. In addition to his scholarly work, Wilson had been assembling a collection of practical political ideas for several years, working them into public speeches as president of Princeton. He was running in 1910 as a progressive, but a conservative progressive, critical of Theodore Roosevelt. President Roosevelt, Wilson charged, had replaced the rule of law with the reign of personal power. Wilson called Roosevelt's progressivism a recipe for arbitrary government, characterized as it was by executive discretion divorced from any constitutional limit. Wilson embraced much of Roosevelt's political analysis, which by 1910 had become progressive conventional wisdom. The professor agreed that large corporations presented a threat to a well-functioning democracy, and backed government action to check corporate influence. "Comparatively small groups of men in control of great corporations wield a power and control over the wealth and the business of the country which makes them seem rivals of the government itself," Wilson said. But he offered a prescription different from Roosevelt's. "Law must be strengthened and adapted to keep them in curb and to make them subservient to the general welfare." Law, not executive discretion, was the solution. The two signaled very different things to Wilson's way of thinking, two wholly different approaches to reform.[25]

Roosevelt offered the country an administrative state, vested with wide latitude to regulate the corporate economy and secure fairness, efficiency, and the people's interests. He rejected regulation by detailed statutes as unworkable and as part of the problem. The corporate economy changed too quickly, businessmen hatched new designs to evade the law too easily, for codified legal prohibitions to do much good. Moreover, the congressmen who wrote the laws were far too susceptible to corporate influence to be effective regulators. No, the way forward, according to Roosevelt, was an independent administrative bureaucracy free from electoral pressures and with the largest possible discretion to issue new regulations and punish recalcitrant corporate actors by fine or prosecution, as necessary.

Wilson was all in favor of economic regulation—in principle, at least—but not by executive fiat. Surrender the power to regulate to a set of independent commissions, and one surrendered the ability to govern oneself. Under Roosevelt's leadership, "we have in fact turned from legal regulation to executive regulation," Wilson warned. "It is that choice which as Democrats we challenge, and challenge with confidence, as opposed to every ancient principle of liberty and of just government." Discretionary executive power threatened democratic freedom. "The government of the United States," he pointed out, "was established to get rid of arbitrary, that is, discretionary executive power." Perhaps the growth of the great corporations did represent a new economic despotism, an oligarchic rule of the powerful few. But Wilson believed that Roosevelt's policies would simply substitute one despotism for another—unbridled presidential and administrative power for unmanaged corporate influence. In both cases, the victim was individual liberty.[26]

Creatively combining the Democrat's populist heritage and the limited government, states' rights strand of party tradition, Wilson accused Roosevelt of making the federal government a master of the people rather than their servant. Roosevelt, Wilson said, wanted a cabal of purported experts to set policy rather than the people's elected legislators. But whatever Roosevelt claimed about neutral, nonpolitical administration, administrators were not neutral; they were human beings, with preferences and political attachments like anyone else. Law was neutral. "Our battle cry must be, 'Back to the reign of law,'" Wilson believed. If there must be regulatory commissions, let them operate according to standardized procedures specifically set down by legislation. Give them uniform rules by which to reach decisions and above all, limit—not expand—their discretion. On Wilson's view, ceding political authority to administrative commissions diminished the people's agency rather than augmented it. Discretionary government regulation fostered a populace deferential to, and ultimately dependent upon, the national state. "We turn more and more with a sense of individual helplessness to the government, begging that it take care of us because we have forgotten how to take care of ourselves," Wilson thought. Better to remember the teachings of Thomas Jefferson and the American founders. "The familiar Jeffersonian maxim that that government is the best which governs least, translated into the terms of modern experience," Wilson concluded, "means that that government is best whose processes least expose the individual to arbitrary interference and the choices of governors." Protect the individual, that was Wilson's mantra. Make him secure in his rights and choices. At the foundation of Wilson's rhetoric was a rationale for reform starkly divergent from Roosevelt's, turning on a distinct conception of political freedom. Wilson urged his fellow Democrats to promote individual liberty rather than any preordained collective interests—or rather, he seemed to take individual choice as the signature interest of every citizen. "Law, and the government as umpire; not discretionary power, and the government as master," Wilson said. This was his program for progressive reform.[27]

The rhetoric was powerful, but the precise details of Wilson's program were, in 1910, far from clear. He blasted the Republicans for adopting a tariff policy that, by his lights, created the very business combinations and special interests that now menaced free government. But he made no specific proposals of his own for tariff reform. He sharply criticized Roosevelt for delegating too much authority to independent agencies but offered only additional criminal prosecutions of wayward companies as an alternative—an approach the Roosevelt administration had tried at some length, and found tedious, expensive, and marginally effective at best in changing corporate behavior. Wilson urged Congress to rewrite the antitrust laws, but, beyond a proposal to make corporate executives personally liable for company malfeasance, he offered few suggestions as to what statutory language would be more potent. Instead of offering new proposals, Wilson ran in 1910 on a platform of progressive staples: administrative reorganization, an eight-hour workday, employer liability laws, extension of the civil service. The details of his unique version of progressive reform were yet to come. But already the central themes were in place: law over executive discretion; government regulation for the advancement of individual liberty.[28]

Wilson's New Jersey campaign catapulted him into the ranks of Democratic presidential contenders. After four successive general election defeats, the Democrats were desperate for a fresh start. William Jennings Bryan, the party's nominee and pall bearer in three of those four electoral debacles, still commanded a considerable following among the rank and file. But his influence was on the wane. Meanwhile, the Roosevelt years in Washington helped stimulate a new generation of Democratic progressives in the South and East, heavily influenced by their party's old populist alliance with its Jacksonian overtones, but committed all the same to progressive reforms. These Democratic progressives supported corporate regulation, labor laws, and municipal reorganization. They also favored vigorous prosecution of the antitrust laws, a drastic downward revision of the protective tariff, and federal support for farmers. In the South, especially, they were stridently racist. Sweeping black disenfranchisement and segregation measures were perhaps the seminal Southern reform of the progressive era. Wilson boasted ties to the progressive Democrats in both South and East, and sympathized with most of their inclinations, including their racism. More importantly to his future in party leadership, his rhetoric offered a promising new combination of progressive themes and more traditional, postwar Democratic emphases. He linked concern for states' rights with the promotion of individual liberty; he called the tariff the mother of the trusts; he criticized Roosevelt's administrative state as detrimental to genuine reform. With his victory in New Jersey in November 1910, the Democrats had found a new voice. And the progressive ferment had produced a formidable challenge to Theodore Roosevelt.[29]

The election results were discouraging for the colonel. For the first time in eighteen years, the Democrats defeated Republicans for control of the House of Representatives, a stunning fifty-eight seat switch. Republicans retained control of the Senate, but not by much. Ten GOP senators lost their jobs in what amounted to a nationwide bloodletting. The year 1910 was a Republican catastrophe. Though he was not himself in office, Roosevelt had been deeply involved in the fall campaign, and he felt the loss acutely. His handpicked gubernatorial candidate went down to defeat in New York, along with most of the Republican congressional slate. Clearly voters were dissatisfied with the party's public feuding and were irritated by President Taft's apparent drift. But beneath the surface discontents, the McKinley-Roosevelt electoral alignment was weakening. The colonel's plan to unite the party had failed. Progressive insurgents and old guard leaders were as acrimoniously divided as ever, and each camp blamed the other for the electoral defeat. With his egotistical, self-aggrandizing maneuvers, Roosevelt had made himself part of the problem. Despite his supposed strategy to effect party reconciliation, he never managed to endorse Taft publicly. If anything, his western speaking tour and the speech at Osawatomie implied just the opposite intention. Roosevelt appeared to be reentering the lists as a political candidate, or as a critic of the White House at the very least. In 1910, the former president had spent months articulating a body of ideas about the role of government and the needs of society that he meant to direct not merely the course of the Republican Party, but the course of American political thought. He had staked out new intellectual territory for progressives, gestured toward a newly energized reform agenda. But few in the party leadership seemed inclined to follow, and certainly not Taft. As he nursed his wounds in the early months of 1911, Roosevelt decided Taft was not a genuine reformer. He was not a progressive. Roosevelt still believed it would be "a serious mistake" to challenge a sitting president for the nomination in 1912, but his doubts were wavering. A movement without a master-spirit was doomed to fail, a people without a prophet, doomed to perish. If he didn't lead, who would?[30]

11

BATTLE FOR THE LORD

Finally, by February Theodore Roosevelt threw off the cloak of retirement and girded to reenter the fray. On the twenty-first he gathered reporters for the most momentous announcement of his political life. "My hat is in the ring," he exclaimed. "[T]he fight is on." The colonel was going to challenge William Howard Taft, his once-loyal subordinate and chosen successor, for the Republican presidential nomination in 1912. He would bid to regain control of the Republican Party and, with it, the progressive moment. Roosevelt convinced himself that Taft had squandered the legacy he left. Taft's self-indulgent indecision and foolish alliance with the congressional leadership threatened the party's electoral future and, more importantly, the future of reform in America, Roosevelt decided. He would not—could not—stand idly by and watch the progressive movement career into disunity, extremism, faction and impotence. He could not allow men like Robert La Follette to assume command. Roosevelt was the master-spirit. Forgetting his own conclusions from the career of Oliver Cromwell about the importance of moderation and self-restraint and ignoring his own role in the travails of the Taft administration, his refusal ever to cede political leadership to his successor or to withdraw from the public eye, Roosevelt charged ahead. He was going to fight in 1912 from a combination of philosophical conviction and shocking personal hubris. He could not have known that the campaign would bring the most insightful, penetrating challenge to his politics ever voiced. He could not have known that his resurrection would mean his eclipse.[1]

However determined Roosevelt might be, however convinced he was of his critical importance, William Howard Taft was not about to stand aside and surrender the nomination. He had been profoundly hurt by Roosevelt's failure to rally to his side and over time came to believe the colonel was slightly unhinged.

"The truth is," he wrote ruefully to a friend, Roosevelt "believes in war and wishes to be a Napoleon and to die on the battle field. He has the spirit of the old berserkers." The congressional leadership and much of the party's Eastern establishment agreed. Roosevelt had become an extremist, they feared. His new nationalism sounded to them too much like state socialism, and they feared that his return to power might well destroy economic prosperity and private enterprise for a generation. Roosevelt, they believed, would allow no obstacle, no constitutional limit, to stand in his way. The party elite regarded the colonel's vitriolic hostility to the federal courts with particular anxiety. To the great consternation of Elihu Root, Henry Cabot Lodge, and other members of the Republican establishment, Roosevelt had voiced support as early as 1910 for popular review of judicial decisions. Now, in a series of incendiary speeches in the winter and spring of 1912, Roosevelt demanded that federal judges who "decide against the power of the people to do elementary justice" be made subject to popular recall. Taft, a once and future judge, was mortified and accused his political mentor of "putting the axe to the tree of well-ordered freedom." The man would topple the entire constitutional order in his bid to force through his agenda, Taft feared. He had to be stopped. Together, Taft and party leaders were going to do everything in their power to deny Roosevelt the nomination.[2]

In 1912, 362 delegates to the Republican national convention were elected by voters in party primaries. State bosses effectively controlled the remaining 706. Following Roosevelt's announcement, Taft swiftly set about securing delegates through the party machinery, employing almost precisely the tactics Roosevelt had used to guarantee his own nomination while president in 1904.[3]

The colonel, however, failed to see the parallel. He accused Taft of stealing the nomination. Trading on his personal popularity, Roosevelt won two hundred and seventy-eight delegates through the party primaries, more than three-quarters of the total available. But Taft, to no one's surprise, captured the vast majority of the seven hundred votes chosen in districts and state party conventions. In Roosevelt's judgment, Taft's actions were anything but legitimate. They proved that everyday voting Republicans wanted him as president, not Taft. Roosevelt did not have time to trifle. He refused to accept defeat. If Taft opposed him, Taft opposed progressivism and the cause of righteousness. "It has become clear beyond a shadow of a doubt that if I had not made the Progressive fight," Roosevelt thundered to a packed assembly on the national convention's penultimate evening, "it would have completely broken down," stymied by "the forces of reaction and political crookedness." The Republican Party had become a den of thieves, he decided, hopelessly sunk in materialism, bossism, and big business corruption. In February he had crossed a personal Rubicon by electing to challenge a sitting president from his own party. Now he burned the bridge behind him. If the Republicans would not have him as their nominee, he would not have them as his party.[4]

The break was momentous. He had been a Republican all his life, through victory and defeat, always opting to work within the party system. He had condemned the mugwumps for bolting the Republican fold in 1884 and for years scorned reformers who attempted to operate without the party machinery, calling them inefficient and utopian. His warrior republicanism emerged from decidedly Republican political commitments—nationalism and an active federal government and social melioration. His politics had been sustained by a Republican electoral coalition. But now, in a testament to his conviction or ambition—or both—Roosevelt reached a different conclusion: the Republicans were finished. They had ceased to be the party of progress and uplift. They refused to be the vehicle for reform. Roosevelt's ideas had finally overwhelmed the Blainite Republican establishment's tolerance for change. He had passed far beyond economic nationalism and industrial development. He favored state activism on a scale they found chilling and justified it with principles—social justice and economic equality—that they regarded as more than vaguely socialist. As Roosevelt saw it, this crusade was but the latest front in the "eternal war against wrong"; his break with the Republicans, the logical outworking of his career's progression. He had grown and changed as he went on in politics; his ideas had matured over time. The Republicans had not. The progressive era demanded a new party to take their place, one committed to genuine change, a party to advance Roosevelt's nationalism and politics of virtue. So he would go on without them. "[W]ith unflinching hearts and undimmed eyes," he told his progressive supporters as he bid the Republicans adieu, "we stand at Armageddon, and we battle for the Lord."[5]

On a humid night in Chicago two months later, the logic of Roosevelt's progressive politics came to fruition. He called it a confession of faith—an appropriate title, because the long, rambling speech brought together the ideas he had been articulating in public since 1905. What critics thought they spied just beneath the surface in Roosevelt's 1907 and 1908 annual messages, and in his speech at Osawatomie, the colonel now made explicit. He proposed a new venture in state-building on a scale hitherto unseen in American history, a reform agenda amounting to nothing short of a full-scale remodel of the American regime. Roosevelt wanted a social welfare state.

"[O]ur aim should be the same in both State and nation; that is, to use the government as an efficient agency for the practical betterment of social and economic conditions throughout the land," he said. For three decades or more, Americans had worried that the circumstances of the modern economy—if not modern life in toto—were undermining the social facts and mores necessary for free, republican government. Roosevelt had long championed the state as a remedial agent of moral reform, a tool to discipline the market and set its bounds. In Chicago he proposed to use the state to fashion a new republican political economy and a better, more just, more virtuous society. He proposed to use the state to advance genuine democracy, a government for the people's good, uniting them in common feeling, calling them to their highest potentials. He called for a politics of moral and social transformation.[6]

"As a people," Roosevelt preached, "we cannot afford to let any group of citizens or any individual citizen live or labor under conditions which are injurious to the common welfare." The industrial economy, unregulated, crushed the poor and laboring classes with wages so low and hours so long no honest worker could hope to advance. The social equality that produced democratic sympathy and fellow-feeling was virtually impossible under such conditions, as Roosevelt knew firsthand from his boyhood in New York. Not to mention that industrial workers maimed by the factories and the mines crippled economic productivity. "Industry, therefore," Roosevelt said, "must submit to such public regulation as will make it a means of life and health, not of death or inefficiency." The time had come for a national industrial commission with "complete power to regulate and control all the great industrial concerns engaged in interstate business —which practically means all of them in the country." Such a commission would have access to all corporate records. It would possess authority to make those records public for review. Additionally, the commission could approve or deny mergers between competitors—effectively preempting the antitrust laws —regulate working conditions, and perhaps fix prices in certain circumstances. The powers the Interstate Commerce Commission exercised over the railroad industry would be wielded by Roosevelt's national industrial commission over corporate business at large. To supplement this new regulatory agency, Roosevelt called again for a national ban on child labor and an end to all tenement labor.[7]

Regulating industry was not enough, however. The social consequences of industrial work had to be addressed and, wherever possible, meliorated. This was partly a matter of national efficiency, but more importantly it was a matter of moral righteousness. "The abnormal, ruthless, spendthrift industry of establishment tends to drag down all to the level of the least considerate," Roosevelt said. In these circumstances, against this economy of degradation, the state would intervene to advance social justice by creating a welfare infrastructure to protect the most vulnerable. Rather than regulate competition to protect the functions of civil society, per the original logic of the economic mugwumps, Roosevelt proposed to replace functions traditionally entrusted to civil society with national state action, in the name of the common welfare. He sought government old-age pensions and basic health insurance, unemployment assistance, the extension of workmen's compensation, and perhaps a nationwide tort insurance system to replace private legal suits between individuals. He renewed his support for federal aid to farmers. He called for a national minimum wage, what he called a living wage "high enough to make morality possible, to provide for education and recreation . . . and to permit reasonable saving." The logic sounded in democratic equality. This welfare infrastructure would allow industrial workers, rural farmers, and those without financial means the ability to participate on a roughly equal footing with other citizens in the democratic life of the nation. In 1905 Roosevelt had proposed to use the government to bring moral order to the industrial economy. Now he proposed to bring moral order to society, to make a better society and better citizens through state action.[8]

Roosevelt was in no mood to see his agenda stymied by unelected judges. His characteristic impatience with the Constitution's separation of powers burst into open contempt—and a plan for revision. "The people themselves must be the ultimate makers of their own Constitution," he instructed. Enough obstruction from federal courts. Their self-reverential antics and stubborn loyalty to "freedom of contract" jeopardized majority rule, Roosevelt concluded. If courts continued to block progressive legislation, checks and balances would mean nothing more than government by judiciary. When courts struck down new laws, they checked the political branches—the legislature and the executive. They checked the people's servants. But who checked the courts? "The courts have here grown to occupy a position unknown in any other country, a position of superiority over both the legislature and the Executive," he said. The colonel had a solution, which he meant as a means to break the separated-powers logjam and reinvigorate majority rule. Subject judicial decisions to popular referendum, he proposed, and judges to popular recall.[9]

When federal courts differed "in their interpretations of the Constitution the people themselves should be given the chance, after full and deliberate judgment," he said, "authoritatively to settle what interpretation it is that their representatives shall thereafter adopt as binding." In other words, Roosevelt proposed to curtail dramatically the power of judicial review. Decisions that conflicted with public opinion could be overturned by a sort of public referendum. Since judges "are chosen to serve the interests of the whole people, they should strive to find out what those interests are," Roosevelt had claimed while president in

1908, "and, so far as they conscientiously can, should strive to give effect to popular conviction when deliberately and duly expressed by the lawmaking body." But Roosevelt by 1912 was advancing more than a theory of statutory interpretation. Not only should judges interpret statutes according to the public meaning at the time of passage, Roosevelt maintained. They should construe the Constitution to permit statutes that gained widespread popular support. The Constitution, to put it plainly, should be interpreted in light of prevailing public opinion, and when that opinion was unclear, or when the judges read it wrongly, the people should be allowed to vote on the court's decision. Roosevelt effectively proposed a form of common-law constitutionalism, as in England, where no written charter bound the Parliament. The statutes adopted by a parliamentary majority were taken to be constitutional per se. The power to make law was effectively the power to alter the constitution. Later in the century, Canada would adopt a variation of this model, perhaps even closer to what Roosevelt had in mind: decisions by the Canadian high court could be overturned by a national plebiscite.[10]

Roosevelt thought that popular sovereignty meant rule by the people, which he interpreted in turn to mean majority rule in the public interest. No document, however venerable, should be allowed to block the people's will as expressed through their elected representatives. That this view was a radical departure—from both the very idea of a written Constitution designed to guide and limit majority rule, and the practice of judicial review as understood at least since John Marshall—seems not to have occurred to Roosevelt, or at least not to have bothered him. His goal was not to protect minority rights or to preserve the balance between branches of government. He was not interested in protecting federalism or the separation of powers. He was interested in abrogating them. His goal was to get progressive legislation, and to get the courts out of the way.[11]

Roosevelt's confession of faith was a ringing call for national reform on a grand scale, for moral and social regeneration through state management. He was on a crusade, and his fellow Progressive Party members—Bull Moosers—were crusaders too. Temperance advocates, social gospel believers, and urban reformers composed some of the more vocal segments of the new Progressive Party. They were lapsed Republicans, most of them, but they showed the fervor of new converts. Their Chicago convention looked and sounded like the nineteenth century revival meetings on the American frontier that pulsed with the voltage of biblical religion. The Chicago delegates sang hymns and made personal commitments to improve themselves and the world. But in place of biblical religion, they embraced social reform. To the delegates, never before had the prospect of a Christian society—an ethical, moral, altruistic commonwealth—seemed so real, so achievable. And indeed, the vision Roosevelt painted, the state-building he advocated, was as bold a project in social reformation as any tried since Thomas Cranmer and the English Protestants remade the Henrician state. Theodore Roosevelt preached to the country democratic collectivism. He championed freedom through communal action, popular rule, and moral uplift achieved by the intervention of the national state. His was the grandest confession of republican collectivism ever heard in the United States. But history is not the story of the inevitable. The day after Roosevelt delivered his vision, Woodrow Wilson accepted the Democratic nomination to challenge him for the presidency and for the future of American politics.[12]

The governor's vacation home at Sea Girt, New Jersey, was called a cottage but looked more like a small mansion. The house was two stories high with three third-story dormers, four chimneys, and a massive covered porch that spanned the entire front side. On the afternoon of August 7, 1912 — hot and hazy with a listless breeze — a photographer had managed to perch himself atop one side of the porch so as to capture for posterity the moment Governor Wilson became the Democratic presidential nominee. On the lawn below, a crowd of several hundred Democratic politicians and well-wishers milled about expectantly, the women wearing white dresses and the men clad in blazers, seersucker pants, and boat hats. "I hand you this formal letter of notification," Kentucky Democrat Ollie James began, as Governor Woodrow Wilson stepped out on the front porch. "I have the honor to request your acceptance." Wilson smiled, took the letter, and with an eager crowd looking on, launched into a pedantic and terrifically boring acceptance speech. "I read it with a cold chilly feeling of disappointment," Lillian Ward of New York's Henry Street Settlement House later recalled. "Mr. Roosevelt's 'Confession' is very exciting and made us feel as if the Social Reformers' Creed was about to become the religion of the politician," she said. But Wilson's speech was dry and stilted. The formal tone made more than a few readers suspect a political hedge. In fact, Wilson anything but hedged. He barraged his listeners with mind-numbing detail.[13]

He called for new antitrust legislation and tariff reform. He endorsed legislation to protect organized labor, promote vocational education, and conserve the country's physical resources. He criticized the so-called money trust combination of private bankers that controlled the flow of the nation's credit. The problem wasn't a lack of policy specificity. The problem was message. And it was one that had beset Wilson since his victory at the Democratic convention in June. The New Jersey governor had muscled his way to the nomination on the strength of his versatile intraparty appeal. He eschewed William Jennings Bryan's classist rhetoric and rejected the Great Commoner's positions on free silver and government ownership of railroads. But Wilson echoed many of Bryan's diagnoses of American ills, including especially the overweening power of the corporations. Wilson also had a relatively strong record of progressive reform in his brief months as governor of New Jersey, including workmen's compensation and public utilities legislation, though he remained cool to progressive enthusiasm for the referendum and recall. At once a Southerner and an Easterner, Wilson seemed likewise to be at once a conservative and a progressive. His elasticity and creative combination of Democratic positions brought him the nomination, but he had yet to find a way to meld his laundry list of policy ideas into an effective election message, as perhaps best symbolized by his oddly ambivalent take on the trusts. While he pressed for new antitrust legislation and excoriated the evils of monopoly, Wilson regarded monopolization with strange quiescence. "I dare say we shall never return to the old order of individual competition, and the order of business upon a great scale of cooperation is, up to a certain point, itself normal and inevitable." That was August 7. Three weeks later, he met Louis D. Brandeis.[14]

Brandeis, a Jewish, activist attorney destined in time for the U.S. Supreme Court, considered himself a Republican. He was in fact a founding member of the National Progressive Republican League and had advised Robert La Follette on antitrust policy. But La Follette was not running in 1912, and Brandeis did not relish his other options. Brandeis regarded Taft skeptically as an ersatz reformer uninterested in any fundamental change. As for Roosevelt, Brandeis believed the colonel's trust policy and indeed the whole of his regulatory approach were fundamentally misguided. In fact, Brandeis disputed the principal tenet of Roosevelt's economic program, which led him to develop one of his own. Corporate bigness, Brandeis argued, was not inevitable and it was not necessarily efficient. On the contrary, growth in corporate size often led to waste and inefficiency as corporate concerns became too large to manage. "[A] unit of business may be too large to be efficient as well as too small," Brandeis concluded. If the twentieth century was really the age of combination, as Roosevelt frequently said, why, Brandeis wondered, had so many combinations failed so miserably. The newspaper trust, the writing paper trust, the upper leather trust, the sole leather trust, the wool trust, the paper bag trust, the international merchant marine trust, the cordage trust, the mucilage trust, and the flour trust—all had collapsed. Of those that remained, most grew their market share only by purchasing competitors, not by outproducing them.[15]

Given their inefficiency, one might expect the market to destroy the trusts on its own. Unfortunately, on Brandeis's analysis, the trusts' mammoth size and market power allowed them to stifle competition by purchasing more efficient producers, driving them out with selective price wars, or leveraging a monopoly in one product line to gain market power in another—product "tying," it was called. Government had not helped matters. State laws allowed corporations to be treated as artificial legal "persons," limiting their liability, while courts extended them constitutional protections, including the right to contract. As a result, Brandeis concluded in language that sounded faintly mugwumpish, corporations had become a state within a state, an economic oligarchy so powerful the "ordinary social and industrial forces existing are insufficient to cope with it."[16]

The solution, however, was not to grow the size of government to manage the corporate economy. Ineffective government regulation was one reason unnatural, economically inefficient trusts persisted. Expanding the size of the national state would only re-create the problems of corporate bigness on a political axis. The state would become unwieldy, choked with too many independent commissions and agencies and administrators to be effectively directed by Congress or managed by the executive. Rather than growing government regulatory power, the better answer was to cut the corporations back by restoring market competition. Unregulated competition consumed itself, Brandeis thought. It allowed some concerns to grow so large they destroyed the entire competitive system. Government should intervene to prevent behavior that stifled competition—prevent price fixing and tying arrangements—not through discretionary regulatory commissions, but through specific written laws. Government should enable private competition to flourish. Competition, not regulation: that was the Brandeis message.[17]

He found a willing pupil in Woodrow Wilson. The attorney's emphasis on restoring market competition through carefully tailored legislation complemented Wilson's critique of the Roosevelt administrative state as arbitrary, unmanageable, and unbound by law. Brandeis's distrust of bigness as at once inefficient and potentially undemocratic played to Wilson's sympathy for the states and his concern for individual rights. Best of all, Brandeis's ideas allowed Wilson to seize the reformist high ground, to claim that he and not Roosevelt—to say nothing of Taft—was the true progressive in the race. "We believe that no methods of regulation ever have been or can be devised to remove the menace inherent in private monopoly and overweening commercial power," Brandeis instructed Wilson. Roosevelt purported to control monopoly, but really his platform endorsed it. The colonel's corporatist nationalism was nothing more than a permanent partnership between government and industry, the old Republican tariff alliance reborn and enlarged to encompass every interstate special interest in the nation. "The difference in the economic policy of the two parties is fundamental and irreconcilable. It is the difference between industrial liberty and industrial absolutism," Brandeis concluded. Here was a theme to organize Wilson's campaign, a thesis broad and fertile enough to sustain attacks on Roosevelt as a corporatist, an executive absolutist, a denizen of special interests, and a sham reformer. Wilson made it his own by making one potent addition. He linked competition and individual liberty. Roosevelt wanted management and moral regeneration. Wilson wanted freedom.[18]

Following his late August meeting with Brandeis, the New Jersey governor took his new message public with gusto. Though the race was nominally three-way, Wilson did not bother much with Taft. The colonel was his quarry. His freshly minted attack on Roosevelt proceeded along two paths. Wilson began with a full-throated call for social and industrial reform on almost every front named by Roosevelt, followed by a blistering condemnation of the Progressive platform—the "irregular Republicans," he called them—for failing to separate big business and government. Wilson's rhetorical offensive functioned splendidly as an electoral tactic, appealing at the same time to the populist, agrarian elements of the Bryan camp and to progressive insurgents who doubted Roosevelt's reform credentials. Wilson reminded the latter of Roosevelt's corporatist leanings and the colonel's apathy toward the antitrust laws. But the governor's rhetoric went further: the colonel, Wilson charged, was a paternalist. He wanted government to plan people's lives. With this language, Wilson was attacking more than Roosevelt's method of trust regulation. He was attacking Roosevelt's conception of politics. Wilson was condemning his opponent's distinctive republicanism.[19]

"A government is intended to serve the people that live under it," Wilson told a crowd of thousands in Williams Grove, Pennsylvania, the very day after he met with Louis Brandeis. "We are only just now beginning to learn how to take care of our people, to prevent accidents . . . to prevent unreasonable hours of labor, to prevent women from being overworked, to prevent young children from being worked at all." This litany of social reform aspirations matched Roosevelt's almost word for word. Wilson was going to concede nothing to the colonel when it came to reformist ideals. Nor did he hesitate to criticize corporations, or, as he tellingly referred to them, monopolies. "These monopolies are so many cars of juggernaut which are in our very sight being driven over men in such ways as to crush their life out of them." The nation's industrial economy cried out for reform and restructuring, and Wilson, like Roosevelt, maintained that the first step, "the immediate business, if you are to have any kind of reform at all, is to set your government free, is to break it away from partnerships and alliances."[20]

But that was where the similarities ended. Having established his and the colonel's agreement on the social questions of the day, Wilson turned to an indictment of Roosevelt's solutions. "Very well, then, what does this platform"—the "variegated Republican" platform—"propose to do?" Wilson brought Brandeis's logic damningly to bear. Roosevelt, he said, "proposes to legalize" the monopolies. The colonel's plan to regulate the trusts via a semi-independent government agency froze their size and influence in place, Wilson charged. "It says in effect: You can't break them up, the only thing you can do is to put them in the charge of the federal government." And then Wilson's really devastating conclusion: "That looks to me like the consummation of the partnership between monopoly and government. Because, when once the government regulates monopoly, then monopoly will have to see to it that it regulates the government." Roosevelt's plan would, if anything, deepen the hold of special interests over the conduct of the national state by inviting agency capture. Roosevelt seemed to imagine that making regulatory commissions independent and unelected would insulate regulators from the political process. But Wilson turned Roosevelt's critique of federal courts as unaccountable back on him. Independence from partisan politics and independence from business interests were two very different things, Wilson noted. In fact, the absence of direct accountability to voters and the relative obscurity of administrators' work might actually facilitate corporation efforts to bend regulators to their point of view. Not to mention the fact that regulation on the scale Roosevelt proposed—government oversight of all interstate businesses—would require a massive increase in the size of the administrative state. "After all this is done, who is to guarantee to us that the government is to be pitiful, that the government is to be righteous, that the government is to be just?" Wilson wondered. Once the government looked after business, who would look after the government?[21]

Wilson propounded an alternative progressivism. Don't regulate the monopolies or try to direct them. Regulate competition. Restore competition. "What has created these monopolies? Unregulated competition," Wilson said. "It has permitted these men to do anything that they chose to do to squeeze their rivals out. . . . We know the processes by which they have done these things. We can prevent those processes by remedial legislation." The nation needed new, specific, remedial antitrust laws to restrict the wrong use of competition and enable the right use to destroy monopoly. There would be no need for the government to go about setting up moral standards or trying to enforce right behavior among monopolists if it would simply allow the market to work. A well-functioning market would provide all the check on monopoly needed. Wilson's proposals aimed to reinvigorate market competition without significant government oversight. Of itself, this intellectual synthesis was creative enough. Wilson wedded populist aspirations to a laissez-faire confidence in the market that managed to unite states' rights Democrats and progressive ones. But focusing on this nexus alone could make Wilson sound more conservative than he really was. The truly unique component of Wilson's thought and the most consequential feature of his progressivism was his emphasis on liberty. For him, market competition was a symbol of individual autonomy, a synonym for personal independence. "[O]urs is a program of liberty," he said, "and theirs is a program of regulation."[22]

Liberty was a word Wilson relished. To understand what he meant by it was to understand his politics. Wilson had been raised a Presbyterian although, contrary to some biographers, hardly a strict Calvinist. His minister-father counted himself a liberal, a believer in humans' altruism and capacity for self-improvement rather than in the gloomy dogma of original sin. The adult Wilson spoke frequently of "fallen human nature" but seemed to take the phrase figuratively, as a metaphor for individuals' inclination to be shortsighted and selfish. Importantly, he believed these limiting traits might be overcome by a determined effort to fight evil—that is, an effort to realize one's inner moral potential and improve one's social environment. He believed that individuals could be agents of progress, both for themselves and for the world around them. Though Wilson, like so many of his contemporaries, set aside the orthodoxy of his forebears, American Calvinism's emphasis on the individual left a lasting impress. He regarded the individual person as the primary moral agent in the cosmos, ahead in significance to society or the family or any other grouping. His historical studies as a young man buttressed this view. He read history as the story of great individuals, of Alexanders, Washingtons, and Abraham Lincolns, men of uncommon ability who rose through their talent and determined self-effort to set the fate of humankind. The moral was simple. It was the individual who accounted for the progress of the human race, the individual's faculty for moral betterment that supplied the dynamic of history.[23]

Therefore, "the hope of society," he wrote in 1898, "lies in an infinite individual variety, in the freest possible play of individual forces." Like Roosevelt, Wilson believed in evolution, an evolution of moral improvement driven by the individual's struggle to climb to his highest potential. But in contrast to the colonel, Wilson laid little emphasis on the realization of a collective identity as the end of evolution. Instead, he retained earlier Whig theorists' interpretation of government and civil society as the products of a contract between free individuals. "What is society?" Wilson asked. "It is an organic association of individuals for mutual aid." Wilson was no traditional Whig, however. Unlike John Locke or Edmund Burke or the American framers, he posited a social contract unconnected to natural rights. Natural rights implied a constant human nature or, at the very minimum, an irreducible human identity common to all humans as humans across time and culture. For Wilson, that was too much. He doubted there was such a thing as "human nature" free-floating outside historical experience any more than there was a set of moral absolutes somehow inscribed on the cosmos. Humans lived in time and space. They were historical creatures whose social experience and moral ideas varied from age to age, place to place. Humans did not necessarily share a particular identity or set of moral commitments. According to Wilson, what humans shared was the capacity for self-development. Society was an association for mutual aid. "Mutual aid to what? To self-development."[24]

Freedom in his view meant the ability to develop oneself and choose one's own ends. This was Wilson's version of the social contract. Individuals formed governments so they might be able to pursue their interests in peace and develop them as they saw fit, without the threat of coercion or physical violence. Bound together in a peaceful society of ordered liberty, parties to the compact realized the benefits of one another's initiatives. What a man did for himself would help others by fostering progress, in which all partook as members of the contractual community. Of course, a people's interests and aims would change over time. A just contract would not bind so strictly as to prevent political change and adjustment to match the people's needs. "Political liberty," Wilson believed, "consists in the best practicable adjustment between the power of the government and the privilege of the individual." Put another way, liberty did not mean one thing for all time. It had no single institutional form or substance. Rather, free government was an inherently circumstantial arrangement, totally dependent on the historical character of the people and their aspirations. "If any one asks me what a free government is," Wilson said, appropriating Burke, "I reply, it is what the people think so."[25]

Wilson propounded a theoretically pragmatic politics in keeping with his underlying intellectual pragmatism. Liberty had no universal meaning for him because human nature had no permanent form. Political freedom was a product of human development. Like William James, John Dewey, Oliver Wendell Holmes, and other leading pragmatists of his day, Wilson's attention to individual choice and humans' historical consciousness shaded into a form of moral antirealism. He suspected a priori arguments made from first principles, especially in morals and politics. To Wilson's way of thinking, the fact that human social needs and moral preferences shifted over time powerfully undermined the notion of moral absolutes. It wasn't that he didn't believe in right and wrong. It was just that he interpreted ethical imperatives as social conventions, the products of social development and humans' evolving capacity for altruism. The language of absolutes unsettled him insofar as it obscured the human element in the creation of moral conventions and potentially stifled further individual development. Wilson's pragmatic case for democracy followed from these premises. In the scheme of things, democratic government was best because democracy gave freest rein to individuals' energies. It was a modest form of government, one that could operate without religious consensus or universal agreement on moral standards. Democracy, for Wilson, was government without metaphysics, government that prized the individual and allowed him to pursue his own ends.[26]

But even democracy had its dangers. If individual rights were not vigilantly protected, democracy could degenerate into coercive majority rule and a watery moral absolutism. "I believe that the principal menace of a democracy is that the disciplinary power of the common thought should overwhelm the individual instinct of man's originative power," Wilson said. The danger in a democratic state was that government might suppress individual energy and coerce individual choice in the name of a collective good. Wilson wanted none of that. "We know that the history of politics has been the history of liberty," he maintained, "a history of the enlargement of the sphere of independent individual action." Liberty required constant, periodic adjustments to keep the appropriate balance, to provide security for the whole and an open field of action for the individual. In Wilson's view, the American state was due for just such an adjustment.[27]

The problem with Roosevelt was that he wanted to adjust in exactly the wrong direction. Corporate power had swelled so large that the individual was dwarfed and his agency threatened. But Roosevelt's nationalist program augmented the power of government at the expense of the individual—it further stifled individual energies by growing the state out of all proportion to private actors. Worse, the Roosevelt state purported to achieve individuals' development for them, to reform citizens even as it reformed the industrial economy. It sought to impose on them a set of predetermined, officially sanctioned ethical rules and standards of behavior. "The modern nation," Roosevelt-apostle Herbert Croly wrote in 1910, "really teaches men what they must feel, what they must think, and what they must do, in order that they may live together amicably and profitably." That was a fair if rhapsodic summary of Roosevelt's formative ambition, his politics of "soulcraft." The whole project struck Wilson as disastrously, illiberally, paternalistically unrealistic.[28]

Wilson doubted that government was competent to carry out moral regeneration, because he denied the right of government to say what moral regeneration meant. How could any one man or group of men claim to know what was best for the whole nation? Who was fit to say that his moral preferences were eternally valid? Moral duties changed over time, Wilson believed, in keeping with pragmatic inclinations; they were hardly immutable laws. The attempt to transform society according to some theoretical ideal, according to one particular iteration of society's historical consciousness, was a fool's errand—and an arrogant one. It implied greater knowledge than humans could have, and it stalled further moral and social progress. Moral order grew from the choices of individuals pursuing their interests. It was a voluntary and organic, bottom-up affair, not top-down. It was not something government could create, and government, Wilson said, had no business trying. "A little group sitting every day in Washington City is not going to have a vision of your lives as a whole," Wilson told his listeners. "You alone know what your lives are like."[29]

The Progressive Party's government-by-independent-agency program was arbitrary and undemocratic because it was philosophically haughty. It suggested that government knew best, that the people needed minders to tell them how to behave and experts to manage industrial affairs for them. But no matter how complex the conditions of national life became, Wilson admonished, "the only way the United States is ever going to be taken care of is by having the voices of all the men in it constantly clamorous for recognition of what justice is as they see the light." Not only were discretionary regulatory commissions liable to agency capture, not only were they too big to manage or maintain. No group of regulators knew better than the American people what the people needed. The notion that popular rule was somehow advanced by regulations made in the interests of the people, but not by the people themselves, was preposterous. And dangerous. "The minute you are taken care of by the government you are wards, not independent men," Wilson warned, and this was true of one's personal, no less than economic, life. "We do not want big-brother government," he thundered. "I do not want a government that will take care of me. I want a government that will make other men take their hands off so I can take care of myself."[30]

Wilson's philosophical pragmatism became a defense of a particular kind of democratic liberty. In the final analysis, liberty was for him a condition, not a practice. Liberty was freedom from external restraint, freedom from undue coercion by other individuals or the state. "[N]o government has ever been beneficent when the attitude of government was that it was taking care of the people," Wilson taught. A government that attempted to impose a moral order was a government that coerced its people. "Freedom consists in the people taking care of government . . . we live our own lives, we know our own lives, it is our own lives that concern us, and we will tell government what we intend."[31]

Stung by Wilson's charges of paternalism, Roosevelt countered that Wilson's anti-establishment talk revealed an outdated philosophy of limited government inimical to progressive aspirations. Roosevelt made much of the New Jersey governor's comment in mid-September that "the history of liberty is a history of the limitation of governmental power, not the increase of it." That "outworn academic doctrine," Roosevelt hammered back, was "the key to Mr. Wilson's position." The former professor believed in a Jeffersonian state, a do-nothing state, Roosevelt said, one that could never find the strength to meet the challenges of the industrial age or unite the American race.[32]

Roosevelt suspected that Wilson, with all his individualist talk, was at base an epicurean materialist who understood neither the circumstances of the industrial age nor America's unique moment in history. "The Democratic platform," he claimed in an argument that formed the crux of his counterattack, "is purely retrogressive and reactionary. There is no progress in it." Wilson's plan to break up the trusts through a reinvigorated, government-monitored market struck Roosevelt as foolishly naïve, and he condemned Wilson's proposals in much the same cadence he had used to blast William Jennings Bryan in 1896.[33]

Wilson's program "represents an effort to go back," he contended, "to put this nation of a hundred million, existing under modern conditions, back to where it was as a nation of twenty-five million in the days of stage coach and canal-boat." But those days were gone forever. The concentration of modern business was "both inevitable and necessary for National and international business efficiency. Does Mr. Wilson deny this?" Wilson's bid to empower anew the competitive market, and his underlying vision of independent producers competing against one another on equal terms, struck Roosevelt as a typical response from the party of Bryan. The orator from the plains never reconciled himself to modernity, Roosevelt thought, and Wilson had not, either.[34]

"In economic terms," Roosevelt wrote a few months after the election, with the issues still fresh in his mind, "the course [Wilson] advocates as part of the 'New Freedom' simply means the old, old 'freedom' of leaving the individual strong man at liberty . . . to prey on the weak and the helpless." Roosevelt equated Wilson's individualism with the individualism of the frontier as he defined it in his histories: solitary action indifferent to its effects on others, the sort of thing that was no longer feasible in an age of combination. If the "plain people" did not unite through the national government and assert their sovereignty over corporations—mega-individuals—those corporations would dominate and destroy the freedom of the plain people. If American citizens did not create with their government a political economy of virtue, moral chaos would ensue, and the race would not progress. Wilson failed to grasp these truths, and he compounded his error by preaching individual self-development as the highest aim of politics. "I profoundly disagree with what seems to be the morality" of Wilson's campaign statements, Roosevelt protested. The governor's consistent appeals to individualism horrified Roosevelt, who identified individual interests held against the greater good of the race as the bane of early twentieth century politics. "Surely it is not necessary," Roosevelt complained, to make a case for progressive reform by "preach[ing] a morality of so basely material a character."[35]

Roosevelt would never tell individuals to do as they pleased — to follow their own interests. He told them to do what was right, what was just, what was required, as his father had told him. He believed that personal development came by striving for a standard of righteousness. All of his life had been about that striving. It was no surprise his politics should have been as well. Wilson's talk of releasing individual energies was foreign to Roosevelt. He wanted to reform individual energies, to control them, direct them, transform them into something higher and worthy. To him, that transformation was the business of politics. Roosevelt's political science was premised on a moral and anthropological teleology starkly at odds with Wilson's more pragmatic intellectual sympathies. Roosevelt's politics were based on the conviction that the people realized their nature and found their agency by living in accord with the enduring moral order of the universe. Put another way, the race progressed by living up to its potential. For Roosevelt, the political corollary was obvious. Unless selfish materialism was driven from politics there could be no progress. Statecraft would degenerate into a welter of competing interest groups clamoring for their own personal projects. Government would end up dealing with Americans based on their class, or ethnic background, or socioeconomic status. "What we Progressives are trying to do," Roosevelt said by way of contrast, "is to enroll rich and poor, whatever their social and industrial position, to stand together for . . . those elementary rights which are the foundation of good citizenship." What Roosevelt was trying to do was unite the nation in a common enterprise of social and moral uplift.[36]

There was a good deal of truth to Roosevelt's interpretation of his opponent's political morality with its faintly epicurean flavor, but his fulminations against Wilson's supposedly retrograde view of federal power fell wide of the mark. Wilson was as much a partisan of positive government as Roosevelt if not quite, at this stage in his career, such an avid nationalist. Nevertheless, Wilson believed the equilibrium of liberty required constant adjustments that the American constitutional system too often prevented. Changing social and economic circumstances demanded policy and perhaps institutional changes to match, in order to facilitate the freest play of individual energies. Or, to put it another way, as individual needs and interests shifted, the needs of the state shifted too. At base, Wilson's conception of open-textured individualism realized and expressed through personal self-development chafed at the limits of constitutional government because it ran at odds with the framers' goal to protect permanent natural rights. Wilson wanted political flexibility and room for growth. The constitutional structure on the other hand limited majority rule and made institutional change difficult. Wilson wanted speed. The constitutional order was slow, deliberate, designed to conserve timeless rights and blunt the effects of human selfishness. In the name of individual liberty, Wilson wanted to rearrange the whole thing.[37]

"The checks and balances which once obtained are no longer effective," Wilson had concluded as a young professor. It was a view he never abandoned. "As at present constituted, the federal government lacks strength because its powers are divided, lacks promptness because its authorities are multiplied, lacks wieldliness because its processes are roundabout, lacks efficiency because its responsibility is indistinct and its action without competent direction." In designing the national government, Wilson believed that the American framers had attempted inexpertly to translate the British parliamentary model to the circumstances of the new world, trying to re-create its triple equipoise of crown, lords, and commons. While Wilson supposed these divisions had appeared to the Constitution's makers as a separation of executive and legislative powers, no doubt thanks to the influence of Baron de Montesquieu, Wilson thought the divisions were in fact merely momentary features of a fluid constitutional system evolving toward the more perfect condition of cabinet government familiar to Wilson in his own day. Like Roosevelt, Wilson admired the British system as he understood it because he believed that it facilitated rather than constrained majority rule. Or, more to the point, the British system facilitated rule by the prime minister. Prime ministerial administration was in effect a sophisticated form of executive government, and Wilson loved its efficiency. The House of Commons, Parliament's dominant branch, was not a law-writing body. Laws were drafted by the cabinet, at the behest of the prime minister. Parliament was instead a law-ratifying institution dominated by the majority party and generally pliant to the cabinet's wishes. Of course cabinets and premiers could be defeated in Parliament and turned out of office. But when in power, they were formidable. No written constitution stood in the way, no parchment barriers blocked them. Cabinet government was swift, flexible, responsive to public opinion, and potent. The cumbersome American system, by contrast, in which Congress wrote the laws, another branch administered them, and yet a third passed on their legitimacy, made coherent social and economic policy difficult to achieve. It made adjustments in the balance of liberty difficult to implement.[38]

For a man who professed to disdain arbitrary executive power, Wilson harbored an almost mystical fascination with great leaders. All individuals contributed to human progress by virtue of their struggle for self-realization, he thought, but gifted men contributed most of all. According to him, the surest way to reform the American constitutional order was to make space for great men. Not surprisingly, Wilson turned to the presidency. He was inspired in part by Theodore Roosevelt. Wilson's academic studies in American political history over the course of the 1890s and the experience of Roosevelt's administration the following decade convinced him the executive office held enormous potential for transformative leadership. Men like Washington, Jackson, Lincoln, and, yes, Roosevelt refashioned the political worlds of their day. Their office allowed them to dominate the legislative agenda, to command the military, to speak directly to the people. The powers afforded the president under Article II were almost kingly, if the president could learn to use them. "The President is at liberty, both in law and conscience, to be as big a man as he can be," Wilson concluded. "His capacity will set the limit; and if Congress be overborne by him, it will be no fault of the makers of the Constitution." The Constitution gave Congress ample powers to offset the president's own. The question, then, was which branch would more effectively marshal the prerogatives at its disposal. In search of a way to overcome the strictures of the constitutional order, Wilson hoped to use the president's institutional endowments to bridge the separation of powers. He sought to translate the office's opinion-making potential into groundswells of public sentiment for specific legislative proposals so strong that Congress could not resist. Using the tools of popular presidential rhetoric developed by Roosevelt himself, Wilson wanted to make the president a party leader on the order of a prime minister. Congress might continue nominally to write the laws, but the president would propose them and largely shape their content. He would shepherd their passage through the legislative chamber via close consultation with congressional leaders. And he would rally the people to keep his party in power and in lockstep under his authority.[39]

Wilson's means for realizing the positivist government he wanted reflected the lessons Wilson learned from Roosevelt's own legislative strategy. But the two men's conceptions of leadership diverged in a way that mirrored and reinforced their different philosophies of politics. Roosevelt conceived the president as the steward of the public welfare, the common servant of all the people who recalled the populace to its common interests. The president was, most essentially, an ethical inspirator and educator preaching a moral standard of conduct and championing the heroic virtues. "I tried my best to lead the people, to advise them, to tell them what I thought was right," Roosevelt said to the Progressive Party convention in Chicago. But "if necessary, I never hesitated to tell them what I thought they ought to hear, even though I thought it would be unpleasant for them to hear it." For Roosevelt, the task of the movement leader was to guide the people, with wisdom and restraint, in order to help them perceive their true interests.[40]

Wilson by contrast taught that "the processes of liberty are that if I am your leader, you should talk to me," not vice versa. "I must listen to the cry of those who are just coming into the lists. I must be very still and hear . . . the next approaching generation." The leader listened to the whispers and wants of the people. He heard their interests and knew their needs. He gave special attention to the quieter among the public, the young, the downtrodden, and the oppressed, and dedicated himself to representing their desires. In sum, the president allowed the people to direct him, and in their voices and opinions discerned a mandate for his leadership. Where Roosevelt found direction in the overarching interests of the nation—in a conception of the common good—Wilson looked to the immediate interests of individuals as they defined them. His approach was inductive. "When you ask which party you are going to support," Wilson told crowds in Buffalo, New York, "you are asking this fundamental question, 'By which means and by which choice can we best serve ourselves?'"[41]

Wilson recognized no common good after the manner of Roosevelt. To the colonel's collectivist, Rousseauesque interpretation of the general will, Wilson opposed a more Lockean variant that eschewed Roosevelt's commitment to moral teleology and character formation. John Locke held that independent individuals chose to form a polity in order to secure certain basic goods, and one above all: self-preservation. The state's mandate was limited to protecting the individual and the schedule of more or less permanent rights derived from his need to survive. Wilson, similarly, viewed the common good as a contractual matter. He saw no reason to speculate, in the vein of Roosevelt, about the principles of righteousness or the perfection of mankind. He certainly did not believe the president should force his own preferences on the nation. The common good was not a matter of metaphysics. Rather, the common good was what individuals had contracted for when they joined civil society—or, put another way, what they would have contracted for had they been given the chance. Following Locke, Wilson believed individuals entered the polity to protect their interests. The general will, then, was nothing more than individual interests in aggregate.[42]

Like Locke, Wilson lowered the aim of democratic politics. He left the quest for personal reformation and moral growth to one side and made individual desires the centerpiece of his politics. But Wilson departed from his intellectual forebear in one very important respect. While Locke saw self-preservation as the person's primary want, Wilson made a substitute. He defined citizens' greatest interest as self-development. Thus his concept of interests, like his concept of individualism generally, proved to be far more open-ended than Locke's and, for that reason, far more hospitable to an activist state and an activist leader. Locke used the person's need for self-preservation to elaborate a series of what he called natural rights, including the rights to life, liberty, and property, all of them founded on the need to survive. He limited the state by allowing it only to protect those rights. Wilson's notion of self-development was susceptible to no such elaboration. It couldn't be expressed in a set of permanent rights. In fact, in Wilson's theory, the nature of rights and the meaning of liberty shifted. They evolved as individuals developed. And the state evolved with them. Unlike Locke, Wilson's thought placed no internal bounds on the growth of state power, so long as that power was directed toward securing the common good defined as individual liberty, individual choice.

Given this interpretation of the social contract, it is no surprise Wilson placed greater emphasis on executive leadership than did Locke or the American founders or almost any of his liberal predecessors. For that matter, he emphasized it even more than Roosevelt. The colonel conceived of leadership as instruction and inspiration, but in his political thought the common good was the main thing. By contrast, leadership was the essence of Wilson's politics. To him democratic liberty consisted of the proper adjustment between the state and the individual. Wilson pictured this adjustment as a fundamentally executive task, based on an interpretation of individual needs. Leadership was, for him, a craft of interpretation. By virtue of his status as the only nationally elected public officer, the president was uniquely placed to understand the people's interests and embody them in policy. He alone was accountable to all the people. He alone could speak on behalf of the whole nation. By interpreting the people's wants and giving them voice and form, the president created a common political agenda—a common politics to unite the nation. He created national unity in his person.[43]

Ultimately, Wilson did not so much abandon Roosevelt's quest for community as transpose it, locating its source in the executive. Given its glorification of the president as national interpreter and emblem, Wilson's idea of democratic leadership had as much potential to be "paternalistic" as Roosevelt's did. His version of the social contract, stripped of the limits of natural rights and tuned instead to open-ended self-development, could sound more like Thomas Hobbes than John Locke, more like a cult of the leader than limited government. Still, Wilson managed to turn his theory to devastating effect on his opponent. A president "must listen to the voices the politician does not hear," Wilson counseled. And then, in a direct slap at Roosevelt, he said, "I must listen to the voices which the self-appointed savior cannot hear." Roosevelt wanted to tell Americans how to live their lives. But "we won't take the dictum of a leader who thinks he knows exactly what should be done for everybody," Wilson declared. "I don't care how benevolent the master is going to be. I will not live under a master." Wilson would not have a politics focused on forming citizens' characters. He would have no paternalistic, government-corporate partnership to manage industrialism's inequalities. Roosevelt wanted to regulate the economy and transform citizens' souls. The Democrat wanted to restore competition and set individuals free to find their own way.[44]

A partisan of positive government or no, Roosevelt was right that Wilson did not advocate a social welfare state. As the campaign wore on, the colonel made every effort to turn Wilson's reluctance against him. "He is against the minimum wage," Roosevelt trumpeted, just as Wilson was against a national ban on child labor, on grounds that legislation under the general commerce clause power would grow the authority of the federal government too much. "His principles," Roosevelt charged, "would prevent us either effectually helping labor or effectually regulating and controlling big business." In contrast, the Progressives knew no such reticence. "We propose to use the whole power of the government to protect all those who, under Mr. Wilson's laissez-faire system, are trodden down in the ferocious, scrambling rush of an unregulated and purely individualistic industrialism." Roosevelt correctly identified a laissez-faire flavor to Wilson's rhetoric, but what he did not see was that Wilson's principles were far from intrinsically libertarian. Wilson balked at the expansion of the federal government because he feared it would stifle individual liberty. But should it turn out that individuals needed a certain minimum standard of personal welfare to develop their potentials and choose their own ends—freedom from fear, freedom from sickness, freedom from want, say—then Wilson's open-textured individualism could justify a social welfare state as easily as it condemned one. His essentially negative conception of liberty could be put to surprisingly positive ends. His individualism perhaps even required positive guarantees from government to remain viable in the modern world.[45]

Whether he intended to or not, Wilson in 1912 was elaborating an alternative, distinctly liberal rationale for activist government, in contrast to Roosevelt's republican, nationalist version. A Wilsonian state intervened to protect individuals' interests, not to promote a moral standard. It sought to expand the number of voices and viewpoints at government's table, not to call on all Americans to realize a common good. Individuals, in Wilson's system, did not require the nation as a source of transcendent meaning. They did not need the glory of triumph to find purpose for their lives. The person's ability to develop himself was the source of his meaning, his ability to select his own life ends the source of his value. Liberty, for Wilson, consisted ultimately of the capacity to choose, as unfettered and unhindered as possible by outside forces. A truly free government, a Wilsonian government, would protect first and foremost the person's ability to choose his way. "[T]he individual must be assured the best means, the best and fullest opportunities, for complete self-development," Wilson believed.[46]

But if individual development was the highest priority and the release of individual energies the greatest good, then surely government should intervene to guarantee every individual the ability to develop himself to the fullest extent possible. Some individuals were stronger than others, after all, better able to realize their interests than their fellows. Similarly, some individuals were more influential and capable of making their voices heard above the political din than their poorer, less educated counterparts. If both sets of citizens were to have their chance at self-development, the disadvantaged would need help from the state. Already in the autumn of 1912 Wilson's rhetoric carried a noticeably egalitarian tone. "I tell you ladies and gentlemen, the men I am interested in are the men who never have their voices heard, who never get a line in the newspapers, who never get a moment on the platform, who never have access to the ears of governors or of anybody who is responsible for the conduct of government." Those were the Americans Wilson said he wanted to help. And though he hesitated out of respect for the Constitution at the more ambitious elements of Roosevelt's social reform plan, Wilson wasn't worried about the constitutional text, for which he had little regard. "[T]he Constitution of the United States is not a mere lawyers' document," he believed. "[I]t is a vehicle of life, and its spirit is always the spirit of the age." Wilson was talking about constitutional custom. He was saying, in effect, the time for the growth of government was not ripe. But national health insurance, old age insurance, disability benefits, unemployment assistance, and free higher education could all be justified as props to individual development. The entire Roosevelt political corpus, in fact, could be premised on a Wilsonian theory. In time, most of it would be.[47]

This did not make Roosevelt's politics and Wilsonian progressivism interchangeable. The twin philosophies may have advanced similar ends, but they fed on separate cores. Wilson's rhetoric of liberty could encompass virtually all of Roosevelt's reform initiatives but not, tellingly, his moral ambitions. Wilson could not accommodate Roosevelt's righteousness. The celebration of individualism at the heart of Wilson's politics jarred with Roosevelt's aim to achieve national greatness by promoting personal virtue. It clashed with Roosevelt's conviction that the business of government was to improve the moral character of citizens, to transform society into a righteous place after the model of the kingdom of God. While Roosevelt held out the state as a moral agent, and regulation as a means to moral order, Wilson rejected the idea that the American people could be reformed. And he emphatically objected to what he took to be the know-it-all quality of Roosevelt's philosophy of government. "I want to frankly say to you that I am not big enough to play Providence, and my objection to the other program is that I don't believe that there is any other man that is big enough to play Providence," Wilson said from the campaign trail. His critique was expansive. In context, his language functioned as a jibe at Roosevelt's regulatory program and the colonel's emphasis on professional, nonpartisan, bureaucratic administration. But more deeply, Wilson's individualist logic indicted the formative strand of Roosevelt's politics as illiberal, even authoritarian. A politics focused on moral improvement was a politics that told individuals what to do, that demanded they conform their interests to a substantive conception of the good. A politics of virtue prioritized certain qualities of character over individual self-development, and regarded individual choice as praiseworthy based on what ends individuals chose.[48]

In sum, Roosevelt's politics endorsed a corporate morality as intrinsic to corporate freedom. Wilson questioned the viability of both concepts. "There is no such thing as corporate liberty," he said flatly. "Liberty belongs to the individual or it does not exist." By the same logic Wilson questioned the notion of communal morality. Moral responsibility was the product of individual choice, he reasoned. Only when individuals freely chose their behavior was it ethically meaningful. The moral nature of human action emerged from the agent's exercise of self-determination and from his capacity to bear the consequences of that determination. Nations were not moral or immoral, righteous or unrighteous. Individuals were. Underwritten by his pragmatic rejection of moral absolutes, Wilson's individualism functioned as an apology for moral pluralism. To endorse a particular conception of the good disrespected individuals by coercing their choice. It prevented them from selecting their own ends and, by extension, from exercising their moral agency. Paradoxically, then, corporate morality actually hindered citizens' moral development by diminishing their opportunities for experimentation. It stifled individual energy. In place of Roosevelt's reformist nationalism Wilson offered a procedural politics centered on advancing personal freedom understood as personal choice. He purged progressivism of its millennialist aims and elevated individual autonomy instead. Let citizens choose their own purposes. Let government protect them in the choice.[49]

Wilson adopted many of Roosevelt's reformist policies but changed Roosevelt's means. He changed Roosevelt's logic. And ultimately he offered the country a different vision of its future. Wilson's unique, liberal progressivism built on Roosevelt's practice and appropriated the reformist aspirations the colonel helped bring to the national scene. From Wilson's cache of reform priorities to his diagnosis of industrialism's ills, from his conception of the presidency to his devotion to positive government, Roosevelt's ideas made Wilson's possible. But the former professor successfully tapped the American past in a way Roosevelt never managed to do. Wilson appropriated the language of American individualism. Roosevelt regarded it as an artifact of history, but Wilson recognized individualism as an enduring American aspiration. The United States was birthed in reaction against oppressive government, and the late colonial and early republican periods, right through the era of the frontier, resounded with talk of personal liberty and the dangers of political power. America's republican tradition was a distinctly individualist one, as Wilson understood, focused on the individual's rights and his freedom to exercise them. Wilson revived these themes and linked them to the progressive cause. He reset Roosevelt's reformist philosophy to an individualist cadence.[50]

By then reinterpreting individualism as self-development, Wilson made the language of individual liberty and rights accessible to the progressives and suggested how the concepts might be fused to the cause of positive government. Wilson's program was indeed an odd amalgam of old ideas and new: a states' rights tone with a centralizing tendency; an individualist ethic in service to a progressive, collectivist agenda. It was also politically potent and intellectually predictive. Wilson's liberal progressivism, his blend of social equality themes and libertarian language, powerfully affected the future of American partisan politics. Both Democrats and Republicans would come to speak its grammar and fight their ideological battles within its bounds. Indeed, his pragmatic, pluralistic defense of democratic government anticipated the dominant Western political theory of the twentieth century. "Pluralism," Oxford professor and liberal philosopher Isaiah Berlin would write in 1958, "seems to me a truer and more humane ideal than the goals of those who seek . . . a 'positive' self-mastery by classes, or peoples, or the whole of mankind." Rooseveltian "positive" liberty, liberty conceived as participation in a collective way of life, in a self-governing community, was all too often a vise that bound the individual, later liberal theorists decided. True freedom was freedom to choose, and that meant freedom to choose one's own ends as well as one's governors. Only the freely choosing individual could be politically free, which meant, by extension, that only a morally pluralistic society could be truly liberal.[51]

Roosevelt had taken up the American republican tradition without its individualist strand. Now Wilson took up individualism to the exclusion of the rest of the republican tradition. Wilson's claims against Roosevelt in the name of personal liberty struck at both the colonel's and the founders' politics. Wilson's individualism ruled out practically any formative politics of any kind. He correctly concluded that a state which sought to encourage particular character traits in its citizens was not neutral with regard to competing conceptions of the good life. In fact, it was precisely because the state embraced a particular conception of the good that it would try to develop corresponding virtues in its citizens. The American founders—including Washington, Adams, Jefferson, and Madison —thought a rights-protecting, self-governing republic was the greatest political good. They believed that only a person who knew and respected the rights of others, a citizen who could deliberate responsibly and consider the common weal, was capable of sharing in self-government. Their constitutional system was meant in part to develop this type of citizen. Roosevelt, on the other hand, conceived racial greatness as the greatest political good, and national righteousness as its touchstone. He advocated a social welfare state, government action far beyond anything the framers imagined, to inspire the conquering virtues and transform society. Both approaches Wilson's political science condemned as inimical to individual freedom, where freedom was understood as the right to choose. Wilson revived republicanism's attention to personal independence but interpreted that independence along a moral rather than economic axis. Independence, in his hands, meant moral autonomy—freedom from a coercive moral community imposed by the state. In place of a republican formative politics, Wilson propounded a public philosophy of individual choice, secured by state action—a procedural politics of positive government for the goal of individual self-development. When historians would write decades later that progressives believed "the state should manifest the values of autonomous individuals conscientiously fulfilling their social responsibility," they would speak of Wilsonian progressivism, of the politics Wilson made.[52]

In propounding his ideas to the country, Wilson highlighted the leading features of Roosevelt's thought as it continued to develop in the second decade of the progressive era. For one thing, Wilson caught Roosevelt's growing statism. He underscored the increasingly ambitious formative project animating Roosevelt's social welfare agenda. He also pointed out the dangers of some aspects of that program: the tendency of regulatory agencies to be captured by the regulated; the loss of democratic accountability with the rise of an independent administrative state; the threat a large, bureaucratized federal government might pose to local institutions and individual liberties. Though Theodore Roosevelt always envisioned himself in the vanguard, the campaign of 1912 showed him to be the one out of sync with the flow of his country's history and politics. Forming citizens' characters according to the needs of self-government had never been tried—or justified—in the way Roosevelt had in mind. Neither the founders nor Lincoln thought statecraft was soulcraft for the purpose of racial greatness, nor did they think that the federal government should undertake soulcraft directly on the scale Roosevelt envisioned. The Constitution and Bill of Rights promoted the levels of government closer to the people as the sources of civic education, and even then the framers meant the primary responsibility for character formation to reside with civil society, with the associations that stood between government and the individual, the church above all. The founders never anticipated, and probably would not have approved, Roosevelt's consolidation of political power in the executive, his direct appeals to the public for the purposes of affecting congressional deliberation, and his attempt to achieve social regeneration through a national welfare state.

More broadly speaking, the man who believed life's meaning was found in struggle and conquest never reconciled himself to his nation's extensive history of rights-talk, and rights-thought. He was always more comfortable speaking about duties rather than rights. Duties and obligations fitted far better with his warrior republicanism. When he did discuss rights, he tended to cast them as instrumental, as stages on the road to the conquering virtues and meaningful triumph. "The object of democracy should be to guarantee each man his rights," Roosevelt said in 1911, "with the purpose that each man shall thereby be enabled better to do his duty." Americans had rarely thought of rights in this fashion, and when they did it was because rights were understood to need the community and other civic institutions to be fully realized, not because rights prepared individuals to achieve for the good of the race.[53]

Roosevelt's dream of a politics of collective transformation, fostered by a powerful national government, reinforced by carefully managed economic conditions, and girded by an overarching sense of racial destiny, was a novelty in American political thought. He gestured to the founders' formative ambition but departed from their communitarian, constitutional vision. He admired Lincoln's teachings on moral equality but did not share the Illinois statesman's underlying fixation on natural rights and the self-evident truths of self-government. He understood the challenges of the industrial age and America's rise to world power, but proposed paths of action substantially different than those the political tradition of his country might have suggested. This is not to say Roosevelt could not have succeeded. Rather, the exceptional quality of Roosevelt's ideas made his effort to achieve them all the more daring, and his defeat the more poignant.

On the evening of October 14, Roosevelt's campaign blew into Milwaukee, Wisconsin, and the colonel struck out by automobile for the auditorium where crowds awaited. His car had only just drawn up to the building when a lone gunman stepped from the shadows and fired into the colonel's chest at point-blank range. Underneath his suit coat, Roosevelt's pallid shirt ran with blood. The doctors wanted him taken to a hospital immediately, but Roosevelt pushed them back and staggered up the steps to the platform. He was not going to stop now.

"Friends, I shall ask you to be as quiet as possible. I don't know whether you fully understand I have just been shot." The colonel unbuttoned his vest to disclose the bloodstained shirt beneath, and the crowd fell instantly silent. "I want to say this about myself. I have altogether too important things to think of to feel concern over my own death. I am telling you the literal truth when I say that my concern is for other things." He paused for a moment, clearly in pain. He believed in the progressive movement, he went on. He believed in social uplift, "in making life a little easier for all our people"; he believed in government for righteousness. If this was his end, so be it. He had done what he returned to do. "Tell the people not to worry for me," he said a day later from his sickbed, the bullet still lodged in his chest. "For always, the army is true. Always the cause is there, and it is the cause for which the people care, for it is the people's cause."[54]

Woodrow Wilson won the election.

12

THE VALLEY OF VISION

Word reached Manhattan late in the morning, borne by shouting newsboys and their extra editions so that by lunchtime every passerby who cared to look or listen knew. Theodore Roosevelt already knew. He didn't need the papers to tell him. In his offices at the *Metropolitan* magazine downtown, he kept to his schedule. He finished dictating letters and signed a few books ahead of his luncheon, and then at the appointed time walked to the Harvard Club wearing his straw hat. Dr. Albert Shaw of the *Review of Reviews* was there, along with the young German-American writer Hermann Hagedorn. The plan was to discuss the reunion of the Progressive and Republican parties, which Roosevelt had been working assiduously to consummate. While his guests talked, however, the colonel said little. He left his meal untouched. The young Hagedorn noted that, behind his glasses, Roosevelt looked stricken.

"Don't give up hope, colonel," Shaw offered when Roosevelt first walked into the dining room. "The news may not be true."

"No," Roosevelt cut him off. He had no tolerance for sentimentality now. "Quentin's dead. Quentin's dead."[1]

A telegram brought the news to Sagamore Hill on July 17, a day before the papers made it public. German fighter pilots had shot down the colonel's youngest son behind enemy lines sometime earlier in the week. Quentin Roosevelt had been a child when his father was president, and now, in 1918, he was but twenty. He was the gentlest of the Roosevelt boys though perhaps also the wildest and most precocious. His antics in the White House—roller skating on the hardwood floors, spitballing the portraits, smuggling a full-grown pony into the mansion elevator—were the stuff of legend. He was the son most like his father, or, perhaps better, he was the boy his father had always wanted most to be. Tall and broad-shouldered, handsome, a natural athlete, Quentin was a nova of vivacity and sheer unabashed boyishness. Theodore never recovered from his grief.

He couldn't help wondering if he was responsible for his son's death. Roosevelt had preached to his boys a stern and unforgiving doctrine of righteous manliness, the same one he had set for himself many years ago. He expected his sons to prove themselves worthy as men, to earn his favor and, with it, their place in the Roosevelt world. All four of them, from Ted to Quentin, heeded his martial example and volunteered for service when war erupted in Europe. "It is rather awful to know that he paid with his life," Roosevelt wrote of Quentin, "and that my other sons may pay with their lives, to try to put in practice what I preached." But ultimately he saw no alternative. The struggle for honor and glory, the battle for righteousness, went hard with every man, just as it did with every nation. This did not mean greatness was not worth having. On the contrary, it was all in this life that was worth having. Goods and kindred may pass away, and the body certainly would, but the nation went on and one's honor with it. To be remembered by a great people, to have shaped and contributed to their greatness—that was immortality. That was worth dying for. He was proud of Quentin's sacrifice, even as he thought privately he should have died in his son's place.[2]

For the man who sat grimly in the Harvard Club that day, this was a season of desolation. Office, influence, the jewel of his family—all had been taken from him, one after another. The American public rejected his leadership in 1912. The Progressive Party disintegrated barely two years later, and Roosevelt found himself turned out in a political wilderness, a statesman without power, without party, and, this time, with few prospects for return. But though bruised and wizened, he forged ahead, galvanized by the last and greatest crisis of his lifetime.

In 1914, the war to end all wars broke over Europe. Roosevelt sensed almost at once that the Western world had come to a turning of the tide. In the face of the European calamity, he gave his warrior republicanism its fullest and final exposition. With a new sense of urgency, Roosevelt trumpeted democratic collectivism. He returned to the warrior virtues, which he cast as both the key to survival in the storm of war and the avenue to success in the industrial future. As darkness fell for him, Roosevelt proclaimed his final vision of the republic.

He sought for a righteous city, powerful enough to defend itself from foes and hasten the advent of civilization worldwide; just enough to provide for the health and security of all its citizens and reward all fairly for their labors; virtuous enough to judge each person on his worth as a man, and not on his wealth or social standing. Though he spent the years after 1912 in a political wilderness, they became for Roosevelt a valley of vision. There he saw what might be and preached it to his countrymen, one last time.

Roosevelt's journey into exile had really begun in February of 1912, when he shattered any remaining hope of Republican unity and sought the presidential nomination for himself. The full ramifications of his choice began to come into focus only after November. Roosevelt lost to Woodrow Wilson by 347 electoral votes. The outcome looked somewhat less severe when viewed through the lens of the popular vote: the Democrat from New Jersey garnered just under forty-three percent of all ballots cast, while Roosevelt won twenty-seven percent and Taft a dismal twenty-three. But adjust the figures as he might, Roosevelt could not escape the reality that he had been decisively defeated. "We have gone down," he told his son Kermit the day after the election, "in a smashing defeat." From a total of over 15 million votes cast, Wilson beat Roosevelt by 2,177,976. In the end, the race was not even close.[3]

Yet wide though the margin was over his nearest competitor, Wilson actually polled 100,000 fewer votes in 1912 than William Jennings Bryan had on his way to defeat by Taft four years earlier. Wilson won approximately 83 percent of those who had voted for Bryan in 1908, while Taft and Roosevelt won, respectively, 40 percent and 46 percent of voters who had cast ballots for Taft in that year. Wilson's achievement, as it turns out, was his ability to hold the existing Democratic coalition intact. He failed to unite the progressives under one standard or expand the Democratic voting bloc. Instead, he made the Democratic Party safe for progressivism, made it electable in a progressive era by refashioning its priorities and justifying them with progressive-sounding rhetoric. Which is to say, Wilson in 1912 brought the Democrats into the political mainstream that Roosevelt had spent a decade creating. Wilson's election signaled the diffusion rather than the concentration of progressive political clout. With all the major parties espousing reform, progressivism became, now more than ever, a generalized climate of opinion. Roosevelt's third-party run hastened this development by crippling the electoral partnership that had kept Republicans in power and in charge of progressive reform for a decade. Just as his presidency had helped spur the emergence of progressive Democrats, his 1912 political maneuvers helped clear the path for their ascent. Whether Taft could have defeated Wilson absent the colonel's meddling was very much an open question, but there is no doubt Roosevelt's campaign made Wilson's victory virtually certain. The Wilson era was due in no small part to the hubris of Theodore Roosevelt.[4]

Wilson's true accomplishment in 1912 was not electoral but intellectual. Perhaps the most noteworthy consequence of Roosevelt's bolt, then, was the new brand of progressivism it allowed to take hold. Once in office, Wilson proved that his political theory was as adaptable as his campaign rhetoric suggested it would be. He pursued the pro-competitive reforms he advocated from the campaign trail, but the New Freedom was only the start of his program. Almost from the first, President Wilson took up regulatory policies advocated by Theodore Roosevelt. The difference was in how he used them, and how he justified them.

In 1913, the Wilson-led Democratic Congress reorganized the nation's banking system with the Federal Reserve Act. The law's linchpin was a Roosevelt-style government board, appointed by the president, with the power to issue currency and to regulate and supervise the country's seven thousand independent banks. A year later Wilson won a new antitrust measure, the Clayton Antitrust Act, which included the measures Wilson propounded in 1912—a prohibition on interlocking directorates, a ban on tying arrangements and anti-competitive price cutting, and stiffer penalties for violating the original Sherman law. But Wilson proved more interested in 1914 in another Roosevelt idea, a Federal Trade Commission that would prevent unfair competition in restraint of trade by issuing administrative orders and assisting the Justice Department with antitrust prosecutions. This body was almost exactly what Roosevelt had been demanding since the end of his presidency, an institution Wilson had called "paternalistic" in 1912. But though he swiftly appropriated major policies from Roosevelt's nationalist program, Wilson invested this filched agenda with an individualist, libertarian rationale. An independent federal reserve board was necessary to break up the money trust, he argued, and prevent a small clique of private bankers from controlling the nation's credit. The board was, in short, a market-corrective mechanism. He justified the Federal Trade Commission on similar grounds. Under Brandeis's tutelage, Wilson became convinced that no one law or set of laws could prevent all the possible practices that thwarted market competition. The commission, then, was a stopgap measure. It would interpret and adapt Congress's general antitrust rules to help prevent the forms of industrial organization and anti-market behavior that stifled competition, but which no one statute could anticipate. The commission would be an independent administrative agency, but one in service to decentralization and the market economy.[5]

As always for Wilson, the market continued to function as a symbol of individual liberty. However many of Roosevelt's policies Wilson adopted, his program remained geared toward releasing individual energies and constructing a neutral framework of individual rights to allow private citizens to pursue their own ends. In time he would embrace national regulation of labor and wages through the commerce clause, another cherished Roosevelt reform. But he did it not to advance collectivist nationalism or moral uplift, but because he wanted to protect the individual and his capacity for self-determination. Wilson gave the country positive government, but for liberal ends. He overcame the inertia of the federalist system with executive leadership, but for the purpose of making the constitutional order efficient and parliamentary rather than morally transformative. With his reforming policies Wilson gradually won over much of the progressive intellectual leadership, including Herbert Croly, imbuing them with his political theory. It was Wilson's neutral, procedural liberalism, not Roosevelt's warrior republicanism, that defined the remainder of the progressive era, and perhaps the century.[6]

Probably not until the mid-term congressional elections of 1914 reduced the Progressive Party presence in Congress to a bare remnant did Roosevelt appreciate what Wilson had accomplished in November of 1912. Wilson had beaten Roosevelt for leadership of the progressive moment. With the Wilsonian Democrats pushing progressive causes, Roosevelt's Bull Moosers faced a difficult task in justifying their existence. America's first-past-the-post electoral system did not as a rule reward minority parties, and so long as both Democrats and Republicans continued to endorse versions of progressive reform, there was little chance Roosevelt's Progressives would ever find the popular support necessary to upset the party establishment.

The Progressive Party withered after 1914. Unable to turn his back on politics, his life-long vocation, Roosevelt returned reluctantly to the Republicans. Yet for all intents and purposes, he was a man without a party. Republican leaders, including Roosevelt's close friend, Henry Cabot Lodge, had resigned themselves to almost certain defeat in 1912 in a gamble to wean the Republican Party from Roosevelt and his increasingly statist republicanism. "It is essential," Vice-President James Sherman said even before the 1912 Republican convention, "both for the life of our party and the continuance of our Government," that Roosevelt be "sidetracked." If Republicans could not win without him, they were just as certain that Roosevelt could not win without *them*, and they wagered that a Roosevelt bolt might prove beneficial to the party in the long run. In rejecting Roosevelt as their presidential nominee, Republicans announced the conclusion of their ten-year dalliance with the regulatory state. And this was no minor event.

Since the close of the Civil War, the Republicans had been the party most consistently associated with federal reform. Their postbellum commitments to a strong national government, territorial expansion, and economic development were the foundation of the electoral alliance that made Roosevelt's regulatory reforms possible. These doctrines were Roosevelt's orthodoxy, they were the ideas he would rearrange and refashion to create his progressivism. But Roosevelt's intellectual development outpaced his party's and eventually diverged from it entirely. He never succeeded in convincing the party leadership that the traditional Republican support for industrialism and economic growth required in the twentieth century a regulatory partnership between business and government. He failed to convert the party elite to his claim that social cohesion and national unity were impossible without a social welfare state.

Roosevelt began to hope in the final years of his presidency that his party, with its proud history of social reform and melioration, with its band of urban reformers and social gospel disciples, might sponsor the advent of a welfare state in America—one calibrated to cultivate the warrior virtues, dissolve class loyalties, produce industrial efficiency, empower collective action, and reawaken the public's moral sense. But neither the Republican leadership nor the workaday voter warmed to that vision. It was too statist, too coercive, too intrusive and expensive to capture the imagination of most Republicans. With Roosevelt's exit in 1912, the party drifted slowly toward the other leading interpretation of its historic commitment to industrial growth: economic liberalism. Republicans embraced an agenda of diminishing interference in the affairs of business. They coupled it with a firm belief in the market and the natural order of the private sector. It would take a catastrophic depression to bring American voters to endorse a social welfare state. Republicans were never more than reluctant converts.

After Roosevelt, the party would turn to large-scale economic regulation only when it could be harmonized with other, preexisting Republican priorities, like economic growth and the tariff. And given Roosevelt's banishment from party leadership, the prospects for an intersection of the Republican agenda and sweeping industrial reform were quite limited. In this sense, even Taft had managed to defeat Roosevelt in 1912. The colonel could come back to the Republicans, but the party was no longer his.[7]

The progressive era was no longer his. Roosevelt abandoned the Republican Party in the summer of 1912 ostensibly in hopes of reclaiming the reins of American politics and political thought. But his impatience and arrogance, his refusal to bide his time and wait for the wheel to turn, hastened his own eclipse. Where in 1905 and 1906 he had made a political moment, artfully matching his ideas to the needs of the day, after 1912 he found himself increasingly unsuited to his time. He preached a politics of transformation but lacked a transformative event, the sort of national cataclysm that might have inspired the country to leave behind its storied past of individualist, libertarian sentiment and embrace the collectivist nationalism he favored. History denied him the towering national crisis his politics demanded. Then came the Great War, with Woodrow Wilson as president.

On May 7, 1915, a German submarine fired on the passenger ship *Lusitania* just off the southwestern coast of Ireland. One thousand, one hundred and ninety-eight passengers drowned amid the wreckage in the frigid Irish Sea, among them 270 women and 94 children; 124 Americans died in the attack. It was the first significant American loss of life in the First World War. Theodore Roosevelt issued a statement to the press demanding immediate action, the sort he believed he would have taken if he was president. The White House, he said, must enforce American rights in international waters — by breaking diplomatic relations with Germany if necessary. "Of course I shall not be satisfied in any delay in asserting . . . our rights," he wrote, "our rights to send ammunitions of war to France and England . . . the right of American citizens to travel freely on belligerent merchant ships on the high seas." Since February, the German high command had been experimenting with a daring campaign of underwater warfare, using submarines to crimp French and British supply lines by torpedoing unarmed allied merchant vessels sailing in international waters. Technically, the strategy was illegal. International law guaranteed unarmed vessels right of passage on the high seas, even in the event of hostilities. But facing a punishing near-blockade by the redoubtable British navy, the Germans were willing to run the risk. Because America was the major neutral nation, its reaction was critical to the success or failure of the German strategy. The Wilson administration made little protest in the early months of the campaign, and, sensing American indecision, Berlin escalated. The *Lusitania* was not a merchant vessel at all; it was a passenger liner. Wilson's response was to call for arbitration.[8]

"Wilson even more than Jefferson has been the apologist for and has given impetus to our very worst [tendencies]," Roosevelt fumed. Though he did not yet advocate war with Germany, Roosevelt regarded the president's neutrality as base. "The kind of 'neutrality' which seeks to preserve 'peace' by timidly refusing to live up to our plighted world and to denounce and take action against such wrong . . . is unworthy of an honorable and powerful people," he said even before the *Lusitania* exploded. The public reaction following the tragedy horrified him. "If ever the American people stood in need of calmness and deliberation it is at this hour," the leading Baptist weekly admonished its readers. When Wilson proposed to expand the regular army and active reserve, the public reaction was hostile — especially among progressives. Church leaders, farm and labor spokesmen, and urban social justice reformers all opposed any move to war. They could not understand what interest Americans could possibly have in a fight between distant European powers, especially when that fight involved control of colonial territory. Roosevelt blamed Wilson.[9]

"The moral sense of our people," he charged, has been "drugged into stupor by the men in high places who taught us that we had no concern with the causes of war, that all combatants were fighting for the same things, that it was our duty to be neutral between right and wrong." Wilson should have been leading the public, Roosevelt thought. He ought to have been helping them to want what they ought to want, to identify their short-term interests with their obligations to keep treaty commitments and oppose wrongdoing. He should have been calling them to righteousness. Instead, Wilson's politics exalted selfish pursuits and encouraged moral indifference.[10]

Roosevelt saw Americans' tepid attitude toward international conflict as the entirely predictable consequence of Wilson's progressivism. The American character always tended toward individualistic materialism, Roosevelt believed. It drifted toward self-absorbed, money-getting parochialism. Wilson facilitated these vices. He enabled them, and the crisis in Europe threw them now into sharp relief. Wilson is "cordially supported by . . . every soft creature, every coward and weakling . . . whose god is money, or pleasure, or ease, and every man who has not got in him both the sterner virtues and the power of seeking after an ideal." Wilson cared nothing for the country's soul, Roosevelt believed. But the colonel did. He cared for national character above all and he was willing to take bold state action to safeguard it. As the menace of war loomed, this was Roosevelt's message to the American people, the latest stanza of a gospel he had preached for the better part of two decades. "The prime work for this nation at this moment is to rebuild its own character," he said. "Let us find our own souls."[11]

For Roosevelt, statecraft was always and inescapably soulcraft, but now he made the connection more explicit, the goal of fostering virtue more immediate, than ever before. He proposed his own version of a national gymnastic, a regimen of practical training and instruction to mold the next generation of American citizens and, through them, the American regime. In short, Roosevelt proposed to inculcate the warrior virtues to get a warrior republic. The chief cornerstone of his effort was mandatory military training for every American boy. "A law should be passed at once making military training universal for our young men, and providing for its immediate application to all young men between 19 and 21." Roosevelt envisioned several months of on-site instruction in shooting, marching, and survival in the open. Boys would live together in barracks on army bases, the training to replicate "actual field-service under war conditions" as nearly as possible. The immediate objective was to alleviate the country's shortage of men and arms. "When once this system has begun fairly to function, we shall be ready at any time to repel the attack of any foreign foe who may make war on us," he claimed. But he had far more ambitious aims than that. His program was meant for peace as well as war, for this time and for the time to come. "I would use the registration of all our men," he explained, "as a basis for further development for training and service in the duties of peace." Specifically, he proposed both young men and women be given "certain fundamental forms of industrial training," by which he meant vocational instruction in manual and mechanical labor for men, and "certain forms of household work and work outside the home" for women.[12]

The impetus for Roosevelt's program was the menace of war, but this was no temporary regimen that Roosevelt wanted. His vision far outstripped the imminent threat to the country's security. He foresaw a new pillar of the American state, a permanent institution to shape the horizons of young American men and women of every generation. Roosevelt's service program was designed to shepherd adolescents' passage from youth to adulthood, baptizing them into a common civic identity forged by shared physical hardship, discipline, and education. More than merely a few weeks of basic military training, Roosevelt proposed a citizen-training school. This was a new national sacrament, to be taken by all members of the nation, a rite that communicated the responsibilities of democratic citizenship and conferred full membership in the state.

"Under this system," Roosevelt said, "the young men would . . . learn those habits of self-reliance and law-abiding obedience which are not only essential to the efficiency of a citizen soldiery," but importantly, are "essential to the efficient performance of civic duties in a free democracy." Mandatory military training would promote equality, a sense of national feeling, and a common ethic of duty. Perhaps thinking of his own father, he insisted that no person could purchase a substitute. No one would be exempt. Every man would be given the honor of serving his country, every child, the honor of knowing his father served.[13]

Roosevelt's program was motivated by his long-pursued goal to replace parochial and class identities with loyalty to the national state. As a result of Roosevelt's gymnastic, "every man, whether he carried a rifle or labored on public works or managed a business . . . would have a clearer conception of his obligations to the State," he said. The relationship between citizens and state was fundamentally reciprocal, on Roosevelt's conception. Only those citizens who served the collective faithfully deserved to be counted full members of the body politic and admitted to its full privileges. He had hinted at this nexus before, this connection between service and rights. But now he proposed to codify it in law. If a young man refused to undergo military training and serve at least six months in the field, Roosevelt would deny him the right to vote. Only if a man contributed to the common defense of the nation was he entitled to help direct its fate. "No man has a right to citizenship in a democracy," Roosevelt held, "if, for any cause whatsoever, he is unwilling to fight."[14]

The same principle held true for women. Female citizens should enjoy equal rights with their male counterparts, but this "privilege" — equal rights — would be "secured on the service each [woman] must render." As he had before, Roosevelt argued for rights as positive, conventional guarantees made by the state to citizens in order to facilitate better service by the individual to the collective. "The woman must bear and rear the children, as her first duty to the state; and the man's first duty is to take care of her and the children." For both men and women, the national state should be the object of service even as it was the source of rights. If American men served together in the military, and American women were trained to raise their children and perform supporting tasks on the home front, the American public would come to share a new sense of national community. In lieu of Wilson's citizenship of self-development, Roosevelt preached a citizenship of shared obligation and virile morality. The longevity of the American republic depended, in the final analysis, on sound moral character, not on "slothful ease and soft selfishness and the loud timidity that fears every species of risk and hardship." It depended on "the virile strength of manliness which clings to the ideal of stern, unflinching performance of duty."[15]

To Roosevelt, the need for virile men at the helm of the state was a simple, if severe, lesson of history. His warrior gymnastic was aimed not only at improving the moral timber of the average citizen, but at securing for the nation a class of warrior leaders equal to the adversities of the century to come. For a project of this radical import, however, he was not willing to trust to education alone. In his mind, the link between moral excellence and racial inheritance was too close. His warrior republicanism had always carried a racial element; it was in many senses a racial statecraft. But the scientific discoveries of the early twentieth century and the pressing need to safeguard America's future against a rising tide of German and Japanese militarism brought the evolutionist strain of Roosevelt's thought back to the surface. Just as he was willing to use the government to cultivate citizens' characters, he was willing now to marshal the powers of the state to shape the country's racial stock. His gymnastic included a program of state-directed eugenics.

With the rediscovery of Gregor Mendel's law of heredity, most biologists by the second decade of the twentieth century had come seriously to doubt Lamarck's theory of transferable adaptations. Organisms could not, the new thinking went, pass personal adaptations to their young. Acquired characteristics were not inheritable. Roosevelt acknowledged this revisionism in 1918, if only grudgingly. "Most scientific men nowadays disbelieve in the inheritance of acquired characteristics," he wrote in a book review on evolutionary theory. But that did not mean character was not transmittable. On the contrary, it suggested character was not as pliable to environment as Lamarckians had thought. The new generation of genetic "hereditarians" certainly believed character traits —everything from habitual drunkenness to criminality—were transmittable from parent to progeny. It was just that once transmitted, the traits could not be easily changed, if at all.[16]

On this theory, the need to protect and preserve the right type of racial stock became all the more urgent. By 1917 and 1918, Roosevelt had added a new cardinal virtue to the constellation of his warrior qualities: the willingness and ability to reproduce. The civic health of the United States was increasingly imperiled, Roosevelt convinced himself, because the country's best citizens—"old stock" Americans with the habits and mores suitable to self-government—were refusing to reproduce in numbers sufficient to keep the American race alive. If birthrates from the first two decades of the twentieth century held, Roosevelt feared, Americans would cease to be a unified race at all. They would be drowned in a sea of polyglot immigrants, some of whom possessed the right racial and personal makeup to become productive members of a great race, but all of whom needed to be "Americanized," inducted into the American racial nation. This could not happen if there were no true Americans left.[17]

"Every student of the subject knows that the United States shares with other English-speaking countries . . . [the] rapid decline of the birth-rate which inevitably signals race decay," Roosevelt lamented. If unchecked, such decline would spell "racial death." Americans' failure to breed was not due to their incapacity. The country had not witnessed a sudden wave of infertility. Rather, Americans—or at least middle-class, Northeastern Americans—were choosing to have smaller families, and Roosevelt regarded this as positively immoral. The heart of the American race dwelled in New England, and "the New England conscience now sadly needs to be awakened to the frightful and fundamental immorality which it has ignored and condoned." A healthy, virile warrior took joy in breeding. It was a mark of his manhood. Moreover, breeding is how the race survived. In this sense, the desire to reproduce was perhaps the first and foundational civic virtue. "The qualities that make men and women eager lovers, faithful, duty-performing, hard-working husbands and wives . . . stand at the foundation of all possible social welfare," he wrote. Those Americans who desired only small families did so for base and selfish reasons, he concluded. The desire to be financially secure had obscured their racial responsibilities and, worse, emasculated their natural impulses. Roosevelt wanted the state to do something about it.[18]

He pushed for new legislation to tax families with only one or two children more heavily than those with three or more. Additionally, Roosevelt thought parents should be given tax deductions for children, increasing in value with the number of offspring. A father "should be exempted an additional $500 of income for each of his first two children, and on an additional $1000 of income for every subsequent child—for we wish to put especial emphasis on the vital need of having the third, and the fourth and the fifth child." Not everyone should get these tax breaks, of course. "The men and women with small or reasonable incomes are the ones who should be encouraged to have children;"—that is, the lower middle classes—"they do not represent a class which will be tempted by such exemption to thriftlessness or extravagances."[19]

The truth of the matter was that Roosevelt did not want just any American reproducing. "Among human beings, as among all other living creatures, if the best specimens do not, and the poorer specimens do propagate, the type will go down." Roosevelt did not hesitate to acknowledge that he was calling for a national eugenic program, which he regarded as not only scientifically sound, but as morally necessary. "I wish very much that the wrong people could be prevented entirely from breeding; and when the evil nature of these people is sufficiently flagrant, this should be done." Specifically, "criminals should be sterilized, and feeble-minded persons forbidden to leave offspring behind them." Targeting his proposed tax benefits to members of particular socioeconomic strata was another way of sifting the desirable from the undesirable. Newly arrived immigrants, the poor, and the indolent rich would all be excluded. The child taxes would encourage only the hardworking and industrious middle classes to reproduce.[20]

Under the influence of crude racial hereditarianism, Roosevelt's formative ambition became a eugenic undertaking. The quest to achieve moral renewal and social transformation blurred into a project to purify the genetic composition of the populace. This aim coexisted somewhat uneasily with his continued calls to construct an American social welfare state able to cultivate the conquering character traits. The rest of his gymnastic, in fact—his plans for military training and industrial education—presupposed that heredity was not determinative, that will and effort could make a difference. In reality, Roosevelt's long-held republicanized Lamarckianism and the new hereditarian science mingled in his mind, the tension between them unresolved. To the degree Roosevelt's attitude toward eugenics occluded his lifelong emphasis on personal reformation through effort and will, it obscured rather than advanced the core concern of his political thought. In this sense, his eugenic program was less a logical extension of his transformative politics than a vulgar caricature. But if nothing else, Roosevelt's eugenic turn illustrated the cast his reformist ambitions could take when united to his racial ideas. His politics sought a moral regeneration so thorough, social reform so drastic and so personal, that he was willing to reform the genetic makeup of the citizenry to accomplish it. He was willing to try to change the very nature of the human person.[21]

From Roosevelt's racialist, militarist gymnastic emerged his final vision of the American nation. Like other political philosophers and state-makers before him, from Socrates to the American founders, Roosevelt premised his politics on getting the right type of citizen. But right for what? Roosevelt strove to get citizens who could sustain a warrior republic. That was his ideal commonwealth, the culmination of his political thought. Roosevelt recognized no tension between his militarist gymnastic and the American way of life, because for him the fighting virtues were the lifeblood of the political community, America's and any other. "[T]here is very little use of solemnly debating such questions as . . . 'How does militarism affect such social values as the sense of the preciousness of human life,'" he told audiences in 1916. The real question, instead, was how a free nation would survive the threat of armed foes without embracing the military virtues. "Belgium," Roosevelt pointed out, "had a very keen sense of the 'preciousness of human life'"—before the German invasion. But Belgium had ceased to exist, because "Belgium had not prepared her military strength so that she could put on her frontiers at least half a million thoroughly armed and trained men of fighting spirit." The warrior qualities of character were eminently, desperately, necessary in the present crisis—necessary to survive—but beyond that, Roosevelt saw them as the foundation of the good life. He dreamed, in his political exile, of a socially cohesive, militarily strong, collectivist democracy. He envisioned a state where citizens found their personal identity in service to the nation, a place where the individual drew his sense of belonging from membership in the national community. Roosevelt's republic prized virtue, but of a certain kind—loyalty to the public weal, vigilance for the honor of the nation, and the courage to protect and defend the state. More ancient than modern, more Spartan than Athenian, Roosevelt's ideal commonwealth was a proud and industrious republic of military virtue.[22]

At the headwaters of the Western political tradition, Socrates taught that the first and greatest virtue was moderation, the virtue befitting the life of philosophic inquiry. The Socratic quest for the personal self-control and political independence necessary for true philosophy inspired the birth of political liberalism. Later, in their own interpretation of the republican heritage, the American founders championed self-reliance, piety, and love of liberty, traits appropriate to the participatory self-government they regarded as man's right by nature. Roosevelt, by contrast to these forebears, deprecated the value of philosophy and free inquiry as a way of life. Their requisites did not inform his idea of political liberty. For him, obedience to the right and duty to the whole were the higher obligations. And while he lauded democracy, he imagined one of a different type than the American founders. Roosevelt understood democratic life as the culmination of racial greatness, the ultimate stage in the moral progress of mankind. Democracy was the form of government where the human person was at last able to realize the ethical commands of Christ through collective activity and achieve the moral community that eluded him in earlier ages. Which is to say, Roosevelt's republic was not particularly liberal at all. It called for collective action rather than independence; self-sacrifice rather than self-development; obedience rather than free inquiry. It was sustained by citizens' ability to fight and conquer, to defend themselves and master their own destinies. It thrived on citizens' loyalty to the state. Democracy, for Roosevelt, was government for the strong, government for the proud, government for the powerful and the just. In a word, democracy was government for the righteous.

Hobbled by age and illness, cast out from the councils of power, Theodore Roosevelt envisioned a righteous city, a secular replacement for the city of God. In Roosevelt's political thought, the righteous republic effected Christ's promised salvation by bringing its citizens to moral excellence. By doing Christ's work it replaced him and his kingdom. Salvation came instead in the city. In the city, the human person discovered himself as "a link in the great chain of creation and causation . . . as an essential part of the whole, whose life must be made to serve the larger and continuing life of the whole." The child of the republic became a part of what Roosevelt in his last year of life called the "great adventure," the timeless, deathless adventure of the nation, of heaven worked out on earth. Roosevelt's vision was statist and coercive, perhaps even socialistic. It directed citizens' moral energies toward the state, exalting the political collective as the final destiny of the human person. His republic made little space for natural rights or personal liberty. It gave little attention to democratic deliberation or constitutional self-rule. It was, in short, the republicanism neither of the framers nor of the English liberals before them. Uniquely American yet inconsonant with much of the American political tradition, breathtakingly ambitious yet conservative, radically religious and yet radically secular, this warrior republic was a Roosevelt original. And already by 1917, it was an anachronism.[23]

Woodrow Wilson marched to reelection in November 1916 promising to keep America out of war. Domestic politics had been swallowed by foreign policy, and in the months after Wilson's victory Republicans looked for guidance to the man who had been preaching preparedness for over two years. They wanted Roosevelt to command their campaign against Wilson's war leadership. The truce between the former president and the party he once led was tenuous and uneasy, and it did not extend to Roosevelt's domestic reform ideas. But it gave the colonel more reason to hope than he had felt in quite some time. If Republicans wanted him to lead the battle against Wilson on the ground of foreign policy, he would. In fact, his final arguments against his political nemesis proceeded as a thinly veiled critique of Wilson's political science, one last bid by Roosevelt to resume leadership of the progressive era. But in the end, the final clash between the two great interpreters of progressivism brought the reform moment to a finish. The war, when it finally came, commandeered Americans' reformist energies and exhausted their taste for change.[24]

From Wilson's politics of self-development came a foreign policy of national self-determination. Ironically, the man who castigated Theodore Roosevelt's political philosophy as Olympian in its transformative ambitions tried to enlist his countrymen to transform the international system, to destroy the rule of the powerful few and replace it with the free self-direction of the peoples of the world. To Roosevelt, Wilson's grand scheme was the height of folly, born of ignorance, arrogance, and moral equivocation. Wilson's "peace without victory" would ultimately prevent a stable peace, Roosevelt charged, and harm the national interests of the United States. He set out in 1917 to convince the country to agree.[25]

Roosevelt began his last political charge, appropriately, with a moral salvo. Even as Wilson's political philosophy warped the American spirit at home, he said, it was endangering America's strategic position abroad. The statecraft of neutral self-development and the foreign policy of neutrality were intellectually linked and morally base. "The kind of 'neutrality' which seeks to preserve 'peace' by timidly refusing to live up to our plighted world . . . is unworthy of an honorable and powerful people," Roosevelt wrote. Wilson's official neutrality policy from the time of war's outbreak until the spring of 1917 sprang from the same immoral impulses as his interest-based political science, Roosevelt believed. Wilson was forever casting the American state as neutral between competing moral forces, whether they were differing conceptions of self-development at home or foreign powers struggling for dominance abroad. He hesitated to side with any one set of warring nations lest he be forced to ask the American people to sacrifice their self-interest to a larger cause. Wilson's politics of self-indulgence bridled at any call to sacrifice. His philosophy of epicurean individualism recoiled from the need to give oneself to a common good or set aside personal gain for national honor.[26]

But there was such a thing as right and wrong, Roosevelt said, and Germany was in the wrong. This "Prussianized Germany," as Roosevelt took to calling it, threatened the future of civilization with its acts of wanton aggression against Belgium and France. Kaiser Wilhelm's state was "autocratic [and] imperialistic," Roosevelt warned, and would be satisfied with nothing less than domination of the European continent. If the United States did not intervene to help the so-called Western Powers—Britain, France, and Russia—then the allied autocracies of Germany, Austria, Serbia, and Italy would win the field and swiftly threaten the United States. Once Germany had entrenched itself in Europe, Roosevelt reasoned, there was nothing to stop it from turning to South America. Roosevelt as president had fended off German advances in the Western Hemisphere on two separate occasions. Expansion of American influence would be severely hampered, if not entirely checked, by any outcome in Europe that made Germany the power center of the international system. The United States could not afford to be neutral. American interests must be protected. Righteousness had to be upheld.[27]

The colonel was correct to discern a connection between Wilson's philosophy of government and his foreign policy, though the link was neither as simple nor as nefarious as Roosevelt implied. Wilson had little experience with international politics. He failed to appreciate the intricacies of the international system's power balance or comprehend the significance of the major powers' strategic interests. To him, "balance of power" was synonymous with international domination by the European colonizers. "Have you ever heard what started the present war?" Wilson asked the Cincinnati Women's City Club in 1916. "If you have, I wish you would publish it, because nobody else has, so far as I can gather. Nothing in particular started it, but everything in general." While Roosevelt located the war's origins in the bellicose and destabilizing imperial ambitions of Wilhelmine Germany, Wilson attributed the conflict to a vague but sinister misunderstanding between the people of the world. "There had been growing up in Europe a mutual suspicion, an interchange of conjectures about what this Government and that Government was going to do," Wilson said. That "complex web of intrigue and spying" was virtually certain, sooner or later, "to entangle the whole of the family of mankind on that side of the water in its meshes." And so it had.[28]

In Wilson's analysis, the major European powers came to occupy the same narrative role as the corporate business interests did in his domestic political story. Both cliques, according to Wilson, ran roughshod over the interests of the people at large in favor of their own selfish priorities. Wilson saw no point in intervening to help one conglomeration of interests prevail over the other, at home or abroad. "America is not interested in seeing one nation or group of nations prevail against another, but she is interested in seeing justice founded upon peace throughout the world." Wilson's prescription for the international system was the same one he trumpeted in his domestic policy: release the energies of the common man, empower his agency. When ongoing German submarine warfare made American neutrality impossible, Wilson called for war not to readjust the systemic balance of power, nor to vanquish the German enemy. Wilson called for war to bring the right of self-determination to peoples everywhere.[29]

"I am proposing," Wilson told Congress January 22, 1917, "that every people should be left free to determine its own polity, its own way of development, unhindered, unthreatened, unafraid, the little along with the great and powerful." The rhetoric could just as well have been drawn from the campaign of 1912. The themes were virtually identical, liberal progressivism applied globally. Liberty, Wilson argued, was the fundamental right to choose one's own way of life and live as one saw fit, and it belonged properly to all people, to nations as well as to individuals. The United States would fight to vouchsafe the right of free choice —the very essence of democratic freedom—to people struggling to be heard across the world.[30]

As he had done in the campaign of 1912, Wilson proposed to enable self-determination by making government a neutral umpire protecting the people's rights. The neutral government he had in mind this time was worldwide in scale. Wilson wanted to found a new international governing body, to be called the League of Nations, that would take the place of armed conflict between states. The League would supplement, but not supplant, national sovereignty. It would draw the nations of the world together to achieve their common interests in peace and freedom. From now on, according to Wilson's program, world powers would rely for their safety on collective security. No more colonies or arms races. No more secret alliances. Wilson's League was to be built on reciprocal pledges by member-states to respect the territorial rights of one another. These pledges were in turn to be backed by a judicial system of sanctions and penalties. Henceforth the Western world, led by the United States, would pursue an altruistic foreign policy, grounded in the universal interest of every nation and every person in free self-development.[31]

Wilson's domestic politics and his foreign policy were philosophically consistent. In both spheres, Wilson aimed to elevate choice and free self-determination as the primary end of statecraft. The man who denigrated Roosevelt's politics as unrealistic ultimately proposed to remake the world order, but not because he believed that the diverse and contesting interests of nation-states could be fully reconciled, any more than he believed that Americans' plural values and life ambitions could be orchestrated into national unison. Rather, Wilson sought to build consensus, at home and abroad, around neutral political procedure. His guiding idea in both realms was to let individuals work out their interests as they saw fit—for what were nations, in the end, but groups of individuals? Government would confine itself to protecting neutral rights and the conditions of free choice. At home, that meant state regulation to revitalize the market and give the disadvantaged equal opportunity. Abroad, it meant collective security to prevent domination by the powerful few and to protect the rights of every nation. That his project failed so spectacularly in its international dimension is a telltale sign that Wilson's politics were not as neutral as he insisted. In fact, the commitment to free self-determination as the greatest political good depended on a host of subordinate moral and political commitments the nations of the world did not necessarily share with the United States. Wilson drastically underestimated the moral and intellectual consensus necessary to sustain his liberty-oriented world order, perhaps because he had for so long maintained that social morality was irrelevant or just not possible.

Wilson's call for a peace without victory left Roosevelt cold. The president totally failed, Roosevelt thought, to appreciate the substantive national interests driving the warring parties. "If the powers were justified in going into this war by their vital interests, then they are required to continue the war until these vital interests are no longer in jeopardy," Roosevelt believed. National interests were stubborn things. By pretending that nations had no vital interests apart from the gauzy right of self-determination, Wilson retreated from reality. "We must endeavor earnestly but with sanity to bring about better world conditions," Roosevelt admonished. But constructing an elaborate edifice of international law on the ill-defined right to self-determination, with no regard for the actual circumstances of actual countries and their widely various political, economic, and security needs, was ridiculous. "Some of these fourteen points are mischievous under any interpretation," Roosevelt said. "Most of them are worded in language so vague and so purely rhetorical that they may be construed with equal justice as having diametrically opposite meanings." It was hard to know exactly what Wilson meant. But what Roosevelt understood, he didn't like.[32]

In perhaps his most powerful argument, Roosevelt pointed out that Wilson's collective security arrangement would commit the United States to routine overseas military intervention even as Wilson sought to reduce American armaments. The president's plan for collective security depended on the territorial guarantees contemplated in his famous Fourteen Points. But who would make good those promises? Roosevelt suspected it would be the United States. "Point thirteen proposes an independent Poland, which is right," Roosevelt offered as an example, "and then proposes that we guarantee its integrity in the event of future war, which is preposterous unless we intend to become a military nation more fit for overseas warfare than Germany is at present." Wilson's new world order would require not only the transformation of the international system, but the transformation of America's place in the world. Roosevelt believed in the United States' messianic destiny, to be sure. He wanted his country to take a more active role in international affairs. But he doubted Wilson's altruism was sustainable. The Democrat's policy was enough to "guarantee our being from time to time engaged in war over matters in which we had no interest whatever," Roosevelt groused. Did Wilson honestly expect Americans to support frequent armed conflict "with the national constabulary to which he desired to reduce our armed forces"? Could he really expect Americans to play the world's policemen with no regard for their own national security or peculiar interests?[33]

If Roosevelt came off sounding uncharacteristically like a skeptic to Wilson's confident idealist, it was because he concluded that Wilson failed to appreciate the primary importance of the nation. Wilson's greatest sin in foreign affairs stemmed from his most glaring weakness in domestic politics. He wasn't nationalist enough. In his crusade to bring American democracy to the world, Wilson failed to understand that American democracy was the singular product of unique historical circumstances. America was more than an idea; it was a nation. It was no good trying to universalize American "values"—those values sprang from a particular way of life that could not be precisely replicated elsewhere. The same was true for every nation. Historical experience, which was to say, evolutionary experience, simply was not fungible. National identity was not fungible.[34]

Roosevelt's racial ideas stood at back of his nationalism. Nations were important things to him because he believed that nations were the locus of racial self-development. They represented the final stage of evolutionary social progress. The American race had won its moral refinement and forged its distinctive way of life through centuries of struggle. The fruits of that labor—self-government—could not be reduced, as Wilson wanted, to a series of international laws. According to Roosevelt, the way to spread democracy was to spread American influence and American racial stock. Like the apostles of manifest destiny before him, Roosevelt viewed American expansion as the most prominent, effective means by which the United States did good for the world. Roosevelt thought that Wilson's reformist scheme not only would fail, but that it was a fool's errand, a distraction from the serious business of preserving American security.

The United States could not contribute to the uplift of humanity if it ceased to exist or, by the same token, if it was hamstrung by ill-conceived collective security arrangements like the kind Wilson glibly endorsed. "[T]he affairs of hither Asia, the Balkan Peninsula, and of North Africa are of prime concern to the powers of Europe, and the United States should be under no covenant to go to war about matters in which its people have no concern and probably no intelligent interest," Roosevelt concluded. He rejected Wilson's calls to join the League of Nations on much the same logic. "We will not surrender our independence to a league of nations any more than to a single nation," he said. The United States would not be tied down.[35]

Roosevelt was no isolationist. While he regarded Wilson's plans for international peace as dangerously quixotic, he did not counsel American retreat. "The United States cannot again completely draw into its shell," he admonished his fellow citizens. Wilson's League was unwise, but the United States "ought to join with the other civilized nations of the world in some scheme that in a time of great stress would offer a likelihood of obtaining just settlements that will avert war." Roosevelt had a counter proposal, an idea he called the world league for the peace of righteousness. The sovereign nation-state was its bricks and mortar.[36]

Rather than a collective security pact, Roosevelt suggested a league that would function as a more traditional alliance, in which member-states took on reciprocal responsibilities pursuant to a treaty. The Roosevelt league would create an international tribunal to settle disputes among member nations, touching everything from trade to colonial territory, excepting, importantly, the vital national interests of territorial integrity and self-defense. Member-states would contribute jurists to the tribunal and pledge both to obey the body's decisions and to provide military force to execute judgments against recalcitrant nations. Only states boasting a reliable domestic legal system, competent armed forces, and demonstrated commitment to keeping treaty obligations could join. Roosevelt anticipated that seventeen countries would qualify as of 1918, including France, England, Germany (properly reformed after the war), Russia, Japan, Brazil, Chile, Argentina, and the United States. His league would be no stand-pat organization. Roosevelt as much as Wilson concluded that the antebellum balance of power could not survive. His proposed alliance sought to engender a more stable and peaceful international system. Its major goal was to provide incentives to nation-states to become more democratic.[37]

"The spread of democracy," Roosevelt said in his own version of the democratic peace theory, "would render it probably a little more unlikely that there would be a repetition of such disastrous warfare." If nation-states wanted to join his league, they would have to adopt an open and fair legal system and operate a government based on the rule of law. Roosevelt hoped the league over time would promote the spread of ordered freedom worldwide.[38]

In its leading features, the Roosevelt league for righteousness anticipated multinational bodies to come. The North Atlantic Treaty Organization, the United Nations Security Council, and the World Trade Organization all bore a resemblance to Roosevelt's league. These later organizations shared telling features in common. All boasted restricted membership based on highly normative criteria; a well-defined decision-making apparatus; a tangible enforcement mechanism; and, in the case of the Security Council especially, an exemption from collective commitments when vital national interests were at stake.[39]

While Wilson imputed a common, overriding interest to every nation—namely, the right to self-determination—and then proposed to construct an international legal order to protect it, Roosevelt sought instead to work with existing state interests as he found them. He believed in a national, but not a global, common good, because to his mind the people of the world did not share the characteristics that made a common good possible. They did not look to a common history, a common language, common political institutions, or common racial destiny. They were too diverse to be one people, too pluralistic to share a set of overarching moral commitments. Roosevelt may have believed that the principles of righteousness were immutable, even universal. But he believed even more strongly that each person learned his duties and discovered his identity in the nation.

Roosevelt made the nation-state his lodestar. He eschewed talk of universal interests or of international law as the guarantor of peace. Wilson's plan to multiply the legal codes governing the conduct of nations frankly baffled the colonel. "Existing treaties are utterly worthless so far as concerns protecting any free, well-behaved people," he thought—and not because they failed sufficiently to recognize the mysterious right to self-determination. The problem was that international law lacked any reliable means of enforcement. "There is no central police power," Roosevelt noted, "and not the least likelihood of one being created." In these circumstances, to rely on the pronouncements of a League of Nations and a host of new treaties mandating reductions in national armaments was to blink reality. Roosevelt could not bear to hear Wilson called an "idealist." To him, the Democrat was a sham reformer, a timid and confused man who did not understand the real world and could not bring himself to take the steps necessary to change it.[40]

In the debate surrounding the Great War, Roosevelt and Wilson seemed on the surface to have switched places. In the months after America's entry in the fighting in 1917, it was Wilson whose reform agenda aimed for transformation,

and Roosevelt who counseled caution, circumspection, and attention to interests. These differences, however, were more apparent than actual. In fact, Wilson's foreign policy flowed from his individualist liberalism, his commitment to
self-development and freedom of choice as the critical elements of democratic
liberty. Roosevelt's interest-based policy, on the other hand, arose from his enduring nationalism, including his racialized interpretation of history and his
unique brand of manifest destiny. His arguments against Wilson's Fourteen
Points and world league would be used in 1919 as a justification for total American withdrawal from the concerns of Europe and the world abroad. But this was
not what he intended. Roosevelt was an expansionist to the end, if not necessarily, by 1918, any longer a colonialist. He still saw the United States as the vanguard of civilization. An international alignment that favored American expansion was his consistent and preeminent priority.[41]

Roosevelt had hoped to persuade his countrymen that withdrawal was impossible and unwise. He hoped to convince them to reject Wilson's individualist liberalism and follow his lead to national greatness and world power. Instead, the
portion of Roosevelt's rhetoric that resonated most was his invective against Wilson's League of Nations and his ringing defense of American sovereignty. Americans in 1918 were not anxious for another adventure. Four decades of dizzying
social and economic upheaval and nearly twenty years of intense, ambitious political reform had taken their toll. The world war was the progressive era's last
great crusade, and, paradoxically, most progressives opposed it. The 1920s would
become a decade of retrenchment, the search for moral order and social justice
characteristic of the early twentieth century replaced by a search for normalcy.
The situation might have been different—history might have been different—
had the progressive moment's most prominent leader not passed into political
exile after 1912. The United States might have entered the war earlier or on different footing. Roosevelt may have prolonged his fellow Americans' interest in regulation and reform. He may have convinced the Republicans to sponsor the advent of America's social welfare state, on his terms and for the purpose of
transforming the national character. Or perhaps not. But Roosevelt would not
wait in 1912, and, as a result, he would never return to power. He spent his final
years an outcast, as the moment passed him by. It was his fate, as his life's afternoon stretched into evening, to watch his dreams fade with the light.

Roosevelt wanted to use the national state to remake society or, to his way of
thinking, to lift American society to its true potential. If the form Roosevelt's ambition took was ultimately illiberal, it was also paradoxically the most progressive
aspect of his thought. Roosevelt suspected particularlist attachments. He disliked traditions that he regarded as backward and outdated. A new national com-

munity, organized and sustained by the federal government, was his answer to the classic republican problem of virtue. Unlike Woodrow Wilson, Roosevelt would dare to rely on virtues, warrior virtues, because he would dare to marshal government to cultivate them. The result was something similar to what Dwight D. Eisenhower would later call "the garrison state": a country directed by its national government, its society modeled on the army, its economy sustained by military expenditure, its rationale, expansion. This was not the America imagined by Thomas Jefferson or James Madison, John Adams, George Washington, or even Alexander Hamilton. It was not the "last best hope on earth" Abraham Lincoln served. Certainly it found no place in the rhetoric of Woodrow Wilson, though Wilson would pursue many a statist policy. Roosevelt's statecraft cared little or nothing for natural rights. It attended not at all to self-evident truths. He referred infrequently to the principles of the Declaration of Independence, and when he did he tended to summarize them as representing "an intense spirit of nationalism." Roosevelt's politics concentrated on instilling the warrior virtues. He strove to prepare America for world power, and to spread American power around the world. He worked, for the whole of his public life, to do his part for the cause of righteousness and to make Americans a great race.[42]

"I believe that at heart the average American man and the average American woman are sound, and that while at the moment they may disregard all appeal, all preaching," Roosevelt said somewhat forlornly after he left the presidency, "yet that sooner or later there will come a deep moral awakening which will stir them to a realization of what is happening before it is too late to undo it." Like many other members of his generation's reform cadre, Roosevelt never stopped hoping and working for moral renewal. For him, moral awakening meant something other than conviction of sin and personal repentance. It meant something different from a return to biblical Christianity. Moral awakening meant righteous behavior, behavior in accord with the virile virtues evolved over millennia in mankind's journey of evolutionary progress, behavior he had learned as a boy in the house of his father.[43]

Roosevelt strove all his life to be worthy of his calling. He expended blood and time and years of toil, faced the sting of bullets and public ridicule, surmounted tragic loss and personal doubt, to try to become a righteous man. He expected the same from his country. Roosevelt's struggle became his religion, and his religion his politics—a politics of effort, strife, strenuosity, and transformation by sheer force of will. His life's journey, a sixty-year spiritual and intellectual odyssey, defined an era and, in the process, changed a nation. Roosevelt contained in his person the major preoccupations and enthusiasms of the age, from the passion for science to the burning concern for moral rejuvenation. He participated in the day's major movements, and led more than a few of them. His politics mirrored the transition from the civic republicanism of the nineteenth century to the modern liberalism of the twentieth. Indeed, in many ways it was a transition he accelerated.

Roosevelt cast the political ideals of nineteenth century republican liberalism as outdated and timeworn. He called economic independence and frontier individualism things of the past. In their stead, he preached a new republicanism of collective action, a republicanism of state regulation and social welfare. He preached a warrior republicanism predicated on the warrior virtues. His ideas and his antics, his adventures and his sermons—really, his whole life story—inspired a generation of American reformers. Though his politics of virtue passed ultimately into the shadows, supplanted by a different progressivism he helped make possible, his vision of collectivist nationalism lived on, nourished by the dislocations of the industrial age, as well as by the institutions Roosevelt helped create: the administrative state and the plebiscitary presidency principally. In time, another Roosevelt would return to Theodore's collectivist vision and find there inspiration for a transformative politics of his own. Whether the Republican Roosevelt would have approved is difficult to say but is beside the point. Already by 1918, Roosevelt's ideas, no less than his life, belonged to history, their fate beyond his ken.

In the autumn of 1918 Roosevelt focused on the present, still working, still hoping, for a great righteous awakening in his lifetime. He hoped though he doubted his countrymen heard him any longer; he soldiered on though he believed the race teetered on the brink of irreversible disaster. He kept the faith even when personal sorrow overtook him and the shadows lengthened.

The results of the 1918 autumn elections were somewhat heartening. Wilson's Democrats suffered badly as voters returned Republican majorities to both houses of Congress. Roosevelt claimed to a foreign correspondent that had America's been a parliamentary democracy, those elections might have returned him to executive office. But these too were the words of a man history had some time ago left behind. Roosevelt was no longer leader of the Republican Party. His warrior republicanism was no longer, if it ever had been, the party's reigning creed. Americans were no longer interested in hearing of heroic sacrifices and martial virtues. They wanted peace and prosperity and a chance to live their lives as they saw fit. They wanted, as time showed, Woodrow Wilson's republic, or at least his rhetoric. But Roosevelt kept up the battle right to the end, trying to discredit Wilson and position himself for yet another presidential run in 1920. As a warrior, he knew the future was not in his control. The best he could do was fight mightily, and hope to be remembered.

Still, Roosevelt was tired, especially after a taxing fall campaign. The malaria his body harbored, a vicious relic from a trip to South America, tormented him. Following a long hospital stay in November and December of 1918, he returned to Sagamore Hill in time for Christmas, sixty years old and ready, after all his battles, for a bit of rest. Just before midnight on January fifth, 1919, Roosevelt laid aside his work for the last time and prepared to sleep. "James," he said to his butler, "will you please put out the light?"

Epilogue

Eulogists hailed Theodore Roosevelt with the reverence and earnest warmth reserved for men who have touched one's soul. They called him an emblem of American manhood, a scion of virility and strength. The New York Assembly praised his "indomitable will, unconquerable courage and power of mental and physical endurance." Many mentioned his laborious journey from fragile youth to energetic adulthood. Others noted his common touch despite his privileged upbringing. Nearly all praised his moral vision and capacity to inspirit, invigorate, inspire. "Today," said Senator Frederick Davenport from the floor of the New York Assembly three days after Roosevelt's death, "there has been laid to rest a great prophet of the whole of the American people."[1]

Yet from the glowing tributes of the New York Assembly to the learned paean by Henry Cabot Lodge—who managed to quote Shakespeare, Wordsworth, John Bunyan, Arthur Hugh Clough, and a medieval Moorish ballad in his forty-three page acclamation—perhaps the most insightful praise came in the homely verse composed for Roosevelt's funeral at Oyster Bay:

> With something of the savant and the sage,
> He was, when all is said and sung, a man;
> The flower imperishable of this valiant age,
> A True American.[2]

A child of wealth, a son of power, elite-educated and politically well-heeled: in so many ways, Theodore Roosevelt could not have been less like the great body of his countrymen. Still, he lent his character to an age and became an American icon because he had, above all, an American mind. The great concerns and preoccupations of his era were his preoccupations. His intellectual and spiritual journey paralleled the trajectory of the nation's own into the twentieth century. The progressive era wrote its political autobiography in him.

Roosevelt captured the imagination of his countrymen with his spirited sermons for righteous living. He stirred them with his calls to focus anew on the meaning and practice of democratic liberty. Roosevelt was the emblematic progressive in part because his experience paralleled that of so many of his fellow reformers, in part because his intellectual development reflected that of the age, but really, for this reason foremost: more than any other national figure of the era, he caught the nation's sudden and intense concern for the preservation of self-government. And he embodied that passion in his politics. The industrial upheaval inspired Roosevelt, as it did so many of his fellow Americans, to grapple forthrightly with the fundamental questions of freedom. It moved him to ponder afresh the moral and intellectual requirements of democratic citizenship; to ask after the best institutional arrangements to sustain free life; to seek a way to reconcile the new industrial economy with republican equality and independence; to articulate the place of a free republic in the world. Roosevelt thought more deeply on these questions and saw farther than most any of his contemporaries, including Woodrow Wilson. He was alive to the basic and enduring problems of liberal democracy, and he practiced a politics to answer them. In an era that might have been dominated by petty squabbles over the distribution of prosperity between triumphant capitalists and a supine lower class, or by parceling out economic prizes to discrete groups to still their clamor, or by smug self-satisfaction about the rise of American industry to world prowess, or by willful failure to see the plight of the poor and dispossessed, Roosevelt and the American people with him refused to be waylaid. They addressed the discontent of their time and insisted, in the process, on considering how to preserve their free republic. Their answers may not always have been wise or consistent, but they had the courage and the character to ask the questions.

That courage and that insight, that refusal to mistake the conditions of liberty with the thing itself, is what made Roosevelt a national icon, and what makes him and his era so different from our own.

This is not to say Roosevelt's politics represent a political holy grail that, if only recovered, would set all things to right. Roosevelt's solutions to the unease of his day and to the permanent problems of free government were controversial even in his own lifetime, and for good reason. Their tendency toward statism, racialism, and coercion is enough to give even the most sympathetic admirer pause.

Roosevelt built his political thought on a philosophy of life as struggle. He believed that humans could wrest meaning from a chaotic cosmos only through self-initiated effort. Consequently, he emphasized conquest to an alarming degree. He tended to treat the most powerful as the most virtuous and equate civilization with superiority of force. His impatient dismissals of Native Americans' land claims, his refusal even to grant a fair airing of grievances, offer an unpleasant case in point. By locating the source of human purpose in human volition or will, Roosevelt ominously suggested there is no ethical structure or moral law embedded in the universe, discernable through well-formed reason and reflection. His life philosophy thus provided no internal restraint on the exercise of the will, and no guide for the proper use of power. While Roosevelt insisted one should fight honorably, and show fairness and even compassion in life's battle, these moral imperatives owe more to his synthesis of Christian thought and evolutionary theory than to his warrior philosophy itself. Roosevelt, left to his own devices, might sound a good deal more like Friedrich Nietzsche.

Roosevelt's tendency to praise power, apart from the justice of its use, was only exacerbated by his racial doctrine. He was a well-educated man who had traveled the world and was known to admire other cultures and civilizations. Nevertheless, his preoccupation with bloodlines, and social evolution generally, skewed his cultural analyses. He drastically underestimated the importance of language, tradition, and religious practice in defining a people. He discounted—to the point of ignoring—the role of ideas in the formation of cultural life and social identity. His thought carries the ugly cast common to those who think all of human life is reducible to biological phenomena, which can, in turn, be manipulated by the wise and strong.

One of the most unsettling implications of Roosevelt's racial ideas is the place they give to the state. He drew no distinction between the race acting as a whole and the national government. The latter was a natural extension of the former, in his view. And if humans found their greatest meaning in the triumphs of the race, as Roosevelt believed they did, the nation-state came to be the focus of all human life. The American founders had countered such a statist view by pointing to natural rights as limits on the power of the political community, indicators of the person's destiny beyond the political realm. Roosevelt rejected this construction and eviscerated the notion of natural rights. For him, there was nothing natural—common to all humans by virtue of their humanity—about rights. They existed to protect the conditions citizens needed in order to achieve for the good of the race. They could be changed by the state from generation to generation.

Roosevelt's concomitant hostility toward private religion, local associations, and other possible sources of civic identity outside the national collective betrayed his troubling belief that race and racial interests were ultimately the only substantive things a people had in common. Besides his implicit denigration of the value of ideas, Roosevelt's conversion of the kingdom of God into the body politic is especially noteworthy. Religion in his hands ceased to circumscribe state action and became instead its impetus. The effect was to reverse the centuries-long trend of Western history and raise the aims of republican politics—dramatically. Roosevelt's politics sought to found on earth the righteous city, to get citizens who were more than independent, deliberative, and unselfish, as in traditional republican politics. Roosevelt sought to make citizens righteous.

The intersection of this inflated formative ambition and Roosevelt's racial ideas proved particularly perilous. Like the ideal republic of Socrates, which also strove to heal the human person in the polity, Roosevelt's warrior republic finally looked to eugenics to reform human nature. His political thought authorized the state to prune and perfect the nation's racial stock in a program of eugenic breeding and sterilization not entirely dissimilar to that pursued by the German Third Reich. The American government's brief foray into eugenic politics has been fiercely and justly condemned, and the demise of Roosevelt's eugenicist statecraft is no loss.

Many of these shortcomings were publicly identified by Woodrow Wilson. In his own brand of progressive politics, Wilson offered a contrasting interpretation of democratic freedom. He construed liberty as the ability of the individual to choose his own path and define his own destiny free of interference from others.[3]

Wilson's liberalism carried the day. In the years following his election in 1912, his Democratic Party gradually adapted Theodore Roosevelt's nationalist regulatory policies to the logic of Wilsonian individualism. As Wilson's campaign rhetoric in 1912 foreshadowed, Democrats became increasingly preoccupied with guaranteeing disadvantaged individuals and groups equal ability to choose their own ends and equal protection from interference when choosing. They turned more frequently to the federal government to provide the conditions of freedom in the form of social and economic security and through redistribution of wealth. This movement culminated with the presidency of Franklin Delano Roosevelt, who once characterized his New Deal as a "satisfactory compromise" between his cousin's New Nationalism and Wilson's New Freedom. In fact, the New Deal represented collectivist nationalism in the service of procedural liberalism: an activist state to secure the conditions for meaningful individual choice, Rooseveltian means to Wilsonian ends.[4]

Wilson's political and intellectual victory affected the Republicans in no less noteworthy, and perhaps in more historically ironic, ways. Left intellectually

adrift after the defeat of William Howard Taft, Republicans continued their bitter infighting. Insurgents backed Wilson's regulatory efforts, which they welcomed as a belated conversion to their cause. Republican conservatives continued to question the wisdom of additional state regulation, pointing to its impact
on business productivity and freedom of contract.

Roosevelt-style national planning enjoyed a brief renaissance under the leadership of Herbert Hoover, the nation's first engineer president and a devotee of
scientific management. Hoover criticized the adversarial relationship between
government and business during the Wilson years and promoted instead state-
sponsored cooperative associations designed to bring government and business
together to foster economic stability, growth, and technological dynamism. Notably absent from Hoover's associationalism, however, was any aspiration to cultivate the warrior virtues or to achieve social transformation. Hoover's was a program of economic prosperity, a procedural politics in its own right. The onset of
the Great Depression and Franklin Roosevelt's arrival in Washington curtailed
the Hoover Republicans' experiment with positive government. As Roosevelt
implemented his New Deal, the GOP adopted a principled opposition to activist government sounding in the rhetoric of individual freedom. They criticized Franklin Roosevelt's collectivist ventures with the logic of Woodrow Wilson. While they eventually accepted the major pillars of the Depression-era
social welfare state, Republicans from the middle of the century forward usually
opposed additional federal programs for economic regulation or redistribution
of wealth as assaults on the individual's right to live his own life.[5]

Since the 1930s, then, most Republicans have embraced a Wilsonian-sound-
ing skepticism about government as an agent of social improvement. They have
largely eschewed Theodore Roosevelt's language of collective solidarity and promoted instead a politics of liberty. This emphasis became particularly pronounced after the presidential candidacy of Barry Goldwater and the rise of the
Goldwater conservatives. Reacting against what they considered to be the excesses of the postwar welfare state and its tendencies toward waste and coercion,
the Goldwater Republicans talked of liberty as the absence of governmental—or
at least bureaucratic—power. Their rhetoric had a distinctly anti-paternalist,
anti-government ring. Democrats, Republicans were charging regularly by the
late 1960s, had become the party of "big-brother government." The GOP, by
contrast, wanted to "get the government off the backs of the people" and release
popular energy. Perhaps the most articulate political spokesman for this libertarian liberalism, once deployed rhetorically by Wilson against Theodore Roosevelt, was the man who led Roosevelt's party but bore Wilson's name. Ronald
Wilson Reagan famously told the American public that "government is not the

solution to our problems. Government is the problem." Wilson could not have said it better himself.[6]

Yet strands of Theodore Roosevelt's thought resurfaced in Reagan's politics and in the work of his neo-conservative compatriots. Alongside his anti-establishment rhetoric of individual freedom, Reagan spoke of renewing national unity and fellow-feeling by making government again the agent of the common good. "It is not my intention to do away with government," he said at his first inaugural. "It is, rather, to make it work." The state, he went on, "can and must provide opportunity, not smother it; foster productivity, not stifle it." Reagan's political strength stemmed, at least in part, from his ability to articulate a vigorous sense of national purpose. He characterized the United States as a righteous city with a mighty mission. "For now it is our task to tend and preserve, through the darkest and coldest nights, that 'sacred fire of liberty,'" Reagan said. He urged Americans to draw together to defeat the Soviet Union, which he called "the focus of evil in the modern world." Reagan campaigned as an unabashed nationalist, and he governed that way, too. While he spoke frequently of cutting back the size of the state, Reagan as president famously grew the federal government rather than shrinking it; federal spending climbed to historic highs on his watch. The occasion for much of this spending was a major military buildup, the chief emblem of his reinvigorated nationalism. Reagan's hawkish foreign policy and concomitant celebration of America's virtues brought millions of former Democrats into the Republican ranks—"Reagan Democrats" they were called—and helped account for his large electoral majorities in the elections of 1980 and 1984. All of which is to suggest that Reagan succeeded politically as much because of his Rooseveltian emphasis on national strength and solidarity as because of his rhetoric of personal freedom.[7]

While Reagan resuscitated, in a gentler form, Roosevelt's nationalism, neo-conservative intellectuals like Irving Kristol rediscovered the moral power of state action. Kristol famously questioned the moral consequences of the Great Society welfare state. He feared that, in the long run, welfare policies would worsen poverty rather than alleviate it by eroding the character traits necessary for personal success, just as they might undermine ordered liberty by destroying the qualities necessary for participatory self-government. This analysis shared Roosevelt's moral concern, albeit from a different angle, and reflected his insight that politics can and does have moral consequences. Other members of the modern conservative coalition went a step further. After the U.S. Supreme Court's decision legalizing abortion in 1973, evangelical Protestants and orthodox Catholics turned to the Republican Party in large numbers, a trend that accelerated over the ensuing two decades. These voters pressed for government to set a moral standard, to become again through its policies a force for national moral renewal. The agenda of the social conservatives and that of the more libertarian Republicans have not always meshed well, and, as the twenty-first century began, party orthodoxy remained in flux, suspended between competing priorities and, if only implicitly, competing visions of democratic freedom.[8]

Even so, in a milieu where the meaning of political labels is still fixed largely by reference to one's position on the New Deal and Great Society programs, almost all Republicans have remained wary of the social welfare state and ambivalent, if not hostile, to its progressive antecedents. Theodore Roosevelt is himself an ambiguous figure in this context. He does not fit well on the contemporary spectrum as either a conservative or a liberal, and while modern Republicans often admire his style, they just as often balk at his politics. Given the history of the party and its current struggles, there is a certain paradox in Republicans' ambivalence toward the progressive era and its iconic leader. It was the Republican Party after all, that, before Woodrow Wilson and even before Theodore Roosevelt, led the nation toward government regulation of industry and social melioration. Republicans are, historically speaking, no strangers to the use of government power. And the party is historically no stranger to internal competition between pro-business, pro-market, laissez-faire partisans on the one hand and moral reformers on the other. Republicans sustained a similar debate at the turn of the last century, one that was resolved for a season by the synthetic politics of Theodore Roosevelt, who sought to make the market good for democracy. In this connection, he and his fellow progressives are the people from whom contemporary Republicans may be apt to learn most.

In the end, despite his political failures and personal shortcomings, despite his repulsive racialism, his statism, and his obsession with power, Roosevelt's politics still hold a kernel of promise for the American future. Roosevelt knew two things worth remembering that contemporary Americans have forgotten.

He knew that liberty is a fundamentally social undertaking. Like ours, his age prized personal freedom, and Woodrow Wilson bested Roosevelt at the polls by making personal choice the end of his political program. But Roosevelt understood that the individual's highest capacities are realized in society. Laboring and learning, creating and worshipping, deliberating and governing: if the individual is able to pursue these activities, we say that she is free. Each requires a particular social context. Roosevelt rightly worried that freedom understood primarily as the right to choose, or as the U.S. Supreme Court has put it more recently, as the "right to define one's own concept of existence, of meaning, [and] of the universe," would obscure the institutional arrangements that made individuals' most important life activities possible. For that matter, liberty-as-choice failed to differentiate between individuals' highest callings and their more base desires; the theory eschewed such "normative" social judgments. Against all this, Roosevelt insisted that some pursuits *are* more worthy than others, and the most important ones—from political deliberation to family life—are possible only in a stable society governed by law and sustained by a healthy sense of the common good. Under the influence of Wilsonian-style liberalism, contemporary Americans have come to think of liberty in a way that is vaguely antisocial. We are vigilant for individual rights, but we have trouble saying what it is that social, political life is affirmatively good for. Roosevelt and the progressives remind us that political life is about practicing and protecting the activities that make us human and make us free.[9]

Roosevelt also knew that politics is a profoundly moral enterprise. For better or worse, the laws a people adopt shape the type of citizens they become. Roosevelt was attentive to this formative relationship from his earliest days as a politician and historian. His study of the American frontier convinced him that only a certain type of citizen can sustain democracy. He spent the rest of his political life attempting to secure the conditions that made for responsible, independent citizens. He warned again and again that an economy that rewarded dishonest gain and exploitation of workers would ultimately undermine the moral rectitude and mutual sympathy between citizens necessary for democratic government. He cautioned that poor working conditions and weak families made for bad citizens. The descent of American politics since the Second World War into a banal project of economic management has encouraged us to forget that political choices implicate citizens' characters. Questions about what economic or social welfare policies we should adopt are really questions about what sort of people we want to become, or that ought to be what the questions are about, anyway. Our politics would benefit if we recovered the link between civic character and liberty.

Long after Roosevelt's death, his rhetoric continues to thrill his countrymen with its exhortations to live better, to be more, to aspire to something nobler. If politics is, as Bismarck said, the art of the possible, Roosevelt's politics illumine possibilities not currently realized on the American political scene. His career, and the career of the era he led, demonstrates that the statecraft of economic growth need not be the sum and substance of democratic life. Politics can be about more than distributing the proceeds of the gross national product or balancing the wants of competing interest groups. If a return to Roosevelt's warrior republicanism is both untenable, given the fading of the moral sources that informed its principles, and undesirable, given its statist, racist, and coercive inclinations, his example may yet help Americans imagine a substantive politics of another kind. It may help them go forward to a new public philosophy attentive to the institutional arrangements and moral requisites necessary for liberty, to a politics focused once more on the practice of self-government and its meaning for our lives.

"Roosevelt was the greatest preacher of righteousness in modern times," Gifford Pinchot once claimed.[10] We could stand to hear his sermons again.

Author's Note

In the half-dozen years I have spent working on this project, I have accumulated a voluminous list of personal debts which I cannot hope to discharge here. Nevertheless, I welcome the opportunity at least to acknowledge those people and institutions that have made this book possible. I would like to begin by thanking David Kennedy. Most everything I know about what it means to be a scholar I learned from him. In the years I have known him, he has acted as my teacher, my adviser, my mentor, and my friend. He was the one who encouraged me to undertake this project those years ago, and his tireless support, learned criticism, and sage counsel have helped make it possible for me to finish it. I am not just a better writer and scholar for having known him, I am a better man.

I would like to thank Professor John Blum, the dean of Roosevelt scholarship, and Professor John Cooper, who has penned the best book yet written on Roosevelt's political thought. Between the two of them, they read the entire manuscript multiple times. Their constructive comments and incisive criticisms have been invaluable to me. Akhil Amar offered timely advice for revision, as did Lewis Gould. I offer my sincere thanks to both of them. My editor at Yale University Press, Chris Rogers, and my reviewers there immeasurably improved the quality of this work, for which I thank them.

I would like to thank St. Paul's School and Stephen Baldock especially for giving me the opportunity to teach some of the brightest students in the United Kingdom and try out more than a few of these ideas on them. St. Paul's also afforded me the chance to continue my research and writing while there, for which I am doubly grateful. In that connection, I also thank the British Library for allowing me access to their vast collection.

The Yale Law School's Reubhausen Fund generously supported my archival research at the Houghton Library at Harvard. I offer my thanks to its contributors. Elizabeth Winthrop, on behalf of the Alsop family, kindly permitted me to quote from several private Roosevelt family letters on deposit at the Houghton Library; my thanks to her and the family. I also thank Judge Eugene Nardelli for graciously sharing a rare volume of Roosevelt eulogies from his personal library.

My family has provided unflagging encouragement over the years without which I would never have finished this project. My mother, father, and sister read drafts, offered editorial input, served as sounding boards, and always believed—especially when I didn't—that I had something to contribute. This book has been their dream as much as it has been mine, and I thank them with my love. From an early age, I was blessed by people in my life who thought I could be a writer. Two teachers, in particular, helped me find my voice along the way. Mark Bubalo and Andy Hagedorn pushed me, challenged me, edited me, and demanded I keep writing, no matter what. I did, in no small part because of them.

Countless others have contributed to this project in one way or another, from library staff to classmates and colleagues. I offer all of them my sincere thanks and gratitude.

NOTES

1. IN THE FATHER'S HOUSE

1. Recollections of Anna Roosevelt Cowles (October 28, 1924), Theodore Roosevelt Collection, Putnam Papers R110.P971, Houghton Library, Harvard University (ARC Recollections, Roosevelt Collection HL, hereinafter). Edwin G. Burrows and Mike Wallace, *Gotham: A History of New York City to 1898* (New York: Oxford University Press, 1999), 746–47. For more on the New York of this period, see James Grant Wilson, *Memorial History of the City of New York: From Its First Settlement to the Year 1892* (New York: New York History Co., 1892), 3:422–38; Theodore Roosevelt, *New York* (New York: Longmans, Green, 1891), 512, 523.

2. William H. Seward, "The Irrepressible Conflict," in *The Works of William H. Seward*, ed. George Baker (Boston: Houghton, 1884), 4:289. Seward's speech was noted in the *New York Times*, October 27, 1858, which Martha Roosevelt may well have seen.

3. John C. Calhoun, *Disquisition on Government, and a Discourse on the Constitution and Government of the United States* (Columbia, S.C.: A. S. Johnston, 1852). See also Harry V. Jaffa, *A New Birth of Freedom: Abraham Lincoln and the Coming of the Civil War* (New York: Rowman and Littlefield, 2000), 403–72.

4. *South Carolina Defines the Causes of Secession*, 1860.

5. Letter from Martha Bulloch to Susan West (October 28, 1858); Martha Bulloch to Susan West (November 1, 1858), Putnam Papers, Roosevelt Collection HL. See also *New York Times*, October 27, 1858; Carleton Putnam, *Theodore Roosevelt: The Formative Years* (New York: Charles Scribner's Sons, 1958), 22.

6. The family never referred to the elder Roosevelt as "Senior," however, and Teedie himself dropped the "Junior" appellation by his early twenties. Theodore Roosevelt, *Autobiography* (New York: Charles Scribner's Sons, 1913), 5. Ibid., 27.

7. Ibid., 7. Theodore Roosevelt, Jr., to Theodore Roosevelt (October 22, 1876), in Roosevelt, *The Letters of Theodore Roosevelt*, ed. Elting E. Morrison et al. (Cambridge: Harvard University Press, 1952–54), 1:18. The elder Theodore's children uniformly attested to his unstinting love and depth of character; he was the greatest man in each of their

lives. See Putnam Papers, ARC Recollections (October 27, 1925), Roosevelt Collection HL. See also Recollections of Corinne Robinson Alsop (CRA Recollections hereinafter), Putnam Papers, Roosevelt Collection HL.

8. Putnam, *Theodore Roosevelt*, 5.

9. ARC Recollections (October 23, 1925), Roosevelt Collection HL. For more on the house, see ARC Recollections and Roosevelt, *Autobiography*, 5–6.

10. See Roosevelt, *Autobiography*, 10. ARC Recollections (October 23, 1925), Roosevelt Collection HL.

11. Martha Bulloch Roosevelt to Mrs. James K. Gracie (October 3, 1869), Roosevelt Collection HL. Theodore Roosevelt, *Diaries of Boyhood and Youth* (New York: Charles Scribner's Sons, 1928), 251ff.

12. See Roosevelt, *Diaries*, 82–165. Henry F. Pringle, *Theodore Roosevelt: A Biography* (London: Jonathan Cape, 1932), 25. Pringle speculates that the junior Roosevelt's fixation on manliness came later, after his adolescence. Roosevelt's journals and the firsthand recollections of family members strongly suggest otherwise.

13. Roosevelt, *Diaries*, 250.

14. See Roosevelt, *Autobiography*, 14–19. See also David McCullough, *Mornings on Horseback* (New York: Simon and Schuster, 1981), 115–16, and 109–28 generally.

15. Roosevelt, *Autobiography*, 17.

16. *Our Young Folks*, January 1865, 38. See, for instance, his toast at San Francisco's Union League Club in 1903 ("Roosevelt," May 14, 1903), in House and Senate Joint Committee of Printing, *Messages and Papers of the President* (New York: Bureau of National Literature, 1914), 15:413. See also his speeches to Stanford University students in 1906 and at Oyster Bay in August of the same year, the latter reported in the *New York Times*, August 7, 1906.

17. "Physical Health," *Our Young Folks*, January 1865, 38ff.

18. Martha Bulloch to Theodore Roosevelt (October 12, 1853), Roosevelt Collection HL. The full courtship correspondence, or what exists of it, is available in the Roosevelt Collection at Houghton Library, Putnam Papers.

19. Theodore Roosevelt to Martha Bulloch (October 2, 1853), Roosevelt Collection HL. CRA Recollections, Roosevelt Collection HL.

20. Martha Bulloch Roosevelt to Theodore Roosevelt (June 6, 1873), Roosevelt Collection HL, quoted by permission of the Alsop family.

21. For example, see Martha Bulloch to Theodore Roosevelt (November 13 and 28, 1853), Roosevelt Collection HL. Martha Stewart Bulloch to Susan West (December 15, 1863), Roosevelt Collection HL.

22. George Beard, *American Nervousness, Its Causes and Consequences* (New York: Putnam, 1881). See also, Tom Lutz, *American Nervousness, 1903: An Anecdotal History* (Ithaca: Cornell University Press, 1991), 2–10; and T. J. Jackson Lears, *No Place of Grace: Anti-Modernism and the Transformation of American Culture, 1880–1902* (New York: Pantheon, 1981), 49–53.

23. Beard, *American Nervousness*, 176, 1–17. For a summary, see Lutz, *American Nervousness*, 2–5.

24. Beard, *American Nervousness*, 115–17, 171–81, 292–346.

25. Lutz, *American Nervousness*, 3.

26. Lears, *No Place of Grace*, 47–58.

27. Sydney E. Ahlstrom, *A Religious History of the American People* (New Haven: Yale University Press, 1972), 433–36. Nathan O. Hatch, *The Democratization of American Christianity* (New Haven: Yale University Press, 1991), 49–124.

28. Beard, *American Nervousness*, 96–133. Lears, *No Place of Grace*, 56–58, 300–6.

29. A. D. Rockwell, *Rambling Recollections: An Autobiography* (New York: P. B. Hoeber, 1920), 261–63. Theodore attempted to send Teedie and younger brother Elliott to a small private school run by his former tutor, John McMullen. Elliott stayed for a time. Kathleen Dalton, *Theodore Roosevelt: A Strenuous Life* (New York: Random House, 2002), 38.

30. See, for example, Teedie's letters while in Dresden, Germany, in Roosevelt, *Letters*, 1:7–12. See also ARC Recollections (August 19, 1929), Roosevelt Collection HL; CRA Recollections, Roosevelt Collection HL. Corinne Roosevelt Robinson, *My Brother Theodore Roosevelt* (New York: Scribner's Sons, 1921), 50.

31. Robinson, *My Brother Theodore Roosevelt*, 50.

32. Theodore Roosevelt to Martha Bulloch Roosevelt (May 19, 1855), Roosevelt Collection HL. Theodore Roosevelt to Martha Bulloch Roosevelt, quoted in Putnam, *Theodore Roosevelt*, 45.

33. Theodore Roosevelt to Martha Bulloch (October 3, 1853), Roosevelt Collection HL. Theodore Roosevelt to Martha Bulloch Roosevelt (May 19, 1855), Roosevelt Collection HL.

34. CRA Recollections, Roosevelt Collection HL. Roosevelt, *Autobiography*, 6. Christian R. Reisner, *Roosevelt's Religion* (New York: Abingdon Press, 1922), 32ff.

35. Theodore Roosevelt to Martha Bulloch Roosevelt (January 1860), Roosevelt Collection HL.

36. Theodore Roosevelt to Theodore Roosevelt, Sr. (June 22, 1873), in Roosevelt, *Letters*, 1:10. Theodore Roosevelt to Christian Reisner, quoted in Reisner, *Roosevelt's Religion*, 257.

37. Theodore Roosevelt to Martha Bulloch (October 3, 1853), Roosevelt Collection HL. CRA Recollections, Roosevelt Collection HL. For more on Mittie's obsession with cleanliness, see Putnam, *Theodore Roosevelt*, 52–54; McCullough, *Mornings on Horseback*, 66–67. Martha Stewart Bulloch to Susan West (August 22, 1859), Roosevelt Collection HL: "Susy darling, have you read those accounts of the great revival of religion in Ireland? It is indeed a most wonderful work of grace. I wish I could see something of the kind here. One Sabbath at Tuckers makes one feel like weeping to think that there is so little love and fear of God." This is precisely the sort of thing her daughter would never write. Martha Stewart Bulloch to Susan West (December 15, 1863), Roosevelt Collection HL.

38. Ahlstrom, *A Religious History*, 763–65. Ralph Waldo Emerson, "The Divinity School Address" (1838), and "The Transcendentalist" (1841), in *The Works of Ralph Waldo Emerson*, ed. George Sampson (London: G. Bell, 1913), vol. 3.

39. See Ahlstrom, *A Religious History*, 772–73. Frederich D. E. Schleiermacher, *Works*, ed. O. Braun and J. Bauer (Leipzig, 1911–13), 4:240–43; 3:81ff. See also F. D. E. Schleiermacher, *The Christian Faith*, ed. H. R. Mackintosh and J. S. Stewart (Philadelphia: Fortress Press, 1976). Schleiermacher's complete works are in thirty volumes. Baruch Spinoza, *Critique of Religion* (1670). Owen Chadwick, *The Secularization of the European Mind in the Nineteenth Century* (Cambridge: Cambridge University Press, 1975), 161–88.

40. Ahlstrom, *A Religious History*, 772–74. Horace Bushnell, *Christ and His Salvation* (New York: Scribner's, 1864). Washington Gladden, *Being a Christian, What It Means and How to Begin* (Boston: Congregational Sunday School and Publication Society, 1876). Henry Ward Beecher, *Evolution and Religion* (New York: Fords, Howard and Hulbert, 1885). James Freeman Clark, *Ten Great Religions* (Boston: Houghton, Osgood, 1880).

41. Walter Rauschenbusch, *Christianity and the Social Crisis* (New York: Macmillan, 1907), 7. Compare Lyman Abbott, *Jesus of Nazareth: His Life and Teachings: Founded on the Four Gospels, and Illustrated by Reference to the Manners, Customs, Religious Beliefs, and Political Institutions of His Times* (New York: Harper, 1868).

42. C. H. Parkhurst, *Madison Square Presbyterian Church to Its First Pastor, the Rev. William Adams . . . A Tribute* (New York, 1880). Clifford Putney, *Muscular Christianity* (Cambridge: Harvard University Press, 2001), 73–74, 75. Carl D. Case, *Masculine in Religion* (Philadelphia: American Baptist Publication Society, 1906). Compare Howard A. Bridgman, "Have We a Religion for Men?" *Andover Review* 13 (April 1890): 390–91.

43. "A Sermonette," *Evangel* 8, July 1896, 15. "Muscular Christianity" is a term coined by historians to describe the cult of religious physicality that swept many mainline Protestant denominations between 1850 and 1920, both in the United States and in Europe (particularly Britain). For a full discussion, see Putney, *Muscular Christianity*, 25–99 particularly. See also Susan Curtis, "The Son of Man and God the Father," in *Meanings for Manhood: Constructions of Masculinity in Victorian America*, ed. Mark C. Carnes and Clyde Griffen (Chicago: University of Chicago Press, 1990), 67–78. Janet Fishburn, *The Fatherhood of God and the Victorian Family: A Study of the Social Gospel in America* (Philadelphia: Fortress Press, 1981).

44. Theodore Roosevelt diaries, summer 1878, quoted in Putnam, *Theodore Roosevelt*, 151.

45. Martha Bulloch Roosevelt to Theodore Roosevelt (October 15, 1873), Roosevelt Collection HL. ARC Recollections (October 23, 1925), Roosevelt Collection HL. The best account of Elliott's relationship with his father is in McCullough, 143–46, 182–86, 368–69. See also Elliott's account of his father's death (February 9, 1878), in Putnam Papers, Roosevelt Collection HL.

46. See Reflections of William E. Dodge, Putnam Papers, Roosevelt Collection HL. See also Putnam, *Theodore Roosevelt*, 48–49.

47. Theodore Roosevelt to Martha Bulloch Roosevelt (December 15, 1861), quoted by permission of the Alsop family. Theodore's wartime correspondence begins in November of 1861 and spans the whole of his time as allotment commissioner. Available in Roosevelt Collection HL.

2. A SMALL, ORNITHOLOGICAL BOY

1. Theodore Roosevelt (August 9, 1871), in Roosevelt, *Diaries of Boyhood and Youth* (New York: Charles Scribner's Sons, 1928), 248–50.

2. Ibid.

3. "Chased by Dogs," part II of an opus which also contains "Rowing to the bottom of the falls" and "I ride on horse back," composed by Teedie in 1869. Theodore Roosevelt Collection, Putnam Papers, Houghton Library, Harvard University (Roosevelt Collection HL, hereinafter, by permission of the Theodore Roosevelt Association). David Livingstone, *Missionary Travels and Researches in Southern Africa* (Philadelphia: J. W. Bradley, 1858). Theodore Roosevelt, *Autobiography* (New York: Charles Scribner's Sons, 1913), 15–19.

4. Roosevelt, *Autobiography*, 16.

5. Mayne Reid, *The Boy Hunters; Or, Adventures in Search of a White Buffalo* (Boston: Ticknor and Fields, 1857). Roosevelt, *Autobiography*, 14–16. Gail Bederman suggests Roosevelt's interest in natural history constituted a psychological displacement of his desire to be a Western hero. The notion of displacement seems a bit strong: Roosevelt never abandoned his interest in the West, for one thing, and retained a quite independent interest in natural history. Still, the imaginative link she identifies between Roosevelt's boyhood adventure stories and his early naturalist fixation seems sound. Bederman, *Manliness & Civilization: A Cultural History of Gender and Race in the United States, 1880–1917* (Chicago: University of Chicago Press, 1995), 175.

6. Roosevelt, *Autobiography*, 18. J. G. Wood, *Animal Picture Book* (London: G. Routledge and Sons, 1851).

7. Roosevelt, *Diaries*, 1.

8. Roosevelt, *Diaries*, 204, 271, 290–91, 308–9. Recollections of Anna Roosevelt Cowles (October 28, 1924), Theodore Roosevelt Collection, Putnam Papers, Houghton Library, Harvard University.

9. Martha Bulloch Roosevelt to Mrs. James K. Gracie (May 1869), Roosevelt Collection HL. Compare Roosevelt's entries of December 13, 1872, with December 19, 1872, and January 10, 1873, for example. Roosevelt, *Diaries*, 290–91, 293, 303.

10. Maybe Reid, *Afloat in the Forest, Or, A Voyage Among the Tree-Tops* (Boston: Ticknor and Fields, 1867), 10–12. Compare R. M. Ballantyne, *Away in the Wilderness; Or, Life Among the Red Indians and Fur Traders of North America* (London: James, Nisbet and Co., 1863); *Battle and Breeze; Or, The Fights and Fancies of British Tar* (London: James, Nisbet and Co., 1869); *Black Ivory: A Tale of Adventure Among the Slavers of East Africa* (London: James, Nisbet and Co., 1874); James Fenimore Cooper, *Afloat and Ashore; Or, The Adventures of Miles Walingford* (Philadelphia, 1844); *Deerslayer: A Tale* (London: Richard Bentley, 1841); *Last of the Mohicans: A narrative of 1757* (New York: Stringer and Townsend, 1854); *Red Rover: A Tale* (Philadelphia: Lea and Blanchard, 1840).

11. Theodore Roosevelt, *The Winning of the West* (New York: G. P. Putnam's Sons, 1889), 1:30–31.

12. Marvin Harris, *The Rise of Anthropological Theory: A History of Theories of Culture* (New York: Crowell, 1968), 83–89, 93–101; Edward Lurie, *Louis Agassiz: A Life in Science* (Chicago: University of Chicago Press, 1960), 252–302. See also Edward Lurie, "Louis Agassiz and the Races of Men," *Isis* 45 (September 1954): 227–42; John S. Haller, Jr., "The Species Problem: Nineteenth Century Concepts of Racial Inferiority in the Origin of Man Controversy," *American Anthropology* 72:1319–29. For an elegant discussion of the polygenist-monogenist debate in America, see Louis Menand, *The Metaphysical Club: A Story of Ideas in America* (New York: Farrar, Strauss and Giroux, 2003), 104–13.

13. Charles Darwin, *On the Origin of Species by Means of Natural Selection, Or The Preservation of Favoured Races in the Struggle for Life* (London: J. Murray, 1861); *Descent of Man, and Selection in Relation to Sex* (London: J. Murray, 1871).

14. Alfred Russell Wallace was one polygenist who held out, and Nathaniel Southgate Shaler another. David N. Livingstone, "Science and Society: Nathan S. Shaler and Racial Ideology," *Transactions of the Institute of British Geographers*, New Series, vol. 9, n. 2 (1984): 181, 183. Richard Hofstadter, *Social Darwinism in America* (New York: George Braziller, 1944), 4–5, 18–19. Alec R. Vidler, *The Church in an Age of Revolution: 1789 to the Present Day* (Baltimore: Penguin, 1961), 114–25.

15. Daniel J. Kevles, *In the Name of Eugenics: Genetics and the Uses of Human Identity* (Cambridge, Mass.: Harvard University Press, 1985), 4–12. Francis Galton, *Hereditary Genius: An Inquiry into Its Laws and Consequences* (London: Macmillan, 1869), 15–48, 289–336 (2006 edition); Francis Galton, *English Men of Science: Their Nature and Nurture* (London: Macmillan, 1874), 1–26, 64–73, 144–234.

16. Galton, *Hereditary Genius*, 11. Kevles, *Name of Eugenics*, 4, 9.

17. Kevles, *Name of Eugenics*, 57ff. Livingstone, "Science and Society," 186.

18. Livingstone, "Science and Society," 186. John S. Haller, Jr., "Concepts of Race Inferiority in Nineteenth-century Anthropology," *J. Hist. Med. Allied Sci.* 25 (1970): 40–51. See also R. M. Young, *Mind, Brain and Adaptation in the Nineteenth Century* (Oxford: Clarendon, 1970). Thomas F. Gossett, *Race: The History of an Idea in America* (Dallas: Southern Methodist University Press, 1963), 54–83.

19. Henry Ward Beecher, *Evolution and Religion* (New York: Fords, Howard and Hulbert, 1885). Lyman Abbott, *The Evolution of Christianity* (Boston: Houghton, Mifflin, 1892).

20. Theodore Roosevelt to Anna Roosevelt (September 21, 1873), by permission of the Alsop family, Roosevelt Collection HL.

21. Reid's *The Boy Hunters* is a prime example of this sort of racially driven narrative, set on the Western frontier. With reference to stories like Reid's and Cooper's, Richard Slotkin has argued that nineteenth and early twentieth century Americans pictured the frontier as a crucible in which English-speaking racial stock was regenerated through violence, conquest, and struggle. Richard Slotkin, *Regeneration Through Violence: The Mythology of the American Frontier, 1600–1860* (Middletown, Conn.: Wesleyan University Press, 1973), 369–93; Richard Slotkin, *The Fatal Environment: The Myth of the Frontier in the Age of Industrialization, 1800–1890* (New York: Atheneum, 1985), 49–106. Frenchman Arthur Gobineau went so far as to suggest in 1853 that the rise and fall of human civilizations could be explained by racial composition. For a full discussion, see

Thomas G. Dyer, *Theodore Roosevelt and the Idea of Race* (Baton Rouge: Louisiana State University Press, 1980), 21–25 and 90–122.

22. Putnam, *Theodore Roosevelt*, 102–5. The Minckwitzes kept the three Roosevelt children on a rigorous study schedule. They rose at half past six, finished breakfast at half past seven, and studied until nine. After a short break, they studied again until half past twelve. Lunch followed, and lessons were resumed until three. Coffee was then served, and they were allowed free time for exercise, sightseeing, or other recreation until supper at seven. After supper, they studied two hours more, getting to bed at ten. Carleton Putnam, *Theodore Roosevelt: The Formative Years* (New York: Charles Scribner's Sons, 1958), 105. Roosevelt, *Autobiography*, 23. Gossett, *Race*, 84–122. Dyer, *Idea of Race*, 2.

23. ARC Recollections (July 8, 1925), Roosevelt Collection HL.

24. ARC Recollections (July 8, 1925), Roosevelt Collection HL. Kathleen Dalton, *Theodore Roosevelt: A Strenuous Life* (New York: Random House, 2002), 29.

25. Roosevelt, *Autobiography*, 28. ARC Recollections (July 8, 1925), Roosevelt Collection HL.

26. Herbert Spencer, *The Principles of Sociology* (London, 1882–98), volume II. "Evolutionary individualism" is the felicitous phrase of Richard Hofstadter. Hofstadter, *Social Darwinism*, 49.

27. Herbert Spencer, *First Principles* (London: Williams and Norgate, 1862), 367. Hofstadter, *Social Darwinism*, 38.

28. Spencer sometimes wrote as if he believed evolution would fill "an immeasurable future." Spencer, *First Principles*, 506. See also Hofstadter, *Social Darwinism*, 36–37. Spencer, *Principles of Sociology*, 1:577.

29. Spencer, *Principles of Sociology*, 2:607ff. Spencer, *The Data of Ethics* (London: Williams and Norgate, 1879), 140. For an excellent summary of Spencer's ethical system, see Frederick Coplestone, *Empiricism, Idealism, and Pragmatism in Britain and America* (New York: First Image Books, 1994 ed.), 136–45. See also Hofstadter, *Social Darwinism*, 39–42. Spencer, *The Man Versus the State* (London: Williams and Norgate, 1884), 78ff.

30. Hofstadter, *Social Darwinism*, 39–42.

31. Roosevelt, "Biological Analogies in History" (June 7, 1910), in *The Works of Theodore Roosevelt*, ed. Hermann Hagedorn (New York: Charles Scribner's Sons, 1923), 12:29.

32. Roosevelt, "Biological Analogies," 12:27.

33. ARC Recollections (October 23, 1925), Roosevelt Collection HL. Dalton, *Theodore Roosevelt*, 53.

3. RACE AND DESTINY

1. Carleton Putnam, *Theodore Roosevelt: The Formative Years* (New York: Charles Scribner's Sons, 1958), 115, 123 n.33.

2. Theodore Roosevelt, *Autobiography* (New York: Charles Scribner's Sons, 1913), 12. Putnam, *Theodore Roosevelt*, 102–5, 119.

3. Recollections of Anna Roosevelt Cowles (October 28, 1924), Theodore Roosevelt Collection, Putnam Papers, Houghton Library, Harvard University (ARC Recollections, Roosevelt Collection HL, hereinafter). Putnam, *Theodore Roosevelt*, 113–14.

4. Putnam, *Theodore Roosevelt*, 126.

5. Ibid., 130.

6. Henry James, *Charles William Eliot, President of Harvard University, 1869–1909* (Cambridge: Riverside Press, 1930), 1:257. Roosevelt, *Autobiography*, 24.

7. James, *Charles William Eliot*, 1:260, 257.

8. Theodore Roosevelt to Theodore Roosevelt, Sr., and Martha Bulloch Roosevelt (February 11, 1877), in Roosevelt, *The Letters of Theodore Roosevelt*, ed. Elting E. Morrison et al. (Cambridge: Harvard University Press, 1952–54), 1:25–26. James, *Charles William Elliott*, 1:250ff. Roosevelt, *Autobiography*, 26–27.

9. Roosevelt, *Autobiography*, 26–27.

10. Nathaniel S. Shaler, *The Autobiography of Nathaniel Southgate Shaler* (New York: Houghton Mifflin, 1909), 26–55, 90–117. "Nathaniel Southgate Shaler," *Dictionary of Scientific Biography* (New York: Scribner, 1979), 12:343–44. "Nathaniel Southgate Shaler," *Science* (New Series) 23, no. 597 (June 8, 1906): 871.

11. Nathaniel S. Shaler, *Nature and Man in America* (New York: C. Scribner's Sons, 1891), viii–ix, 1–31, 147–207, 277–83. David N. Livingstone, "Science and Society: Nathan S. Shaler and Racial Ideology," *Transactions of the Institute of British Geographers*, New Series, vol. 9, no. 2 (1984): 183. John S. Haller, "The Species Problem: Nineteenth Century Concepts of Racial Inferiority in the Origin of Man Controversy," *American Anthropology* 72:1321–29. Alfred R. Wallace, "The Origin of Human Races and the Antiquity of Man Deduced from the Theory of 'Natural Selection,'" *Journal of Anthropological Sociology* 2: clviii–clxxvii. Nathaniel S. Shaler, *The Neighbor: The Natural History of Human Contacts* (New York: Houghton Mifflin, 1904), 252, 236–59 generally. Livingstone, "Science and Society," 183–84.

12. Jean Lamarck, *Zoological Philosophy* (1809); *Natural History of Invertebrates* (1815).

13. Thomas G. Dyer, *Theodore Roosevelt and the Idea of Race* (Baton Rouge: Louisiana State University Press, 1980), 38–40. George W. Stocking, Jr., "Lamarckianism in American Social Science: 1890–1915," *Journal of Historical Ideas* 23:239–56. Derek Freeman, "The Evolutionary Theories of Charles Darwin and Herbert Spencer," *Current Anthropology* 15 (September 1974): 211–21.

14. Shaler, *The Interpretation of Nature* (Boston: Houghton Mifflin, 1893), 146ff. Dyer, *Idea of Race*, 6–7, 21–44. Livingstone, "Science and Society," 185.

15. Shaler, *The Neighbor*, 23, 21–27, 29–50. Thomas F. Gossett, *Race: The History of an Idea in America* (Dallas: Southern Methodist University Press, 1963), 84–122, 281. See also Nathaniel S. Shaler, *The United States of America. A Study of the American Commonwealth, Its Natural Resources, People, Industries, Manufactures, Commerce, and Its Works in Literature, Science, Education, and Self Government* (New York: D. Appleton, 1894), 1270–1311. W. Stull Holt, "The Idea of Scientific History in America," *Journal of the History of Ideas* 1, no. 3 (June 1940): 352–62.

16. Livingstone, "Science and Society," 185.

17. Shaler, *The Neighbor*, 138ff, 332ff. Shaler, "The Nature of the Negro," *The Development of Segregationist Thought* (Homewood, Ill.: Dorsey, 1968), 57. Shaler, *The Story of Our Continent: A Reader in the Geography and Geology of America* (Boston: Ginn, 1890), 159. Dyer, *Idea of Race*, 6–7. Livingstone, "Science and Society," 192–97.

18. Dyer, *Idea of Race*, 6–7, 37–39.

19. Ray Allen Billington, *The Genesis of the Frontier Thesis: A Study in Historical Creativity* (San Marino: Huntington Library, 1971), 3–8. More generally, see Paul F. Boller, Jr., *American Thought in Transition: The Impact of Evolutionary Naturalism, 1865–1900* (Chicago: Rand McNally, 1969), 1–21, 47–69.

20. Putnam, *Theodore Roosevelt*, 137–38, 131. David McCullough, *Mornings on Horseback* (New York: Simon and Schuster, 1981), 202–6. Roosevelt, *Autobiography*, 25. Theodore Roosevelt to Anna Roosevelt (October 13, 1879), in Roosevelt, *Letters*, 1:42.

21. Pringle makes much of Roosevelt's loss in the boxing title match, a loss which he once misreported as a win. The claimed psychological insight seems overdrawn, as Roosevelt elsewhere recalled the outcome correctly. Henry F. Pringle, *Theodore Roosevelt: A Biography* (London: Jonathan Cape, 1932), 33. McCullough, *Mornings on Horseback*, 209–10.

22. Putnam, *Theodore Roosevelt*, 177, 220.

23. Stephen Skowronek, *Building a New American State: The Expansion of National Administrative Capacities, 1877–1920* (Cambridge, U.K.: Cambridge University Press, 1982), 61. Robert Marcus, *Grand Old Party: Political Structure in the Gilded Age, 1880–1896* (New York: Oxford University Press, 1971), 41–102.

24. Lewis L. Gould, *Grand Old Party: A History of the Republicans* (New York: Random House, 2003), 62–63. David M. Jordan, *Roscoe Conkling of New York: Voice in the Senate* (Ithaca, N.Y.: Cornell University Press, 1971), 61–84. Donald Barr Chidsey, *The Gentleman from New York: A Life of Roscoe Conkling* (New Haven: Yale University Press, 1935), 80–92.

25. Gould, *Grand Old Party*, 63. Skowronek, *Building a New American State*, 25–26, 61. McCullough, *Mornings on Horseback*, 171.

26. Skowronek, *Building a New American State*, 59–60. Gould, *Grand Old Party*, 65–68. Jordan, *Roscoe Conkling*, 80.

27. Gould, *Grand Old Party*, 73–77.

28. Putnam, *Theodore Roosevelt*, 245. Kathleen Dalton, *Theodore Roosevelt: A Strenuous Life* (New York: Random House, 2002), 66. Henry Brooks Adams, "Civil Service Reform," *North American Review* 190, no. 225 (October 1869): 456. Skowronek, *Building a New American State*, 54.

29. McCullough, *Mornings on Horseback*, 173–74. Skowronek, *Building a New American State*, 60–61.

30. McCullough, *Mornings on Horseback*, 173–75. Gould, *Grand Old Party*, 96.

31. Jordan, *Roscoe Conkling*, 281–87. Skowronek, *Building a New American State*, 60. Gould, *Grand Old Party*, 90–97. *New York Herald*, November 9, 1877.

32. McCullough, *Mornings on Horseback*, 176–77. *New York Tribune*, October 30, 1877.

33. *New York Tribune*, December 13, 1877. McCullough, *Mornings on Horseback*, 178–79. Gould, *Grand Old Party*, 96.

34. Putnam, *Theodore Roosevelt*, 245. Theodore Roosevelt to Theodore Roosevelt, Sr. (December 8, 1877), in Roosevelt, *Letters*, 1:30–31. Theodore Roosevelt to Theodore Roosevelt, Jr. (December 16, 1877), Putnam Papers, Roosevelt Collection HL.

35. Skowronek, *Building a New American State*, 61. Gould, *Grand Old Party*, 96.

36. ARC Recollections (October 23, 1925), Roosevelt Collection HL. See Elliott Roosevelt's account of his father's death (February 9, 1878), Putnam Papers, Roosevelt Collection HL. Corinne Roosevelt Robinson, *My Brother Theodore Roosevelt* (New York: Scribner's Sons, 1921), 105.

37. Putnam, *Theodore Roosevelt*, 151, 178. Christian R. Reisner, *Roosevelt's Religion* (New York: Abingdon Press, 1922), 81. Roosevelt, *Autobiography*, 57.

4. THE CODE OF A WARRIOR

1. Theodore Roosevelt, *Hunting Trips of a Ranchman: An Account of the Big Game of the United States and Its Chase with Horse, Hound, and Rifle*, in *The Works of Theodore Roosevelt*, ed. Hermann Hagedorn (New York: Charles Scribner's Sons, 1923), 1:183.

2. Roosevelt, *Hunting Trips*, 15.

3. Theodore Roosevelt, *Autobiography* (New York: Charles Scribner's Sons, 1913), 55–56. Carleton Putnam, *Theodore Roosevelt: The Formative Years* (New York: Charles Scribner's Sons, 1958), 217–18. Kathleen Dalton, *Theodore Roosevelt: A Strenuous Life* (New York: Random House, 2002), 16 n.4. See also James C. Mohr, *The Radical Republicans and Reform in New York During Reconstruction* (Ithaca, N.Y.: Cornell University Press, 1973), 29–60, 69–75.

4. Roosevelt, *Autobiography*, 56. Putnam, *Theodore Roosevelt*, 243–44.

5. Putnam, *Theodore Roosevelt*, 240–44.

6. Putnam, *Theodore Roosevelt*, 245–46. Lewis L. Gould, *Grand Old Party: A History of the Republicans* (New York: Random House, 2003), 99–100. Robert Marcus, *Grand Old Party: Political Structure in the Gilded Age, 1880–1896* (New York: Oxford University Press, 1971), 74–75. Paul Grondahl, *I Rose Like a Rocket: The Political Education of Theodore Roosevelt* (New York: Free Press, 2004), 65–67, 69–74.

7. *New York Evening Post*, November 7, 1881. Putnam, *Theodore Roosevelt*, 248–49.

8. Roosevelt private diary (January 7, 1882), Putnam Papers, Roosevelt Collection, Houghton Library, Harvard University HL. Roosevelt, *Autobiography*, 92. Putnam, *Theodore Roosevelt*, 252. *New York Sun*, January 25, 1882. Phillip Garbutt to Carleton Putnam, Putnam Papers, Roosevelt Collection HL.

9. Unidentified Democratic newspaper, Roosevelt Albany Scrapbook, Putnam Papers, Roosevelt Collection HL. *Morning Journal*, February 25, 1883, editorial, "Let Us Have Progress." *New York Sun*, February 25, 1883.

10. *New York Times*, October 13, 1882. *New York Tribune*, October 13, 1882. Theodore Roosevelt, "Phases of State Legislation," in *Essays on Practical Politics* (New York: G. P. Putnam's Sons, 1888), 34.

11. Roosevelt, "Phases of State Legislation," 11. Roosevelt, "Machine Politics in New York," in *Essays*, 51.

12. Putnam, *Theodore Roosevelt*, 259. Roosevelt, "Machine Politics in New York," 51. Roosevelt, "Phases of State Legislation," 28.

13. Putnam, *Theodore Roosevelt*, 261–62, 264. Roosevelt, "Machine Politics in New York," 48. Grondahl, *Rose Like a Rocket*, 89–98.

14. Roosevelt, "Machine Politics in New York," 48, 62.

15. Putnam, *Theodore Roosevelt*, 283, 304–5. *New York Evening Post*, March 16, 1883. Grondahl, *Rose Like a Rocket*, 112–15.

16. Roosevelt, "Machine Politics in New York," 61, 65. Roosevelt's assessment of the secret strength of political associations tracks Stephen Skowronek's later analysis. Stephen Skowronek, *Building a New American State: The Expansion of National Administrative Capacities, 1877–1920* (Cambridge, U.K.: Cambridge University Press, 1982), 30. See also Richard Hofstadter, *The Age of Reform: From Bryan to F.D.R.* (New York: Knopf, 1955), 174–86.

17. Roosevelt, "Machine Politics in New York," 73–74. Theodore Roosevelt to unnamed correspondent: "Dear Sir: It will give me great pleasure to join the Civil Service Association. . . . I am heartily in accord with any movement tending towards the improvement of the 'spoils' system — or, I should say, to its destruction. Very Sincerely Yours, Theodore Roosevelt" (December 31, 1881). Putnam Papers, Roosevelt Collection HL.

18. Gerald W. McFarland, "The New York Mugwumps of 1884: A Profile," *Political Science Quarterly* 71, no. 1 (March 1963): 40–58. Gordon S. Wood, "The Massachusetts Mugwumps," *The New England Quarterly* 33, no. 4 (December 1960): 435–51.

19. Roosevelt, "Machine Politics in New York," 46–47. Gould, *Grand Old Party*, 90–97. John Morton Blum, *The Republican Roosevelt* (Cambridge, Mass.: Harvard University Press, 1954), 9–14.

20. The precise contents of the second telegram are unknown, but upon receiving it Roosevelt left the floor of the assembly immediately. Putnam, *Theodore Roosevelt*, 384–87.

21. Roosevelt private diary (February 14, 1884), Roosevelt Collection HL.

22. Roosevelt, *Hunting Trips*, in *Works*, 1:8.

23. Edmund Morris inaccurately implies Roosevelt stopped suffering from asthma once he was married. His private diaries and correspondence reveal otherwise. The hunting trip with Elliott to Illinois occurred over the summer of 1880, before Roosevelt's wedding to Alice. Elliott had spent months on a ranch in Texas in 1876–77. See Roosevelt, *Hunting Trips*, in *Works*, 1:90–95.

24. Putnam, *Theodore Roosevelt*, 151.

25. The children's book was entitled *Hero Tales from American History* (1895), authored jointly with Henry Cabot Lodge. The text consists of twenty-six chapters treating various American heroes. Roosevelt wrote fourteen of the twenty-six, eight especially for the volume and the other six as pieces for *St. Nicholas* in May through October of 1895. Roosevelt, *Works*, 10:1–150.

26. Theodore Roosevelt, *The Winning of the West* (New York: G. P. Putnam's Sons, 1889), 1:xxi, xxxiv; 4:4.

27. Edward A. Freeman, *Comparative Politics* (New York, 1873). Herbert Baxter Adams, *The Study of History in American Colleges and Universities* (Washington, D.C., 1887); Herbert Baxter Adams, *The Germanic Origins of New England Towns* (Baltimore, Md., 1882). John W. Burgess, "The Methods of Historical Study and Research in Columbia University," in *Methods of Teaching History*, ed. G. Stanley Hall (Boston, 1883), 220. John Fiske, *The Critical Period of American History* (New York, 1888); *The Beginnings of*

New England; Or, the Puritan Theocracy in Its Relation to Civil and Religious Liberty (New York, 1889), chapter 1. See generally, Edward Norman Saveth, "Race and Nationalism in American Historiography: The Late Nineteenth Century," *Political Science Quarterly* 54, no. 3 (September 1939): 421–41. David N. Livingstone, "Science and Society: Nathan S. Shaler and Racial Ideology," *Transactions of the Institute of British Geographers*, New Series, vol. 9, n. 2 (1984): 187–88. Richard Hofstadter, *Social Darwinism in America* (New York: George Braziller, 1944), 172ff. Richard Hofstadter, *The Progressive Historians: Turner, Beard, Parrington* (New York: Knopf, 1968), 35–43, 65–71.

28. Livingstone, "Science and Society," 188. Adrian Hastings, *The Construction of Nationhood: Ethnicity, Religion, and Nationalism* (Cambridge, U.K.: Cambridge University Press, 1997), 115ff.

29. Roosevelt, *Winning of the West*, 1:168, 27, 4:2–4, 1:103. See also Roosevelt, *Works*, 12:40, 13:247.

30. Roosevelt, *Winning of the West*, 1:106.

31. For example, see Plato's *Republic*, book VIII. Allan Bloom, preface and interpretive essay, in *The Republic of Plato* (New York: Basic Books, 1991 edition), vii–xxiv, 307–436, and also 437 n.1.

32. Roosevelt, *Winning of the West*, 4:2.

33. Roosevelt, *Winning of the West*, 1:27.

34. Nathaniel S. Shaler, *The United States of America. A Study of the American Commonwealth, Its Natural Resources, People, Industries, Manufactures, Commerce, and Its Works in Literature, Science, Education, and Self Government* (New York: D. Appleton, 1894), 1270–72. Roosevelt, *Works*, 12:37.

35. Roosevelt, *Works*, 12:38.

36. Roosevelt, *Winning of the West*, 2:108.

37. Frederick Jackson Turner, "The Significance of the Frontier in American History," in Frederick J. Turner, *The Frontier in American History* (New York, 1920), 1–2. Turner, review in *The Dial*, August 1889, in Ray Allen Billington, *Frederick Jackson Turner: Historian, Scholar, Teacher* (New York: Oxford University Press, 1973), 83.

38. Roosevelt, *Winning of the West*, 1:86, 124.

39. Roosevelt, *Winning of the West*, 1:50, 86; 2:6, 145. That phrase, "regeneration through violence," belongs to Richard Slotkin. Slotkin has emphasized the violent strains in the mythology of the Western frontier, present throughout the seventeenth, eighteenth, and nineteenth centuries, but which Roosevelt in some senses crystallized. A recurring theme in the boyhood literature of Roosevelt's day, as Slotkin has shown, is white boys' achievement of manhood by becoming like Indian warriors, even as they remain the Indians' superiors. Slotkin, *Regeneration Through Violence: The Mythology of the American Frontier 1600–1860* (Middletown, Conn.: Wesleyan University Press, 1973), 3–56, 313–93. Richard Slotkin, *The Fatal Environment: The Myth of the Frontier in the Age of Industrialization, 1800–1890* (New York: Atheneum, 1985), 49–106. Slotkin, *Gunfighter Nation: The Myth of the Frontier in Twentieth Century America* (New York: Atheneum,

1992). The acquisition of identity through violence against and at the hands of Native Americans is an old theme in American history. See Jill Lepore, *King Phillip's War and the Origins of American Identity* (New York: Knopf, 1998).

40. Roosevelt, *Winning of the West*, 1:192, 1:50.

41. Roosevelt, private diaries (August 21, 1884), Putnam Papers, Roosevelt Collection HL. Roosevelt, *Hunting Trips*, in *Works*, 1:32–34.

42. Roosevelt, *Hunting Trips*, in *Works*, 1:393–96. Compare Roosevelt, *The Wilderness Hunter* (1893), in *Works*, 2:380.

43. Roosevelt, *Winning of the West*, 1:67.

44. Roosevelt quoted in Christian R. Reisner, *Roosevelt's Religion* (New York: Abingdon Press, 1922), 257. Theodore Roosevelt to Anna Roosevelt (September 20, 1886), Putnam Papers, Roosevelt Collection HL. Roosevelt, "The Search for Truth in a Reverent Spirit" (December 2, 1911), in *Works*, 12:118.

45. For a sample of evangelical opposition to Darwinism in this period, see Charles Hodge, *What Is Darwinism?* (New York, 1874). On the other side of the dispute, see Asa Gray's *Darwiniana: Essays and Reviews Pertaining to Darwinism* (New York, 1876) and John Fiske's *Cosmic Philosophy* (Boston, 1875) and *Destiny of Man: Viewed in the Light of His Origin* (New York, 1884). Roosevelt, *Works*, 12:138.

46. Roosevelt, *Works*, 12:128. Roosevelt, "Kidd's Social Evolution," *North American Review*, 161 (1895): 94–109.

47. Thomas Hobbes originated this school of thought for the early modern period, with his *Leviathan* (1660) and other works. Humans must impose an order of their own creation on an essentially unknowable universe, he instructed. Hobbes believed that "there is no natural harmony between the human mind and the universe," in the words of one of the twentieth century's greatest Hobbes scholars, Leo Strauss. For a full discussion, see Strauss, *Natural Right and History* (Chicago: University of Chicago Press, 1950), 166–202. David Hume followed in Hobbes's footsteps and was a favorite of late nineteenth and early twentieth century scientific progressives. See especially Hume, *An Enquiry Concerning Human Understanding* (1748).

48. Roosevelt, "How Not to Help Our Poorer Brother" (January 1897), in *Works*, 16:383.

49. Roosevelt, *Autobiography*, 210. Roosevelt, *Works*, 12:54, 73.

50. Roosevelt, speech at the Sorbonne (April 23, 1910), in *Works*, 15:354.

51. Elting E. Morrison, "Introduction," in Roosevelt, *The Letters of Theodore Roosevelt*, ed. Elting E. Morrison et al. (Cambridge, Mass.: Harvard University Press, 1952–54), 5:xiv.

52. Roosevelt, *Works*, 15:374, 369. Roosevelt's battle-centric view of life accentuated a late nineteenth and early twentieth century emphasis on "male passion" as an important element of masculinity. See Anthony Rotundo, *American Manhood* (New York: Basic Books, 1993), 227–48.

53. Roosevelt, *Works*, 12:54.

54. This particular pronouncement came in a speech in the United Kingdom, 1910. See Roosevelt, *Works*, 12:58.

55. Roosevelt, *Winning of the West*, 2:187, 241. Roosevelt, *Works*, 12:58.

56. Roosevelt, *Winning of the West*, 1:241.
57. *Dickinson Press*, October 3, 1885. Dalton, *Theodore Roosevelt*, 95.
58. Hermann Hagedorn, *Roosevelt in the Bad Lands* (New York: Houghton Mifflin, 1921), 407–10, 411.

5. APOSTLE OF EXPANSION

1. For criticism of Roosevelt's decision to remain a regular Republican, see the somewhat opportunistic indignation of the *New York World*, July 20, 1884. For a defense of Roosevelt, see the *Boston Herald*, July 20, 1884. Carleton Putnam, *Theodore Roosevelt: The Formative Years* (New York: Charles Scribner's Sons, 1958), 390ff. Stephen Skowronek, *Building a New American State: The Expansion of National Administrative Capacities, 1877–1920* (Cambridge, U.K.: Cambridge University Press, 1982), 68–69.
2. Skowronek, *Building a New American State*, 68–69. Lewis L. Gould, *Grand Old Party: A History of the Republicans* (New York: Random House, 2003), 106–13. Putnam, *Theodore Roosevelt*, 274–75.
3. *New York Times*, May 29, 1883. Gould, *Grand Old Party*, 82–85, 90–93. Robert Marcus, *Grand Old Party: Political Structure in the Gilded Age, 1880–1896* (New York: Oxford University Press, 1971), 129–50. Charles W. Calhoun, "Political Economy in the Gilded Age: The Republican Party's Industrial Policy," *Journal of Policy History* 8 (1996): 292–309.
4. *New York Tribune*, November 15, 1893. Roosevelt and Lodge's scheming is preserved in Henry Cabot Lodge, ed., *Selections from the Correspondence of Theodore Roosevelt and Henry Cabot Lodge, 1884–1918* (New York: Charles Scribner's Sons, 1925); see, e.g., 1:139, 177, 351; 2:274, 279. William C. Widenor, *Henry Cabot Lodge and the Search for an American Foreign Policy* (Berkeley, Calif.: University of California Press, 1980), 101–20.
5. Roosevelt, *The Works of Theodore Roosevelt*, ed. Hermann Hagedorn (New York: Charles Scribner's Sons, 1923), 12:54.
6. Roosevelt, *Winning of the West* (New York: G. P. Putnam's Sons, 1889), 1:22. Roosevelt, *The Naval War of 1812; Or, The History of the United States Navy During the Last War with Great Britain, to Which Is Appended an Account of the Battle of New Orleans* (1894; repr., New York: Random House, 1999), 252.
7. Roosevelt, *Naval War*, 252. Compare *Winning of the West*, 3:2.
8. See Roosevelt, *Winning of the West*, 4:4, for example.
9. Roosevelt, *Winning of the West*, 1:xxxiii. Niall Ferguson has recently argued that England entered the colonial race partly as a result of jealousy of Spain, and determination to match Spanish wealth and beat the Spanish at their own game of territorial expansion. Ferguson, *Empire: How Britain Made the Modern World* (London: Penguin Press, 2003), 4–14. Roosevelt, *Winning of the West*, 2:376; 1:xxxii; 4:125–30. Theodore Roosevelt to Henry Cabot Lodge, in Lodge, *Correspondence* (October 27, 1894), 1:139, (December 4, 1896), 243–44, (June 17, 1897), 267. Henry C. Lodge, "Our Blundering Foreign Policy," *The Forum*, 19 (1895): 8–17. Julius W. Pratt, "The 'Large Policy' of 1898," *Mississippi Valley Historical Review* 19, no. 2 (September 1932): 231–36.

10. Edward Norman Saveth, "Race and Nationalism in American Historiography: The Late Nineteenth Century," *Political Science Quarterly* 54, no. 3 (September 1939): 422–28.

11. Roosevelt, *Messages and Papers of the President* (New York: Bureau of National Literature, 1914), 15:6659. Roosevelt in Raleigh, *New York Times*, October 20, 1905. Roosevelt, *Messages and Papers*, 15:6659. Roosevelt, *Winning of the West*, 1:193, 183–86.

12. Roosevelt, *Winning of the West*, 2:170. Roosevelt, *Works*, 15:366, 369.

13. Roosevelt, *Messages and Papers*, 6659. Roosevelt, *Winning of the West*, 2:47–48.

14. Roosevelt, *Messages and Papers*, 6659. Roosevelt, *Works*, 12:57–58.

15. Theodore Roosevelt, in *Wichita Daily Eagle*, July 5, 1900. See also Howard K. Beale, *Theodore Roosevelt and the Rise of America to World Power* (Baltimore: Johns Hopkins Press, 1956), 70. John Winthrop, "City upon a Hill" (1630), in *Speeches That Changed the World*, ed. Owen Collins (Louisville, Ky.: Westminster John Knox Press, 1999), 63–65. Sydney E. Ahlstrom, *A Religious History of the American People* (New Haven: Yale University Press, 1972), 124–32, 135–50. Edwin Scott Gaustad, *A Religious History of America* (New York: Harper and Row, 1966), 147–63.

16. Pauline Maier, *American Scripture: Making the Declaration of Independence* (New York: Vintage Books, 1997), 47–90. [Madison], *The Federalist* (Cambridge, Mass: Belknap Press of Harvard University Press, 1961), Number 14; George Washington, "Circular to the States," *George Washington: Writings*, ed. John Rhodehamel (New York: Penguin, 1997), 316–26; "First Inaugural Address," 730–33; "Farewell Address," 962–77.

17. Brooks Adams, "Unpublished Biography of John Quincy Adams," quoted in Charles Vevier, "American Continentalism: An Idea of Expansion, 1845–1910," *The American Historical Review* 65, no. 2 (January 1960): 333–34.

18. *Memorial of Asa Whitney*, February 24, 1846 (Senate Executive Document, 29th Congress, 1st sess., IV, no. 161), 8–9. Vevier, "American Continentalism," 327–28. See also Margaret L. Brown, "Asa Whitney and His Pacific Railroad Publicity Campaign," *Mississippi Valley Historical Review*, 20 (September 1933): 209–24.

19. John L. O'Sullivan, "The Great Nation of Futurity," *The United States Democratic Review* 6, no. 23 (1839): 426–30. This vision is animated by a postmillennial eschatology typical of American Christianity in this period. Ahlstrom, *A Religious History*, 600. George E. Baker, ed., *The Works of William Seward* (New York: Redfield, 1853–54), 1:91, 247–49.

20. U.S. Congress, Senate, Senator Stephen A. Douglas in support of the acquisition of Oregon, 28th Cong., 2d sess., *Congressional Globe* 14, no. 15 (February 4, 1845): 225–27.

21. U.S. Congress, Senate, Senator Stephen A. Douglas in support of the annexation of Texas, 28th Cong., 2d sess., *Congressional Globe* 14, no. 6 (January 6, 1845): 95–97. See also Douglas in support of the acquisition of Oregon, *Congressional Globe*, 225–27; Harry V. Jaffa, *Crisis of the House Divided: An Interpretation of the Issues in the Lincoln-Douglas Debates* (Garden City, N.Y.: Doubleday, 1959), 63–103.

22. Frank Ninkovich has correctly argued that Roosevelt framed his foreign policy prescriptions with the rhetoric of spreading civilization—white, European civilization. Ninkovich, "Theodore Roosevelt: Civilization as Ideology," *Diplomatic History* 10 (Summer 1986): 221–45.

23. Roosevelt, *Winning of the West*, 1:88, 31, 86, 87.

24. Roosevelt, *Winning of the West*, 4:17, 1:241.

25. Roosevelt, *Winning of the West*, 3:44, 45–46, 41–46 generally. Niccolo Machiavelli, *The Prince*, trans. Harvey C. Mansfield (Chicago: University of Chicago Press, 1985), 61–62, 68–71.

26. Richard W. Turk, *The Ambiguous Relationship: Theodore Roosevelt and Alfred Thayer Mahan* (New York: Greenwood Press, 1987), 37ff. Peter Clarke, *Hope and Glory: Britain 1900–1990* (London: Penguin, 1996), 8.

27. Vevier, "American Continentalism," 224–25. Howard K. Beale, *Theodore Roosevelt and the Rise of America to World Power*, 447. Henry C. Ide, "Our Interest in Samoa," *North American Review* 165 (1897): 155–73.

28. Roosevelt to Henry Cabot Lodge (October 27, 1894), in Lodge, *Correspondence*, 1:139. David F. Trask, *The War with Spain in 1898* (New York: Macmillan, 1981), 45–46. Ivan Musicant, *Empire by Default: The Spanish-American War and the Dawn of the American Century* (New York: Henry Holt, 1998), 10–37, 105–6.

29. Widenor, *Henry Cabot Lodge*, 80–86. Roosevelt, *Naval War of 1812*, xxiv.

30. Alfred Thayer Mahan, *The Influence of Sea Power upon History, 1660–1783* (Boston, 1890), 6–9, 25–29, 82–89. See also Alfred Thayer Mahan, "The United States Looking Outward," *The Atlantic Monthly* (1890): 816–24. Theodore Roosevelt to H. C. Lodge (September 21, 1897), in Lodge, *Correspondence*, 1:278–79. H. C. Lodge to Theodore Roosevelt (May 31, 1898), in Lodge, *Correspondence*, 1:302. Trask, *The War with Spain in 1898*, 13. Turk, *Ambiguous Relationship*, 37. Roosevelt biographers have tended to overemphasize the influence of Captain Mahan on Roosevelt's thinking. Charles and Mary Beard helped fuel this line of interpretation with their conspiratorial suggestions about a Roosevelt-Lodge plot to launch war against Cuba in order to take the Philippines. Charles A. Beard and Mary R. Beard, *The Rise of American Civilization* (New York: Macmillan, 1927), 2:375–76. But see John A. S. Grenville and John Berkeley Young, *Politics, Strategy, and American Diplomacy: Studies in Foreign Policy, 1873–1917* (New Haven: Yale University Press, 1966). Henry Pringle also overaccented Mahan's influence. Henry F. Pringle, *Theodore Roosevelt: A Biography* (London: Jonathan Cape, 1932), 172.

31. Abraham Lincoln, speech in Peoria, Illinois, October 1854, in *Abraham Lincoln: A Documentary Portrait Through His Speeches and Writings*, ed. Don E. Fehrenbacher (Stanford: Stanford University Press, 1964), 72. Jaffa, *Crisis of the House Divided*, 84–103.

32. Roosevelt to Lodge (October 27, 1894), in Lodge, *Correspondence*, 1:139. Vevier, "American Continentalism," 229–30.

33. Marcus, *Grand Old Party*, 129–38. Skowronek, *Building a New American State*, 75–78.

6. THE FATE OF COMING YEARS

1. James F. Richardson, *The New York Police: Colonial Times to 1901* (New York: Oxford University Press, 1970), 246–67. Theodore Roosevelt, *Autobiography* (New York: Charles Scribner's Sons, 1913), 172–73, 194–97, 204–5. Jacob A. Riis, *The Making of an Ameri-*

can (New York: Macmillan, 1947), 257–59. Riis, *How the Other Half Lives: Studies Among the Tenements of New York* (New York: Charles Scribner's Sons, 1890), 82–91.

2. Henry Cabot Lodge to Theodore Roosevelt (August 10, 1895), in Henry Cabot Lodge, ed., *Selections from the Correspondence of Theodore Roosevelt and Henry Cabot Lodge, 1884–1918* (New York: Charles Scribner's Sons, 1925), 1:163.

3. Robert Higgs, *Crisis and Leviathan: Critical Episodes in the Growth of American Government* (New York: Oxford University Press, 1987), 84–87.

4. Roosevelt, "The Menace of the Demagogue" (October 15, 1896), in *The Works of Theodore Roosevelt*, ed. Hermann Hagedorn (New York: Charles Scribner's Sons, 1923), 16:396. Theodore Roosevelt to Anna Roosevelt Cowles (November 8, 1896), in Roosevelt, *The Letters of Theodore Roosevelt*, ed. Elting E. Morrison et al. (Cambridge: Harvard University Press, 1952–54), 1:565–66.

5. Lewis L. Gould, *Reform and Regulation: American Politics from Roosevelt to Wilson* (New York: Knopf, 1986), 6–8. Stephen Skowronek, *Building a New American State: The Expansion of National Administrative Capacities, 1877–1920* (Cambridge, U.K.: Cambridge University Press, 1982), 50. Robert Marcus, *Grand Old Party: Political Structure in the Gilded Age, 1880–1896* (New York: Oxford University Press, 1971), 27–29.

6. Arthur S. Link and Richard L. McCormick, *Progressivism* (Arlington Heights, Va.: Harlan Davidson, 1983), 18.

7. Albro Martin, "The Troubled Subject of Railroad Regulation in the Gilded Age—A Reappraisal," *Journal of American History* 61 (1974): 343–44.

8. Marc Allen Eisner, *Regulatory Politics in Transition* (Baltimore: Johns Hopkins University Press, 1993), 32. Link and McCormick, *Progressivism*, 13. Solon Justus Buck, *The Granger Movement: A Study of Agricultural Organization and Its Political, Economic and Social Manifestations 1870–1880* (Cambridge, Mass: Harvard University Press, 1913), 80–123, 143–238. Buck traced railroad rate regulation to the efforts of Western grain farmers in the early 1870s. Buck, *Granger Movement*, 3–39. In fact, the coalition for reform was far broader. See George H. Miller, *Railroads and the Granger Laws* (Madison, Wis.: University of Wisconsin Press, 1971), 16–23, 161–71.

9. Martin, "Railroad Regulation in the Gilded Age," 344. Hans Thorelli, *The Federal Antitrust Policy: Origination of an American Tradition* (Baltimore: Johns Hopkins Press, 1955), 58–60. Skowronek, *Building a New American State*, 127. George J. Stigler, "The Origin of the Sherman Act," in *The Rise of Big Business and the Beginnings of Antitrust and Railroad Regulation 1870–1900*, ed. Robert F. Himmelberg (New York: Garland Publishing, 1994), 377–78. Eisner, *Regulatory Politics*, 32.

10. *Wabash v. Illinois*, 118 U.S. 557 (1886). The Supreme Court had nine years earlier declared the exact same state regulations valid. *Munn v. Illinois*, 94 U.S. 113 (1877). Link and McCormick, *Progressivism*, 18. Eisner, *Regulatory Politics*, 32.

11. Link and McCormick, *Progressivism*, 20. Eisner, *Regulatory Politics*, 33. Gould, *Grand Old Party*, 116–19, 124–25.

12. Gould, *Grand Old Party*, 125–27.

13. Samuel P. Hays, *Conservation and the Gospel of Efficiency: The Progressive Conservation Movement, 1890–1912* (Cambridge, Mass: Harvard University Press, 1959), 266–71.

14. Richard Hofstadter, *Social Darwinism in America* (New York: George Braziller, 1944), 107, 113. Edward Bellamy, *Looking Backwards* (New York, 1888).

15. Theodore Roosevelt, *American Ideals and Other Essays Social and Political* (New York: G. P. Putnam's Sons, 1898), 7. Link and McCormick, *Progressivism*, 18. For an account of the strike from May to July, 1894, and an assessment of the damage caused, see United States Strike Commission, "Report on the Chicago Strike," June–July 1894, Senate Executive Document No. 7, 53rd Congress, 3rd session.

16. James Livingston, *Origins of the Federal Reserve System: Money, Class and Corporate Capitalism, 1890–1913* (Ithaca, N.Y.: Cornell University Press, 1986), 41. Roosevelt, *American Ideals*, 8. Melvyn Dubofsky, "Labor Organizations," in *Encyclopedia of American Economic History: Studies of the Principal Movements and Ideas*, ed. David William Voorhees et al. (New York: Charles Scribner's Sons, 1980), 531–32.

17. Andrew Carnegie, *Triumphant Democracy; or Fifty Years' March of the Republic* (New York, 1886), 1.

18. Roosevelt, "The Menace," in *Works*, 16:394. Roosevelt, *American Ideals*, 8–9.

19. Roosevelt, *Works*, 16:351. Roosevelt, *American Ideals*, 7. Roosevelt, "New York," in *Works*, 10:539. Roosevelt, *Works*, 10:539.

20. Roosevelt, "The Vice-Presidency," in *Works*, 16:367, 369. Roosevelt, *American Ideals*, 7–8.

21. Roosevelt, *American Ideals*, 9, 7.

22. Roosevelt, "The Menace," in *Works*, 16:394.

23. Roosevelt, "The Vice-Presidency," 16:361, 367, 369.

24. Gould, *Grand Old Party*, 119–22.

25. John C. Calhoun, *Disquisition on Government, and a Discourse on the Constitution and Government of the United States* (1853; repr. New York: Macmillan, 1953), 19–40, 45–54.

26. Edmund S. Morgan, "Slavery and Freedom: The American Paradox," *Journal of American History* 59 (1972): 5–29. Caroline Robbins, *The Eighteenth-Century Commonwealthmen: Studies in the Transmission, Development and Circumstance of English Liberal Thought from the Restoration of Charles II Until the War with the Thirteen Colonies* (Cambridge, Mass.: Harvard University Press, 1959), 3–21, 378–86. J. G. A. Pocock, "Machiavelli, Harrington, and English Political Ideologies in the Eighteenth Century," *William and Mary Quarterly* 22 (October 1965): 549–83. J. G. A. Pocock, *The Machiavellian Moment: Florentine Political Thought and the Atlantic Republican Tradition* (Princeton, N.J.: Princeton University Press, 1975), 462–552. Alexander Keyssar, *The Right to Vote: The Contested History of Democracy in the United States* (New York: Basic, 2000), 172–222.

27. Julian P. Boyd, ed., *The Papers of Thomas Jefferson*, 18 vols. (Princeton, N.J.: Princeton University Press, 1950), 8:426, 682. Thomas Jefferson to John Jay (August 23, 1785), in Merrill D. Peterson, ed., *Jefferson Writings* (New York: Library of America, 1984), 818. Compare John Adams, "U" to the *Boston Gazette*, August 29, 1763; C. Bradley Thompson, *John Adams and the Spirit of Liberty* (Lawrence, Kans.: University Press of Kansas, 1998), 47ff.

28. Gordon S. Wood, *The Creation of the American Republic, 1776–1787* (Chapel Hill, N.C.: University of North Carolina Press, 1969), 18–28.

29. Livingston, *Origins of the Federal Reserve*, 42–45. Eisner, *Regulatory Politics*, 27–28.

30. Paul Uselding, "Manufacturing," in *Encyclopedia of American Economic History*, 402–11. Hofstadter, *Age of Reform*, 218. Eisner, *Regulatory Politics*, 28. Higgs, *Crisis and Leviathan*, 79–84.

31. Eisner, *Regulatory Politics*, 28–29. Gould, *Reform and Regulation*, 24. In 1998 dollars, average 1900 per capita income was approximately $4,748, compared to $32,000 in 1998. Not only has inflation increased since the turn of the last century, the size and productivity of the American economy has grown dramatically. Joint Economic Committee, U.S. Senate, *The United States Economy at the Beginning and End of the 20th Century*, 106th Cong., 1st sess., 1999.

32. Albro Martin, *Enterprise Denied: Origins of the Decline of American Railroads, 1897–1917* (New York: Columbia University Press, 1971), 5–7, 10. Eisner, *Regulatory Politics*, 28–29.

33. Eisner, *Regulatory Politics*, 4, 29–30. Richard A. Easterlin, "Population," in *Encyclopedia of American Economic History*, 170. Walter I. Trattner, *From Poor Law to Welfare State: A History of Social Welfare in America* (New York: Free Press, 1989), 148.

34. Trattner, *Poor Law to Welfare State*, 148–49. Easterlin, "Population," 170. Eisner, *Regulatory Politics*, 30. Hofstadter, *Age of Reform*, 174–86.

35. Foster Rhea Dulles and Melvyn Dubofsky, *Labor in American History*, 4th ed. (Arlington Heights, Ill.: Harlon Davidson, 1984), 121–41, 196. Link and McCormick, *Progressivism*, 29–30. Trattner, *Poor Law to Welfare State*, 156. Eisner, *Regulatory Politics*, 29–32.

36. Naomi R. Lamoreaux, "Industrial Organization and Market Behavior: The Great Merger Movement in American Industry," in *The Rise of Big Business and the Beginnings of Antitrust and Railroad Regulation 1870–1900*, ed. Robert F. Himmelberg (New York: Garland, 1994), 169–71.

37. Edward A. Purcell, Jr., *Brandeis and the Progressive Constitution: Erie, the Judicial Power, and the Politics of the Federal Courts in Twentieth-Century America* (New Haven: Yale University Press, 2000), 15, 60–62.

38. Theodore Roosevelt, *Hunting Trips of a Ranchman: An Account of the Big Game of the United States and Its Chase with Horse, Hound, and Rifle* (1885), in *Works*, 1:20.

39. Roosevelt, "The Menace," 16:401.

40. Roosevelt, *American Ideals*, 9–10.

41. *The Outlook* magazine (April 8, 1911), in Roosevelt, *Works*, 12:184–96. Roosevelt, *American Ideals*, 9–10.

42. Roosevelt, *American Ideals*, 10.

43. Ibid., 43, 9–10.

44. Roosevelt, "The City in Modern Life," in *Works*, 14:204–13. Link and McCormick, *Progressivism*, 29.

45. Roosevelt, *Works*, 14:204–13; Roosevelt, "Phases of State Legislation," in *Essays*, 61–65. Skowronek, *Building a New American State*, 30. Kathleen Dalton, *Theodore Roosevelt: A Strenuous Life* (New York: Random House, 2002), 83.

46. Theodore Roosevelt, *Winning of the West* (New York: G. P. Putnam's Sons, 1889), 1:116.

47. Link and McCormick, *Progressivism*, 20. Eisner, *Regulatory Politics*, 32. Gould, *Grand Old Party*, 126–27.

48. Ivan Musicant, *Empire by Default: The Spanish-American War and the Dawn of the American Century* (New York: Henry Holt, 1998), 99–100. Roosevelt, *American Ideals*, 13.

49. "True Americanism," in *The Essential Theodore Roosevelt*, ed. John Gabriel Hunt (New York: Gramercy Books, 1994), 3. Roosevelt, speech to the Hamilton Club (April 10, 1899), in *Essential Theodore Roosevelt*, 35, 37–38.

50. David F. Trask, *The War with Spain in 1898* (New York: Macmillan, 1981), 52–53, 79–81. Theodore Roosevelt to George Dewey (February 25, 1898), in Roosevelt, *Letters*, 1:785. Roosevelt to H. C. Lodge (September 26, 1898), in Lodge, *Correspondence*, 1:349. Anna Bulloch to Martha Bulloch Roosevelt (September 1861), Putnam Papers, Theodore Roosevelt Collection, Houghton Library, Harvard University.

51. Theodore Roosevelt to his children (May 6, 1898), in *Works*, 21:471–72.

7. MASTER-SPIRIT

1. Theodore Roosevelt, *Oliver Cromwell* (New York: Charles Scribner's Sons, 1900), 190, 191–92, 236–37.

2. Roosevelt, *Oliver Cromwell*, 6.

3. Roosevelt, *Oliver Cromwell*, 180, 182–83, 225, 20.

4. Roosevelt, *Oliver Cromwell*, 112, 142, 114.

5. Roosevelt, "Second Annual Message to the State of New York," in *The Works of Theodore Roosevelt*, ed. Hermann Hagedorn (New York: Charles Scribner's Sons, 1923), 17:48–54.

6. "First Annual Message to the State of New York," in Roosevelt, *Works*, 17:9–11. Roosevelt, "Second Annual Message," 17:48–54.

7. Roosevelt, *Oliver Cromwell*, 142, 239, 240–41.

8. Carleton Putnam, *Theodore Roosevelt: The Formative Years* (New York: Charles Scribner's Sons, 1958), 151–52.

9. Theodore Roosevelt to Henry Cabot Lodge (September 23, 1901), in Roosevelt, *The Letters of Theodore Roosevelt*, ed. Elting E. Morrison et al. (Cambridge: Harvard University Press, 1952–54), 3:150. Hermann Hagedorn, *Roosevelt in the Bad Lands* (New York: Houghton Mifflin, 1921), 411. Edmund Morris, *Theodore Rex* (New York: Random House, 2001), 10–11. Theodore Roosevelt to Henry Cabot Lodge (September 9, 1901), in Roosevelt, *Letters*, 3:142.

10. *New York Times*, September 15, 1901.

11. Lewis L. Gould, *The Presidency of Theodore Roosevelt* (Lawrence, Kans.: University Press of Kansas, 1991), 24–25. Charles S. Olcott, *William McKinley* (Boston: Houghton Mifflin, 1916), 2:382. Stephen Skowronek, *The Politics Presidents Make* (Cambridge, Mass.: Harvard University Press, 1993), 231–34, 238–40.

12. Gould, *Presidency of Theodore Roosevelt*, 25. David Brady et al., "Heterogeneous Parties and Political Organization: The U.S. Senate, 1880–1920," *Legislative Studies Quarterly*

14, no. 2 (May 1989): 209–10. Horace Samuel Merrill and Marion Galbraith Merrill, *The Republican Command, 1897–1913* (Lexington, Ky.: University Press of Kentucky, 1971), 5, 93–115.

13. Brady, "Heterogeneous Parties," 210–11. Duncan MacRae, "The Relation Between Roll Call Votes and Constituencies in the Massachusetts House of Representatives," *American Political Science Review* 46:1046–55. David Rothman, *Politics and Power: The U.S. Senate 1869–1901* (Cambridge, Mass: Harvard University Press, 1966), 58–61, 71–108.

14. Robert Marcus, *Grand Old Party: Political Structure in the Gilded Age, 1880–1896* (New York: Oxford University Press, 1971), 138–42.

15. 15 U.S.C. § 1 (1890). The Case of Monopolies, King's Bench 1603. *Mitchell v. Reynolds*, King's Bench 1711. See, for instance, the Court's decision in *United States v. E. C. Knight Company*, 156 U.S. 1 (1895), where a narrow majority decided "commerce" did not include manufacturing — only the interstate trade in goods manufactured.

16. *United States v. Trans-Missouri Freight Assoc.*, 166 U.S. 290 (1897). Naomi R. Lamoreaux, "Industrial Organization and Market Behavior: The Great Merger Movement in American Industry," in *The Rise of Big Business and the Beginnings of Antitrust and Railroad Regulation 1870–1900*, ed. Robert F. Himmelberg (New York: Garland, 1994), 169–71. Marc Allen Eisner, *Regulatory Politics in Transition* (Baltimore: Johns Hopkins University Press, 1993), 29. Thomas K. McCraw, "Rethinking the Trust Question," in *Regulation in Perspective: Historical Essays*, ed. Thomas K. McCraw (Cambridge: Harvard University Press, 1981), 32. Vincent P. Carosso, *Investment Banking in America: A History* (Cambridge, Mass.: Harvard University Press, 1970), 29–50.

17. Lamoreaux, *Rise of Big Business*, 171. Eisner, *Regulatory Politics*, 55. *Iowa State Register* (Des Moines), August 8, 1901. Skowronek, *Politics*, 250–51. Arthur S. Link and Richard L. McCormick, *Progressivism* (Arlington Heights, Va.: Harlan Davidson, 1983), 18–20, 27.

18. Cornelius C. Regier, *The Era of the Muckrakers* (Chapel Hill, N.C.: University of North Carolina Press, 1932), 13–14, 17, 35–37, 50. Harold S. Wilson, *McClure's Magazine and the Muckrakers* (Princeton, N.J.: Princeton University Press, 1970), 81–103, 129–47.

19. Roosevelt, "Second Annual Message," in *Works*, 17:49, 49–50.

20. Roosevelt, *Oliver Cromwell*, 189. Regier, *Era of Muckrakers*, 109.

21. Roosevelt, *Oliver Cromwell*, 189.

22. Washington Gladden, *Social Salvation* (New York: Houghton Mifflin, 1901), 2.

23. Sydney E. Ahlstrom, *A Religious History of the American People* (New Haven: Yale University Press, 1972), 785–804. Richard Hofstadter, *Social Darwinism in America* (New York: George Braziller, 1944), 106–9. Paul Monroe, "English and American Socialism: An Estimate," *The American Journal of Sociology* 1, no. 1 (July 1895): 50–68. John Spargo, "Christian Socialism in America," *The American Journal of Sociology* 15, no. 1 (July 1909): 16–20. Gaius Glenn Atkins, "The Crusading Church at Home and Abroad," *Church History* 1, no. 3 (September 1932): 131–49. David B. Danbom, *The World of Hope: Progressives and the Struggle for an Ethical Public Life* (Philadelphia: Temple University Press, 1987), 40–79.

24. Gladden, *Social Salvation*, 9, 14.

25. Gladden, *Social Salvation*, 9, 7, 15.
26. Gladden, *Social Salvation*, 24, 6.
27. Ahlstrom, *A Religious History*, 435–36, 600. Walter Rauschenbusch, *Christianizing the Social Order* (New York: Macmillan, 1912), 90, 83–95. Hofstadter, *Social Darwinism*, 108–9.
28. Gladden, *Social Salvation*, 15, 40, 136.
29. Gladden, *Social Salvation*, 90, 30–31.
30. Roosevelt, *Oliver Cromwell*, 49–50.
31. Richard T. Ely, *Ground Under Our Feet* (New York: Macmillan, 1938), 140, 154. Mary O. Furner, *Advocacy and Objectivity: A Crisis in the Professionalization of American Social Science, 1865–1905* (Lexington, Ky.: University of Kentucky Press, 1975), 68–80. Joseph Dorfman, "Henry Carter Adams: The Harmonizer of Liberty and Reform," in Henry Carter Adams, *Relations of the State to Industrial Action* (New York: Columbia University Press, 1954), 2–7. "Henry Carter Adams 1851–1921," *Journal of Political Economy* 30, 2 (April 1922): 201–11.
32. Adams, *Relations of the State*, 71–73, 78, 83, 86–87.
33. Adams, *Relations of the State*, 89–90.
34. Adams, *Relation of the State*, 94, 92/quoting J. B. Clark, *The Philosophy of Wealth* (Boston: Ginn, 1886), 156–57, 93. Furner, *Advocacy and Objectivity*, 71–72.
35. Adams, *Relation of the State*, 97–98. Nancy Cohen, *The Reconstruction of American Liberalism, 1865–1914* (Chapel Hill, N.C.: University of North Carolina Press, 2002), 179–84.
36. Adams, *Relations of the State*, 104–5.
37. Adams, *Relations of the State*, 124–25, 127. Stephen Skowronek, *Building an American State: The Expansion of National Administrative Capacities, 1877–1920* (Cambridge, U.K.: Cambridge University Press, 1982), 133.
38. Adams, *Relations of the State*, 117. Eisner, *Regulatory Politics*, 42. Stephen Skowronek, *Politics*, 231–34. Professionalizing administration through merit appointments was a long-standing ambition of civil service reformers. For example, Dorman B. Eaton, *The Civil Service in Great Britain: A History of Abuses and Reform and Their Bearing on American Politics* (New York: Harper and Brothers, 1880), 361–428. E. L. Godkin, "The Monopolists and the Civil Service," *The Nation* 32, no. 835 (June 1881): 453.
39. Skowronek, *Building an American State*, 179–81.
40. Roosevelt, "Second Annual Message," in *Works*, 17:164. Arthur M. Johnson, "Theodore Roosevelt and the Bureau of Corporations," *Mississippi Valley Historical Review* 45 (1959): 571–93.
41. Johnson, "Bureau of Corporations," 574, 576–77, 578.
42. Johnson, "Bureau of Corporations," 577–79. *Northern Securities v. United States*, 193 U.S. 197 (1904).
43. Eisner, *Regulatory Politics*, 52–54. *Interstate Commerce Commission v. Cincinnati, New Orleans, and Texas Pacific Railway*, 167 U.S. 479 (1897) (holding the Interstate Commerce Act's language too ambiguous to confer rate-making authority on the Interstate Commerce Commission). See also *ICC v. Texas and Pacific Railway*, 162 U.S. 197 (1896) (refusing to defer to the commission's findings of fact).

44. Eisner, *Regulatory Politics*, 54–55.

45. Roosevelt, Address at Providence, Rhode Island (August 23, 1902), in *Works*, 18:77–78.

46. Theodore Roosevelt, *Winning of the West* (New York: G. P. Putnam's Sons, 1889), 4:3. Regier, *Era of Muckrakers*, 198. "What the Election Showed," *World's Work* 9 (December 1904): 5561.

47. James T. Kloppenberg, *Uncertain Victory* (New York: Oxford University Press, 1986), 300.

8. WARRIOR REPUBLICANISM

1. Lewis L. Gould, *Reform and Regulation: American Politics from Roosevelt to Wilson* (New York: Knopf, 1986), 50–53, 127.

2. Roosevelt, Inaugural Address, March 4, 1905, in House and Senate Joint Committee of Printing, *Messages and Papers of the President* (New York: Bureau of National Literature, 1914), 15:7060. George Washington, "Circular to the States" (June 8, 1783), in *George Washington: Writings*, ed. John Rhodehamel (New York: Library of America, 1997), 516–26.

3. George Washington, *Writings*, 516–26. Converting Christian teachings on individual conscience and personal obedience to God, flowing from a personal relationship with God, into a political theory of natural rights, was the particular province of post-Reformation, Anglo-American Puritans. See James Harrington's *Oceana* (1656), for instance, as well as the writings of Cotton and Increase Mather. The political sermons delivered from American pulpits during the late colonial and early republican periods also reflect this biblically inspired rights doctrine. See Ellis Sandoz, ed., *Political Sermons of the Founding Era: 1730–1805* (New York: Liberty Fund, 1995), vols. 1–2. John Adams reflects on the God-given quality of natural rights, and on Scripture's role in revealing them, in his *Thoughts on Government*. See also Washington's First Inaugural Address and his Farewell Address, as well as the Adams-Jefferson correspondence (1812–26), for thoughts on the same theme. Lester J. Cappon, ed., *The Adams-Jefferson Letters* (Chapel Hill: University of North Carolina Press, 1959).

4. Roosevelt, in House and Senate Joint Committee of Printing, *Messages and Papers of the President* (New York: Bureau of National Literature, 1914), 15:7060.

5. Roosevelt, *Messages and Papers*, 15:7060.

6. Washington, *Writings*, 516–26.

7. Roosevelt, *Messages and Papers*, 15:7061.

8. Ibid.

9. Lewis L. Gould, *The Presidency of Theodore Roosevelt* (Lawrence, Kans.: University Press of Kansas Press, 1991), 144–45.

10. Gould, *Presidency of Theodore Roosevelt*, 137–39. Marc Allen Eisner, *Regulatory Politics in Transition* (Baltimore: Johns Hopkins University Press, 1993), 34.

11. Gould, *Presidency of Theodore Roosevelt*, 149–50. Arthur M. Johnson, "Theodore Roosevelt and the Bureau of Corporations," *Mississippi Valley Historical Review* 45 (1959): 578–79. Harold S. Wilson, *McClure's Magazine and the Muckrakers* (Princeton, N.J.: Princeton University Press, 1970), 137–41. Cornelius C. Regier, The *Era of Muckrakers*

(Chapel Hill, N.C.: University of North Carolina Press, 1932), 55. Ida M. Tarbell, *History of the Standard Oil Company* (New York: McClure Phillips, 1904), vii–viii.

12. Stephen Skowronek, *The Politics Presidents Make* (Cambridge, Mass.: Harvard University Press, 1993), 238–39.

13. Gould, *Presidency of Theodore Roosevelt*, 147–48. Theodore Roosevelt to Lyman Abbott (January 11, 1905), in Roosevelt, *The Letters of Theodore Roosevelt*, ed. Elting E. Morrison et al. (Cambridge: Harvard University Press, 1952–54), 4:1100.

14. Roosevelt, "Fourth Annual Message," in *The Works of Theodore Roosevelt*, ed. Hermann Hagedorn (New York: Charles Scribner's Sons, 1923), 17:251, 257, 258.

15. Ibid., 17:262–63.

16. Skowronek, *Building an American State*, 251–52. Gabriel Kolko, *Railroads and Regulation: 1877–1916* (Princeton, N.J.: Princeton University Press, 1965), 5. Kolko, *The Triumph of Conservatism: A Reinterpretation of American History, 1900–1916* (New York: Free Press, 1963), 83–98, 111–12.

17. *New York Times*, May 22, 1905. Gould, *Reform and Regulation*, 82.

18. Jeffrey K. Tulis, *The Rhetorical Presidency* (Princeton: Princeton University Press, 1987), 97–101. John Morton Blum, *The Progressive Presidents: Roosevelt, Wilson, Roosevelt, Johnson* (New York: Norton, 1980), 24–30, 37–51, 59–60.

19. Roosevelt quoted in *New York Times*, October 20, 1905.

20. Roosevelt, fifth annual message, in *Works*, 15:327. Jane Addams, *Twenty Years at Hull-House* (New York: Macmillan, 1910), 135.

21. Roosevelt, *Works*, 15:328.

22. Theodore Roosevelt, *Autobiography* (New York: Charles Scribner's Sons, 1913), 437–38. Roosevelt quoted in *New York Times*, May 10, 1905. Roosevelt, fifth annual message, 15:250, 318, 317.

23. Roosevelt, fourth annual message, in *Works*, 15:251. Roosevelt, second annual message, in *Works*, 15:165.

24. Roosevelt, fifth annual message, in *Works*, 15:318.

25. Theodore Roosevelt to Edgar Aldrich (August 1, 1911), in Roosevelt, *Letters*, 7:319–20. Theodore Roosevelt to William Henry Moody (September 21, 1907), in Roosevelt, *Letters*, 5:802. Theodore Roosevelt to Elihu Root (August 16, 1906), in Roosevelt, *Letters*, 5:368.

26. Roosevelt, first annual message, *Messages and Papers*, 6646. Roosevelt, *Autobiography*, 439.

27. Roosevelt quoted in *New York Times*, January 31, 1905. Roosevelt, fourth annual message, *Messages and Papers*, 7052.

28. Roosevelt, fifth annual message, *Messages and Papers*, 7354. Roosevelt, *Autobiography*, 442. Roosevelt, quoted in *Topeka Daily Capital*, October 21, 1905.

29. Alexander Hamilton, *The Farmer Refuted*, 1775, available in Hamilton's *Papers*, ed. Harold C. Syrett and Jacob Cooke (New York: Columbia University Press, 1961–79), 1:88. John Adams, *The Works of John Adams*, ed. Charles Francis Adams (Boston: Little, Brown, 1856), 4:555.

30. This "ontological" vs. "chronological" heuristic was suggested to me by Harry V. Jaffa, *A New Birth of Freedom: Abraham Lincoln and the Coming of the Civil War* (New York:

Rowman and Littlefield, 2000), 414–15. Hamilton, *The Farmer Refuted*, in *Papers*, 1:88ff.

31. Roosevelt, *Autobiography*, 437. Theodore Roosevelt, *Winning of the West* (New York: G. P. Putnam's Sons, 1889), 1:146, 173, for example.

32. Roosevelt, *Autobiography*, 437.

33. Compare Roosevelt-the-historian's view to George Bancroft, *History of the United States*, vols. 1–6 (Boston, 1834), 1:311–24, 415–28; 3:107–21, 481–82; 6:5–23, 311–67, 441–57. See also Bancroft, *The History of the Formation of the Constitution of the United States*, vols. 1–2 (New York, 1882), 2:321–35. Edward Norman Saveth, "Race and Nationalism in American Historiography: The Late Nineteenth Century," *Political Science Quarterly* 54, no. 3 (September 1939): 421–22.

34. Roosevelt, *Autobiography*, 372.

35. Roosevelt quoted in *New York Times*, October 20, 1905.

36. "Who It Is That Suffers," Franklin County *Repository and Transcript*, 20 June 1860, 4, col. 2. The *Repository and Transcript* of Franklin County, Pennsylvania, was, in the words of its rival *Valley Spirit*, "the embodiment of the Republican Party in Franklin County." Franklin County Republicans in the mid-nineteenth century were characterized by dedication to free labor ideas, in a manner typical of rank and file Republicans (and many Northerners of either party). The pages of the *Repository and Transcript* between 1856 and 1864 are an excellent entrée to the free labor creed as believed and practiced by non-elites. Jefferson, "Notes on the State of Virginia," in *Jefferson Writings*, ed. Merrill D. Peterson (New York: Library of America, 1984), 290–91. Frederick J. Blue, *The Free Soilers: Third Party Politics, 1848–54* (Urbana, Ill.: University of Illinois Press, 1973), 81–103.

37. Roosevelt, "Nationalism and the Working Man," in *Works*, 19:102.

38. Roosevelt, "The New Nationalism," in *Works*, 19:16.

39. John Adams, *Works*, 6:219. [Madison], *The Federalist* (Cambridge, Mass: Belknap Press of Harvard University Press, 1961), Number 10, 132–36.

40. [Madison], *Federalist*, Number 51, 355–58.

41. Roosevelt, fifth annual message, in *Works*, 17:320.

42. Arthur S. Link and Richard L. McCormick, *Progressivism* (Arlington Heights, Va.: Harlan Davidson, 1983), 32. William Allen White, *Autobiography* (New York: MacMillan, 1951), 146.

43. David M. Kennedy, "Introduction," in *Progressivism: The Critical Issues* (Boston: Little, Brown, 1971), vii, xiii. Robert Higgs, *Crisis and Leviathan: Critical Episodes in the Growth of American Government* (New York: Oxford University Press, 1987), 113–16.

44. Historians advocating the agrarian thesis include John D. Hicks, *The Populist Revolt: A History of the Farmers' Alliance and the People's Party* (Minneapolis: University of Minnesota Press, 1931); C. Vann Woodward, *Origins of the New South, 1877–1913* (Baton Rouge: Louisiana State University Press, 1951); Russel B. Nye, *Midwestern Progressive Politics: A Historical Study of Its Origins and Development, 1870–1950* (East Lansing: Michigan State College Press, 1951). The "status revolution" theory was first tested by George E. Mowry in both *The California Progressives* (Berkeley: University of California Press, 1951) and *The Era of Theodore Roosevelt, 1900–1912* (New York: Harper, 1958).

Richard Hofstadter gave this thesis its classic expression in his *The Age of Reform: From Bryan to F.D.R.* (New York: Knopf, 1955). Samuel P. Hays, *The Response to Industrialism, 1885–1914* (Chicago: University of Chicago Press, 1957), and Robert H. Wiebe, *The Search for Order, 1877–1920* (New York: Hill and Wang, 1967), reformulated Mowry's and Hofstadter's status theory to postulate that it was a young, forward-looking middle class of professionals, rather than a fearful group of fading elitists, who spurred reform. But J. D. Buenker and Peter Filene have demonstrated conclusively that no single progressive "movement" existed. J. D. Buenker, "The Progressive Era: A Search for Synthesis," *Mid-America* 51 (1969): 175–93. Peter G. Filene, "An Obituary for the Progressive Movement," *American Quarterly* 22, no. 1 (Spring 1970): 20–34. And Edward Purcell correctly argues that diverse interest groups united in support of reform to protect their diverse interests through the federal government. Edward Purcell, Jr., "Ideas and Interests: Business and the Interstate Commerce Act," *Journal of American History* 54 (December 1967): 561–78.

45. Roosevelt, fifth annual message, in *Works*, 17:315–400. Gould, *Presidency of Theodore Roosevelt*, 159–63. Skowronek, *Building an American State*, 257. Theodore Roosevelt to William Boyd Anderson (May 5, 1906), in Roosevelt, *Letters*, 5:258–59. Theodore Roosevelt to Edward Payson Bacon (May 8, 1906), in Roosevelt, *Letters*, 5:260. Eisner, *Regulatory Politics*, 56.

46. Upton Sinclair, *The Jungle* (New York: Jungle, 1906). Regier, *Era of Muckrakers*, 135–36.

47. *New York World*, December 6, 1905.

9. THE PROGRESS OF A PROGRESSIVE

1. William Henry Harbaugh, *Power and Responsibility: The Life and Times of Theodore Roosevelt* (New York: Farrar, Straus and Cudahy, 1961), 250–52.

2. Arthur S. Link and Richard L. McCormick, *Progressivism* (Arlington Heights, Va.: Harlan Davidson, 1983), 32.

3. Robert M. La Follette, *Autobiography: A Personal Narrative of Political Experiences* (Madison: La Follette, 1913), 387–89.

4. Cornelius C. Regier, *The Era of the Muckrakers* (Chapel Hill, N.C.: University of North Carolina Press, 1932), 108–12.

5. Roosevelt, "The Man with a Muck-Rake," in *The Works of Theodore Roosevelt*, ed. Hermann Hagedorn (New York: Charles Scribner's Sons, 1923), 5:712–24.

6. La Follette, *Autobiography*, 211. Roosevelt, "The Man with a Muck-Rake," 5:721ff. Regier, *Era of Muckrakers*, 198. Harold S. Wilson, *McClure's Magazine and the Muckrakers*, (Princeton, N.J.: Princeton University Press, 1970), 168–70. Harbaugh, *Power and Responsibility*, 264–67.

7. La Follette, *Autobiography*, 387. Link and McCormick, *Progressivism*, 32–33.

8. Harbaugh, *Power and Responsibility*, 261. Roosevelt, *Works*, 19:18, 17:258, 580.

9. Edmund Burke, *Reflections on the Revolution in France* (Oxford: Oxford University Press, 1993 ed.), 58–59. See also Burke, *Letters to a Member of the National Assembly* (1791); *Appeal from the New to the Old Whigs* (1791); and *Letters on a Regicide Peace* (1796).

10. Roosevelt, fifth annual message, in *Works*, 15:337.

11. Samuel P. Hays, *Conservation and the Gospel of Efficiency* (Cambridge, Mass.: Harvard University Press, 1959), 266–70.

12. Roosevelt, sixth annual message, in *Works*, 15:429. Burke, *Reflections*, 21. Roosevelt, second annual message, in *Works*, 15:165. Roosevelt, third annual message, in *Works*, 15:200.

13. Roosevelt, fifth annual message, in *Works*, 15:316. Roosevelt, "The Menace," in *Works*, 16:405, 404. Roosevelt, sixth annual message, in *Works*, 15:429.

14. Roosevelt, sixth annual message, in *Works*, 15:429. Roosevelt, Union League Speech, *New York Times*, January 31, 1905.

15. Roosevelt, eighth annual message, in *Works*, 17:577–78.

16. Roosevelt, seventh annual message, in *Works*, 17:493; 577, 578–79.

17. Roosevelt, *Works*, 17:577.

18. Gabriel Kolko, *Railroads and Regulation: 1877–1916* (Princeton: Princeton University Press 1965), 5ff. See also Gabriel Kolko, *The Triumph of Conservatism: A Reinterpretation of American History, 1900–1916* (New York: Free Press, 1963), 4–10, 72–78. Robert H. Wiebe, *The Search for Order, 1877–1920* (New York: Hill and Wang, 1967). A number of studies conducted after Kolko's and Wiebe's books were published revealed the extent to which businessmen attempting to influence regulatory legislation on both the national and state levels were forced to compromise on their major positions. Stephen Skowronek, *Building a New American State: The Expansion of National Administrative Capacities, 1877–1920* (Cambridge: Cambridge University Press, 1982), 130. Link and McCormick, *Progressivism*, 64. Albro Martin, *Enterprise Denied: Origins of the Decline of American Railroads, 1897–1917* (New York: Columbia University Press, 1971), 341.

19. Roosevelt, second annual message, in *Works*, 15:172–73. Theodore Roosevelt to Standwood Mencken (January 10, 1917), in Roosevelt, *The Letters of Theodore Roosevelt*, ed. Elting E. Morrison et al. (Cambridge: Harvard University Press, 1952–54), 8:1144. Samuel P. Hays, *Conservation and the Gospel of Efficiency: The Progressive Conservation Movement, 1890–1912* (Cambridge, Mass: Harvard University Press, 1959), 268–71.

20. Robert Nisbet, *The Quest for Community: A Study in the Ethics of Order and Freedom* (San Francisco: Institute for Contemporary Studies, 1990 ed.), 96, 125–35, 23. Gordon S. Wood, *Creation of the American Republic, 1776–1787* (Chapel Hill, N.C.: University of North Carolina Press, 1969), 3–90. Roosevelt, *Works*, 17:584.

21. Theodore Roosevelt to Kermit Roosevelt (January 6, 1903), in *Works*, 21:489.

22. *Youngstown Sheet & Tube Co. v. Sawyer*, 343 U.S. 579 (1952).

23. Theodore Roosevelt to William R. Thayer (August 21, 1916), in Roosevelt, *Letters*, 8:1103. Frederick W. Marks III, *Velvet on Iron: The Diplomacy of Theodore Roosevelt* (Lincoln, Neb.: University of Nebraska Press, 1979), 38–47. Edmund Morris, "'A Few Pregnant Days': Theodore Roosevelt and the Venezuelan Crisis of 1902," *Theodore Roosevelt Association Journal* 15 (Winter 1989): 2–13. Lewis L. Gould, *The Presidency of Theodore Roosevelt* (Lawrence, Kans.: University Press of Kansas, 1991), 76–80.

24. Richard W. Turk, *The Ambiguous Relationship: Theodore Roosevelt and Alfred Thayer Mahan* (New York: Greenwood Press, 1987), 52–53. Roosevelt, third annual message, in *Works*, 17:243–44. Richard L. Lael, *Arrogant Diplomacy: U.S. Policy Toward Colombia, 1903–1922* (Wilmington, Del.: Scholarly Resources, 1987), 1–19.

25. Philippe Bunau-Varilla, *Panama: The Creation, Destruction, and Resurrection* (New York: McBride, Nast and Company, 1914), 311. Alfred Thayer Mahan, usually a Roosevelt defender, privately concluded his Panama actions violated international law. Turk, *Ambiguous Relationship*, 53. For a contemporary's defense of Roosevelt, see William Howard Taft, *Our Chief Magistrate and His Powers* (New York: Columbia University Press, 1916), 93–112. For a survey of newspaper reactions, see "The Panama Revolution," *Literary Digest* 27 (November 14, 1903): 650.

26. Oscar Kraines, "The President Versus Congress: The Keep Commission, 1905–1909: The First Comprehensive Presidential Inquiry into Administration," *Western Political Quarterly* 23, no. 1 (March 1970): 5–54. Harold Pinkett, "Keep Commission, 1905–1909: A Rooseveltian Effort for Administrative Reform," *Journal of American History* 52, no. 2 (September 1965): 297–312. Skowronek, *Building a New American State*, 183–84.

27. Hays, *Conservation and the Gospel of Efficiency*, 3–18. James Penick, Jr., *Progressive Politics and Conservation: The Ballinger-Pinchot Affair* (Chicago: University of Chicago Press, 1968), 6–17.

28. Hays, *Conservation and the Gospel of Efficiency*, 73–85, 123–35, 143. Penick, *Progressive Politics and Conservation*, 11–17, 34.

29. Hays, *Conservation and the Gospel of Efficiency*, 133. Carl E. Hatch, *The Big Stick and the Congressional Gavel: A Study of Theodore Roosevelt's Relations with His Last Congress, 1907–1909* (New York: Pageant Press, 1967), 27–57. Stephen Skowronek, *The Politics Presidents Make* (Cambridge, Mass., 1993), 250. Lewis L. Gould, *The Presidency of Theodore Roosevelt* (Lawrence, Kans.: University Press of Kansas, 1991), 203–4.

30. Theodore Roosevelt, *Autobiography* (New York: Charles Scribner's Sons, 1913), 67.

31. Alexander Hamilton, "Speech to the New York Ratifying Convention" (June 21, 1788), in *The Papers of Alexander Hamilton*, ed. Harold C. Syrett, 26 vols. (New York: Columbia University Press, 1961–79), 5:36–37. Hamilton, "Constitutionality of the Bank," February 23, 1791, in *The Reports of Alexander Hamilton*, ed. Jacob E. Cooke (New York: Harper and Row, 1964), 84.

32. [Hamilton], *The Federalist* (Cambridge, Mass: Belknap Press of Harvard University Press, 1961), Number 68, 443. Skowronek, *Building a New American State*, 172–73.

33. Roosevelt, *Autobiography*, 372. Hamilton quoted in Mortin J. Frisch, ed., *Selected Writings and Speeches of Alexander Hamilton* (Washington, D.C.: American Enterprise Institute for Public Policy Research, 1985), 6.

34. Hamilton, in Frisch, *Selected Writings*, 8.

35. Roosevelt, eighth annual message, in *Works*, 17:584–85, 586.

36. Roosevelt, eighth annual message, in House and Senate Joint Committee of Printing, *Messages and Papers of the President* (New York: Bureau of National Literature, 1914), 7198, 7229. Roosevelt, address to American Bar Association, *New York Times*, October 26, 1905. Theodore Roosevelt to George Otto Trevelyan (June 19, 1908), in Roosevelt, *Letters*, 7:1086. Christopher S. Yoo et al., "The Unitary Executive During the Third Half-Century, 1889–1945," *Notre Dame Law Review* 80, no. 1 (2004): 30–39.

37. Roosevelt, *Autobiography*, 476, 487; 476–513 generally.

38. Roosevelt, *Autobiography*, 210. See, for instance, Roosevelt's fifth annual message, in *Works*, 15:317.

39. Roosevelt, *Autobiography*, 487.

40. For example, Washington Gladden, *Tools and the Man* (Boston: Houghton Mifflin, 1893); *Christianity and Socialism* (New York: Eaton and Mains, 1905); *The Labor Question* (New York: Pilgrim, 1911).

41. Roosevelt, eighth annual message, in *Works*, 17:510–11.

42. Roosevelt, *Autobiography*, 367. Arthur Link, Ray Stannard Baker, Gabriel Kolko, and Martin Sklar are just a few of the prime examples in this category. See Link and McCormick, *Progressivism*, 35–36; Kolko, *The Triumph of Conservatism*, 57–78, 279–87; Martin J. Sklar, "Woodrow Wilson and the Political Economy of Modern Liberalism," *Studies on the Left* 1 (1960): 17–47. David M. Kennedy has noted that "most American academic historians have thought of themselves as the political heirs of the Progressive tradition." See Kennedy, "Introduction," in *Progressivism: The Critical Issues*, ed. David M. Kennedy (Boston: Little, Brown, 1971), xiii. Regier, *Era of the Muckrakers*, 108.

43. Regier, *Era of the Muckrakers*, 108. Other muckrakers came to share similarly jaded views of Roosevelt. Wilson, *McClure's Magazine and the Muckrakers*, 242–43. *New York Times*, January 12, 1906.

44. Gould, *Presidency of Theodore Roosevelt*, 19–46.

45. David W. Southern, *The Malignant Heritage: Yankee Progressives and the Negro Question, 1901–1914* (Chicago: Loyola University Press, 1968), 33–35; 26–54 generally. Jack Temple Kirby, *Darkness at the Dawning: Race and Reform in the Progressive South* (Philadelphia: Lippincott, 1972), 7–22, 57–88. Theodore Roosevelt, "The Negro in America" (June 4, 1910), in *Works*, 14:194. Gail Bederman, *Manliness & Civilization: A Cultural History of Gender and Race in the United States, 1880–1917* (Chicago: University of Chicago Press, 1995), 197.

46. Theodore Roosevelt, *America and the World War* (1915), in *Works*, 18:135.

10. A PROPHET'S RETURN

1. Robert S. La Forte, "Theodore Roosevelt's Osawatomie Speech," *The Kansas Historical Quarterly* 32, no. 2 (Summer 1966): 187.

2. *Osawatomie Graphic*, August 25, 1910. La Forte, "Osawatomie Speech," 187–200.

3. Lewis L. Gould, *Grand Old Party: A History of the Republicans* (New York: Random House, 2003), 174–77. Patricia O'Toole, *When Trumpets Call: Theodore Roosevelt After the White House* (New York: Simon and Schuster, 2005), 78. Arthur S. Link, *Wilson*, 5 vols (Princeton, N.J.: Princeton University Press, 1947), 1:177.

4. Link, *Wilson*, 1:178. O'Toole, *When Trumpets Call*, 178–96. Gould, *Grand Old Party*, 175–76.

5. Marc Allen Eisner, *Regulatory Politics in Transition* (Baltimore: Johns Hopkins University Press, 1993), 57. Stephen Skowronek, *Building a New American State: The Expansion of National Administrative Capacities, 1877–1920* (Cambridge, U.K.: Cambridge University Press, 1982), 263–64.

6. James Penick, Jr., *Progressive Politics and Conservation: The Ballinger-Pinchot Affair* (Chicago: University of Chicago Press, 1968), 107–36, 161–64. Lewis L. Gould, *Reform and Regulation: American Politics from Roosevelt to Wilson* (New York: Knopf, 1986), 135–36. William Henry Harbaugh, *Power and Responsibility: The Life and Times of Theodore Roosevelt* (New York: Farrar, Straus and Cudahy, 1961), 387–88.

7. Gould, *Reform and Regulation*, 135–36. Harbaugh, *Power and Responsibility*, 387–88. Cornelius C. Regier, *Era of the Muckrakers*, (Chapel Hill, N.C.: University of North Carolina Press, 1932), 114–15.

8. Theodore Roosevelt to Henry Cabot Lodge (April 11, 1910), in Henry Cabot Lodge, ed., *Selections from the Correspondence of Theodore Roosevelt and Henry Cabot Lodge, 1884–1918* (New York: Charles Scribner's Sons, 1925), 2:367–74.

9. *Topeka Daily Capitol*, September 1, 1910. *Osawatomie Globe*, September 1, 1910. La Forte, "Osawatomie Speech," 187–200.

10. Theodore Roosevelt, "The New Nationalism," in *The Works of Theodore Roosevelt*, ed. Hermann Hagedorn (New York: Charles Scribner's Sons, 1923), 19:27.

11. Ibid., 19:10.

12. Herbert Croly, *The Promise of American Life* (New York: Capricorn, 1909, 1964 ed.), 173–74; 167–75 generally.

13. Jean-Jacques Rousseau, *The Social Contract* (1762) in *The Essential Rousseau* (New York: Meridian, 1983), 27; 27–124 generally. See also *Discourses on the Origins of Inequality* (1754), 125–202.

14. Roosevelt, *Works*, 19:20.

15. Roosevelt, *Works*, 19:29.

16. Roosevelt, *Works*, 19:20, 17–19.

17. Roosevelt, *Works*, 19:28, 19.

18. Roosevelt, *Works*, 19:25–26, 21, 24.

19. Roosevelt, *Works*, 19:27.

20. Harbaugh, *Power and Responsibility*, 392–93. *New York Sun*, September 1, 1910. *New York Tribune*, September 1, 1910. George E. Mowry, *Theodore Roosevelt and the Progressive Movement* (Madison, Wis.: University of Wisconsin Press, 1946), 144.

21. *Kansas City Star*, September 1, 1910.

22. Woodrow Wilson to George Harvey (November 15, 1910), in Link, *Wilson*, 1:213.

23. "Mr. Gladstone: A Character Sketch," *University of Virginia Magazine*, April 1880, in *Public Papers of Woodrow Wilson*, ed. Ray Stannard Baker and William E. Dodd (New York: Harper, 1925), 19:401–26. The books were entitled *Congressional Government: A Study in American Politics* (1884; repr. Gloucester, Mass.: Peter Smith, 1973); *Division and Reunion 1829–1889* (New York: Longmans, Green, 1893); *The State: Elements of Practical and Historical Politics* (Boston: D. C. Heath, 1898); *A History of the American People*, vols. 1–5 (New York: Harper, 1901); *Constitutional Government* (New York: Columbia University Press, 1908). Daniel D. Stid, *The President as Statesman: Woodrow Wilson and the Constitution* (Lawrence, Kans.: University Press of Kansas, 1998), 9.

24. James Kearney, *The Political Education of Woodrow Wilson* (New York: Century, 1926), 9–10. Link, *Wilson*, 1:116–17.

25. Wilson, "Speech to the National Democratic Club" (April 13, 1908), in *Public Papers*, 2:25.

26. Wilson, *Public Papers*, 2:25.

27. Link, *Wilson*, 1:115. Wilson, *Public Papers*, 2:30.

28. Wilson, "The Author and Signers of the Declaration of Independence," *North American Review*, vol. 186 (September 1907): 22–33. Link, *Wilson*, 1:163.

29. Jack Temple Kirby, *Darkness at the Dawning: Race and Reform in the Progressive South* (Philadelphia: Lippincott, 1972), 7–22, 57–88, 155–76. Arthur S. Link and Richard L. McCormick, *Progressivism* (Arlington Heights, Va.: Harlan Davidson, 1983), 99–100.

30. Gould, *Grand Old Party*, 179–81. Theodore Roosevelt to William Allen White (January 24, 1911), in Roosevelt, *The Letters of Theodore Roosevelt*, ed. Elting E. Morrison et al. (Cambridge, Mass.: Harvard University Press, 1952–54), 7:213–14.

11. BATTLE FOR THE LORD

1. *New York Times*, February 22, 1912.

2. Taft, in John Milton Cooper, *The Warrior and the Priest: Woodrow Wilson and Theodore Roosevelt* (Cambridge, Mass.: The Belknap Press of Harvard University Press, 1983), 154. Address at Columbus, Ohio (February 12, 1912), in *The Works of Theodore Roosevelt*, ed. Hermann Hagedorn (New York: Charles Scribner's Sons, 1923), 19:163–97; Roosevelt, address at Carnegie Hall (March 20, 1912), in *Works*, 19:200–24; Roosevelt, address at Philadelphia (April 10, 1912), in *Works*, 19:255–71.

3. Patricia O'Toole, *When Trumpets Call: Theodore Roosevelt After the White House* (New York: Simon and Schuster, 2005), 159, 171.

4. O'Toole, *When Trumpets Call*, 171–83. Roosevelt, "Speech to the Convention" (June 17, 1912), in *Works*, 19:287.

5. Roosevelt, "Confession of Faith" (August 7, 1912), in *Works*, 19:411.

6. Ibid., 19:351.

7. Ibid., 19:372, 388–89.

8. Ibid., 19:369–70, 374–76, 390, 406.

9. Ibid., 19:368.

10. Ibid., 19:368.

11. Ibid., 17:601–2; 19:369–70.

12. Arthur S. Link and Richard L. McCormick, *Progressivism* (Arlington Heights, Va.: Harlan Davidson, 1983), 41–42.

13. Arthur S. Link, *Wilson*, 5 vols. (Princeton: Princeton University Press, 1947), 1:261–67, 472–75. Wilson, "Acceptance Speech" (August 7, 1912), in *Public Papers of Woodrow Wilson*, ed. Ray Stannard Baker and William E. Dodd (New York: Harper, 1925), 2:464.

14. Wilson, "Acceptance Speech," 2:464. Martin J. Sklar, "Woodrow Wilson and the Political Economy of Modern Liberalism," *Studies on the Left* 1 (1960): 23.

15. Louis D. Brandeis, "Trusts, Efficiency, and the New Party," *Collier's*, vol. 49 (September 14, 1912): 14, 15. Philippa Strum, *Brandeis: Beyond Progressivism* (Lawrence, Kans.: University Press of Kansas, 1993), 75–77, 79–80. Link, *Wilson*, 1:488–89. Brandeis, "Trusts, the Export Trade, and the New Party," *Collier's*, vol. 49 (September 21, 1912): 10–11, 33. Thomas K. McGraw, *Prophets of Regulation: Charles Francis Adams, Louis D. Brandeis, James M. Landis, Alfred E. Kahn* (Cambridge, Mass.: Belknap Press of Harvard University, 1984), 108–12.

16. Strum, *Beyond Progressivism*, 155. McGraw, *Prophets of Regulation*, 108–9.

17. Brandeis, "Trusts, Efficiency, and the New Party," 14–15. Strum, *Beyond Progressivism*, 83–85. Link, *Wilson*, 1:491–92.

18. Link, *Wilson*, 1:492. William Diamond, *The Economic Thought of Woodrow Wilson* (Baltimore: The Johns Hopkins Press, 1943), 130.

19. For example, Woodrow Wilson, Speech at Tremont Temple (September 27, 1912), in *A Crossroads of Freedom: The 1912 Campaign Speeches of Woodrow Wilson*, ed. John Wells Davidson (New Haven: Yale University Press, 1956), 290–91.

20. Wilson, "Acceptance Speech," in *Crossroads*, 65. Wilson, "Labor Day Speech" (September 2, 1912), in *Crossroads*, 75, 77. Roosevelt, *Autobiography* (New York: Macmillan, 1913), 437.

21. Wilson, "Labor Day Speech," in *Crossroads*, 77, 78.

22. Wilson, "Labor Day Speech," in *Crossroads*, 79; Diamond, *The Economic Thought of Woodrow Wilson*, 75–82, 91–97.

23. Scot J. Zentner, "Liberalism and Executive Power: Woodrow Wilson and the American Founders," *Polity* 26, no. 4 (Summer 1994): 579–99. Merle Curti, "Woodrow Wilson's Conception of Human Nature," *Midwest Journal of Political Science* 1, no. 1 (May 1957): 4–6, 13. John Morton Blum, *Woodrow Wilson and the Politics of Morality* (Boston: Little, Brown, 1956), 5–13.

24. Woodrow Wilson, *The State: Elements of Practical and Historical Politics* (Boston: D. C. Heath, 1898), 633.

25. Woodrow Wilson, *Papers of Woodrow Wilson*, ed. Arthur Link, 67 vols. (Princeton, N.J.: Princeton University Press, 1966), 17:71–72, 70. Wilson, "The Puritan," in *Public Papers of Woodrow Wilson*, ed. Ray Stannard Baker and William E. Dodd (New York: Harper, 1925), 1:366.

26. James T. Kloppenberg, *Uncertain Victory* (New York: Oxford University Press, 1986), 26–46, 64–114.

27. Wilson, "The Puritan" (December 22, 1900), in *Public Papers*, 1:366. Wilson, *An Old Master and Other Political Essays* (New York: Charles Scribner's Sons, 1893), 83–84.

28. Herbert Croly, *The Promise of American Life* (1909; New York: Capricorn, 1964 ed.), 284.

29. Wilson, September 4, 1912, in *Crossroads*, 112.

30. Ibid.

31. Wilson, September 2, 1912, in *Crossroads*, 81, 80, 78; October 28, 1912, in *Crossroads*, 491.

32. Wilson, "Address to the New York Press Club," September 9, 1912, in *Crossroads*, 130. Roosevelt, "Limitation of Government Power" (September 14, 1912), in *Works*, 19:420, 419.

33. Roosevelt, "Limitation of Government Power (September 14, 1912), in *Works*, 19:420, 419.

34. Ibid. Roosevelt, "Confession of Faith," in *Works*, 19:403. Roosevelt, *Autobiography*, 590.

35. Roosevelt, *Autobiography*, 597.

36. Roosevelt, "The Leader and the Cause" (October 14, 1912), in *Works*, 19:445.

37. Zentner, "Liberalism and Executive Power," 584.

38. Wilson, *Congressional Government: A Study in American Politics* (Boston: Houghton Mifflin, 1898), 6, 318, 295–333. Wilson's real complaint with the division of sovereignty in a tripartite, federalist arrangement is that it stymies the sort of legislation he thought was necessary for the country's health. In other words, Wilson's political science seems to be politically driven and highly normative.

39. Woodrow Wilson, *Constitutional Government in the United States* (New York: Colum-

bia University Press, 1908), 70–71. Wilson came to this conclusion somewhat belatedly, having earlier treated the president as a constitutional cipher. Terri Bimes and Stephen Skowronek, "Woodrow Wilson's Critique of Popular Leadership: Reassessing the Modern-Traditional Divide in Presidential History," *Polity* 29, no. 1 (Autumn 1996): 40–48. Compare Jeffrey Tulis, *The Rhetorical Presidency* (Princeton: Princeton University Press, 1987), 117–44.

40. Roosevelt, *Works*, 19:410. Roosevelt, eighth annual message, in *Works*, 17:602–3.

41. Wilson, September 20, 1912, in *Crossroads*, 227.

42. Wilson, September 2, 1912, in *Crossroads*, 83–84. John Locke, *Two Treatises on Government*, ed. Peter Laslett (Cambridge, U.K., 1960 edition), 269–82, 318–30, 350–63.

43. Zentner, "Liberalism and Executive Power," 581–84, 590–98. Bimes and Skowronek, "Woodrow Wilson's Critique of Popular Leadership," 41–48.

44. Compare Thomas Hobbes, *Leviathan*, ed. C. B. MacPherson (Harmondsworth, U.K.: Penguin, 1968), 228–39, 261–74. Wilson, September 20, 1912, in *Crossroads*, 228, 237, 238.

45. Roosevelt, address in San Francisco (September 14, 1912), in *Works*, 19:428–29. Compare Isaiah Berlin's well-worn distinction between positive and negative liberty. Berlin, "Two Concepts of Liberty," in *The Proper Study of Mankind: An Anthology of Essays* (New York: Farrar, Straus, Giroux, 1997), 191–242. While Wilson's thought anticipates Berlin's in many respects, it also suggests that the divide between the two concepts is not as crisp as Berlin would have it. Indeed, Berlin's preferred definition of liberty as "freedom from" turns out to depend on a set of "freedoms to" — most notably, freedom to choose, and the positive guarantees of security, welfare, and belonging that make meaningful choice possible. Put a slightly different way, Berlin's apparently neutral, procedural conception of liberty conceals a substantive account of the individual as a creature whose highest purpose is found in uncoerced self-direction and who deserves social and political support to make that self-direction effective.

46. Wilson, *The State*, 633.

47. Wilson, *Constitutional Government*, 69. John Milton Cooper, *The Warrior and the Priest: Woodrow Wilson and Theodore Roosevelt* (Cambridge, Mass.: Belknap Press of Harvard University Press, 1983), 213–14.

48. Wilson, *Crossroads*, 80.

49. Wilson, *Constitutional Government*, 16, 18. Alan L. Seltzer, "Woodrow Wilson as 'Corporate Liberal': Toward a Reconsideration of Left Revisionist Historiography," *Western Political Quarterly*, vol. 30 (1977): 192–93.

50. E. M. Hugh-Jones, *Woodrow Wilson and American Liberalism* (New York: MacMillan, 1949), 277–82.

51. Isaiah Berlin, "Two Concepts of Liberty," 241–42. The root of Berlin's political thought was his moral anti-realism. Compare "The Divorce Between the Sciences and the Humanities," 326–58; "Giambattista Vico and Cultural History," in *Isaiah Berlin: The Crooked Timber of Humanity: Chapters in the History of Ideas*, ed. Henry Hardy (Princeton, N.J.: Princeton University Press, 1990), 49–69.

52. Kloppenberg, *Uncertain Victory*, 357.

53. Roosevelt, "Nationalism and Democracy," in *Works*, 19:141.

54. Roosevelt, "The Leader and the Cause," in *Works*, 19:441, 442. Roosevelt, "The Stricken Standard-Bearer" (October 16, 1912), in *Works*, 19:453.

12. THE VALLEY OF VISION

1. Hermann Hagedorn notes (July 18, 1918), Theodore Roosevelt Collection, Houghton Library, Harvard University (Roosevelt Collection HL, hereinafter).
2. Theodore Roosevelt to Anna Cabot Mills Lodge (September 20, 1907), in Roosevelt, *The Letters of Theodore Roosevelt*, ed. Elting E. Morrison et al. (Cambridge: Harvard University Press, 1952–54), 5:800. Theodore Roosevelt to William B. Crawford (July 24, 1918), in Kathleen Dalton, *Theodore Roosevelt: A Strenuous Life* (New York: Random House, 2002), 503. Compare Theodore Roosevelt to King George V (July 22, 1918), in Roosevelt, *Letters*, 8:1353–54; Theodore Roosevelt to Richard Derby (August 5, 1918), in Roosevelt, *Letters*, 8:1357; Theodore Roosevelt to James Bryce (August 7, 1918), in Roosevelt, *Letters*, 8:1358.
3. Theodore Roosevelt to Kermit Roosevelt (November 5, 1912), in H. W. Brands, *T. R.: The Last Romantic* (New York: Basic, 1997), 725.
4. Arthur S. Link and Richard L. McCormick, *Progressivism* (Arlington Heights, Va.: Harlan Davidson, 1983), 43–45. Link, *Wilson*, 5 vols. (Princeton, N.J.: Princeton University Press, 1947), 1:527. Lewis L. Gould, *Grand Old Party: A History of the Republicans* (New York: Random House, 2003), 194–98.
5. Link, *Wilson*, 2:199–236. Philippa Strum, *Brandeis: Beyond Progressivism* (Lawrence, Kans.: University Press of Kansas, 1993), 85–87. Louis D. Brandeis to Woodrow Wilson (June 14, 1913), in *Woodrow Wilson: Life and Letters*, ed. Ray Stannard Baker (Garden City, N.Y.: Doubleday, Page and Co., 1939), 3:133–15. Marc Allen Eisner, *Regulatory Politics in Transition* (Baltimore: Johns Hopkins University Press, 1993), 27–28, 62–63. Brandeis's own conversion to Roosevelt nationalism was incomplete, and the dysfunction of the Federal Trade Commission, which he helped design, reflected his ambivalence. Thomas K. McCraw, *Prophets of Regulation: Charles Francis Adams, Louis D. Brandeis, James M. Landis, Alfred E. Kahn* (Cambridge, Mass: Harvard Belknap Press, 1984), 114–35.
6. David Steigerwald, "The Synthetic Politics of Woodrow Wilson," *Journal of the History of Ideas* 50, no. 3 (Summer 1989): 465–84. Herbert Croly, "The Two Wilsons," *The New Republic*, vol. 7 (September 9, 1916): 129. I. M. Tarbell, "A Talk with the President of the United States," *Collier's*, vol. 58 (October 28, 1916): 5–6. Link, *Wilson*, 5:117–29.
7. Lewis L. Gould, *Reform and Regulation: American Politics from Roosevelt to Wilson* (New York: Knopf, 1986), 148–75.
8. Link, *Wilson*, 3:312–57. E. R. May, *The World War and American Isolation* (Cambridge, Mass.: Harvard University Press, 1959), 131. Theodore Roosevelt to J. C. O'Laughlin (May 13, 1915), Roosevelt Collection HL.
9. Theodore Roosevelt to A. B. Hart (June 1, 1915), in Roosevelt, *Letters*, 8:927. Theodore Roosevelt, *America and the World War* (New York: Charles Scribners' Sons, 1915), xi. Link, *Wilson*, 3:375, 4:18–26.
10. Theodore Roosevelt, *The Foes of Our Own Household* (New York: George H. Doran, 1917), 15.
11. Theodore Roosevelt to Anna Bulloch Roosevelt (May 19, 1915), quoted in Link, *Wilson*, 3:383. Roosevelt, "Fear God and Take Your Own Part" (1916), in *The Works of Theodore Roosevelt*, ed. Hermann Hagedorn (New York: Charles Scribner's Sons, 1923), 20:300–301.

12. Roosevelt, *Foes*, 48–49, 51. Theodore Roosevelt, "The Great Adventure" (1918), in *Works*, 21:280–81.

13. Roosevelt, *America and the World War*, 210, 124–25.

14. Roosevelt, "Fear God," 20:298–99. Theodore Roosevelt to S. Stanwood Menken (January 10, 1917), in Roosevelt, *Letters*, 8:1147.

15. Roosevelt, *Foes*, 51, 239. Roosevelt, *America and the World War*, 127.

16. Daniel J. Kevles, *In the Name of Eugenics: Genetics and the Uses of Human Identity* (Cambridge, Mass.: Harvard University Press, 1985), 44–45, 85. Richard Hofstadter, *Social Darwinism in America* (New York: George Braziller, 1944), 161–62. Roosevelt, "The Origin and Evolution of Life" (January 16, 1918), in *Works*, 12:159.

17. Roosevelt, "Our Neighbors, the Ancients" (September 30, 1911), in *Works*, 12:174.

18. Roosevelt, "Race Decadence" (April 8, 1911), in *Works*, 12:184, 186–87. Roosevelt, *Foes*, 235, 264.

19. Roosevelt, *Foes*, 265–66. Kevles, *In the Name of Eugenics*, 183.

20. Roosevelt, *Foes*, 264. Roosevelt, "Twisted Eugenics" (January 3, 1914), in *Works*, 12:201.

21. Kevles, *In the Name of Eugenics*, 70–75.

22. Roosevelt, "Fear God," in *Works*, 20:264–65.

23. Roosevelt, *The Great Adventure*, in *Works*, 21:263, 264–65.

24. Douglas B. Craig, *After Wilson: The Struggle for the Democratic Party, 1920–1934* (Chapel Hill, N.C.: University of North Carolina Press, 1992), 1–29.

25. Link, *Wilson*, 5:106–61. Link and McCormick, *Progressivism*, 106–11.

26. Roosevelt, "Problems of Power" (May 31, 1913), in *Works*, 12:241.

27. Roosevelt, *America and the World War*, xi.

28. Woodrow Wilson, October 27, 1916, quoted in Link, *Wilson*, 5:149.

29. Woodrow Wilson, November 2, 1916, quoted in Link, *Wilson*, 5:151. Woodrow Wilson, "Fourteen Points Speech," in *Public Papers of Woodrow Wilson*, ed. Ray Stannard Baker and William E. Dodd (New York: Harper and Brothers, 1925), 3:159–61. E. M. Hugh-Jones, *Woodrow Wilson and American Liberalism* (New York: Macmillan, 1949), 227.

30. Wilson, *Public Papers*, 3:159–61.

31. Link, *Wilson*, 5:266–68. Harley Notter, *The Origins of the Foreign Policy of Woodrow Wilson* (New York: Russell and Russell, 1965), 519–29.

32. Roosevelt, *America and the World War*, 78, 59.

33. Roosevelt, "League of Nations II," *Kansas City Star*, December 2, 1918. "What Are the Fourteen Points?" *Kansas City Star*, October 30, 1918.

34. For an insightful discussion of Roosevelt's and Henry Cabot Lodge's (mostly) shared view on this issue, see William C. Widenor, *Henry Cabot Lodge and the Search for an American Foreign Policy* (Berkeley, Calif.: University of California Press, 1980), 326–27.

35. Roosevelt, *Foes*, 17.

36. Roosevelt, "League of Nations I," *Kansas City Star*, November 17, 1918.

37. League proposals were a dime a dozen during the war years; neither Roosevelt nor Wilson originated the idea. And in fact, Roosevelt's version was strikingly similar to proposals endorsed by Henry Cabot Lodge and William Howard Taft, among others. Widenor, *Search for American Foreign Policy*, 266–67.

38. Roosevelt, *America and the World War*, 105–13, 237–40, 529, 39–40. Roosevelt, "The Great Adventure," in *Works*, 21:346–48.

39. John Milton Cooper, *The Warrior and the Priest: Woodrow Wilson and Theodore Roosevelt* (Cambridge, Mass.: Belknap Press of Harvard University Press, 1983), 281–82, 331–35.

40. Roosevelt, *America and the World War*, 105–6.

41. Widenor, *Search for American Foreign Policy*, 300–48.

42. Roosevelt, *Foes*, 102. Dwight D. Eisenhower, "Radio Address to the American People on the National Security and Its Costs" (May 9, 1953), in *Public Papers of the Presidents of the United States* (Washington, D.C.: United States Government Printing Office, 1953), paper no. 35.

43. Roosevelt, *Works*, 12:192.

EPILOGUE

1. For the assembly's resolution, Senator Davenport's speech, and a representative sample of eulogies, see *State of New York: A Memorial to Theodore Roosevelt* (New York, 1919), 27, 28, and passim.

2. *New York Memoriam*, 29.

3. Contrast with Lincoln's comments on political "salvation" in his Senate campaign speech of July 10, 1858. See also Harry V. Jaffa, *Crisis of the House Divided: An Interpretation of the Issues in the Lincoln-Douglas Debates* (Garden City, N.Y.: Doubleday, 1959), 308–30.

4. Arthur M. Schlesinger, *The Politics of Upheaval, 1935–1936* (Boston: Houghton Mifflin, 1960), 561. David M. Kennedy, *Freedom from Fear: The American People in Depression and War, 1929–45* (New York: Oxford University Press, 2000), 363–80. Richard Hofstadter, *The American Political Tradition and the Men Who Made It* (New York: Knopf, 1948), 311. John Milton Cooper, *The Warrior and the Priest: Woodrow Wilson and Theodore Roosevelt* (Cambridge, Mass.: Belknap Press of Harvard University Press, 1983), 352–53, 357–58.

5. Ellis W. Hawley, "Herbert Hoover, the Commerce Secretariat, and the Vision of an 'Associative State,' 1921–1928," *Journal of American History*, vol. 61 (June 1974): 116–40. Kennedy, *Freedom From Fear*, 70–103.

6. Cooper, *Warrior and the Priest*, 354–57. Jonathan M. Schoenwald, *A Time for Choosing: The Rise of Modern American Conservatism* (New York: Oxford University Press, 2001), 7–13, 124–61.

7. Ronald Reagan, First Inaugural Address, in *Speaking My Mind: Selected Speeches* (New York: Simon and Schuster, 1989), 62.

8. Irving Kristol, *Neo-Conservatism: The Autobiography of an Idea* (New York: Free Press, 1996, 1995), 43–74, 200–204. George H. Nash, *The Conservative Intellectual Movement in America, since 1945* (New York: Basic, 1976), 57–83, 154–87.

9. *Casey v. Pennsylvania*, 505 U.S. 833, 851 (1992) (plurality opinion).

10. Gifford Pinchot, "Roosevelt, the Man of Abundant Life," *Natural History*, 1919, 15.

INDEX